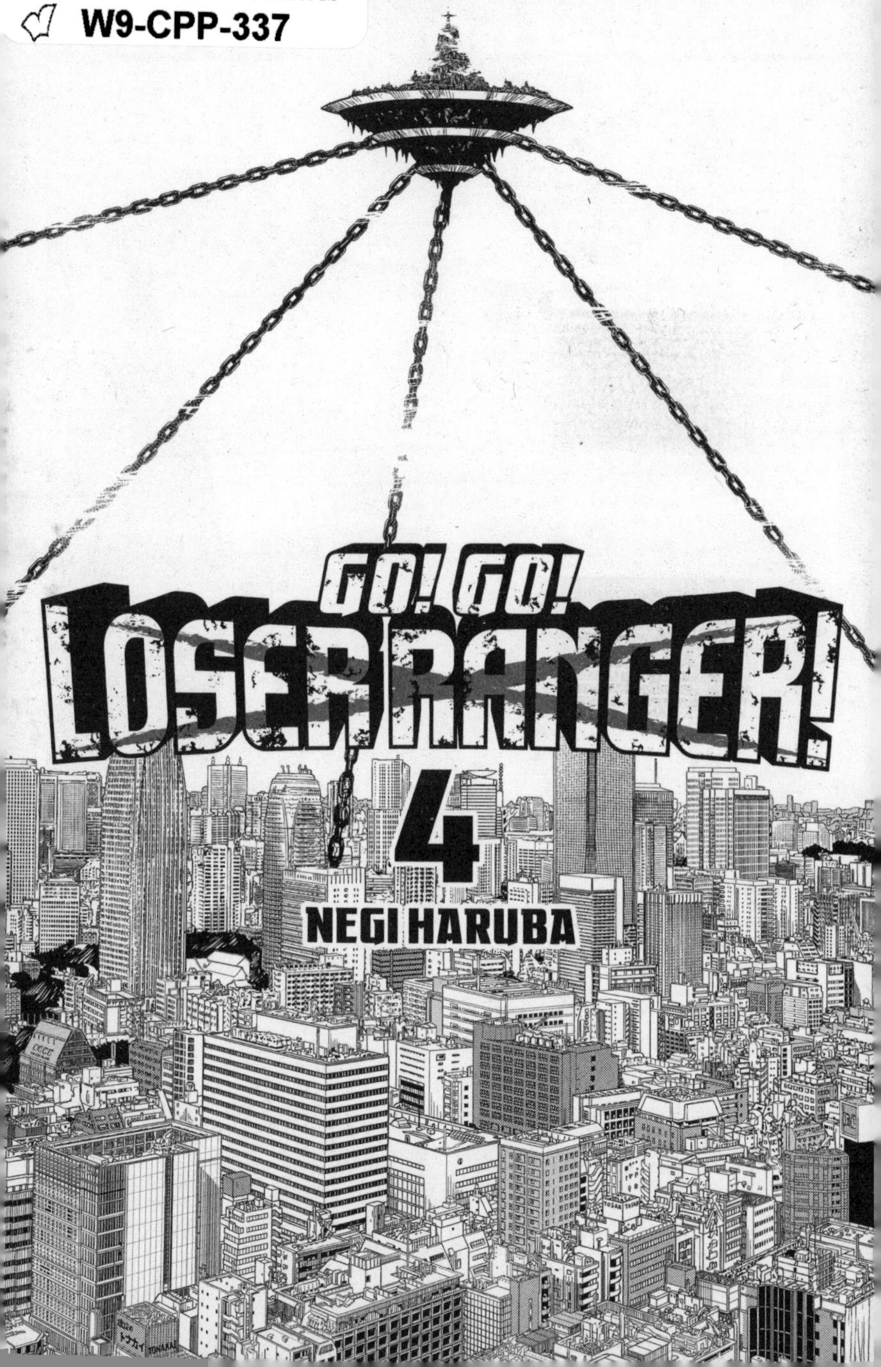
GO! GO!
LOSER RANGER!
4
NEGI HARUBA

CHARACTER PROFILES

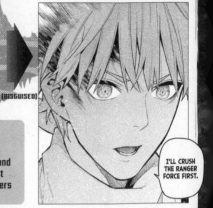

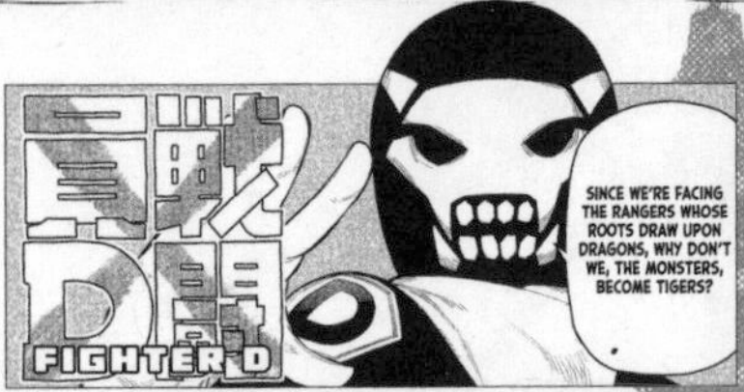
FIGHTER D
SINCE WE'RE FACING THE RANGERS WHOSE ROOTS DRAW UPON DRAGONS, WHY DON'T WE, THE MONSTERS, BECOME TIGERS?

[DISGUISED]

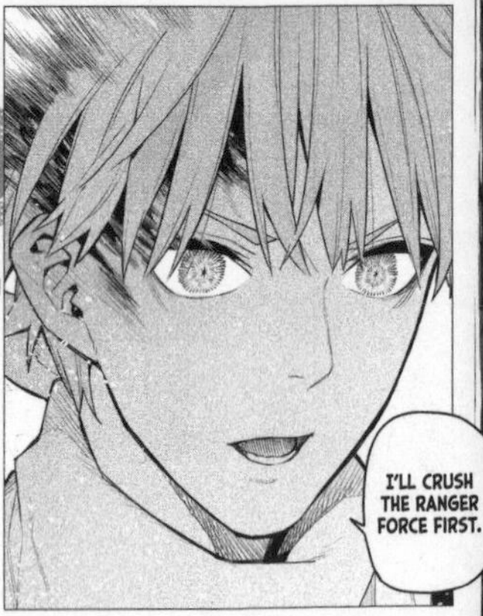
I'LL CRUSH THE RANGER FORCE FIRST.

FIGHTER D

A rank-and-file member of the fighters known as "Dusters." He has decided to join hands with Hibiki in order to put an end to the war by mimicking him and infiltrating the Ranger Force once more. His current goal is to be promoted to a full member of the Rangers in order to get closer to the Dragon Keepers.

RECRUITS

GREEN SQUAD

Stealth specialists who attack from the shadows.

SOUJIROU ISHIKAWA

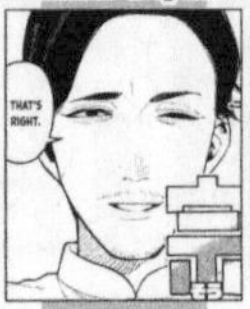
THAT'S RIGHT.

The oldest cadet. Has taken the final exam multiple times.

ANGEL USUKUBO

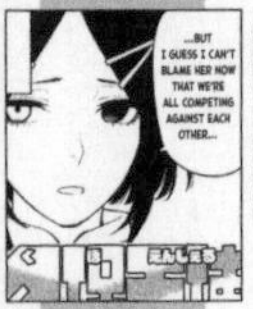
...BUT I GUESS I CAN'T BLAME HER NOW THAT WE'RE ALL COMPETING AGAINST EACH OTHER...

A girl with an unusual eye. Gloomy vibes.

YELLOW SQUAD

Weaker fighters, but have the brains to act as the Ranger Force's backbone.

ANGELICA YUKINO

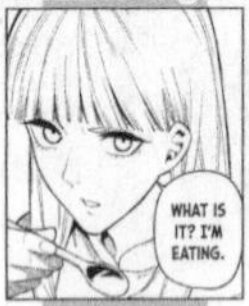
WHAT IS IT? I'M EATING.

Focuses on efficiency. Has a sharp tongue.

YAMATO KURUSU

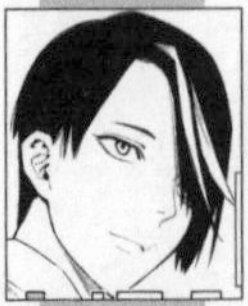

Hibiki's best friend [?]. Playboy tendencies.

RED SQUAD

Monster-hunting shock troops.

KAI SHION

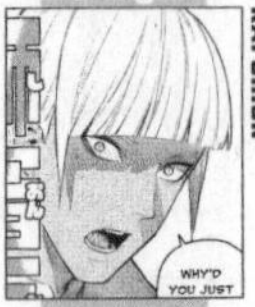
WHY'D YOU JUST

Hates monsters for killing his older brother.

HIBIKI SAKURAMA

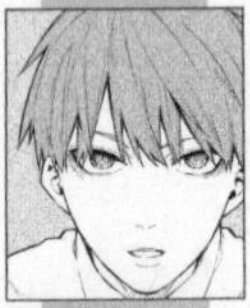

[Fighter D]

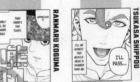

BLUE SQUAD

Managerial specialists who are big picture thinkers and excel at coordinating with allies.

EIGEN URABE

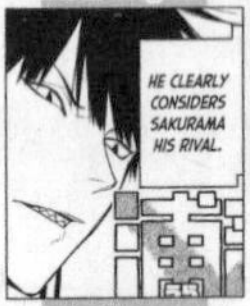
HE CLEARLY CONSIDERS SAKURAMA HIS RIVAL.

Is fueled by his rivalry with Hibiki.

RANMARU KOGUMA

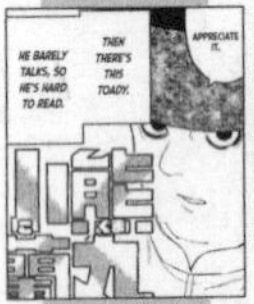
APPRECIATE IT.
THEN THERE'S THIS TOADY.
HE BARELY TALKS, SO HE'S HARD TO READ.

Sucks up to Urabe. Doesn't talk much.

PINK SQUAD

Rear-guard support specialists.

RENREN AKEBAYASHI

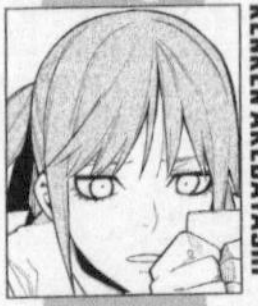

Skilled at acrobatic movements. Perceptive.

TSUKASA SHIPPOU

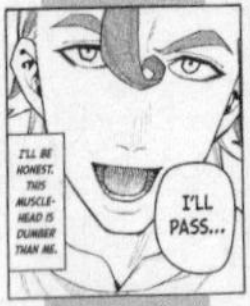
I'LL PASS...
I'LL BE HONEST. THIS MUSCLE-HEAD IS DUMBER THAN ME.

Musclehead. Not smart, but a good fighter.

WHAT IS THE WHITE DRAGON'S NEST FINAL EXAM?

1: Exam takes place over three days.
2: Test period for each day is thirty minutes, modeled after actual Sunday Showdowns.
3: During the above period, cadets must take keys from the exam proctors acting as monsters who match their squad color, then escape the field.

Exam passed!

Cadets now have the right to be scouted by the individual Squadrons!

...Because there's only one key of each color, test takers who share a color aren't actually allies. They're rivals who must fight over a single key!

THE DIVINE DRAGON RANGERS: THE DRAGON KEEPERS

AKA. THE RANGER FORCE

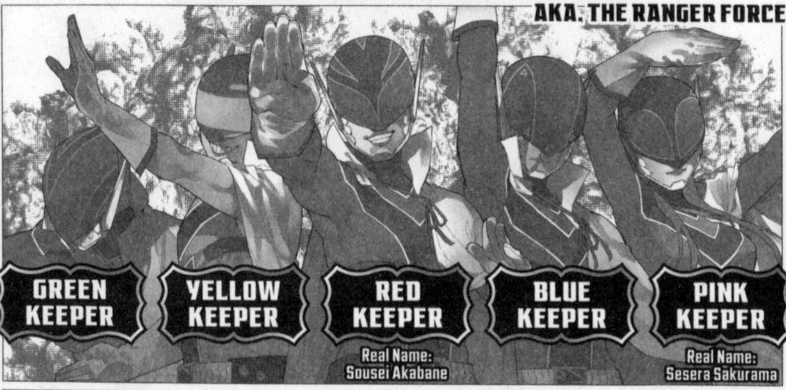
GREEN KEEPER
YELLOW KEEPER
RED KEEPER
Real Name: Sousei Akabane
BLUE KEEPER
PINK KEEPER
Real Name: Sesera Sakurama

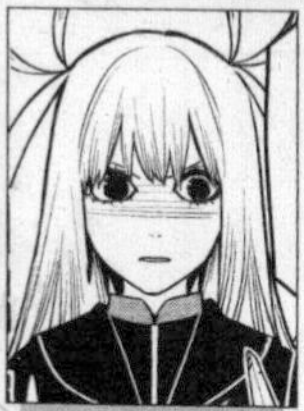

KANON HISUI

Green Squad's Junior First Rank.

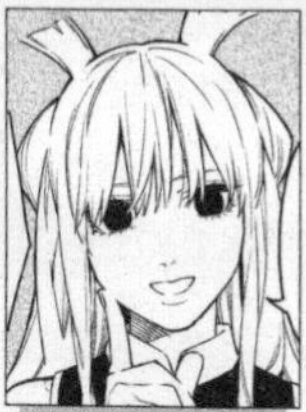

YUMEKO SUZUKIRI

Yellow Squad's Junior First Rank. Plotting to crush the Ranger Force.

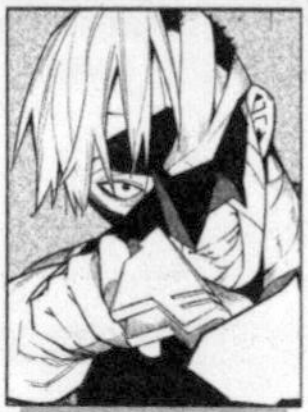

SHUN TOKITA

Red Squad's Senior Third Rank. Red Squadron's rising star who was once defeated by D. Now acting as a monster for the exam in place of Junior First Rank Himura.

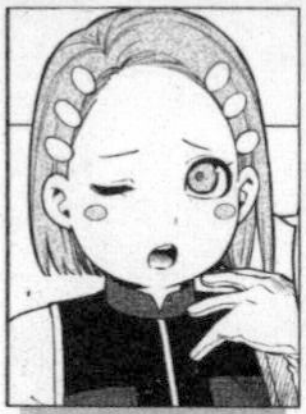

KOMACHI AIZOME

Blue Squad's acting Junior First Rank.

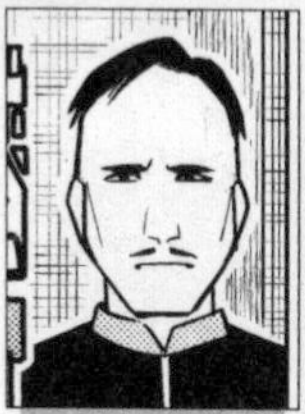

MASURAO NADESHIKO

Pink Squad's No. 2.

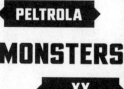

MONSTERS

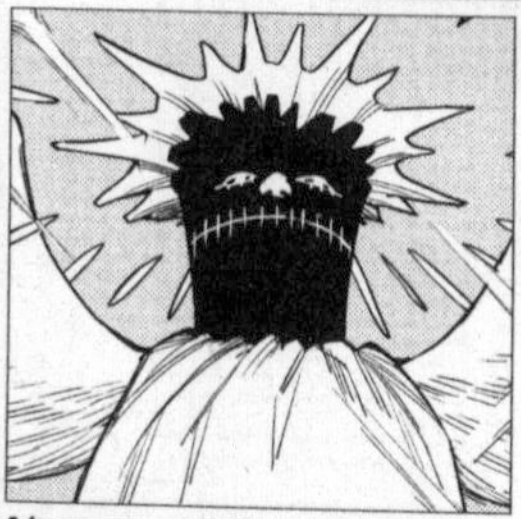

PELTROLA

A boss monster. Thought to have been destroyed by the Dragon Keepers but is actually still alive.

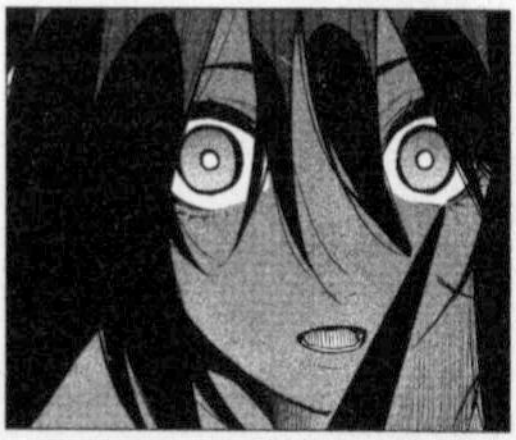

XX (EXES)

A fighter. A proud monster girl who, rather than stay behind in the floating fortress, continued her all-out resistance even after the leaders of the monsters were defeated by the Dragon Keepers.

JUST READ THIS SHORT SUMMARY AND YOU'RE GOOD TO GO!

D has mimicked Hibiki and infiltrated the Ranger Force once more. He now seeks to be promoted to a full member of the Force in order to get closer to the Dragon Keepers! Having learned the true nature of the final exam, he knows that either he or Shion will be promoted, not both. It's now time for the second day of the final exam...!

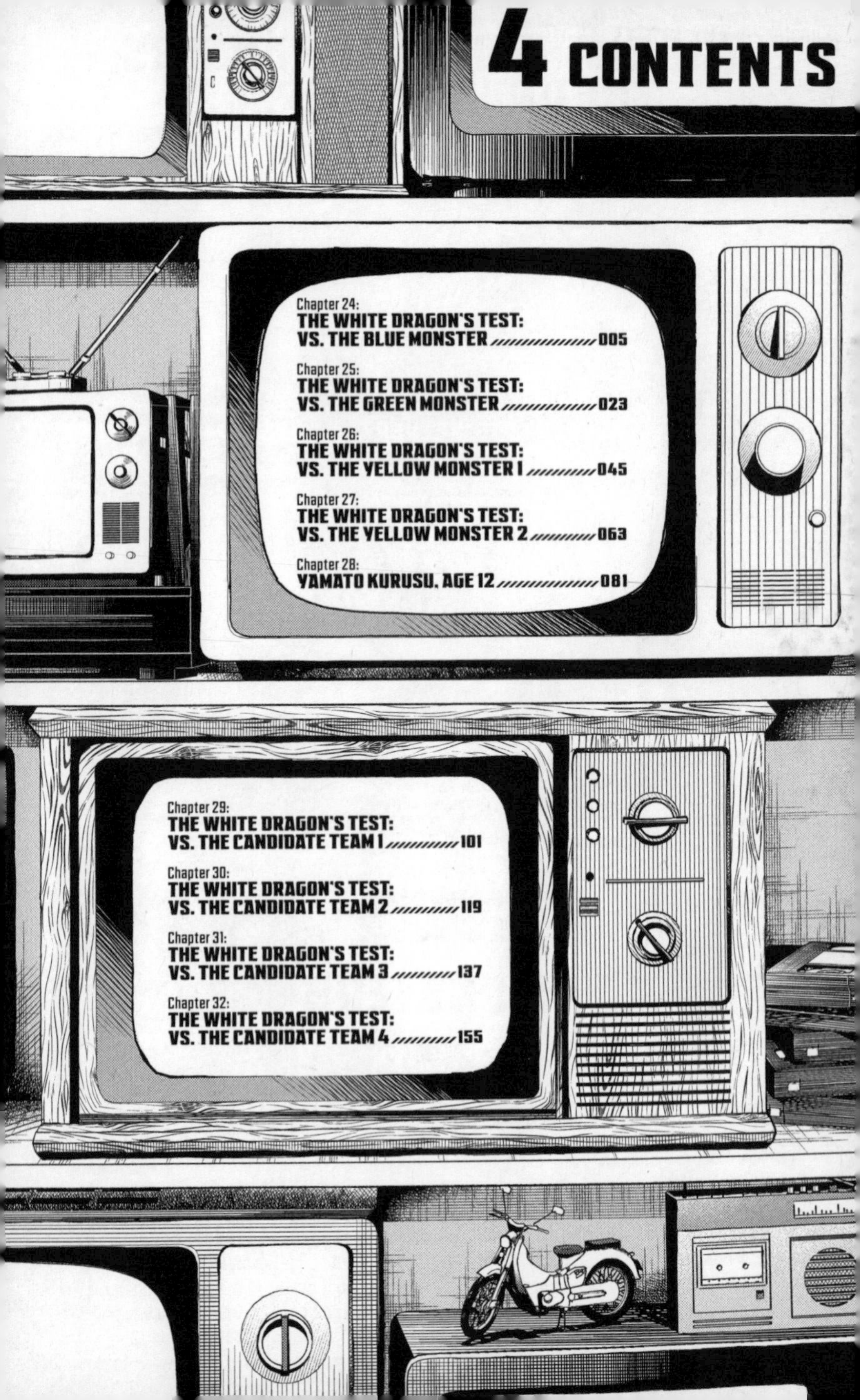

4 CONTENTS

Chapter 24: THE WHITE DRAGON'S TEST: VS. THE BLUE MONSTER

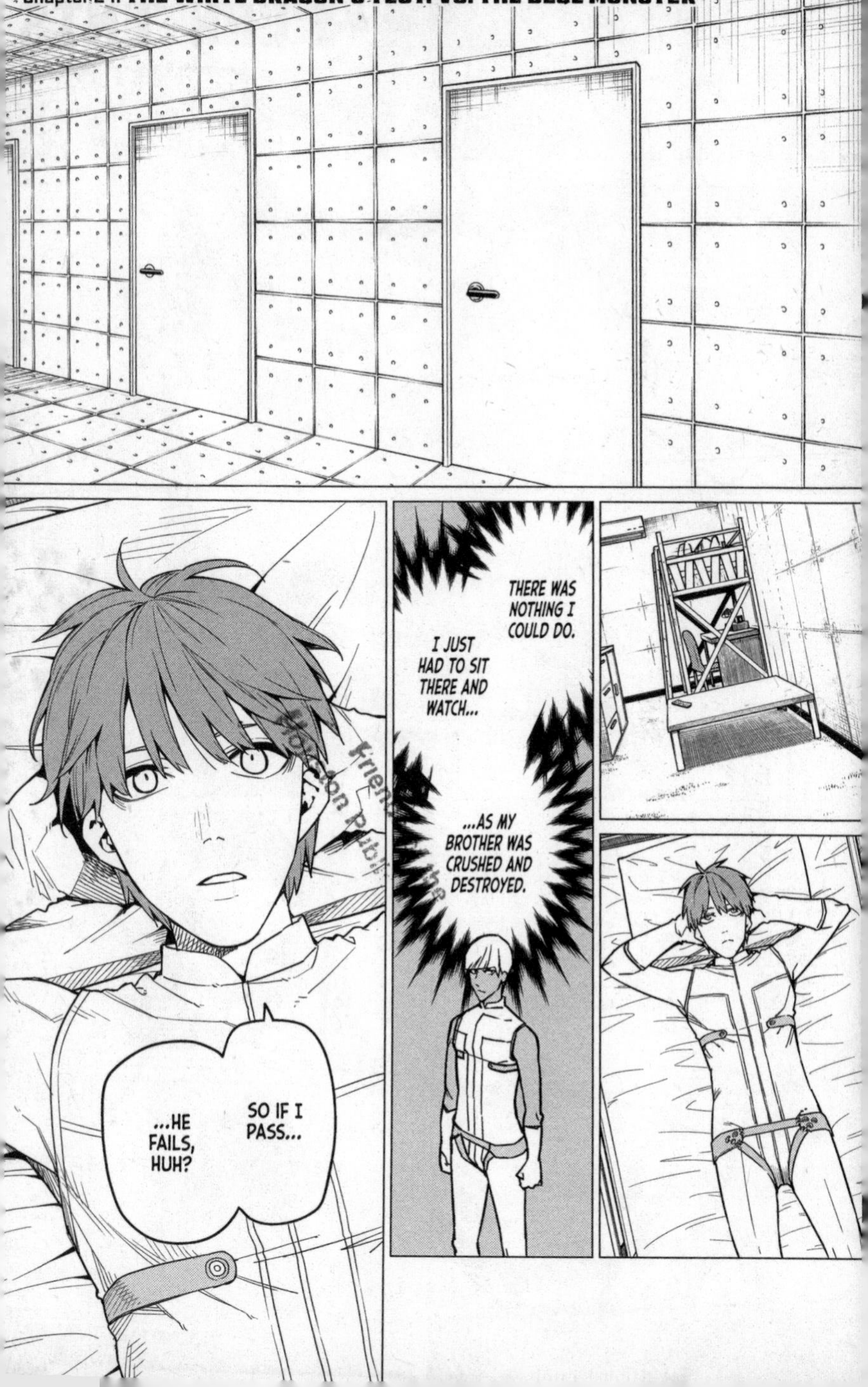
THERE WAS NOTHING I COULD DO.
I JUST HAD TO SIT THERE AND WATCH...
...AS MY BROTHER WAS CRUSHED AND DESTROYED.
SO IF I PASS...
...HE FAILS, HUH?

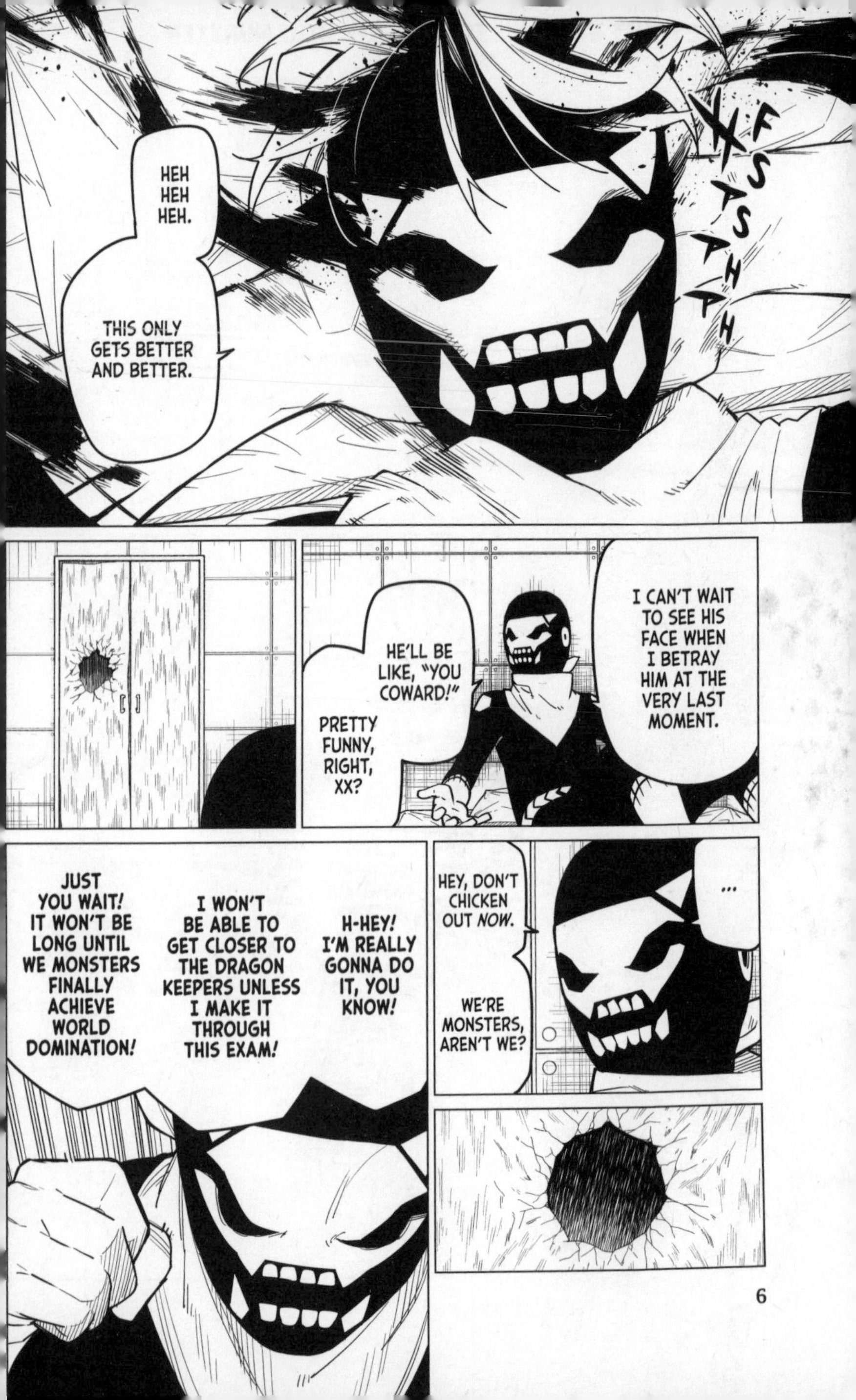
HEH HEH HEH.
THIS ONLY GETS BETTER AND BETTER.
I CAN'T WAIT TO SEE HIS FACE WHEN I BETRAY HIM AT THE VERY LAST MOMENT.
HE'LL BE LIKE, "YOU COWARD!"
PRETTY FUNNY, RIGHT, XX?
...
HEY, DON'T CHICKEN OUT *NOW*.
WE'RE MONSTERS, AREN'T WE?
H-HEY! I'M REALLY GONNA DO IT, YOU KNOW!
I WON'T BE ABLE TO GET CLOSER TO THE DRAGON KEEPERS UNLESS I MAKE IT THROUGH THIS EXAM!
JUST YOU WAIT! IT WON'T BE LONG UNTIL WE MONSTERS FINALLY ACHIEVE WORLD DOMINATION!

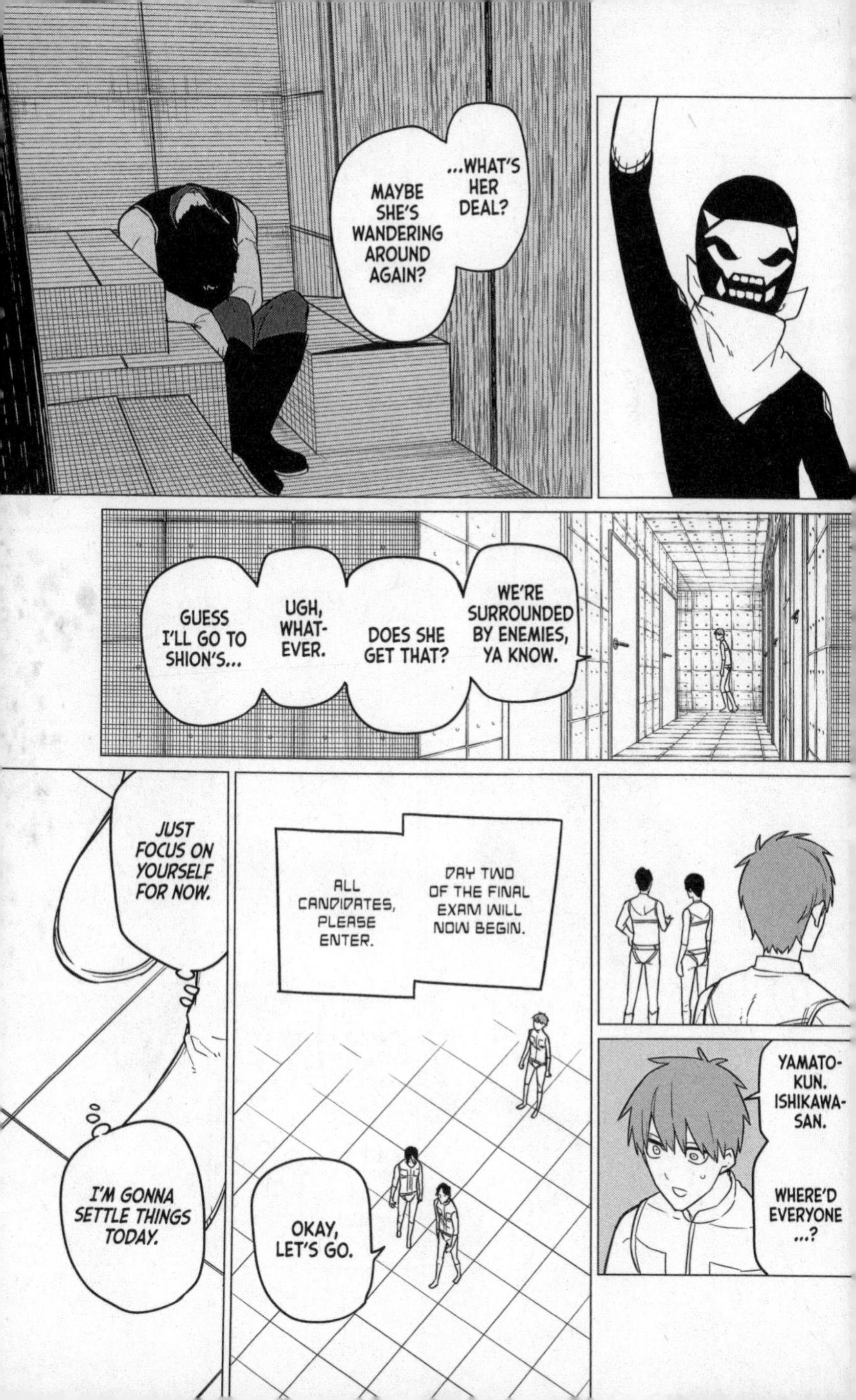
...WHAT'S HER DEAL?
MAYBE SHE'S WANDERING AROUND AGAIN?
WE'RE SURROUNDED BY ENEMIES, YA KNOW.
DOES SHE GET THAT?
UGH, WHAT-EVER.
GUESS I'LL GO TO SHION'S...
YAMATO-KUN. ISHIKAWA-SAN.
WHERE'D EVERYONE ...?
DAY TWO OF THE FINAL EXAM WILL NOW BEGIN.
ALL CANDIDATES, PLEASE ENTER.
OKAY, LET'S GO.
JUST FOCUS ON YOURSELF FOR NOW.
I'M GONNA SETTLE THINGS TODAY.

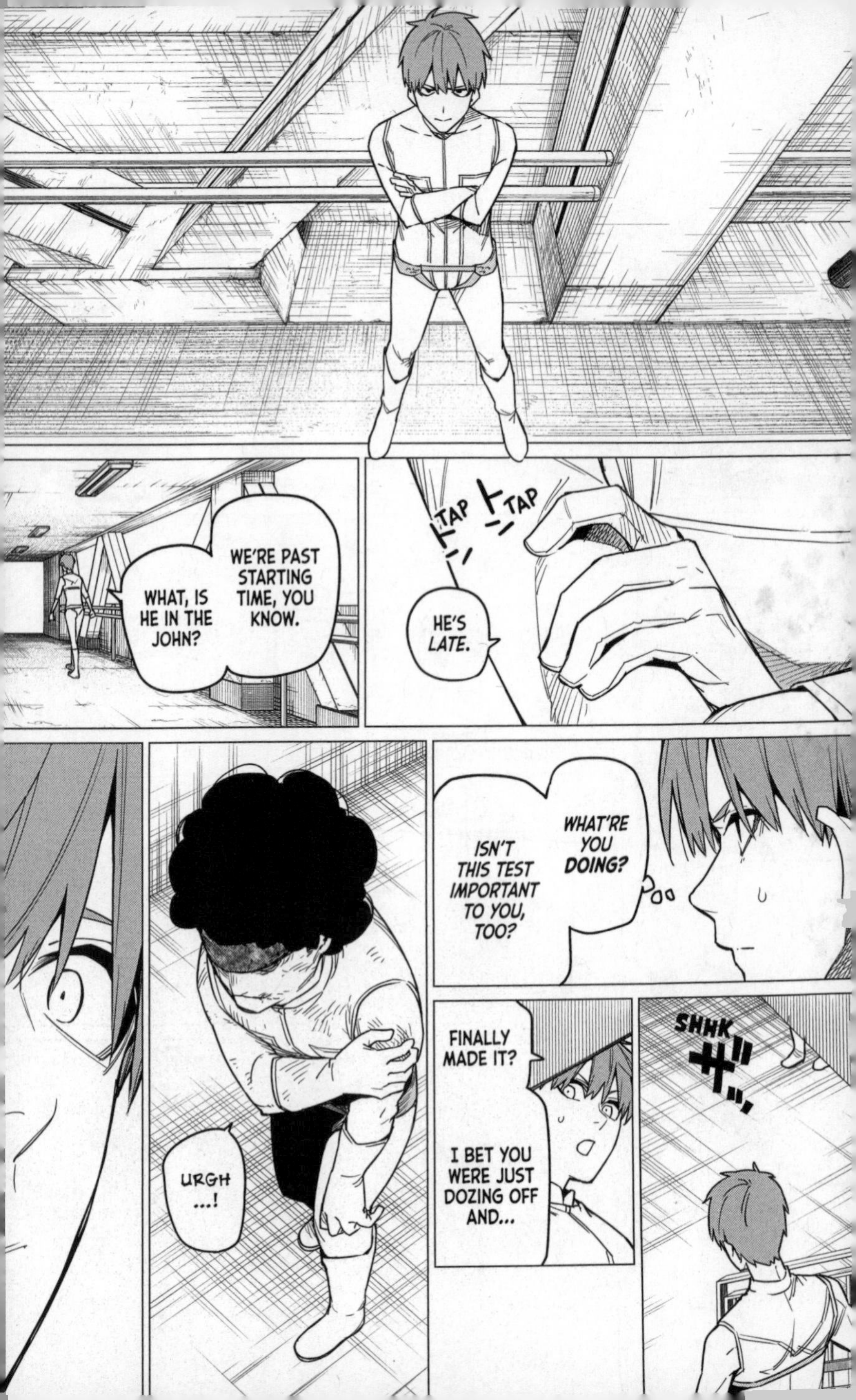
TAP TAP
HE'S LATE.
WE'RE PAST STARTING TIME, YOU KNOW.
WHAT, IS HE IN THE JOHN?
WHAT'RE YOU DOING?
ISN'T THIS TEST IMPORTANT TO YOU, TOO?
SHHK
FINALLY MADE IT?
I BET YOU WERE JUST DOZING OFF AND...
URGH ...!

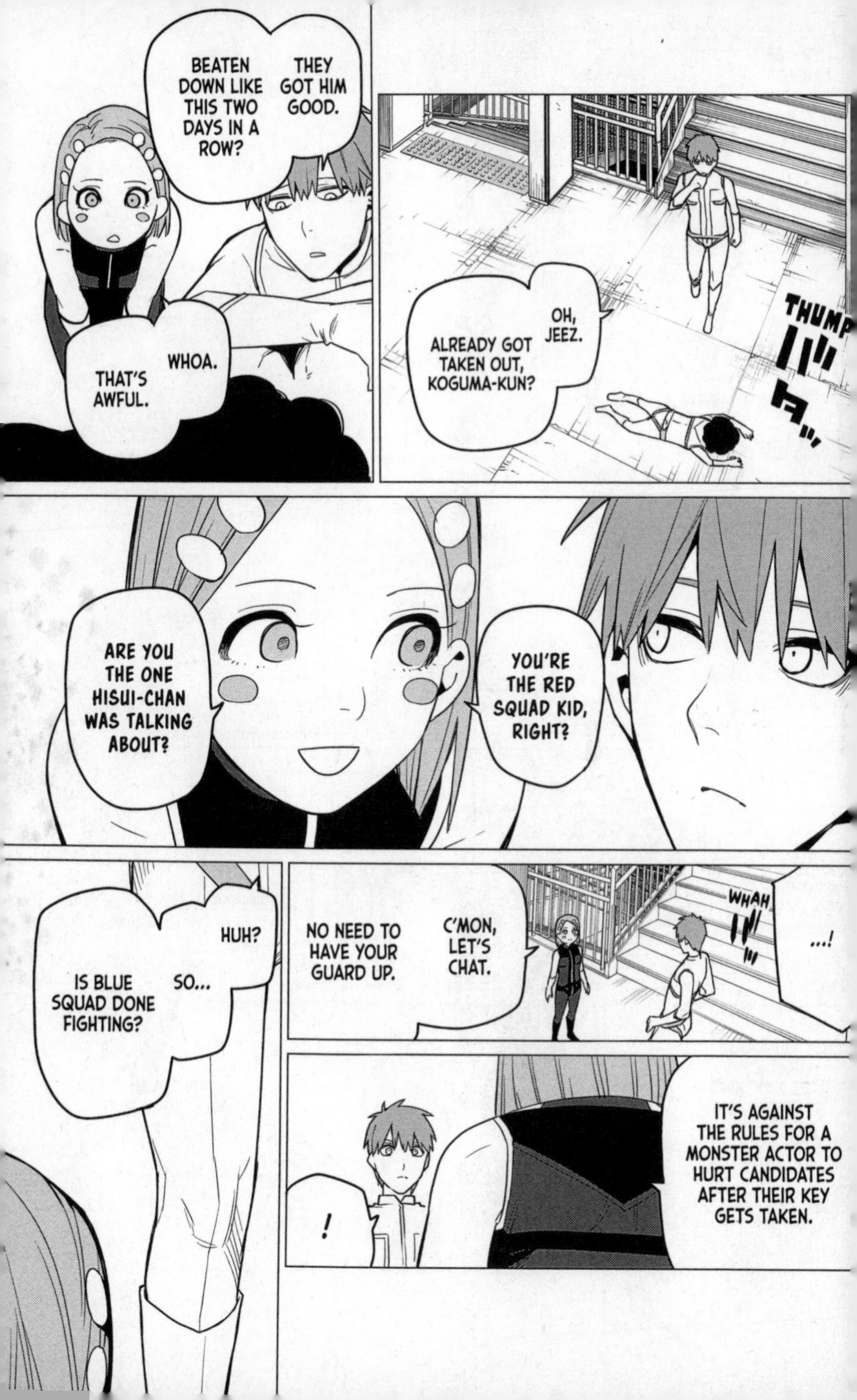
THUMP
OH, JEEZ.
ALREADY GOT TAKEN OUT, KOGUMA-KUN?
THEY GOT HIM GOOD.
BEATEN DOWN LIKE THIS TWO DAYS IN A ROW?
WHOA.
THAT'S AWFUL.
YOU'RE THE RED SQUAD KID, RIGHT?
ARE YOU THE ONE HISUI-CHAN WAS TALKING ABOUT?
...!
WHAH
C'MON, LET'S CHAT.
NO NEED TO HAVE YOUR GUARD UP.
IT'S AGAINST THE RULES FOR A MONSTER ACTOR TO HURT CANDIDATES AFTER THEIR KEY GETS TAKEN.
!
HUH?
SO...
IS BLUE SQUAD DONE FIGHTING?

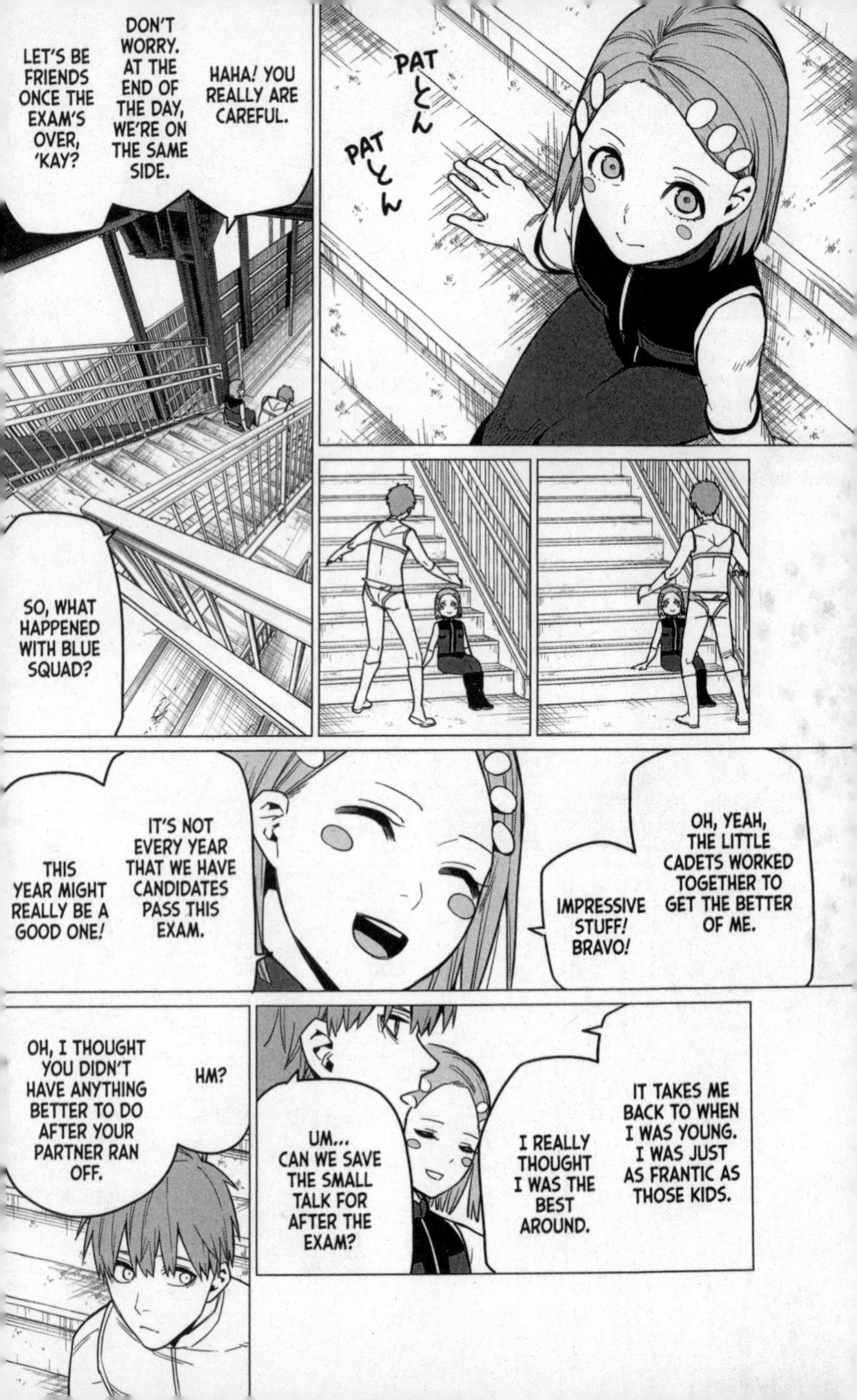
PAT とん
PAT とん
HAHA! YOU REALLY ARE CAREFUL.
DON'T WORRY. AT THE END OF THE DAY, WE'RE ON THE SAME SIDE.
LET'S BE FRIENDS ONCE THE EXAM'S OVER, 'KAY?
SO, WHAT HAPPENED WITH BLUE SQUAD?
OH, YEAH, THE LITTLE CADETS WORKED TOGETHER TO GET THE BETTER OF ME.
IMPRESSIVE STUFF! BRAVO!
IT'S NOT EVERY YEAR THAT WE HAVE CANDIDATES PASS THIS EXAM.
THIS YEAR MIGHT REALLY BE A GOOD ONE!
IT TAKES ME BACK TO WHEN I WAS YOUNG. I WAS JUST AS FRANTIC AS THOSE KIDS.
I REALLY THOUGHT I WAS THE BEST AROUND.
UM... CAN WE SAVE THE SMALL TALK FOR AFTER THE EXAM?
HM?
OH, I THOUGHT YOU DIDN'T HAVE ANYTHING BETTER TO DO AFTER YOUR PARTNER RAN OFF.

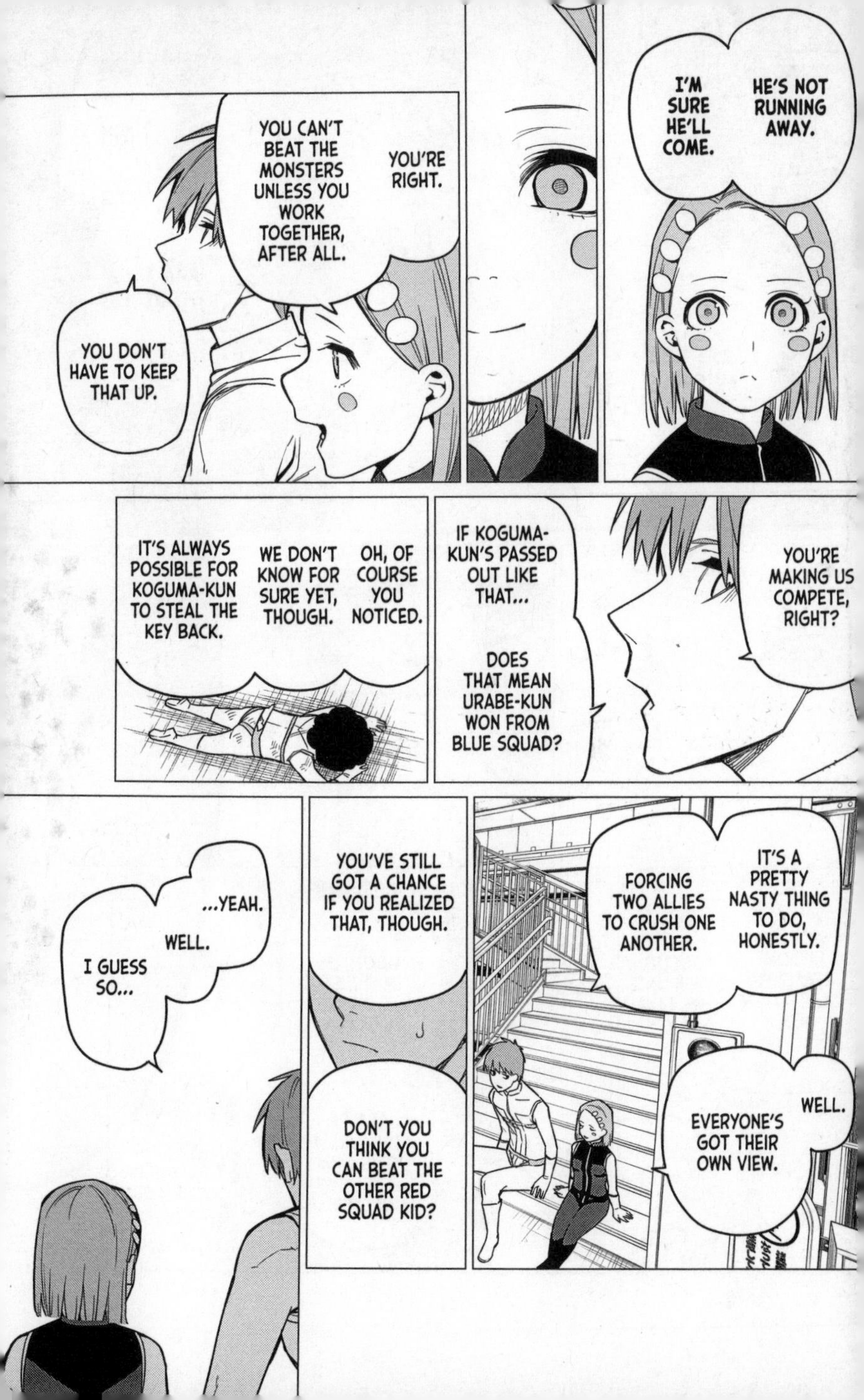
HE'S NOT RUNNING AWAY.
I'M SURE HE'LL COME.
YOU'RE RIGHT.
YOU CAN'T BEAT THE MONSTERS UNLESS YOU WORK TOGETHER, AFTER ALL.
YOU DON'T HAVE TO KEEP THAT UP.
YOU'RE MAKING US COMPETE, RIGHT?
IF KOGUMA-KUN'S PASSED OUT LIKE THAT...
DOES THAT MEAN URABE-KUN WON FROM BLUE SQUAD?
OH, OF COURSE YOU NOTICED.
WE DON'T KNOW FOR SURE YET, THOUGH.
IT'S ALWAYS POSSIBLE FOR KOGUMA-KUN TO STEAL THE KEY BACK.
IT'S A PRETTY NASTY THING TO DO, HONESTLY.
FORCING TWO ALLIES TO CRUSH ONE ANOTHER.
WELL.
EVERYONE'S GOT THEIR OWN VIEW.
YOU'VE STILL GOT A CHANCE IF YOU REALIZED THAT, THOUGH.
DON'T YOU THINK YOU CAN BEAT THE OTHER RED SQUAD KID?
...YEAH.
WELL.
I GUESS SO...

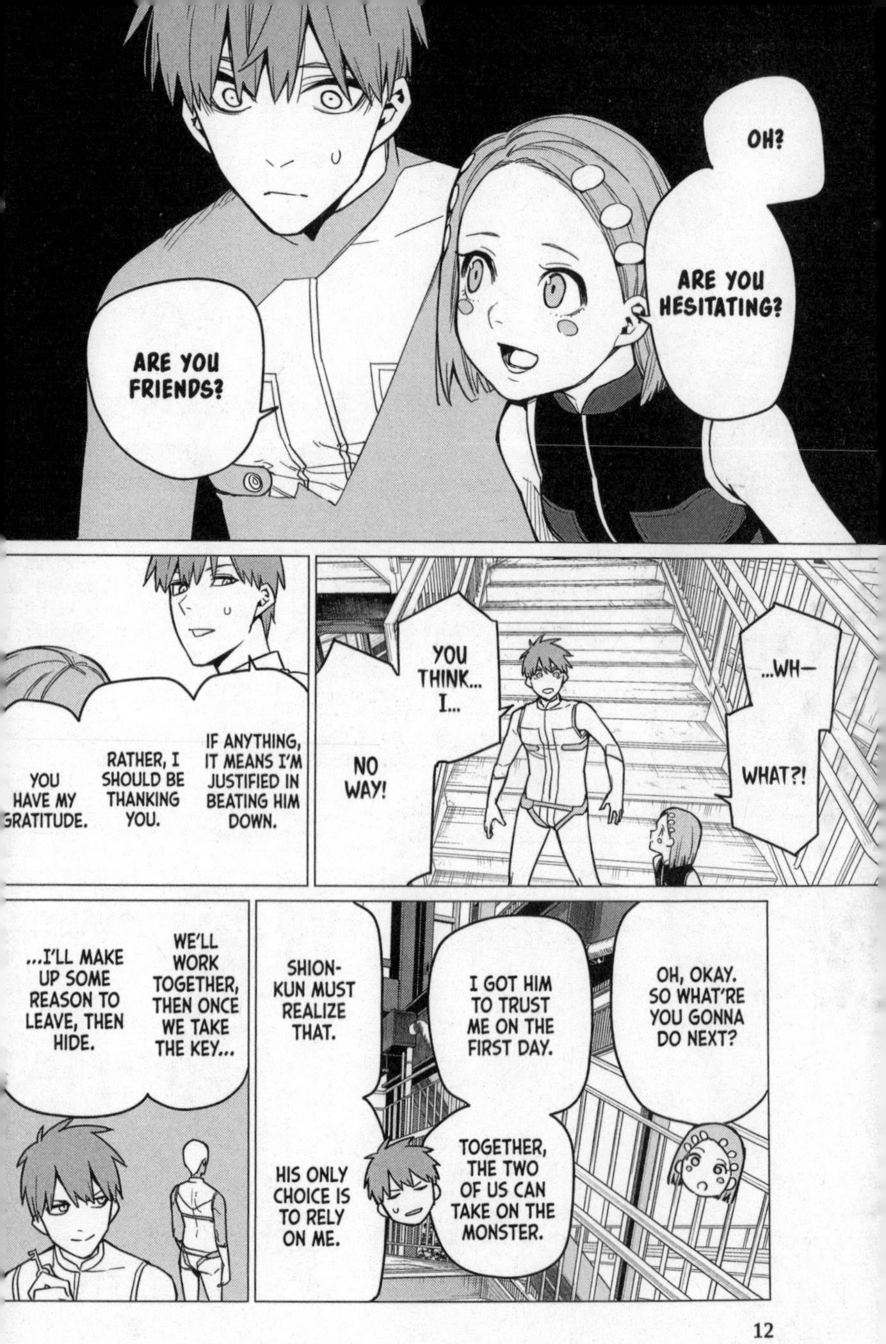
OH?
ARE YOU HESITATING?
ARE YOU FRIENDS?
...WH—
WHAT?!
YOU THINK... I...
NO WAY!
IF ANYTHING, IT MEANS I'M JUSTIFIED IN BEATING HIM DOWN.
RATHER, I SHOULD BE THANKING YOU.
YOU HAVE MY GRATITUDE.
OH, OKAY. SO WHAT'RE YOU GONNA DO NEXT?
I GOT HIM TO TRUST ME ON THE FIRST DAY.
TOGETHER, THE TWO OF US CAN TAKE ON THE MONSTER.
SHION-KUN MUST REALIZE THAT.
HIS ONLY CHOICE IS TO RELY ON ME.
WE'LL WORK TOGETHER, THEN ONCE WE TAKE THE KEY...
...I'LL MAKE UP SOME REASON TO LEAVE, THEN HIDE.

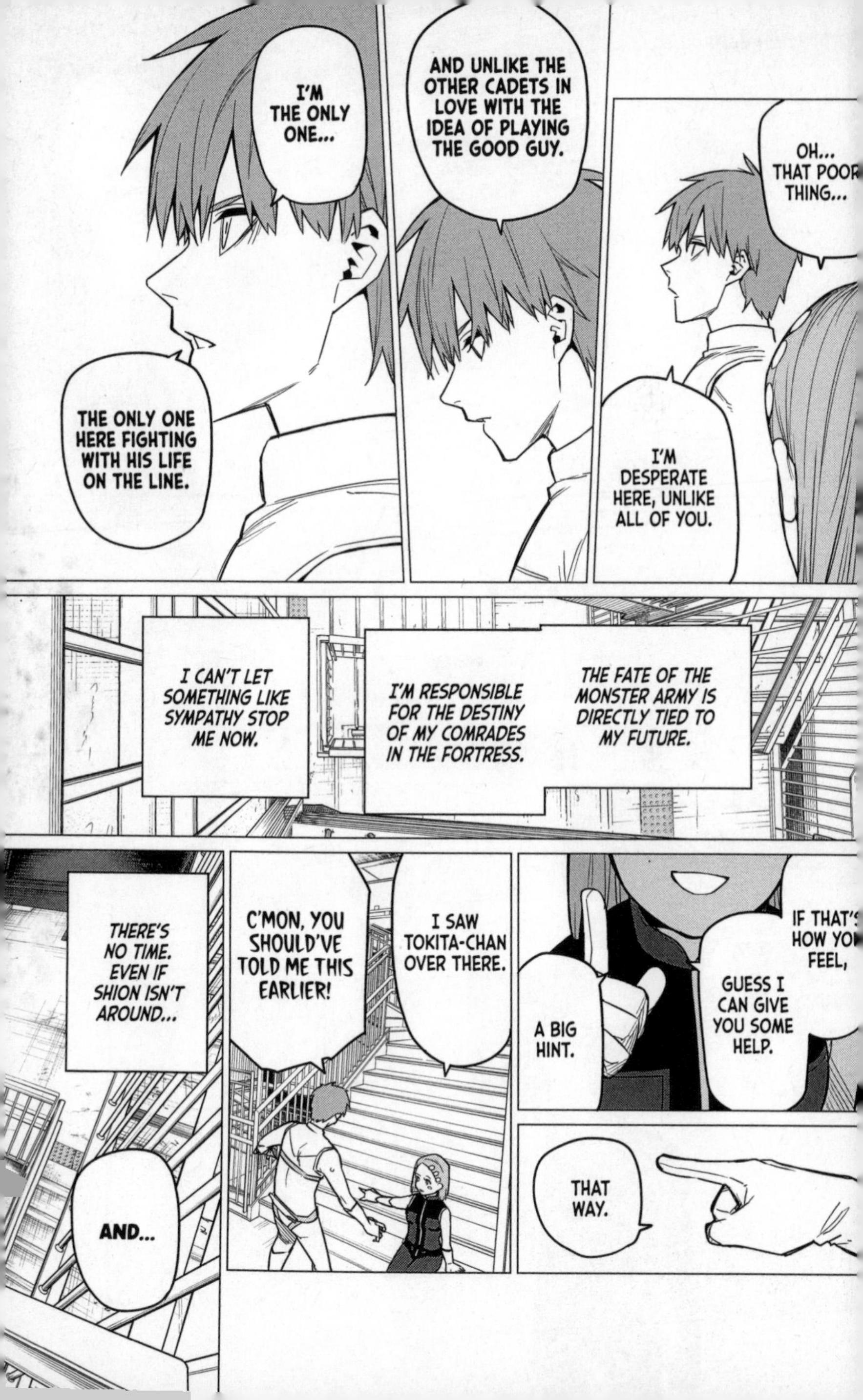

OH... THAT POOR THING...
I'M DESPERATE HERE, UNLIKE ALL OF YOU.
AND UNLIKE THE OTHER CADETS IN LOVE WITH THE IDEA OF PLAYING THE GOOD GUY.
I'M THE ONLY ONE...
THE ONLY ONE HERE FIGHTING WITH HIS LIFE ON THE LINE.
THE FATE OF THE MONSTER ARMY IS DIRECTLY TIED TO MY FUTURE.
I'M RESPONSIBLE FOR THE DESTINY OF MY COMRADES IN THE FORTRESS.
I CAN'T LET SOMETHING LIKE SYMPATHY STOP ME NOW.
IF THAT'S HOW YO FEEL,
GUESS I CAN GIVE YOU SOME HELP.
A BIG HINT.
THAT WAY.
I SAW TOKITA-CHAN OVER THERE.
C'MON, YOU SHOULD'VE TOLD ME THIS EARLIER!
THERE'S NO TIME. EVEN IF SHION ISN'T AROUND...
AND...

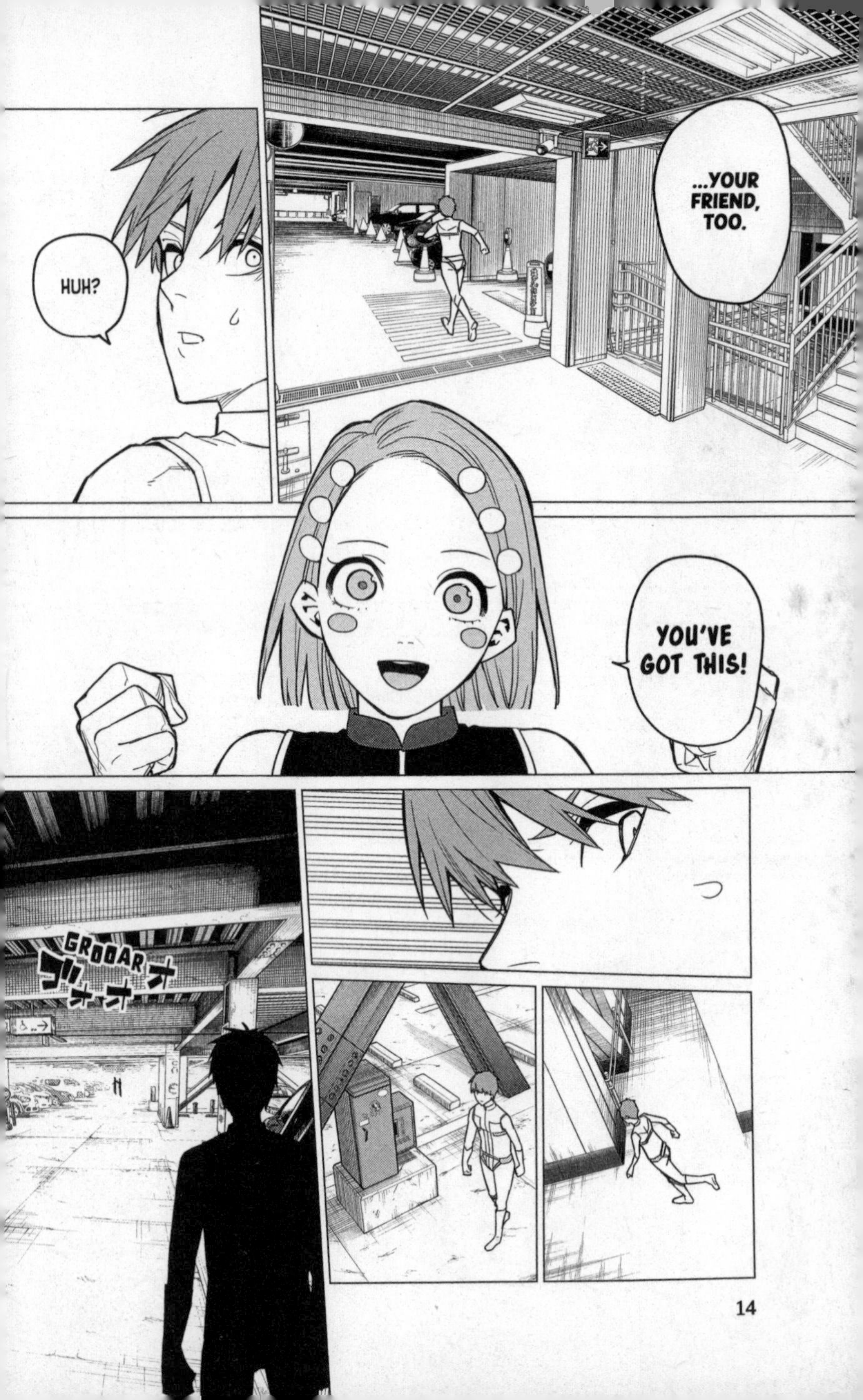
...YOUR FRIEND, TOO.
HUH?
YOU'VE GOT THIS!
GROOAR

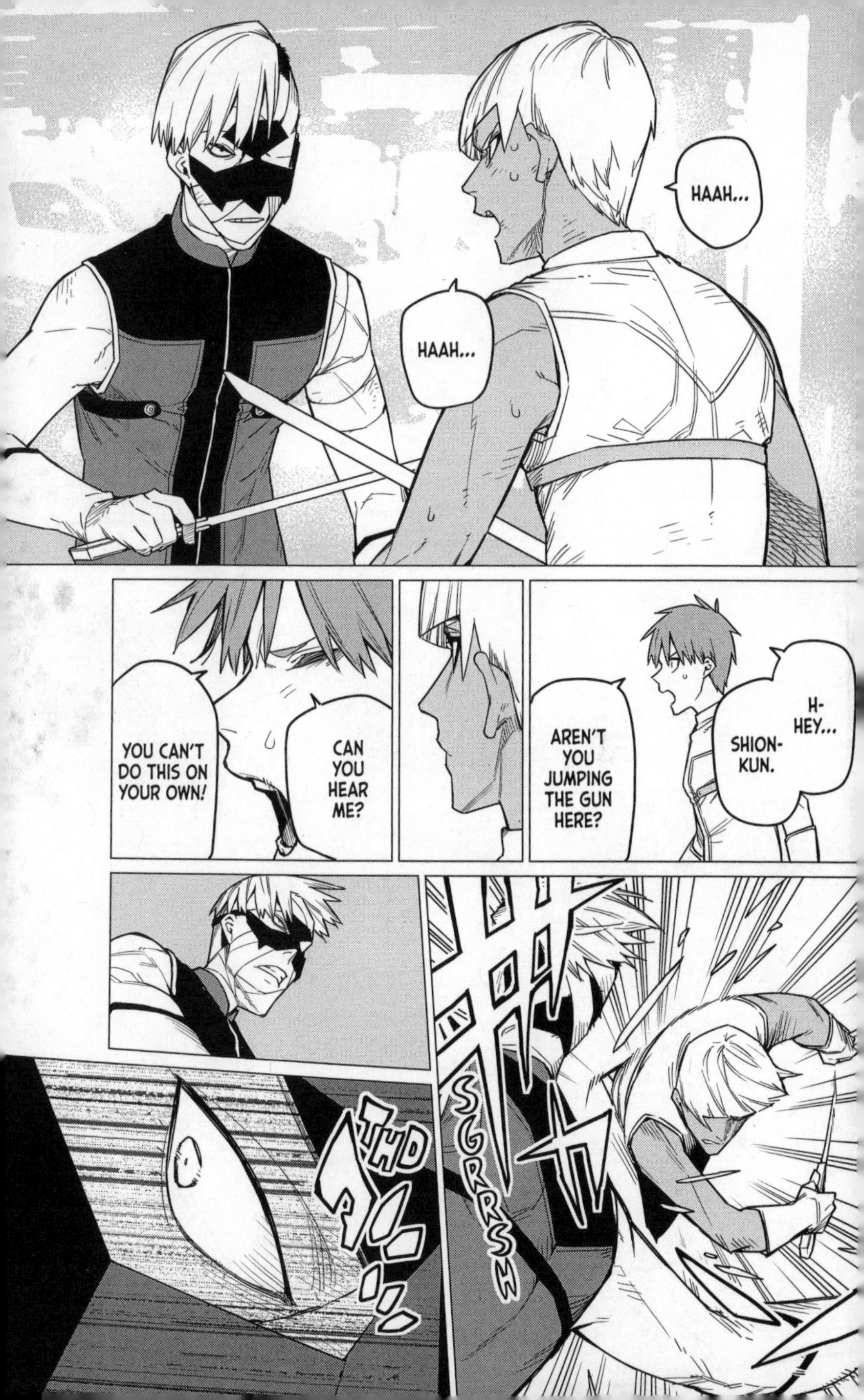
HAAH...
HAAH...
H-HEY... SHION-KUN.
AREN'T YOU JUMPING THE GUN HERE?
CAN YOU HEAR ME?
YOU CAN'T DO THIS ON YOUR OWN!
SGRRSH
THD

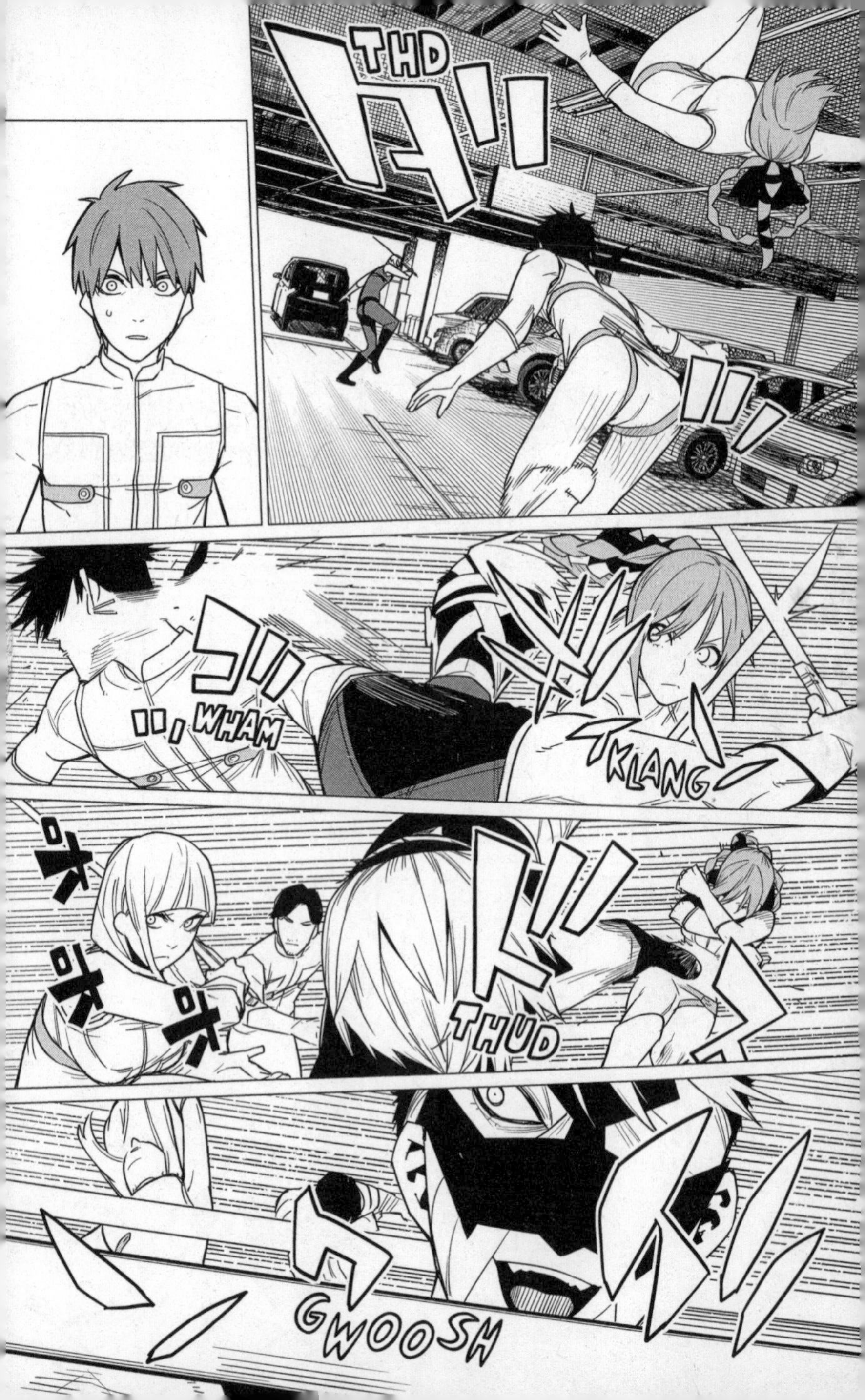
THD
KLANG
WHAM
THUD
GWOOSH

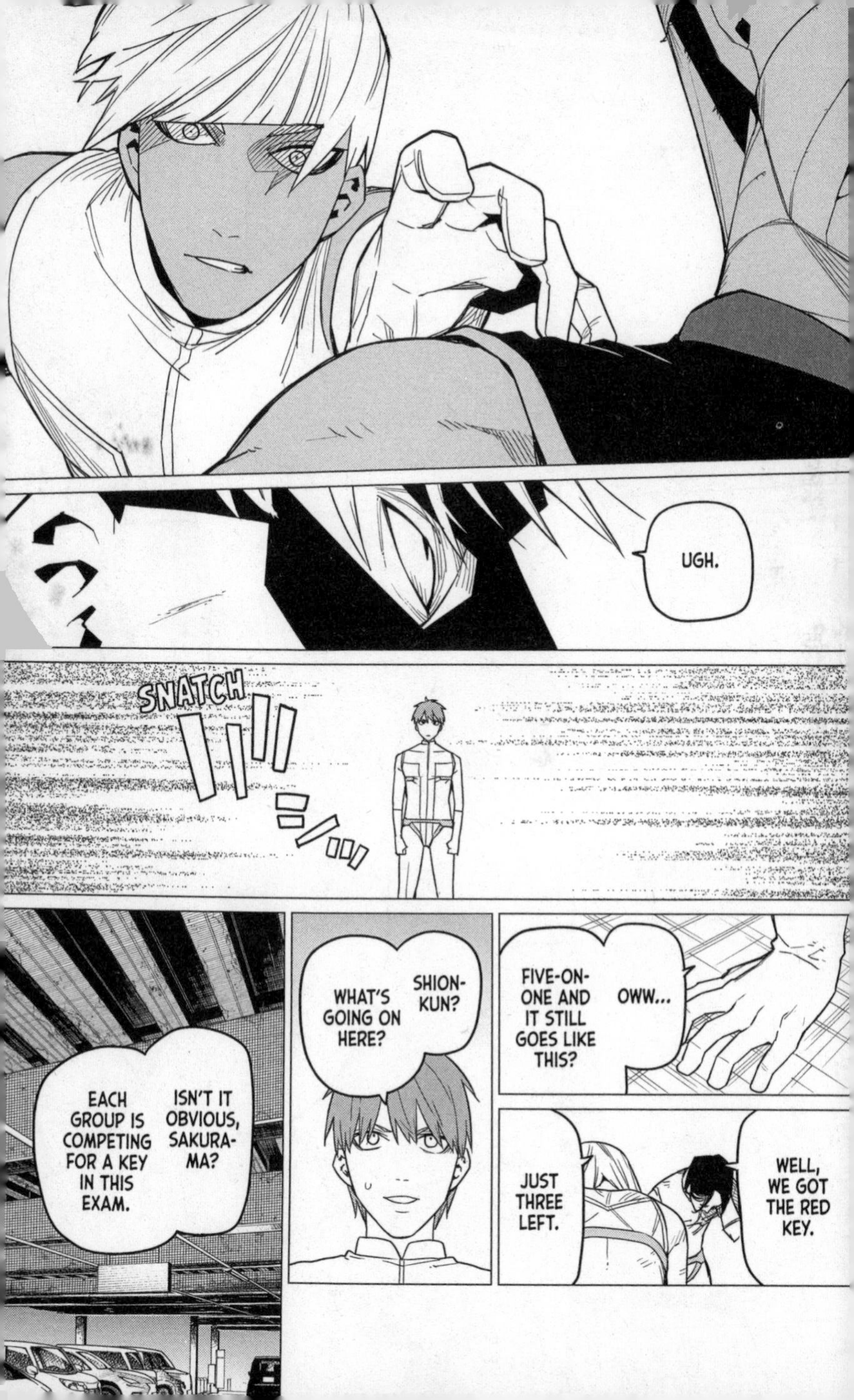
UGH.
SNATCH
OWW...
FIVE-ON-ONE AND IT STILL GOES LIKE THIS?
WELL, WE GOT THE RED KEY.
JUST THREE LEFT.
SHION-KUN?
WHAT'S GOING ON HERE?
ISN'T IT OBVIOUS, SAKURA-MA?
EACH GROUP IS COMPETING FOR A KEY IN THIS EXAM.

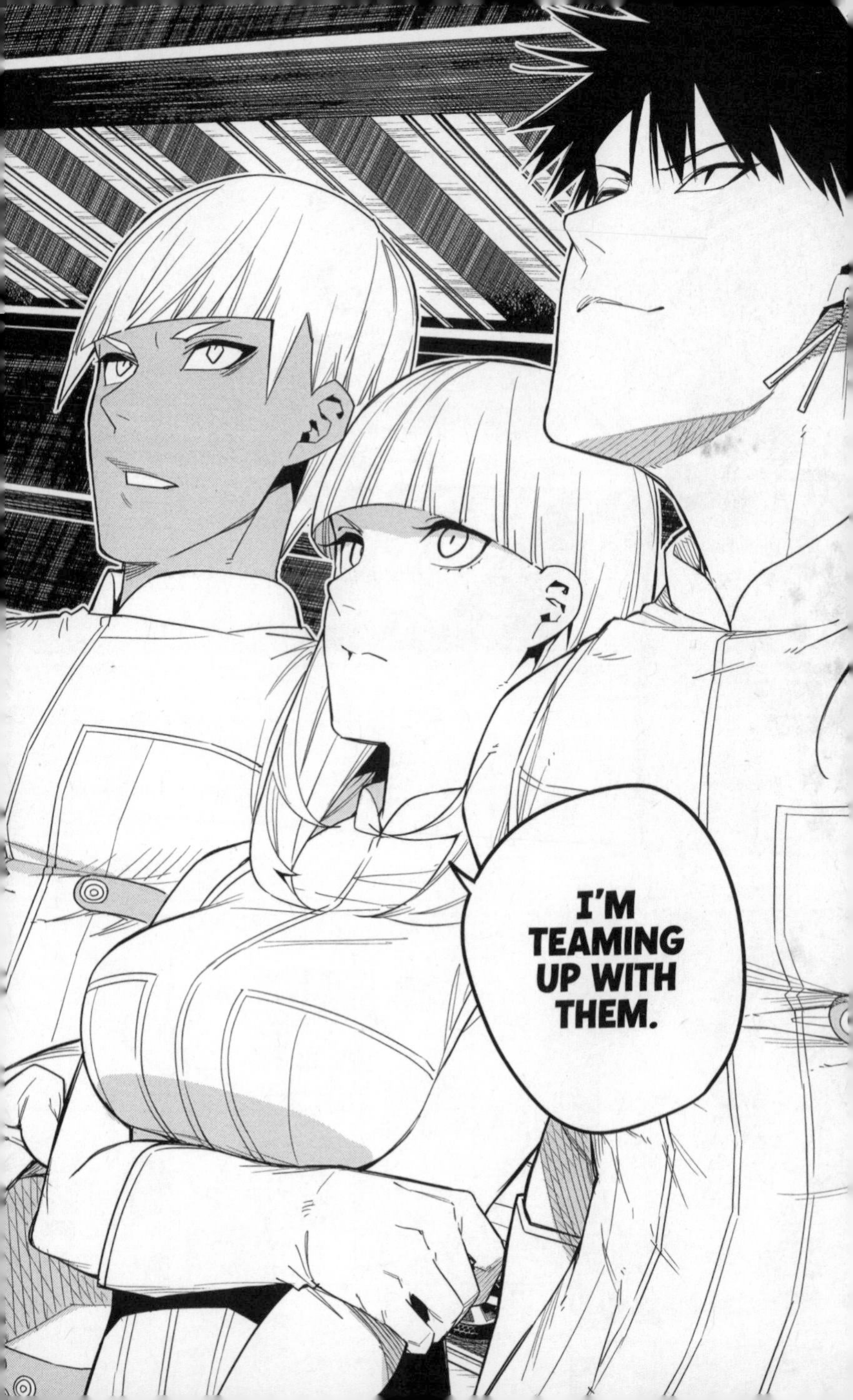
I'M TEAMING UP WITH THEM.

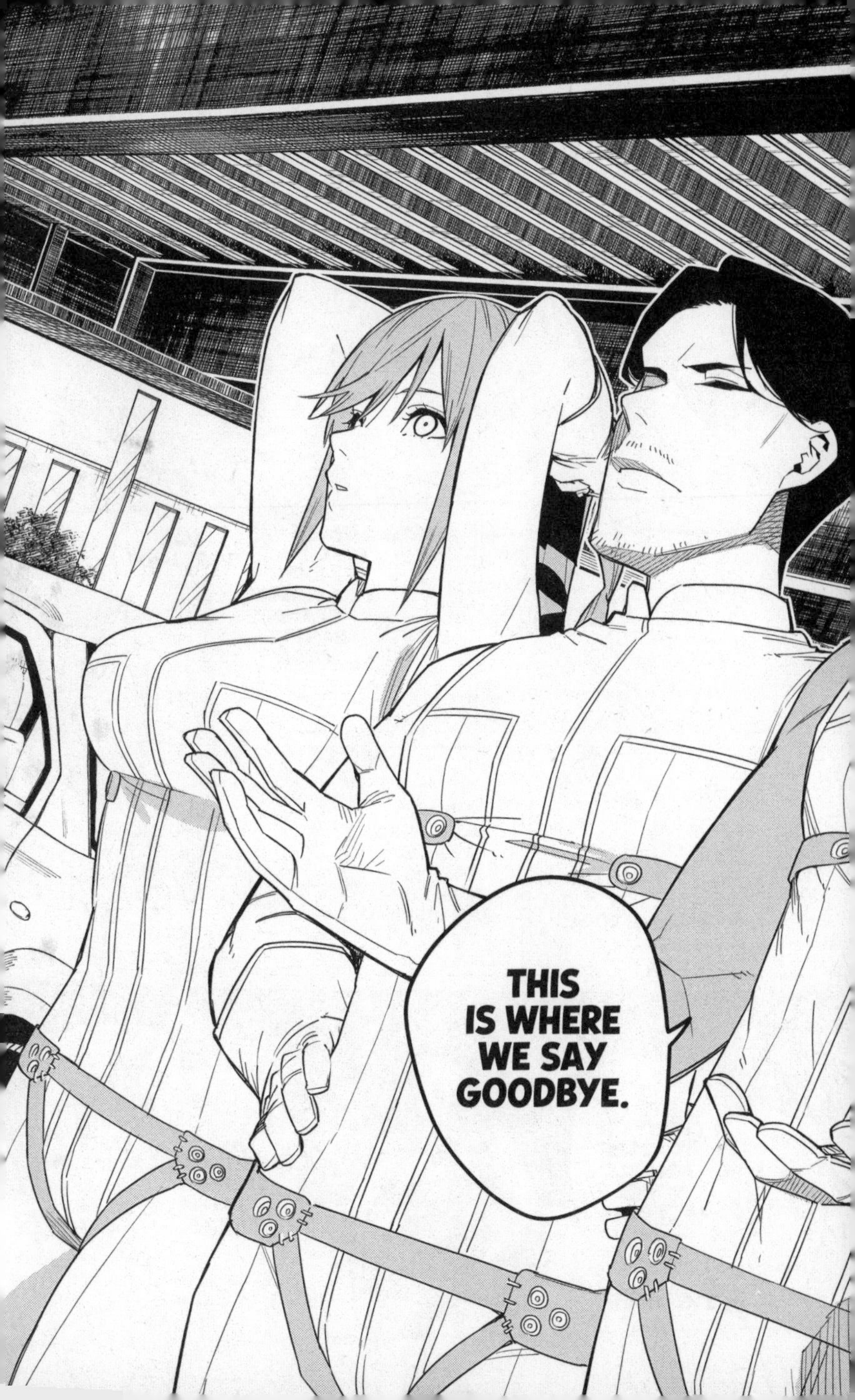
THIS IS WHERE WE SAY GOODBYE.

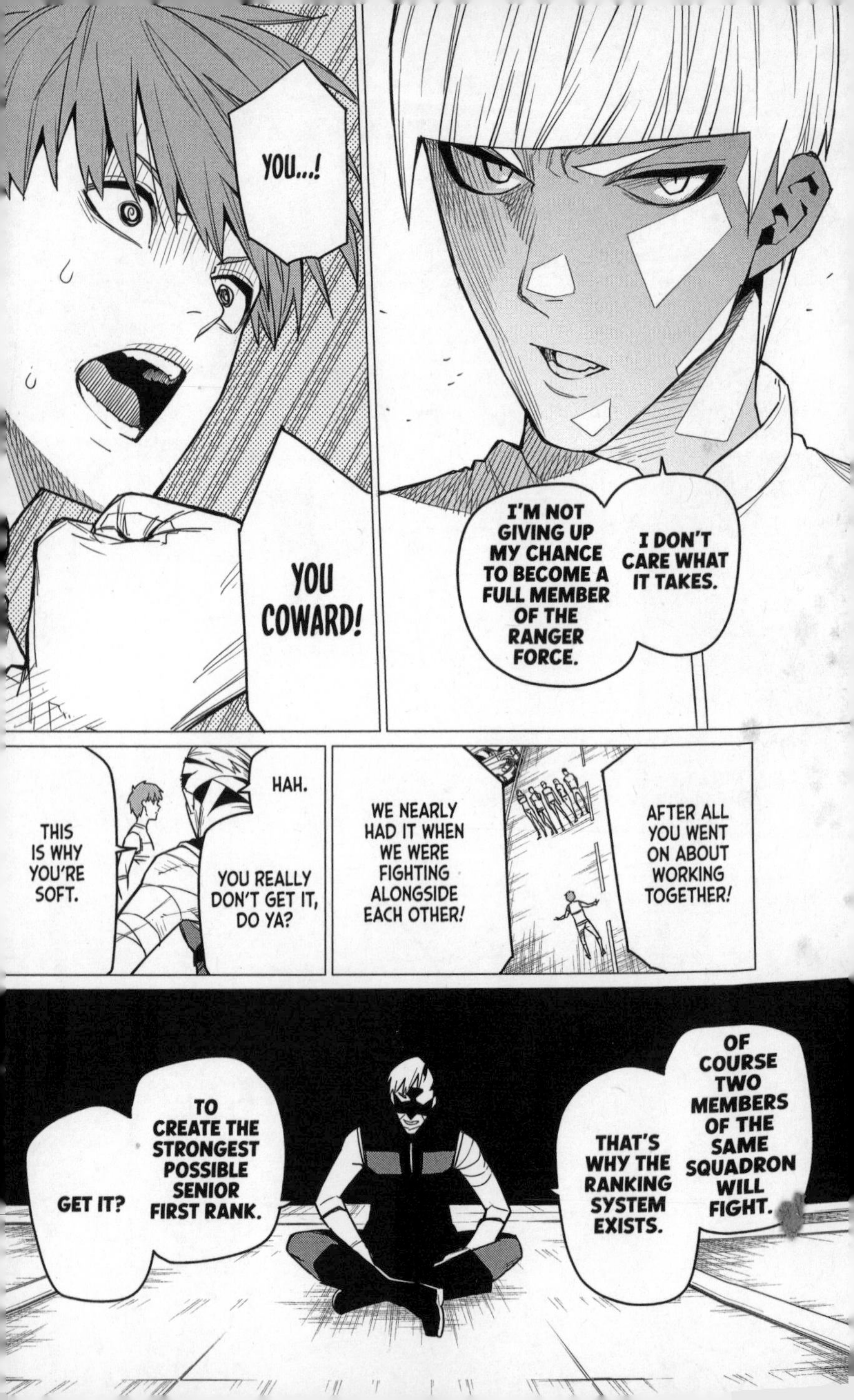
I DON'T CARE WHAT IT TAKES.
I'M NOT GIVING UP MY CHANCE TO BECOME A FULL MEMBER OF THE RANGER FORCE.
YOU...!
YOU COWARD!
AFTER ALL YOU WENT ON ABOUT WORKING TOGETHER!
WE NEARLY HAD IT WHEN WE WERE FIGHTING ALONGSIDE EACH OTHER!
HAH.
YOU REALLY DON'T GET IT, DO YA?
THIS IS WHY YOU'RE SOFT.
OF COURSE TWO MEMBERS OF THE SAME SQUADRON WILL FIGHT.
THAT'S WHY THE RANKING SYSTEM EXISTS.
TO CREATE THE STRONGEST POSSIBLE SENIOR FIRST RANK.
GET IT?

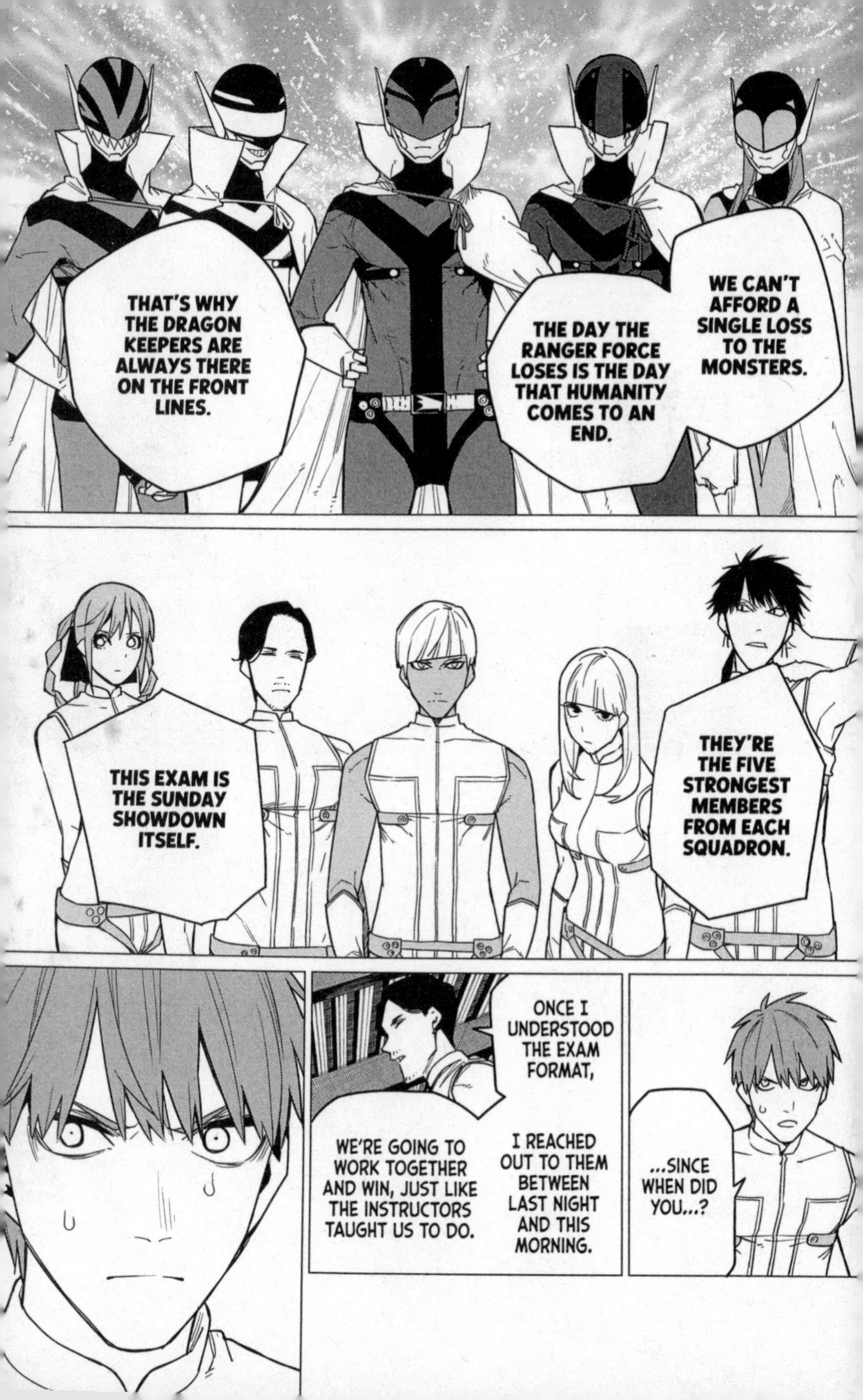
WE CAN'T AFFORD A SINGLE LOSS TO THE MONSTERS.
THE DAY THE RANGER FORCE LOSES IS THE DAY THAT HUMANITY COMES TO AN END.
THAT'S WHY THE DRAGON KEEPERS ARE ALWAYS THERE ON THE FRONT LINES.
THEY'RE THE FIVE STRONGEST MEMBERS FROM EACH SQUADRON.
THIS EXAM IS THE SUNDAY SHOWDOWN ITSELF.
...SINCE WHEN DID YOU...?
ONCE I UNDERSTOOD THE EXAM FORMAT,
I REACHED OUT TO THEM BETWEEN LAST NIGHT AND THIS MORNING.
WE'RE GOING TO WORK TOGETHER AND WIN, JUST LIKE THE INSTRUCTORS TAUGHT US TO DO.

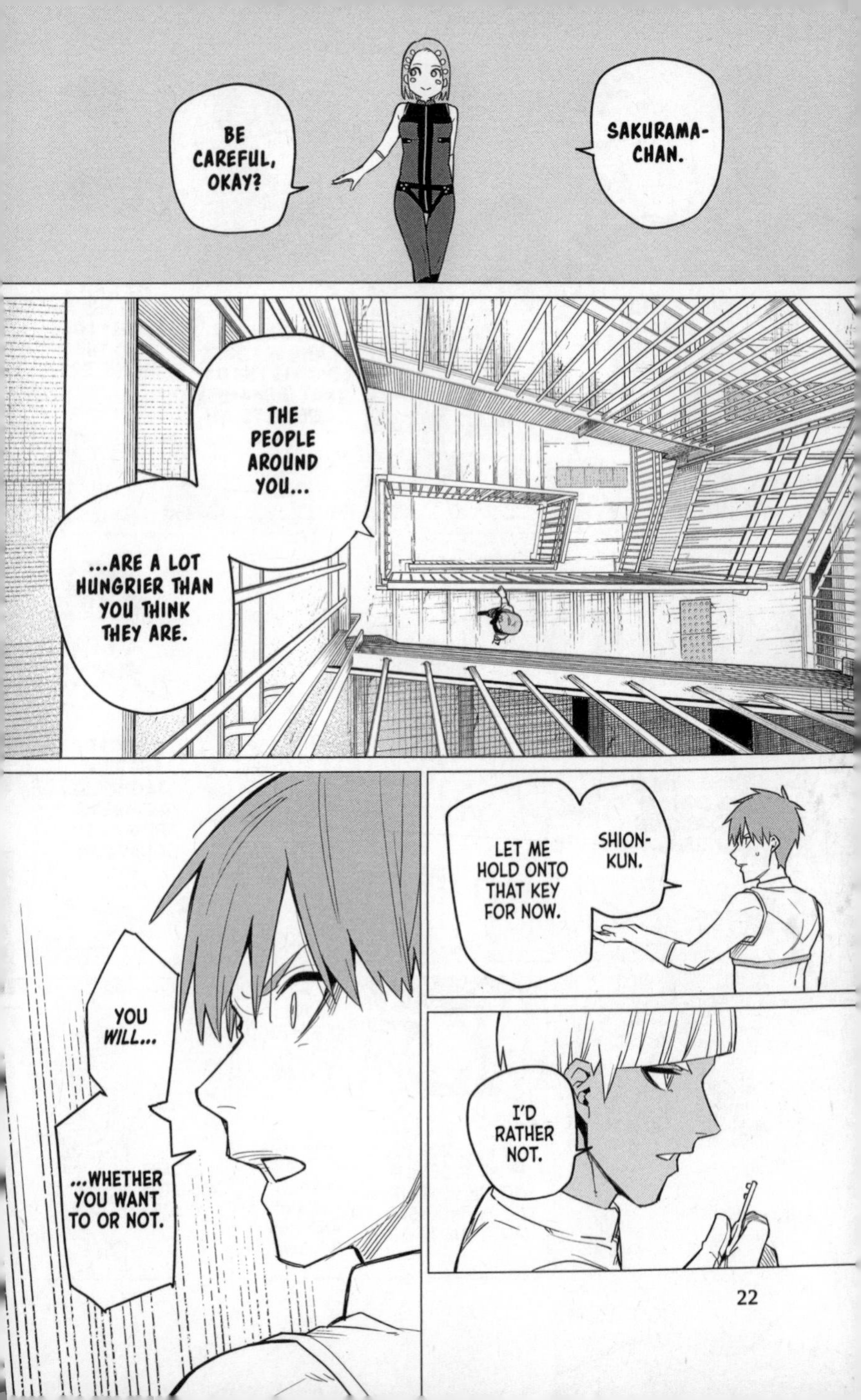
SAKURAMA-CHAN.
BE CAREFUL, OKAY?
THE PEOPLE AROUND YOU...
...ARE A LOT HUNGRIER THAN YOU THINK THEY ARE.
SHION-KUN.
LET ME HOLD ONTO THAT KEY FOR NOW.
I'D RATHER NOT.
YOU WILL...
...WHETHER YOU WANT TO OR NOT.

Chapter 25: THE WHITE DRAGON'S TEST: VS. THE GREEN MONSTER

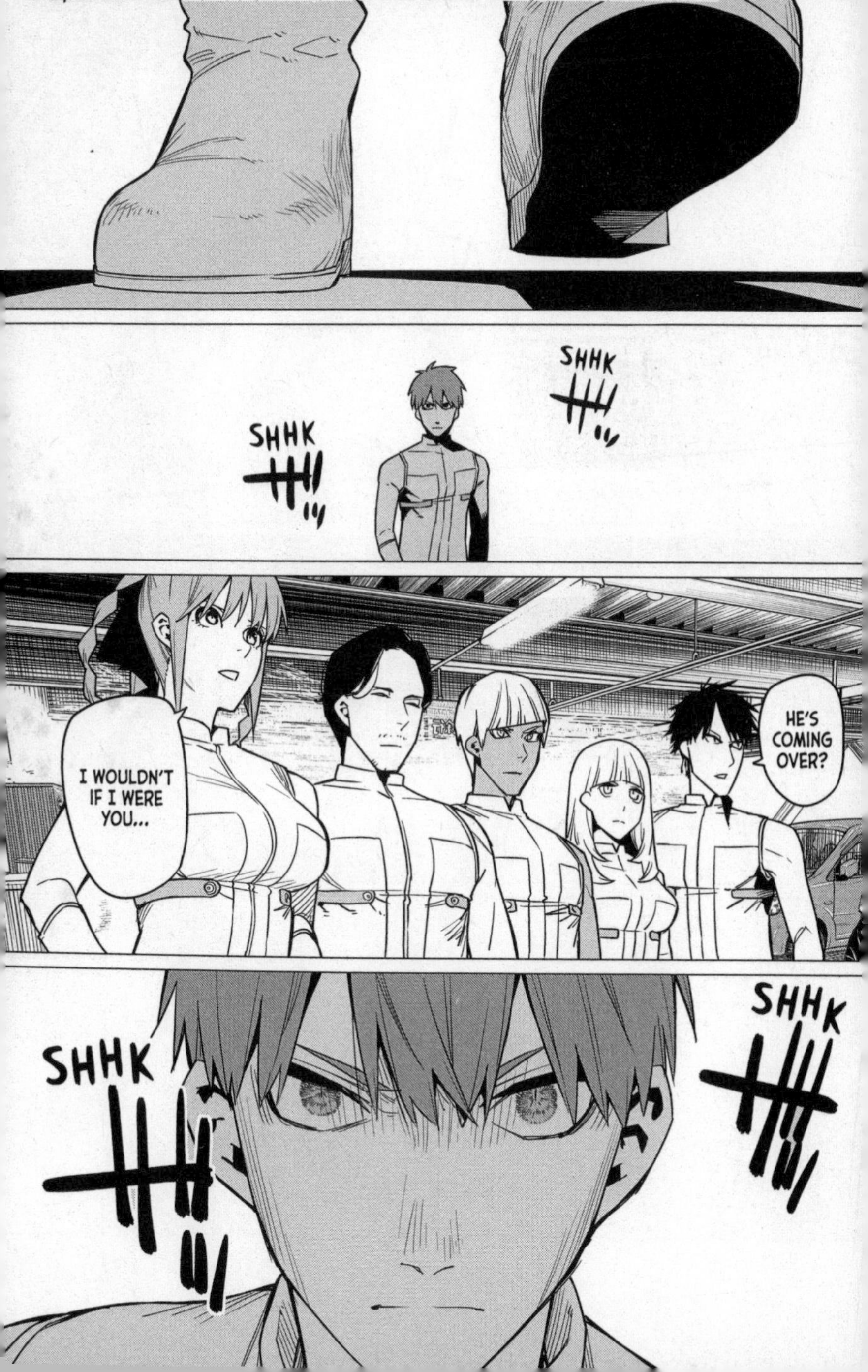
SHHK
SHHK
HE'S COMING OVER?
I WOULDN'T IF I WERE YOU...
SHHK
SHHK

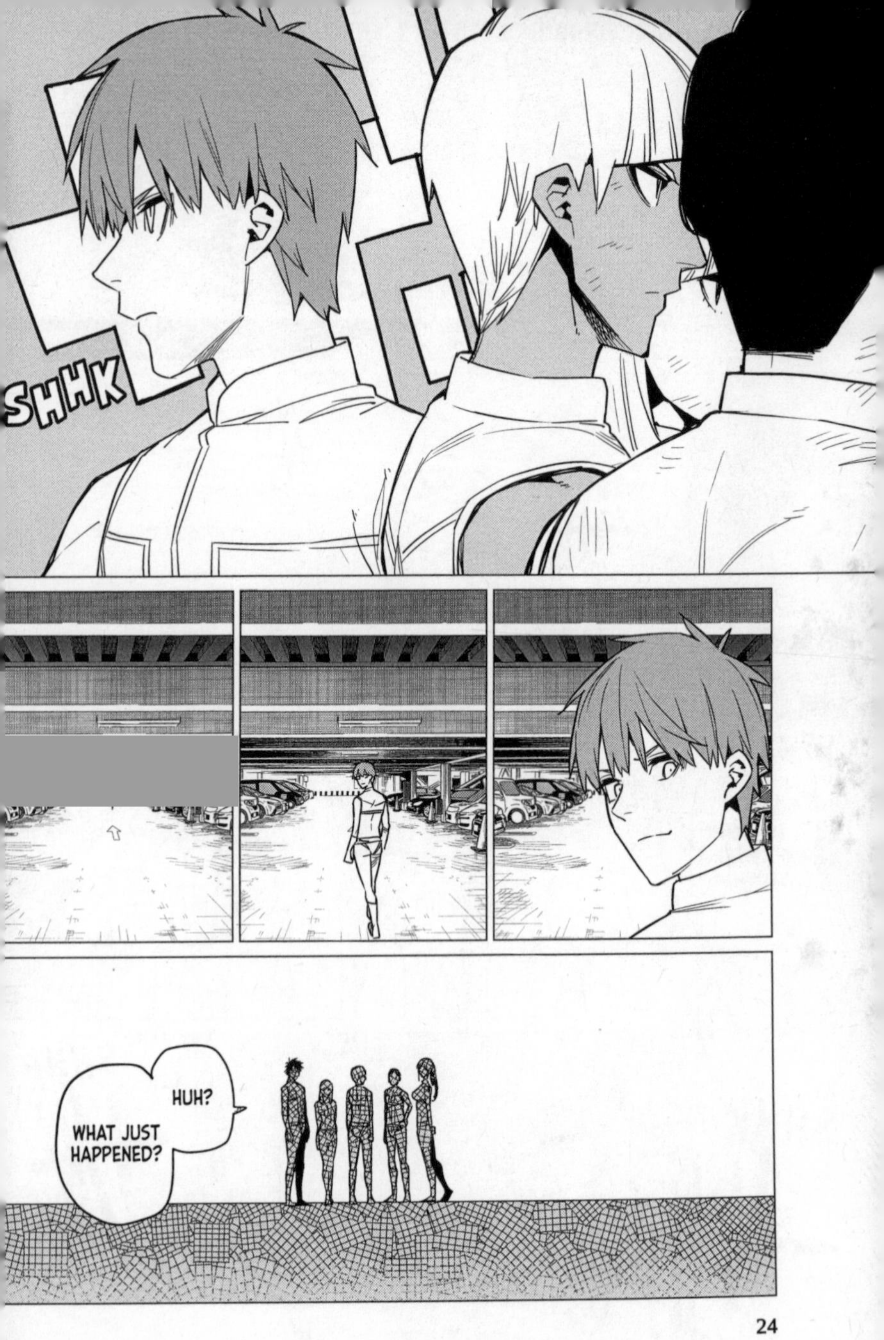
SHHK
HUH?
WHAT JUST HAPPENED?

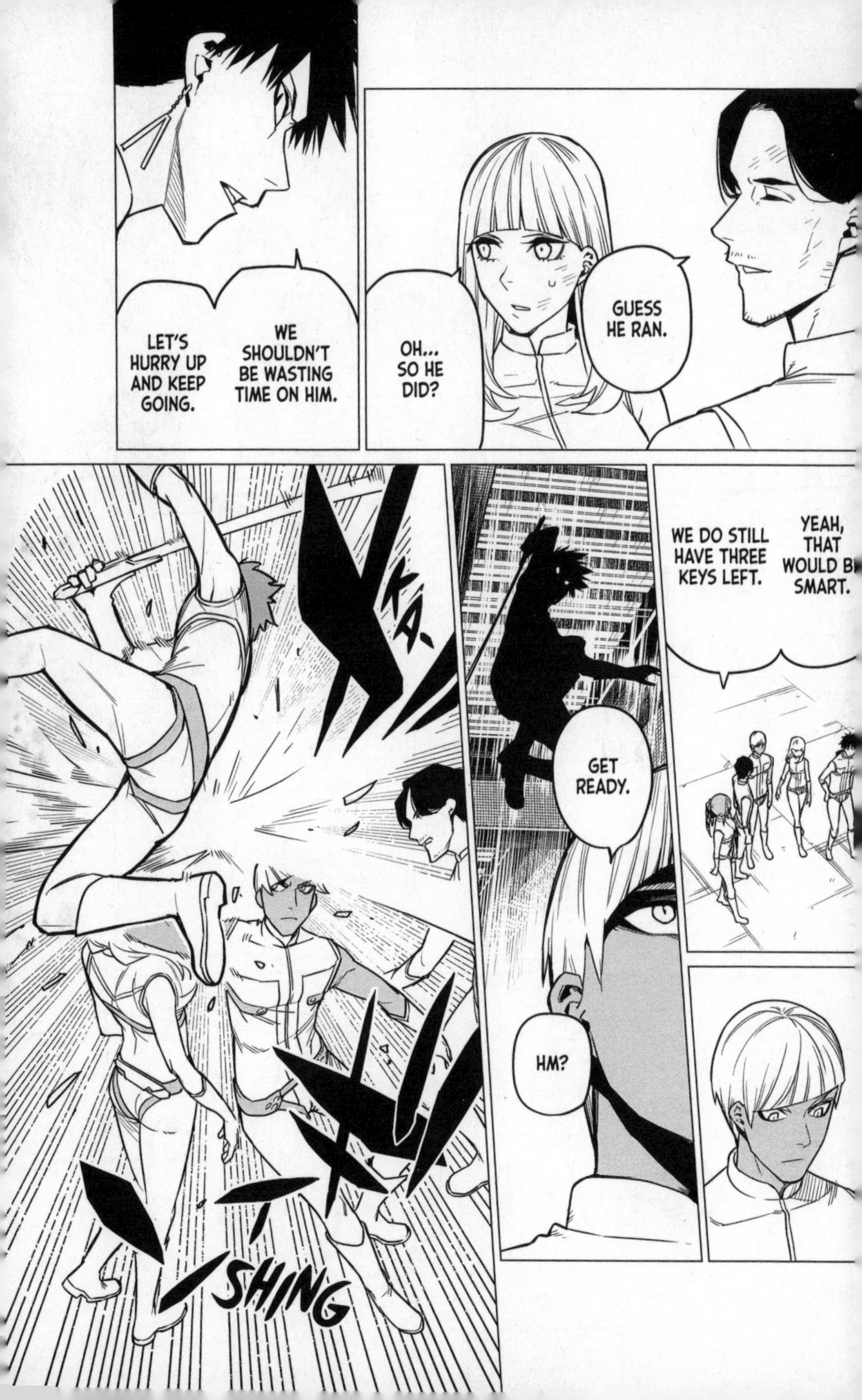
GUESS HE RAN.
OH... SO HE DID?
WE SHOULDN'T BE WASTING TIME ON HIM.
LET'S HURRY UP AND KEEP GOING.
YEAH, THAT WOULD B SMART.
WE DO STILL HAVE THREE KEYS LEFT.
GET READY.
HM?
KA-
SHING

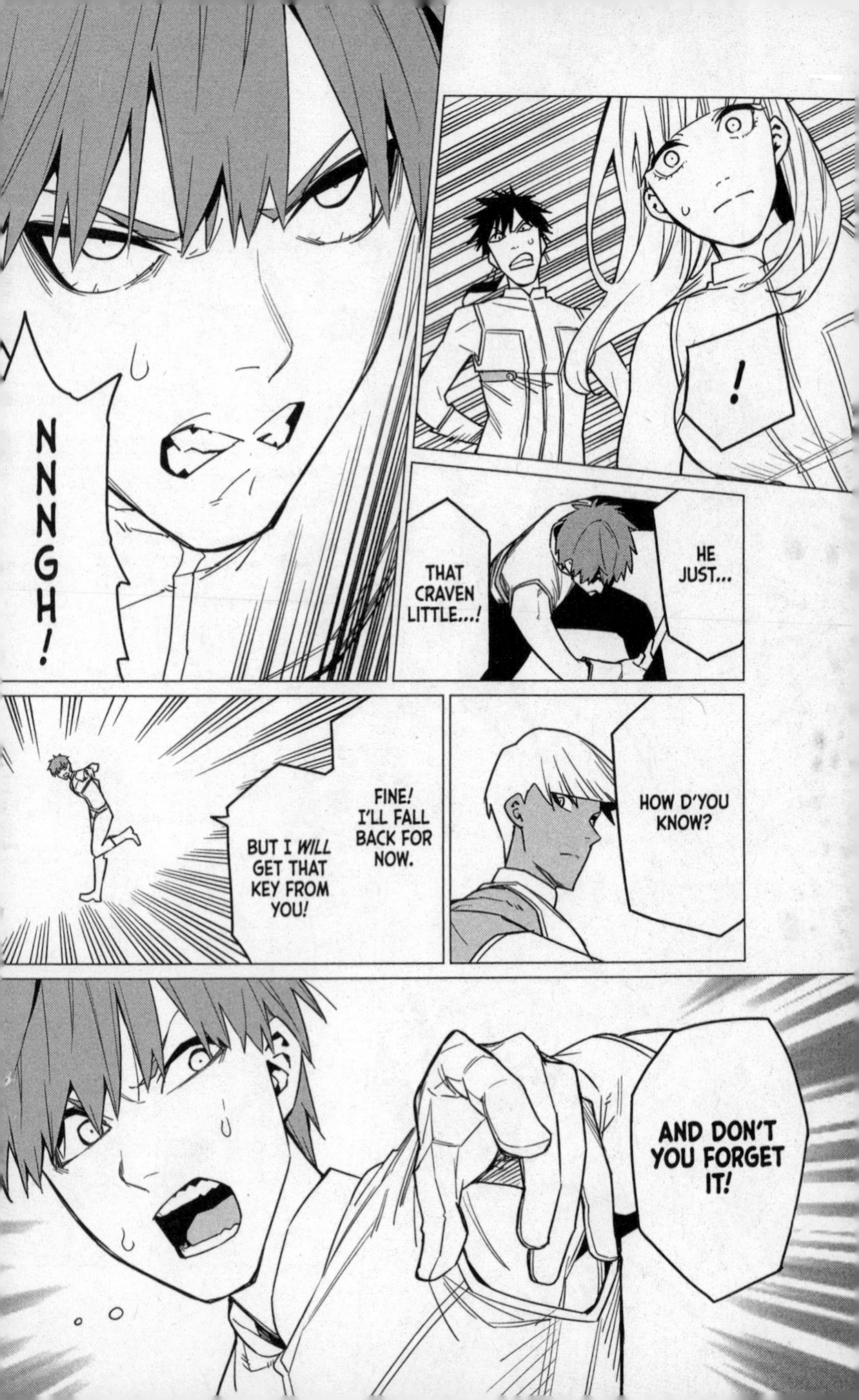
!
HE JUST...
THAT CRAVEN LITTLE...!
NNNGH!
HOW D'YOU KNOW?
FINE! I'LL FALL BACK FOR NOW.
BUT I *WILL* GET THAT KEY FROM YOU!
AND DON'T YOU FORGET IT!

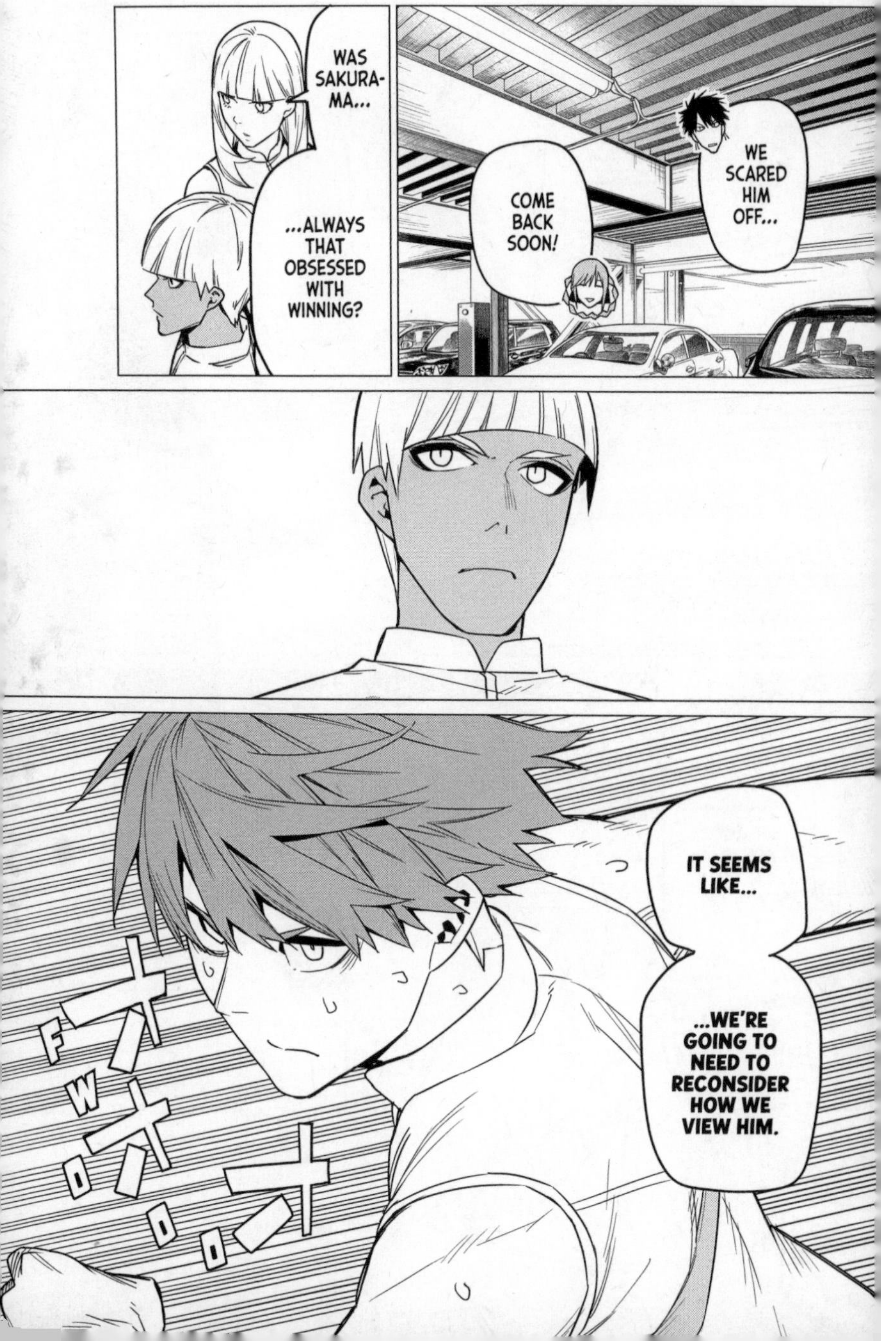
WE SCARED HIM OFF...
COME BACK SOON!
WAS SAKURAMA...
...ALWAYS THAT OBSESSED WITH WINNING?
IT SEEMS LIKE...
...WE'RE GOING TO NEED TO RECONSIDER HOW WE VIEW HIM.
FWOOO

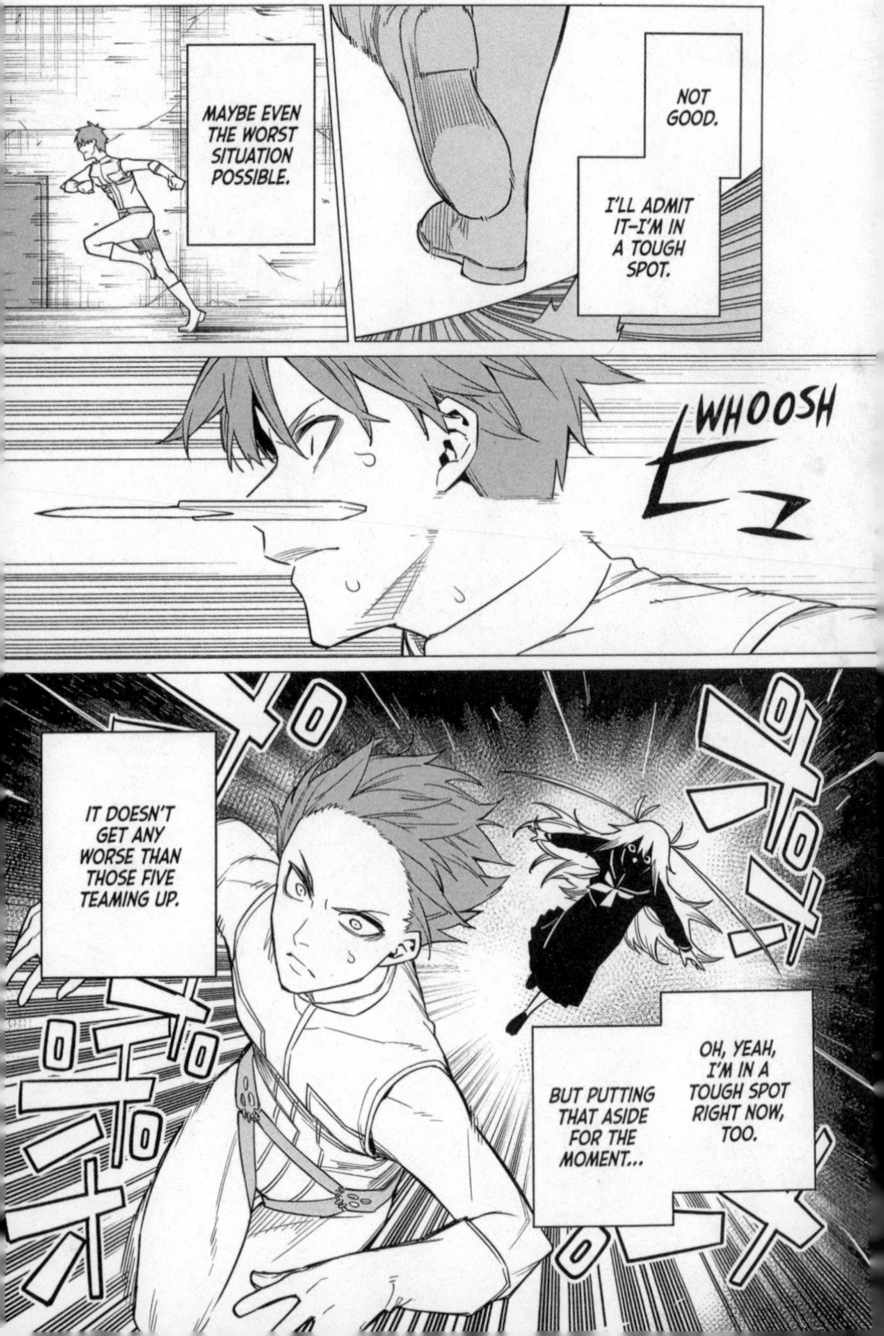
NOT GOOD.
I'LL ADMIT IT—I'M IN A TOUGH SPOT.
MAYBE EVEN THE WORST SITUATION POSSIBLE.
WHOOSH
IT DOESN'T GET ANY WORSE THAN THOSE FIVE TEAMING UP.
OH, YEAH, I'M IN A TOUGH SPOT RIGHT NOW, TOO.
BUT PUTTING THAT ASIDE FOR THE MOMENT...

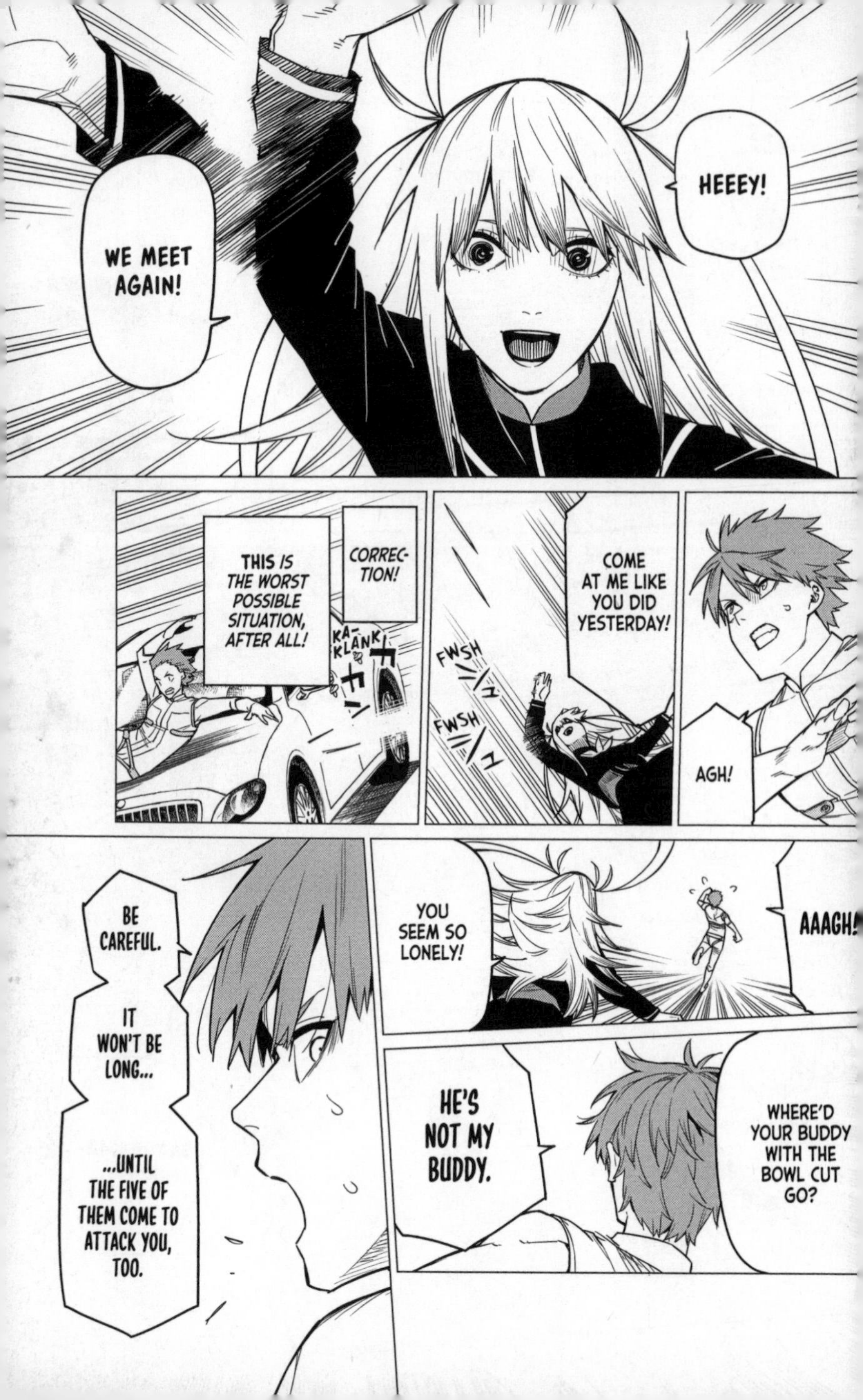
HEEEY!
WE MEET AGAIN!
AGH!
COME AT ME LIKE YOU DID YESTERDAY!
FWSH
FWSH
CORRECTION!
THIS *IS* THE WORST POSSIBLE SITUATION, AFTER ALL!
KA-KLANK
AAAGH!
YOU SEEM SO LONELY!
WHERE'D YOUR BUDDY WITH THE BOWL CUT GO?
HE'S NOT MY BUDDY.
BE CAREFUL.
IT WON'T BE LONG...
...UNTIL THE FIVE OF THEM COME TO ATTACK YOU, TOO.

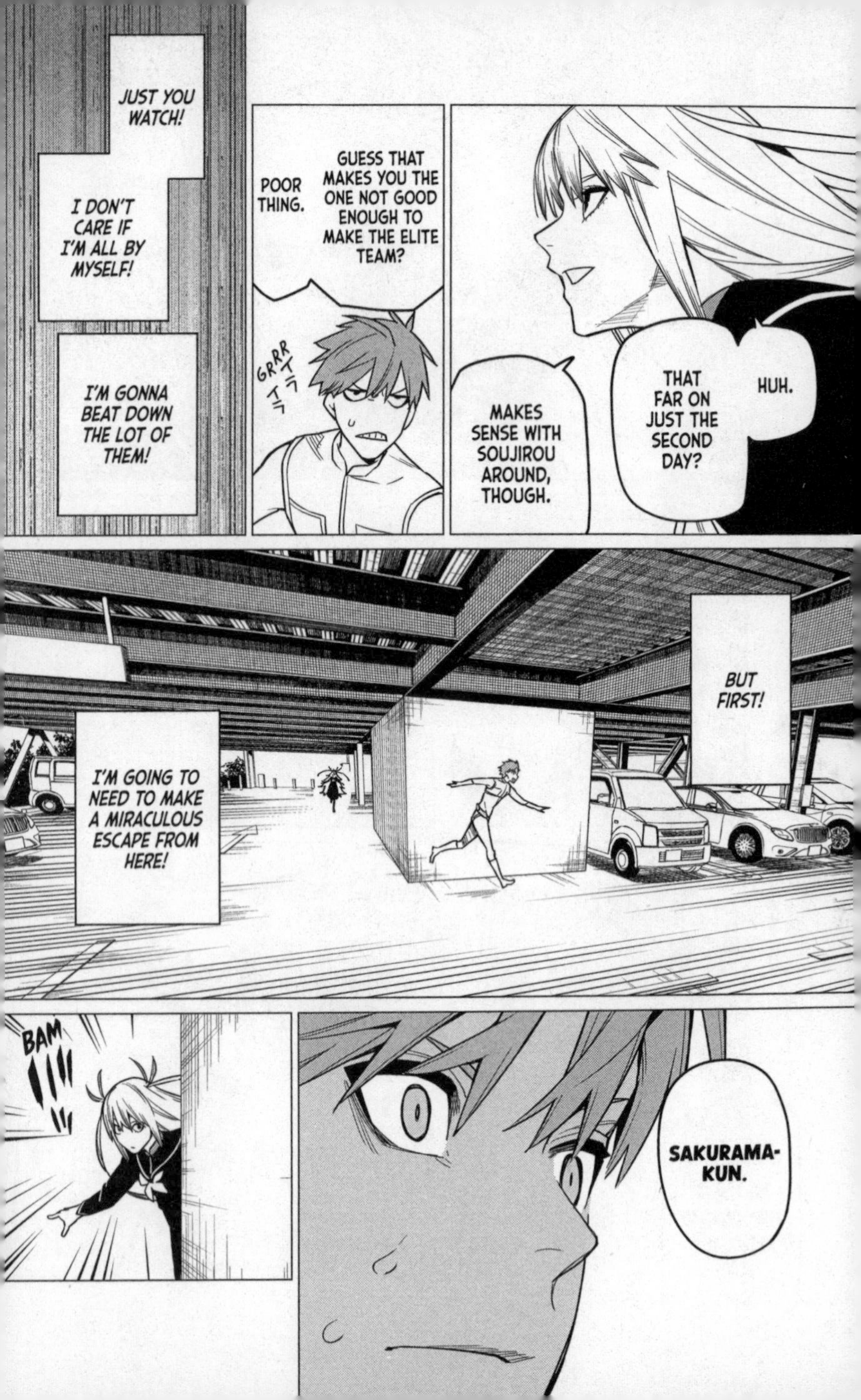
HUH.
THAT FAR ON JUST THE SECOND DAY?
MAKES SENSE WITH SOUJIROU AROUND, THOUGH.
GUESS THAT MAKES YOU THE ONE NOT GOOD ENOUGH TO MAKE THE ELITE TEAM?
POOR THING.
GRRR
JUST YOU WATCH!
I DON'T CARE IF I'M ALL BY MYSELF!
I'M GONNA BEAT DOWN THE LOT OF THEM!
BUT FIRST!
I'M GOING TO NEED TO MAKE A MIRACULOUS ESCAPE FROM HERE!
SAKURAMA-KUN.
BAM

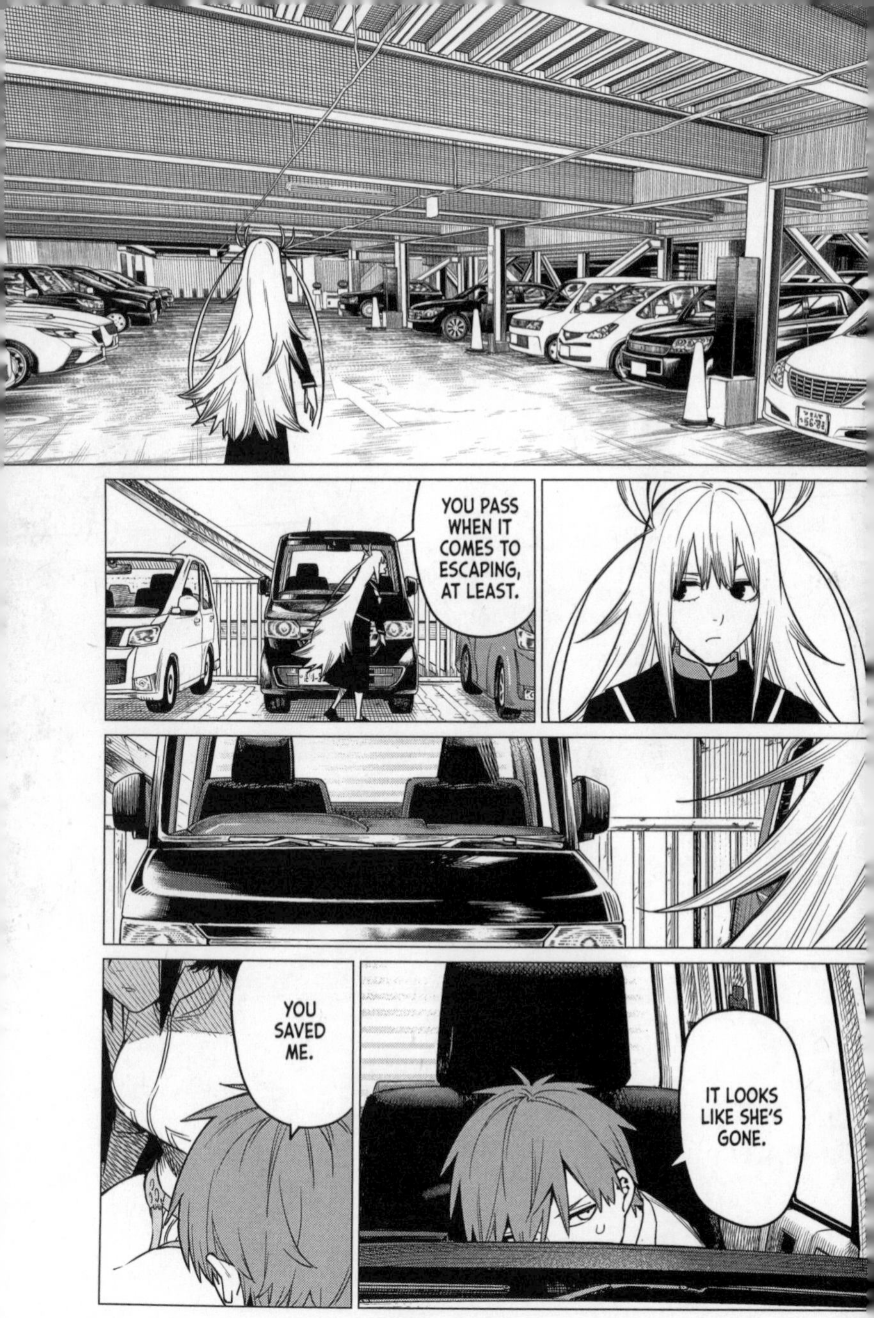
YOU PASS WHEN IT COMES TO ESCAPING, AT LEAST.
IT LOOKS LIKE SHE'S GONE.
YOU SAVED ME.

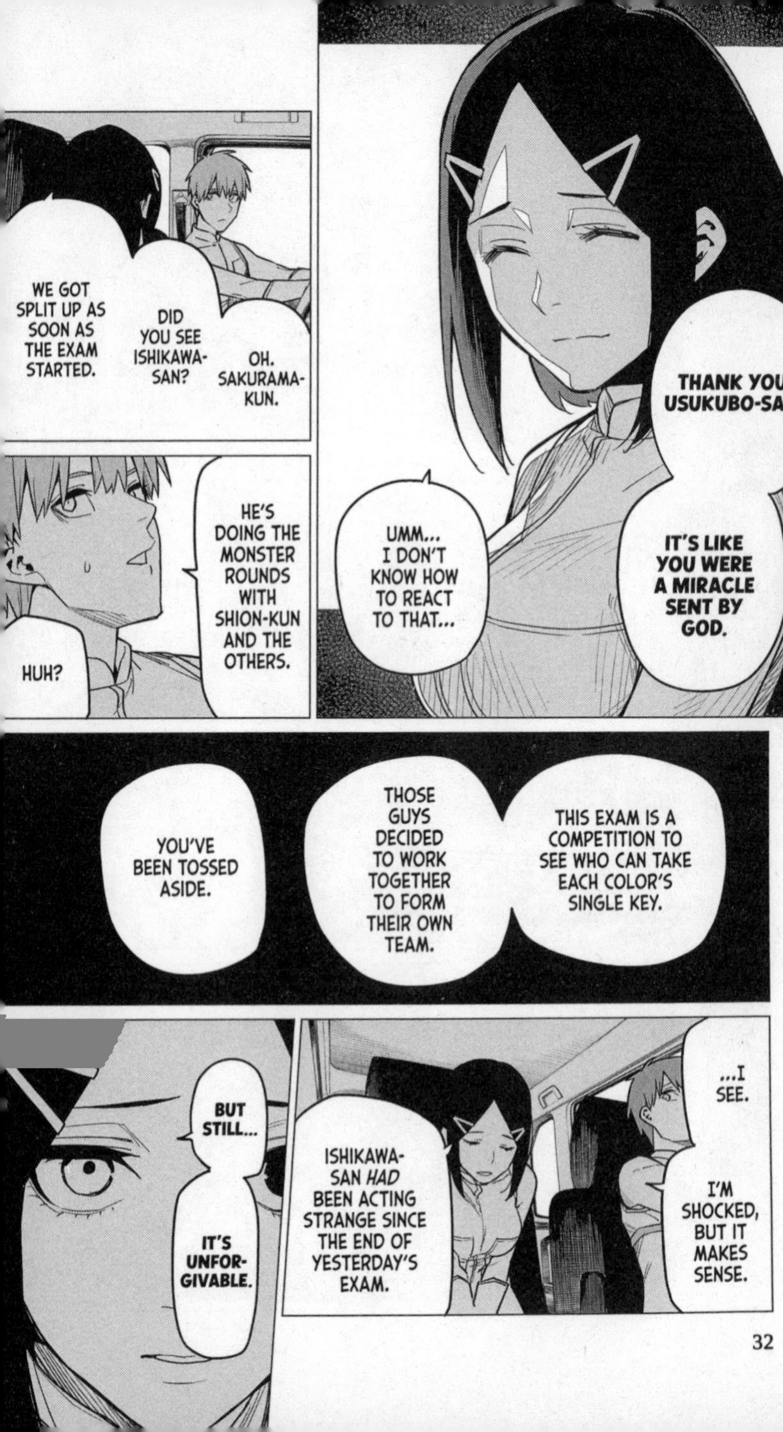
THANK YOU, USUKUBO-SAN.
IT'S LIKE YOU WERE A MIRACLE SENT BY GOD.
UMM... I DON'T KNOW HOW TO REACT TO THAT...
OH. SAKURAMA-KUN.
DID YOU SEE ISHIKAWA-SAN?
WE GOT SPLIT UP AS SOON AS THE EXAM STARTED.
HE'S DOING THE MONSTER ROUNDS WITH SHION-KUN AND THE OTHERS.
HUH?
THIS EXAM IS A COMPETITION TO SEE WHO CAN TAKE EACH COLOR'S SINGLE KEY.
THOSE GUYS DECIDED TO WORK TOGETHER TO FORM THEIR OWN TEAM.
YOU'VE BEEN TOSSED ASIDE.
...I SEE.
I'M SHOCKED, BUT IT MAKES SENSE.
ISHIKAWA-SAN *HAD* BEEN ACTING STRANGE SINCE THE END OF YESTERDAY'S EXAM.
BUT STILL...
IT'S UNFORGIVABLE.

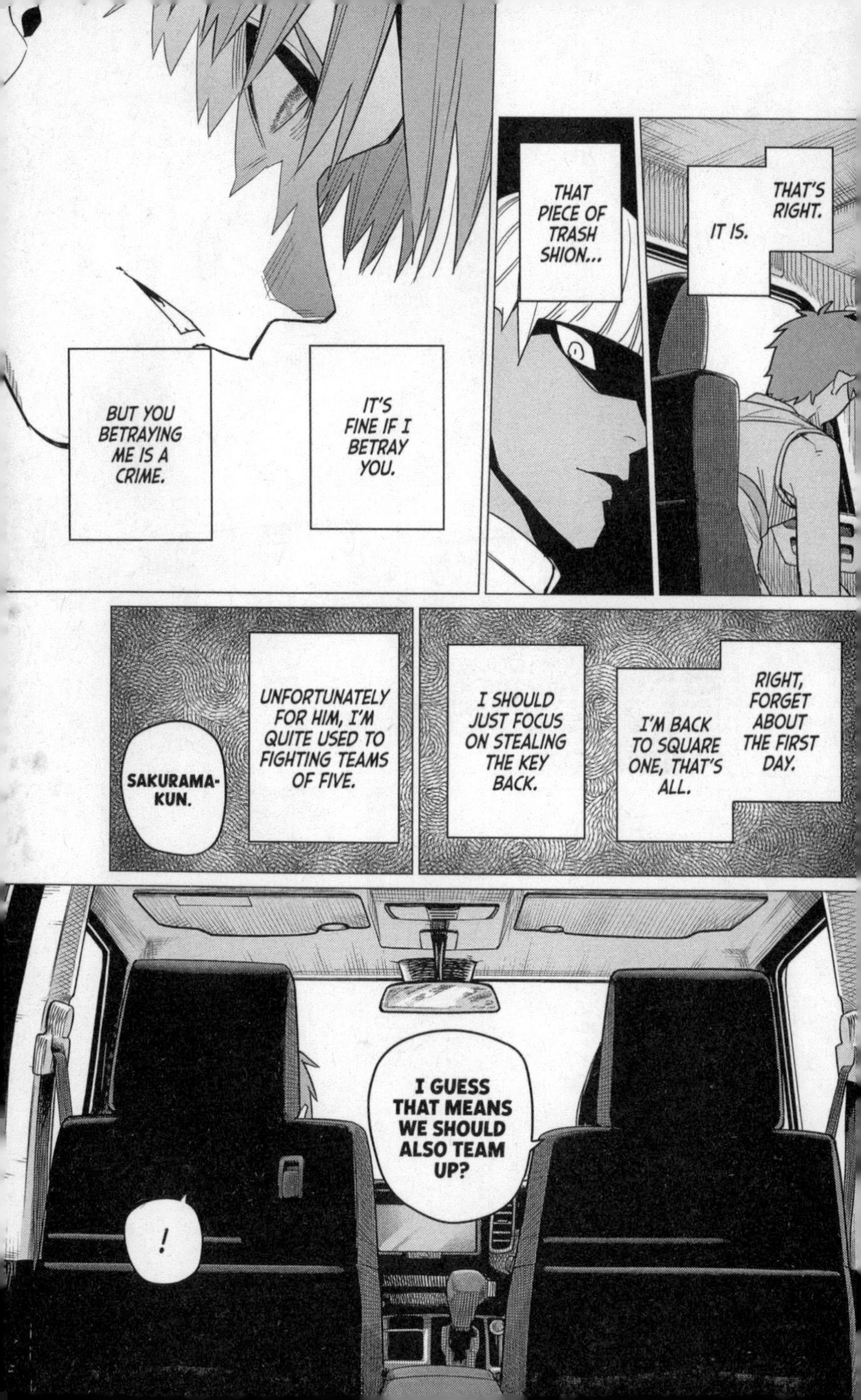
THAT'S RIGHT.
IT IS.
THAT PIECE OF TRASH SHION...
IT'S FINE IF I BETRAY YOU.
BUT YOU BETRAYING ME IS A CRIME.
RIGHT, FORGET ABOUT THE FIRST DAY.
I'M BACK TO SQUARE ONE, THAT'S ALL.
I SHOULD JUST FOCUS ON STEALING THE KEY BACK.
UNFORTUNATELY FOR HIM, I'M QUITE USED TO FIGHTING TEAMS OF FIVE.
SAKURAMA-KUN.
I GUESS THAT MEANS WE SHOULD ALSO TEAM UP?
!

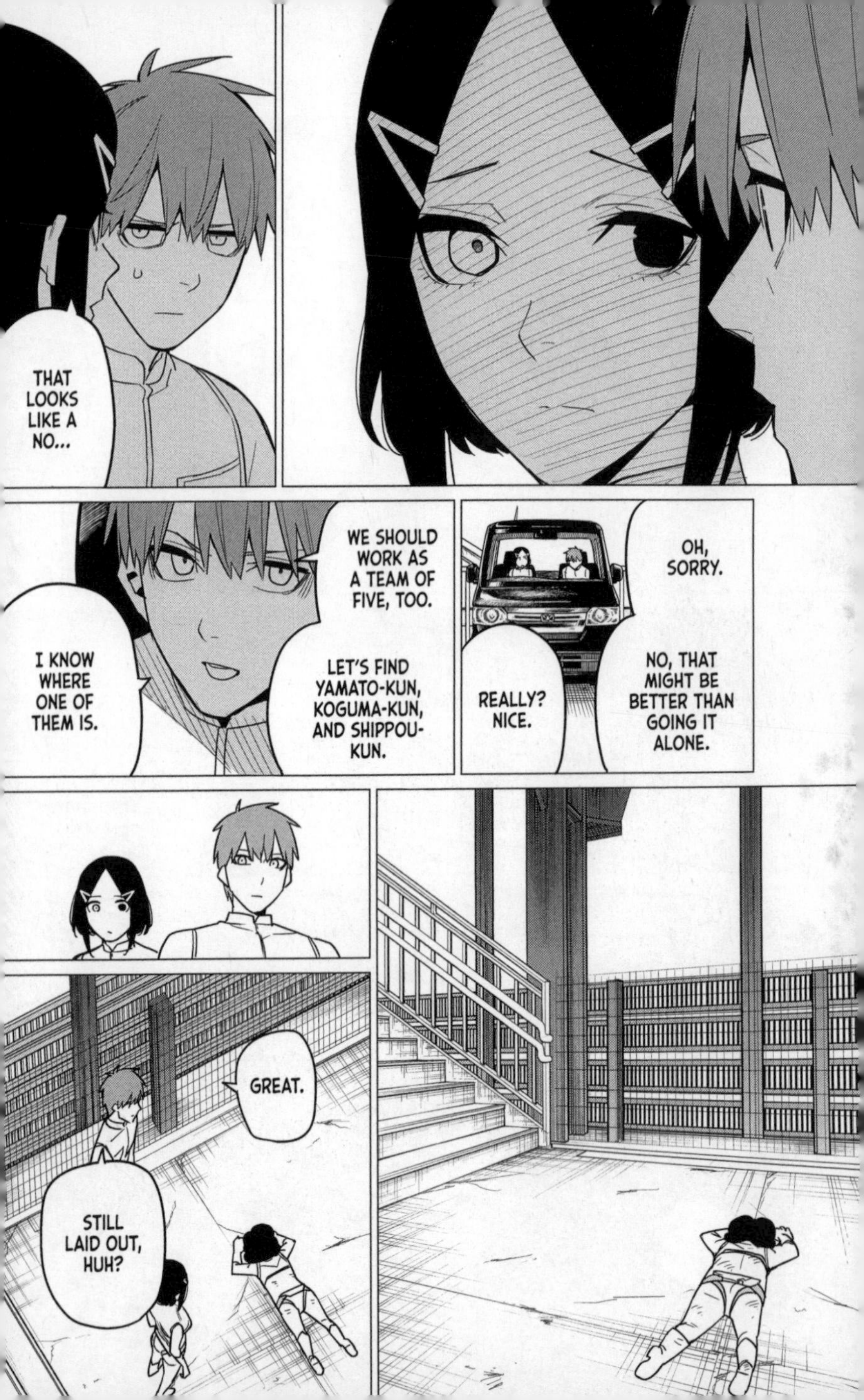
THAT LOOKS LIKE A NO...
OH, SORRY.
NO, THAT MIGHT BE BETTER THAN GOING IT ALONE.
REALLY? NICE.
WE SHOULD WORK AS A TEAM OF FIVE, TOO.
LET'S FIND YAMATO-KUN, KOGUMA-KUN, AND SHIPPOU-KUN.
I KNOW WHERE ONE OF THEM IS.
GREAT.
STILL LAID OUT, HUH?

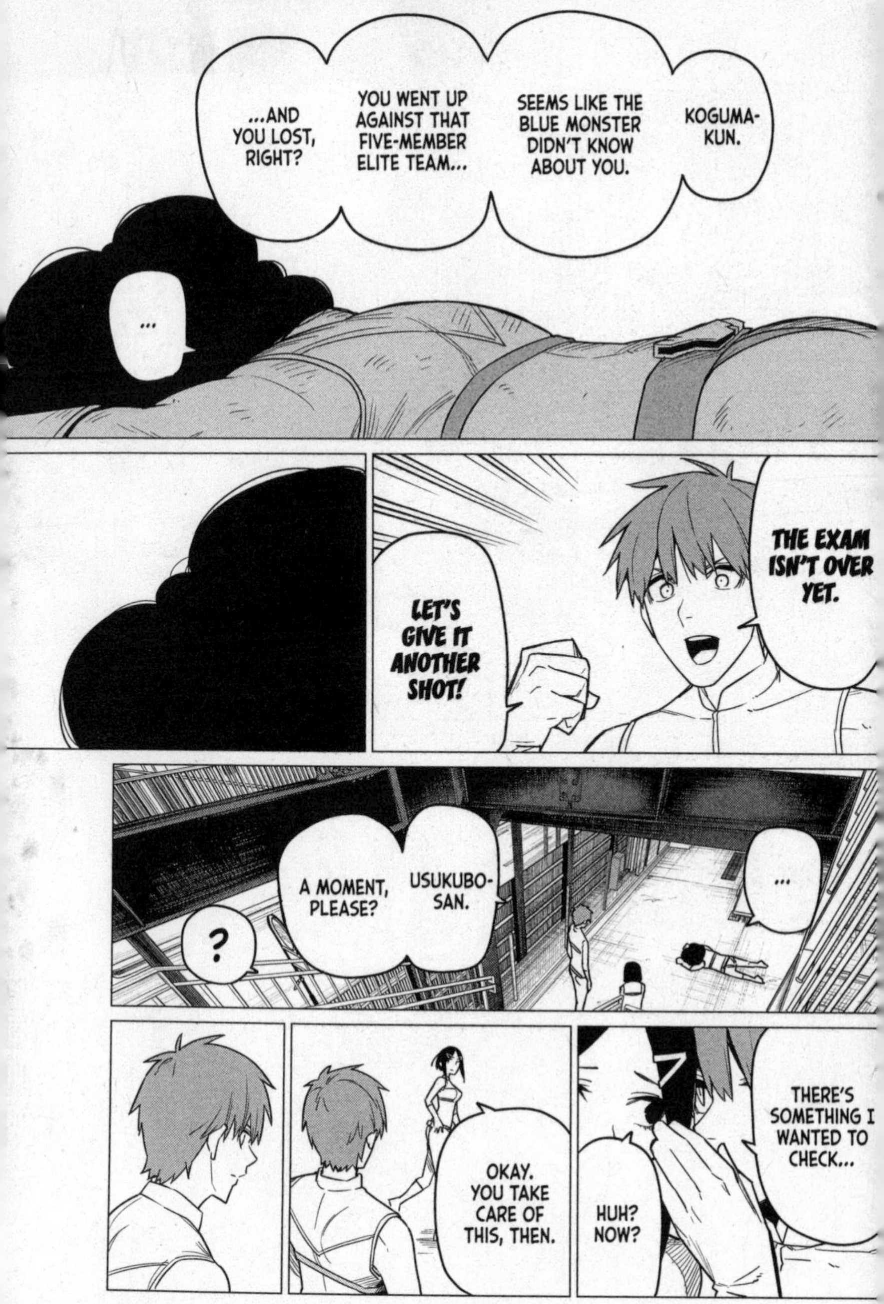
KOGUMA-KUN.
SEEMS LIKE THE BLUE MONSTER DIDN'T KNOW ABOUT YOU.
YOU WENT UP AGAINST THAT FIVE-MEMBER ELITE TEAM...
...AND YOU LOST, RIGHT?
...
THE EXAM ISN'T OVER YET.
LET'S GIVE IT ANOTHER SHOT!
...
USUKUBO-SAN.
A MOMENT, PLEASE?
?
THERE'S SOMETHING I WANTED TO CHECK...
HUH? NOW?
OKAY. YOU TAKE CARE OF THIS, THEN.

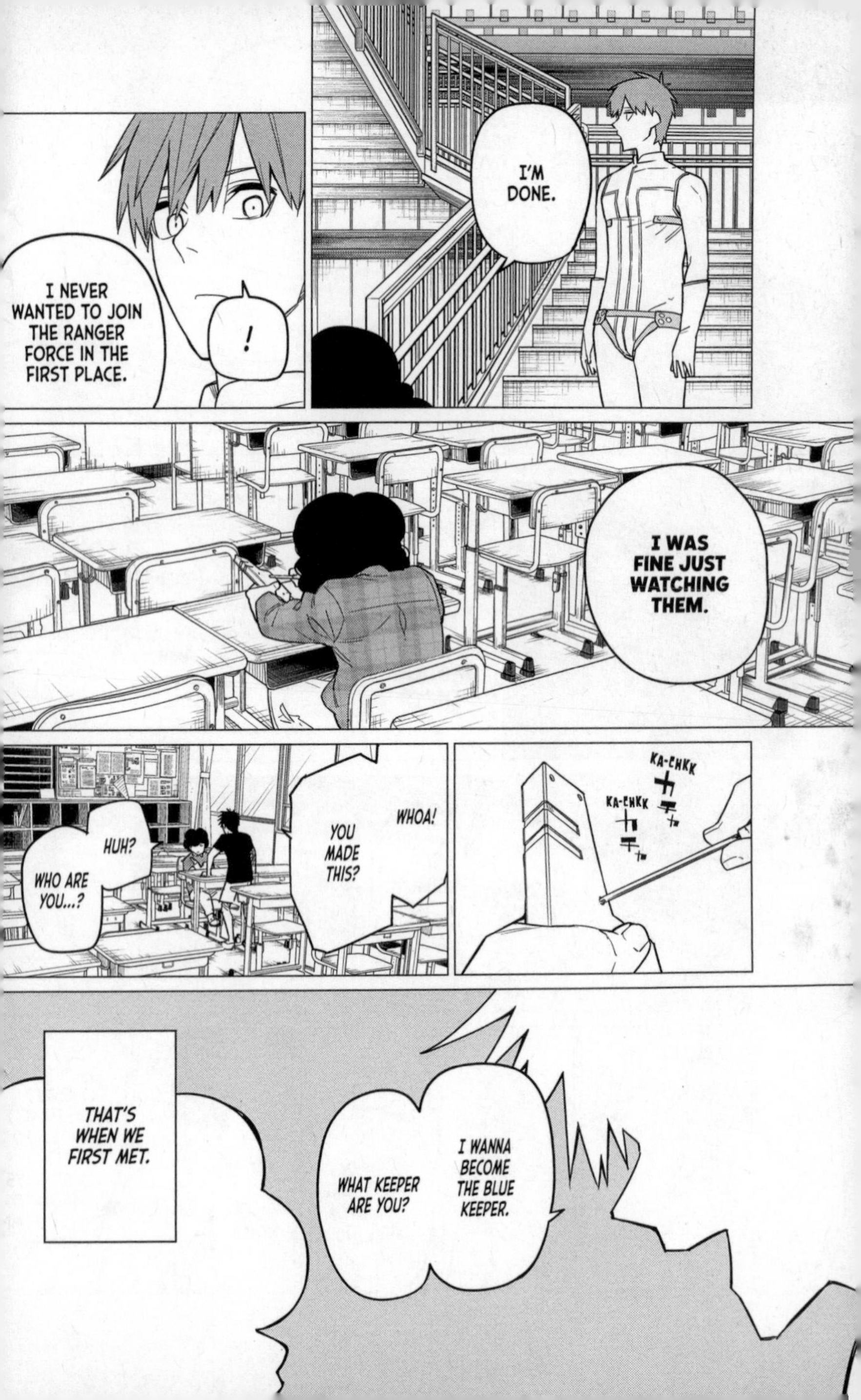
I'M DONE.
!
I NEVER WANTED TO JOIN THE RANGER FORCE IN THE FIRST PLACE.
I WAS FINE JUST WATCHING THEM.
KA-CHKK
KA-CHKK
WHOA!
YOU MADE THIS?
HUH?
WHO ARE YOU...?
I WANNA BECOME THE BLUE KEEPER.
WHAT KEEPER ARE YOU?
THAT'S WHEN WE FIRST MET.

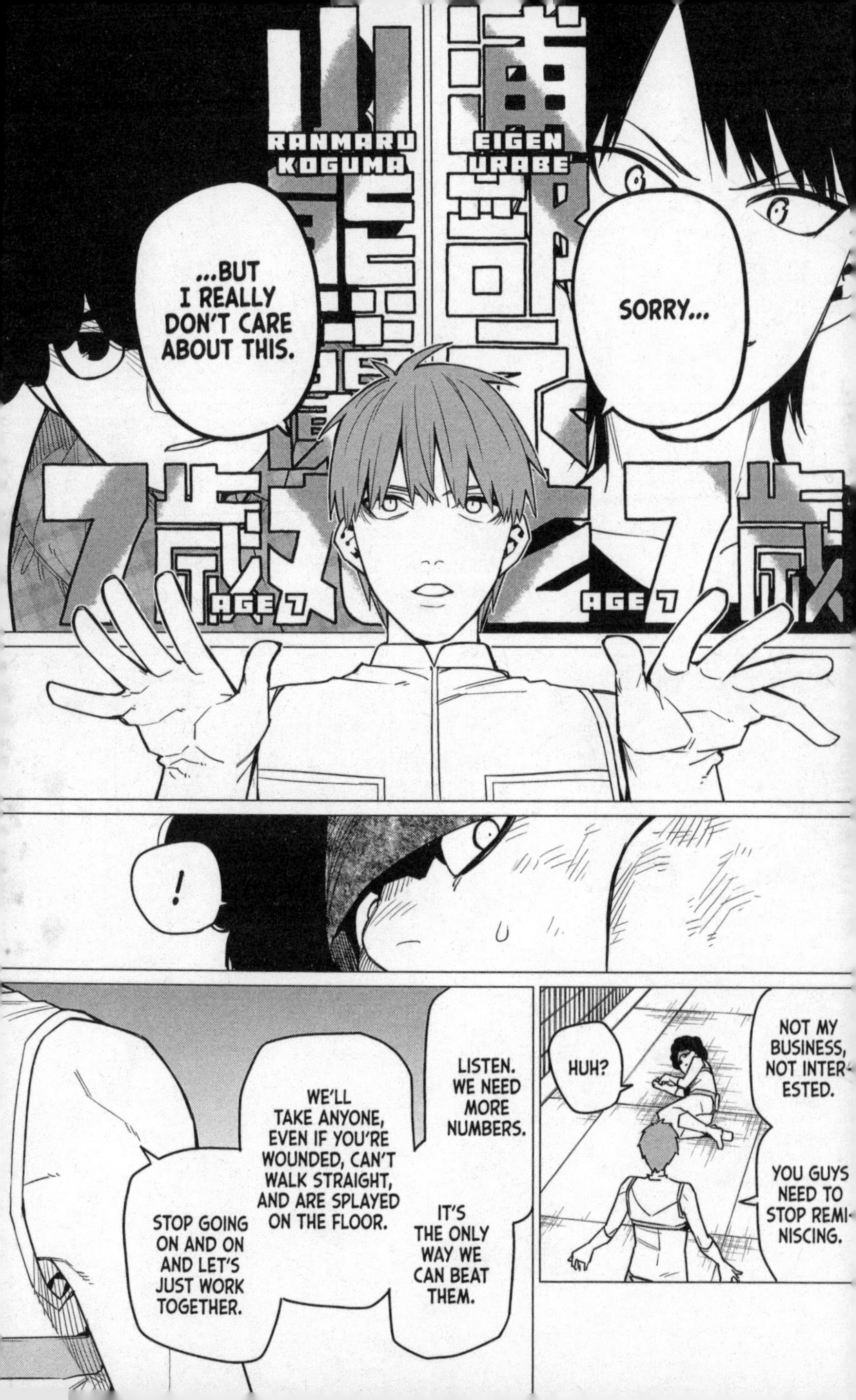
EIGEN URABE
SORRY...
AGE 7
RANMARU KOGUMA
...BUT I REALLY DON'T CARE ABOUT THIS.
AGE 7
!
NOT MY BUSINESS, NOT INTERESTED.
HUH?
YOU GUYS NEED TO STOP REMINISCING.
LISTEN. WE NEED MORE NUMBERS.
WE'LL TAKE ANYONE, EVEN IF YOU'RE WOUNDED, CAN'T WALK STRAIGHT, AND ARE SPLAYED ON THE FLOOR.
IT'S THE ONLY WAY WE CAN BEAT THEM.
STOP GOING ON AND ON AND LET'S JUST WORK TOGETHER.

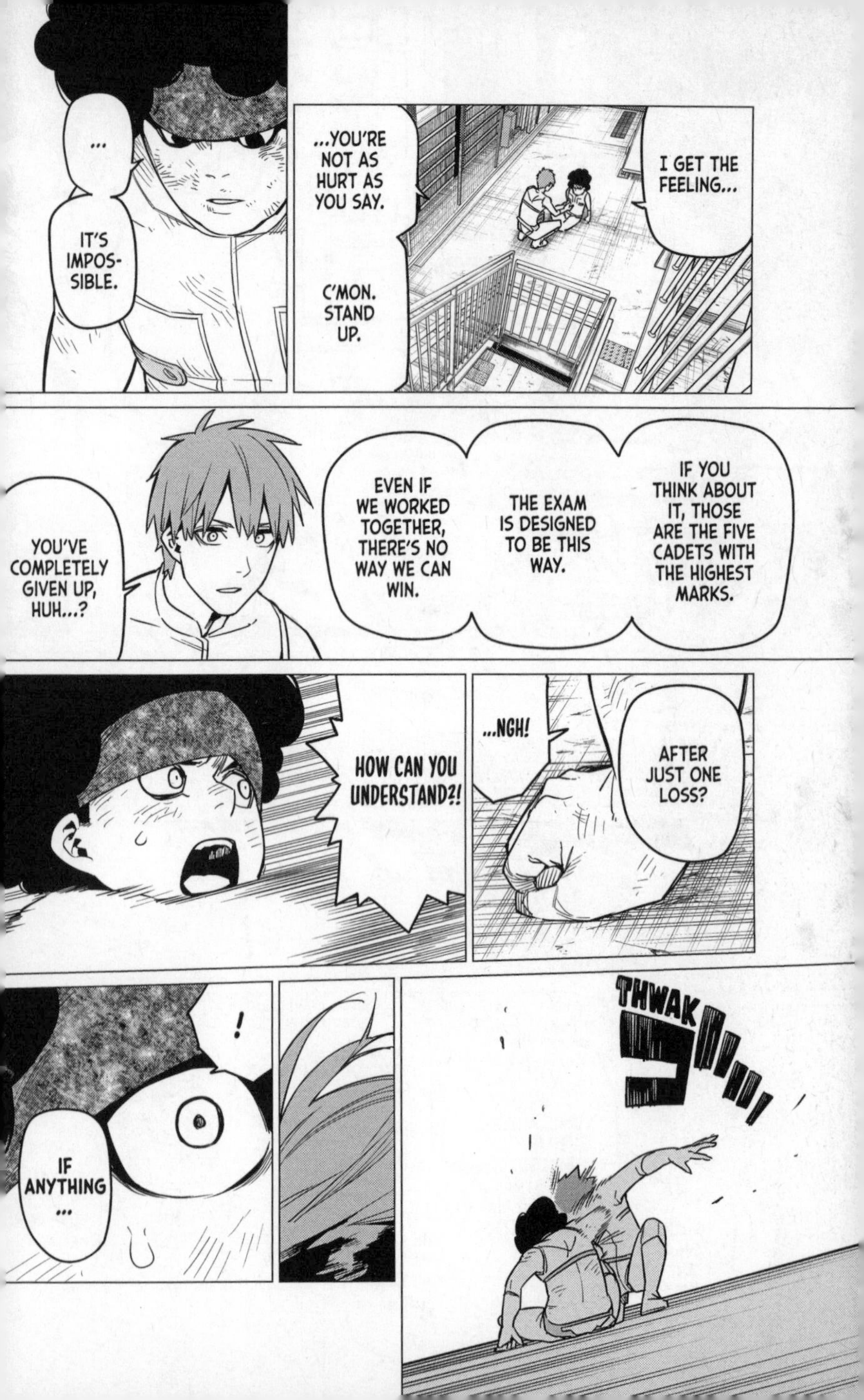
I GET THE FEELING...
...YOU'RE NOT AS HURT AS YOU SAY.
C'MON. STAND UP.
...
IT'S IMPOS-SIBLE.
IF YOU THINK ABOUT IT, THOSE ARE THE FIVE CADETS WITH THE HIGHEST MARKS.
THE EXAM IS DESIGNED TO BE THIS WAY.
EVEN IF WE WORKED TOGETHER, THERE'S NO WAY WE CAN WIN.
YOU'VE COMPLETELY GIVEN UP, HUH...?
AFTER JUST ONE LOSS?
...NGH!
HOW CAN YOU UNDERSTAND?!
THWAK
!
IF ANYTHING...

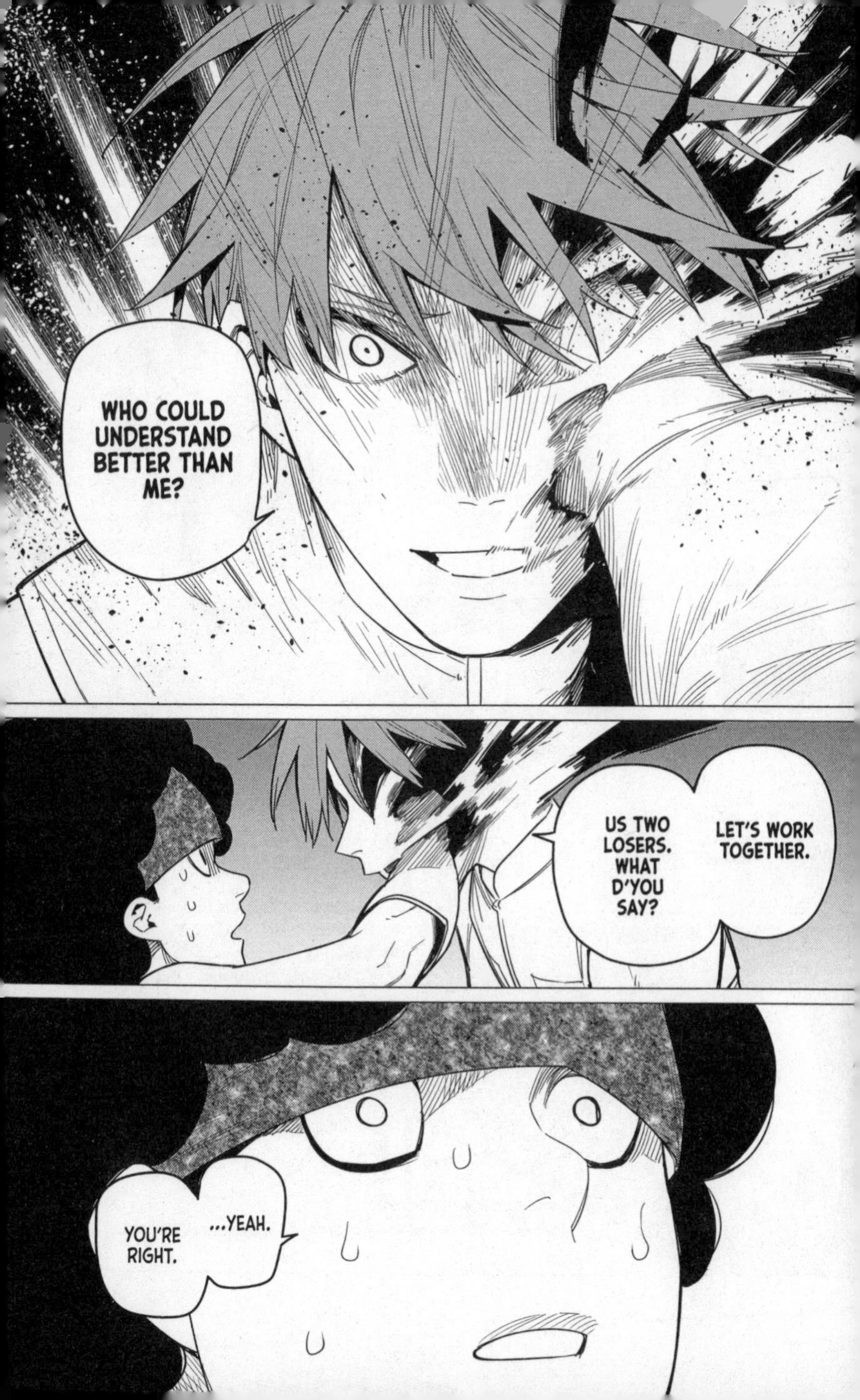
WHO COULD UNDERSTAND BETTER THAN ME?
LET'S WORK TOGETHER.
US TWO LOSERS. WHAT D'YOU SAY?
...YEAH.
YOU'RE RIGHT.

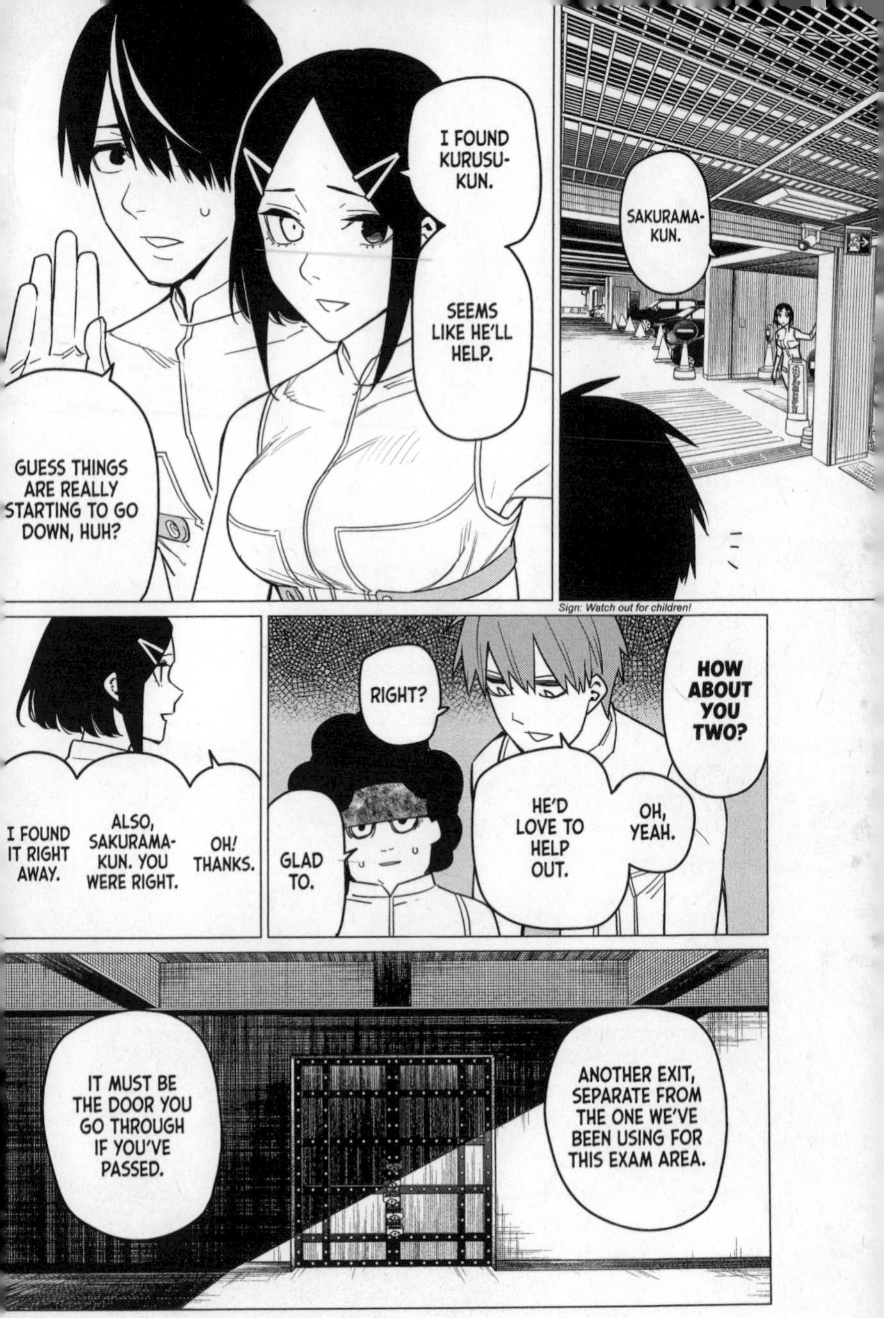
SAKURAMA-KUN.
I FOUND KURUSU-KUN.
SEEMS LIKE HE'LL HELP.
GUESS THINGS ARE REALLY STARTING TO GO DOWN, HUH?
HOW ABOUT YOU TWO?
OH, YEAH.
HE'D LOVE TO HELP OUT.
RIGHT?
GLAD TO.
OH! THANKS.
ALSO, SAKURAMA-KUN. YOU WERE RIGHT.
I FOUND IT RIGHT AWAY.
ANOTHER EXIT, SEPARATE FROM THE ONE WE'VE BEEN USING FOR THIS EXAM AREA.
IT MUST BE THE DOOR YOU GO THROUGH IF YOU'VE PASSED.
Sign: Watch out for children!

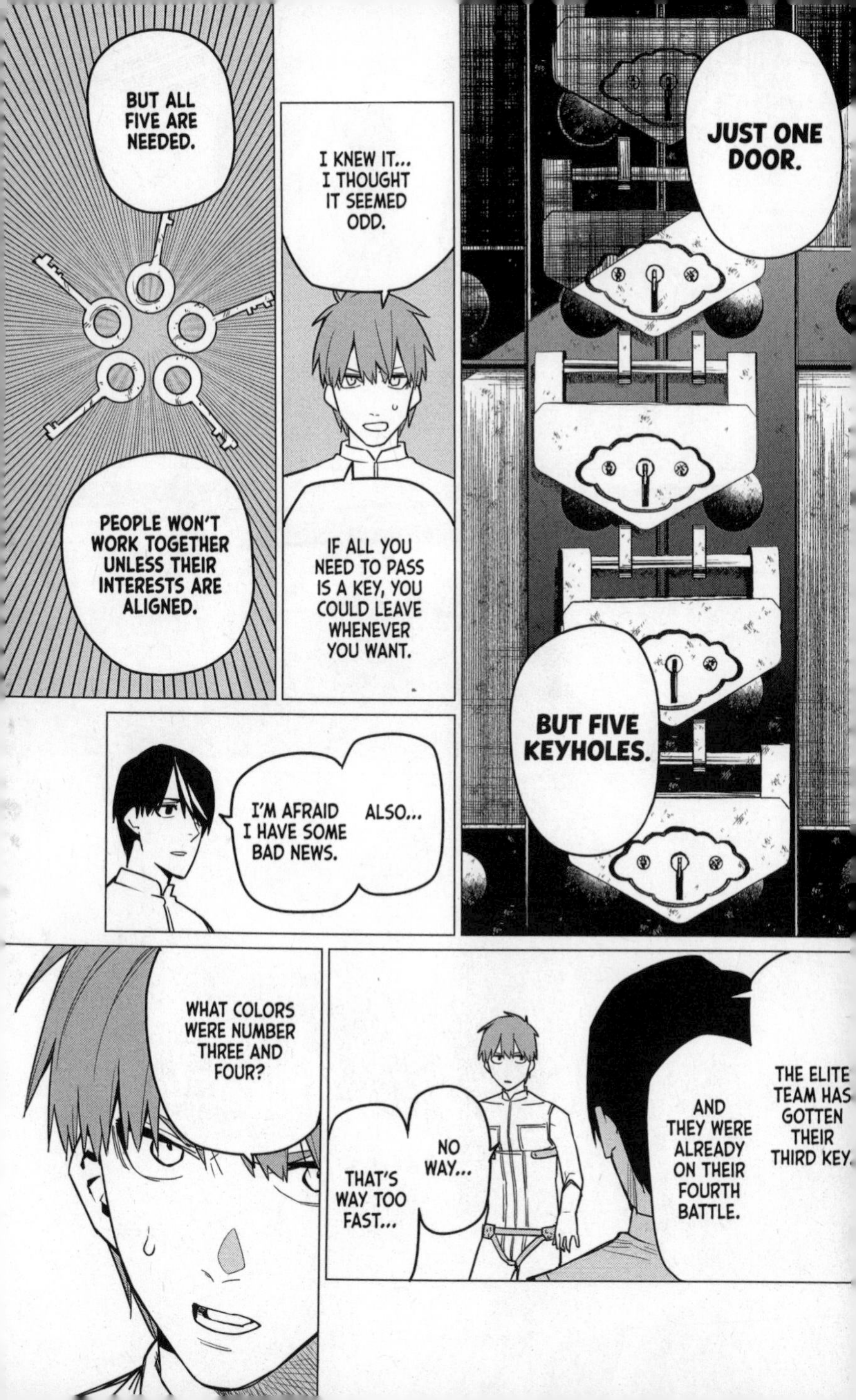
JUST ONE DOOR.
BUT FIVE KEYHOLES.
I KNEW IT... I THOUGHT IT SEEMED ODD.
IF ALL YOU NEED TO PASS IS A KEY, YOU COULD LEAVE WHENEVER YOU WANT.
BUT ALL FIVE ARE NEEDED.
PEOPLE WON'T WORK TOGETHER UNLESS THEIR INTERESTS ARE ALIGNED.
ALSO...
I'M AFRAID I HAVE SOME BAD NEWS.
THE ELITE TEAM HAS GOTTEN THEIR THIRD KEY.
AND THEY WERE ALREADY ON THEIR FOURTH BATTLE.
NO WAY...
THAT'S WAY TOO FAST...
WHAT COLORS WERE NUMBER THREE AND FOUR?

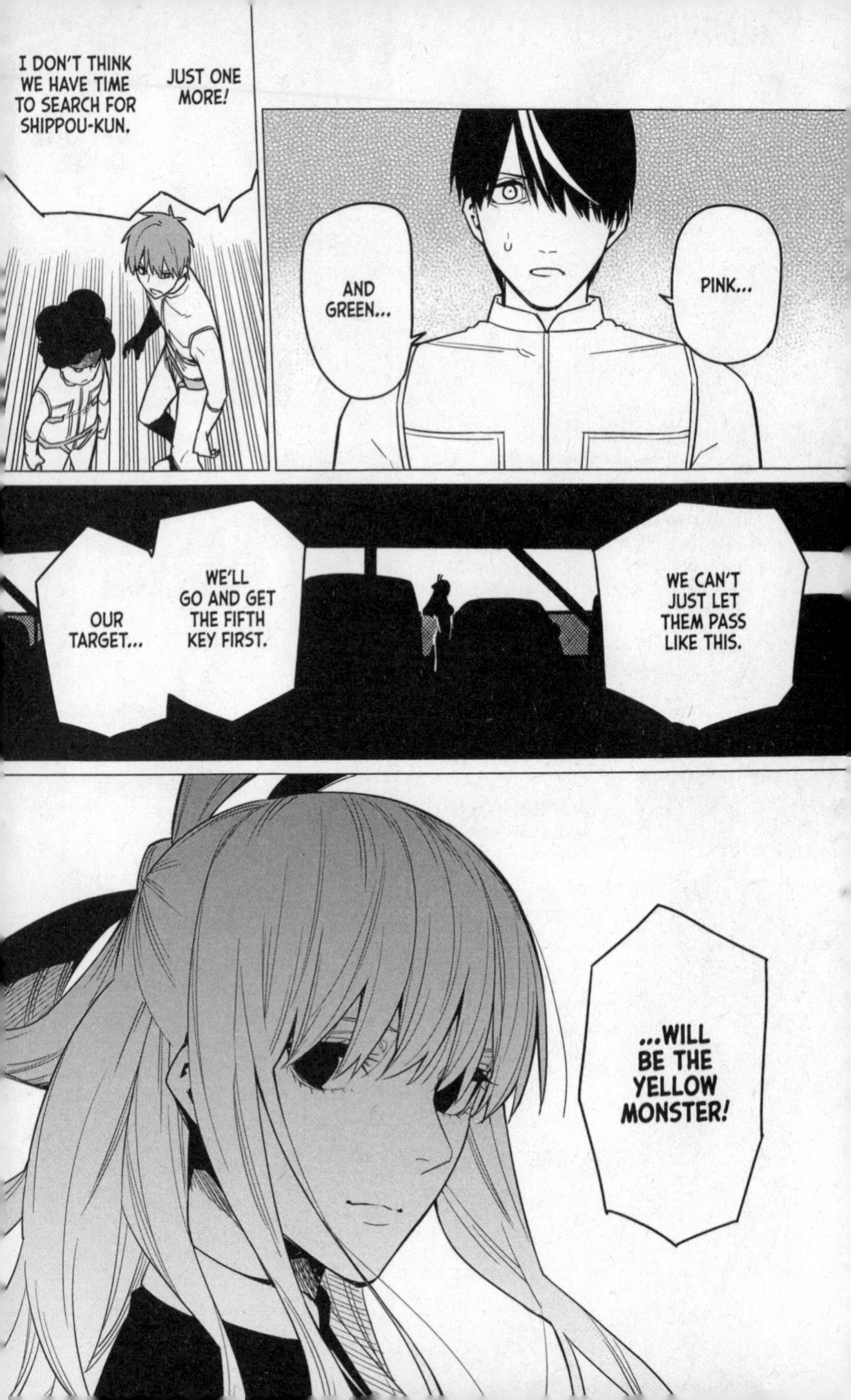
PINK...
AND GREEN...
JUST ONE MORE!
I DON'T THINK WE HAVE TIME TO SEARCH FOR SHIPPOU-KUN.
WE CAN'T JUST LET THEM PASS LIKE THIS.
WE'LL GO AND GET THE FIFTH KEY FIRST.
OUR TARGET...
...WILL BE THE YELLOW MONSTER!

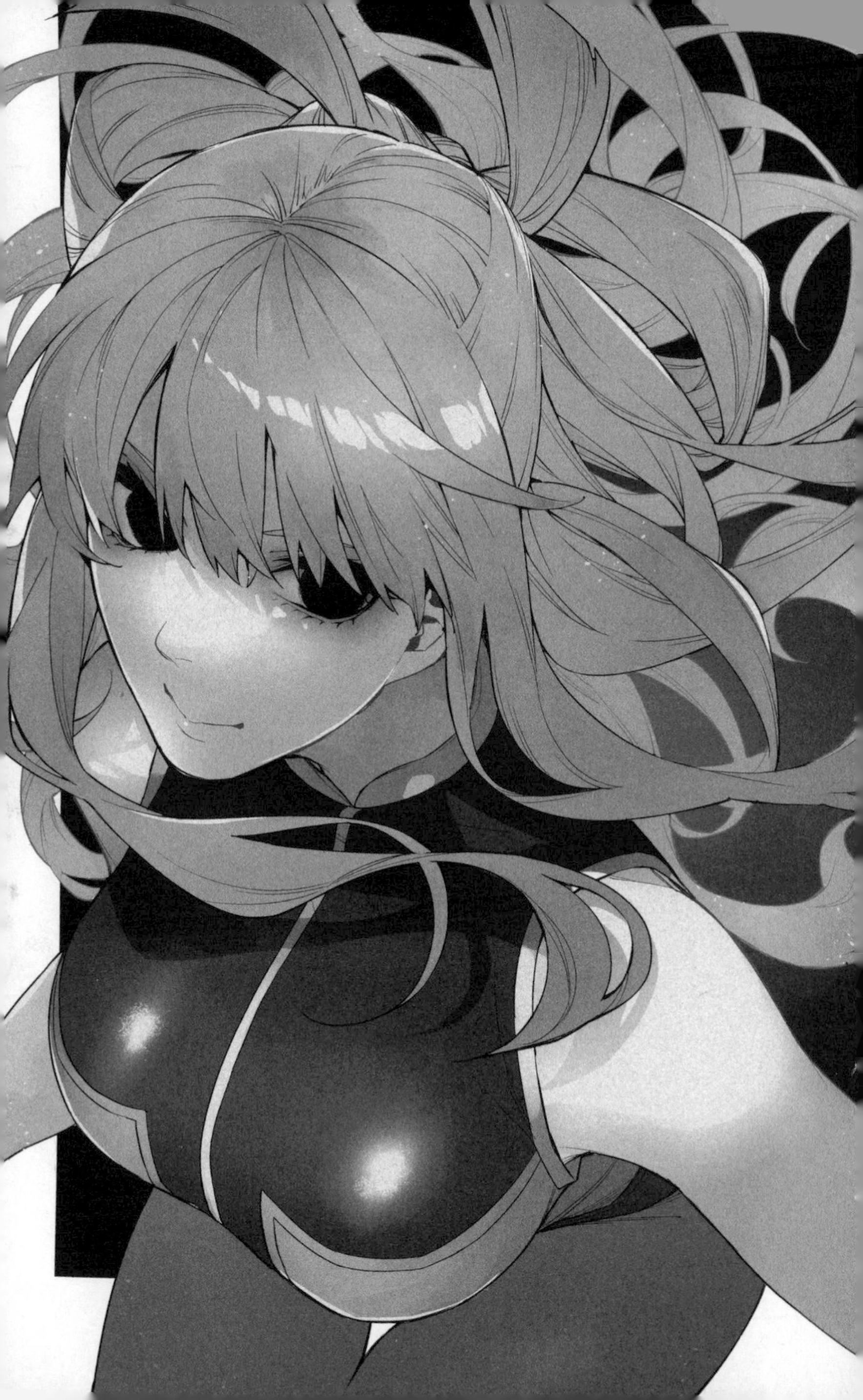

GO! GO!
LOSER RANGER!

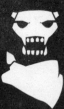

Chapter 26: THE WHITE DRAGON'S TEST: VS. THE YELLOW MONSTER 1

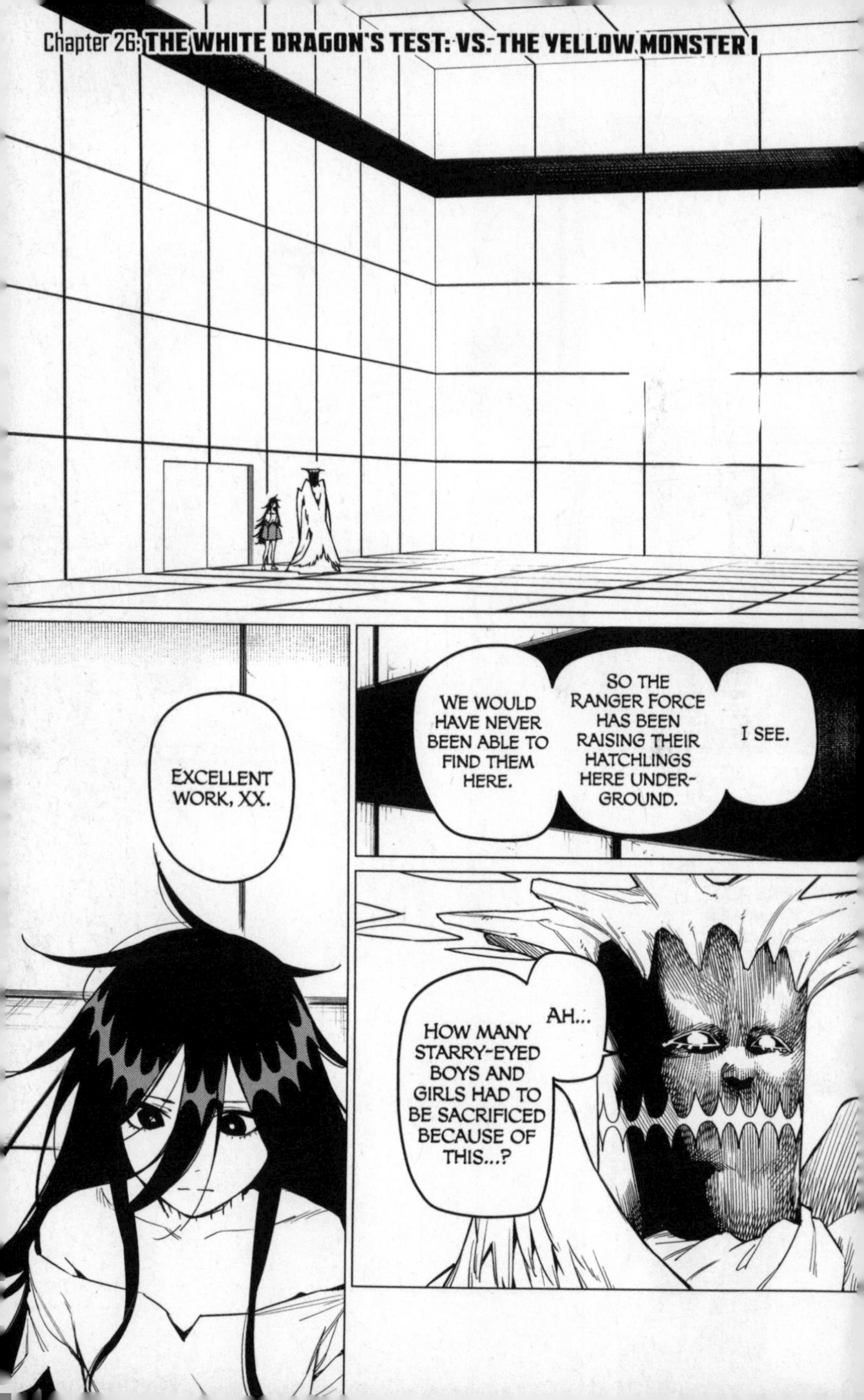
I SEE.
SO THE RANGER FORCE HAS BEEN RAISING THEIR HATCHLINGS HERE UNDER-GROUND.
WE WOULD HAVE NEVER BEEN ABLE TO FIND THEM HERE.
AH...
HOW MANY STARRY-EYED BOYS AND GIRLS HAD TO BE SACRIFICED BECAUSE OF THIS...?
EXCELLENT WORK, XX.

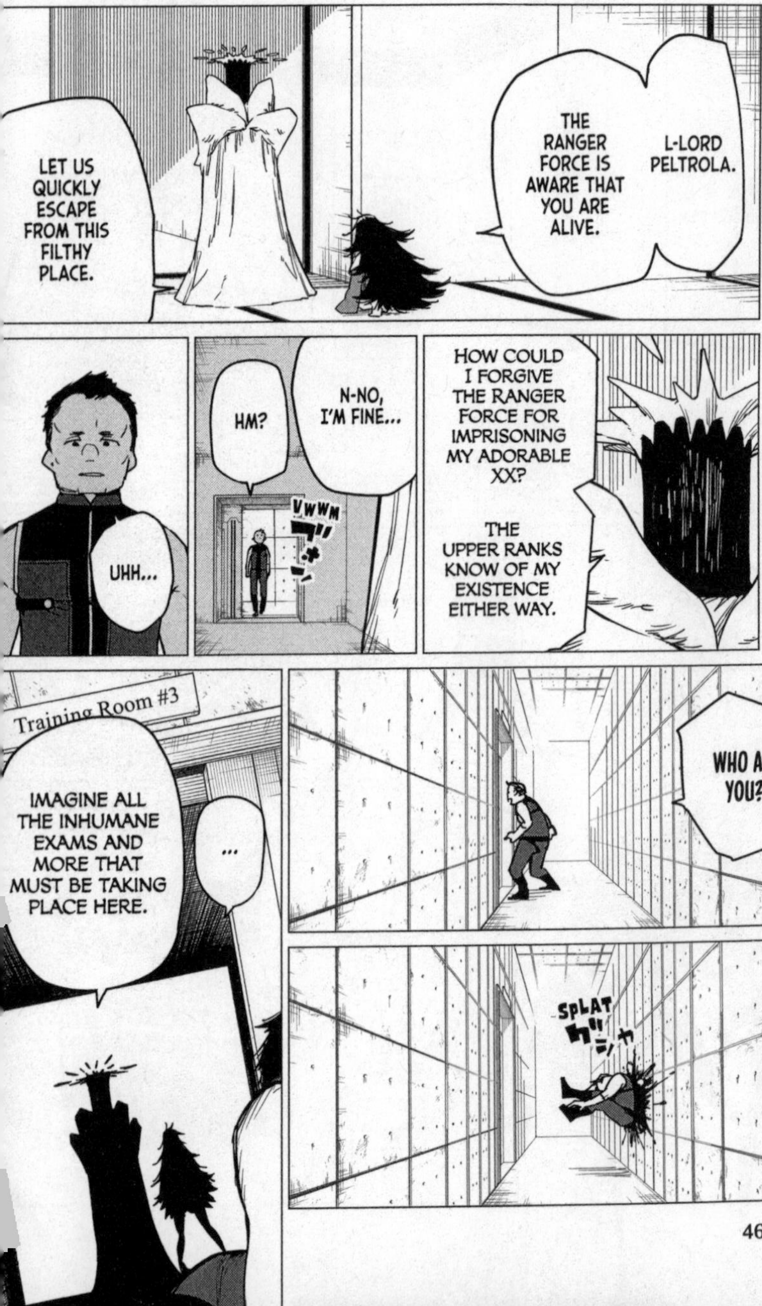

L-LORD PELTROLA.
THE RANGER FORCE IS AWARE THAT YOU ARE ALIVE.
LET US QUICKLY ESCAPE FROM THIS FILTHY PLACE.
HOW COULD I FORGIVE THE RANGER FORCE FOR IMPRISONING MY ADORABLE XX?
THE UPPER RANKS KNOW OF MY EXISTENCE EITHER WAY.
N-NO, I'M FINE...
HM?
VWWM
UHH...
WHO ARE YOU?!
SPLAT
Training Room #3
IMAGINE ALL THE INHUMANE EXAMS AND MORE THAT MUST BE TAKING PLACE HERE.
...

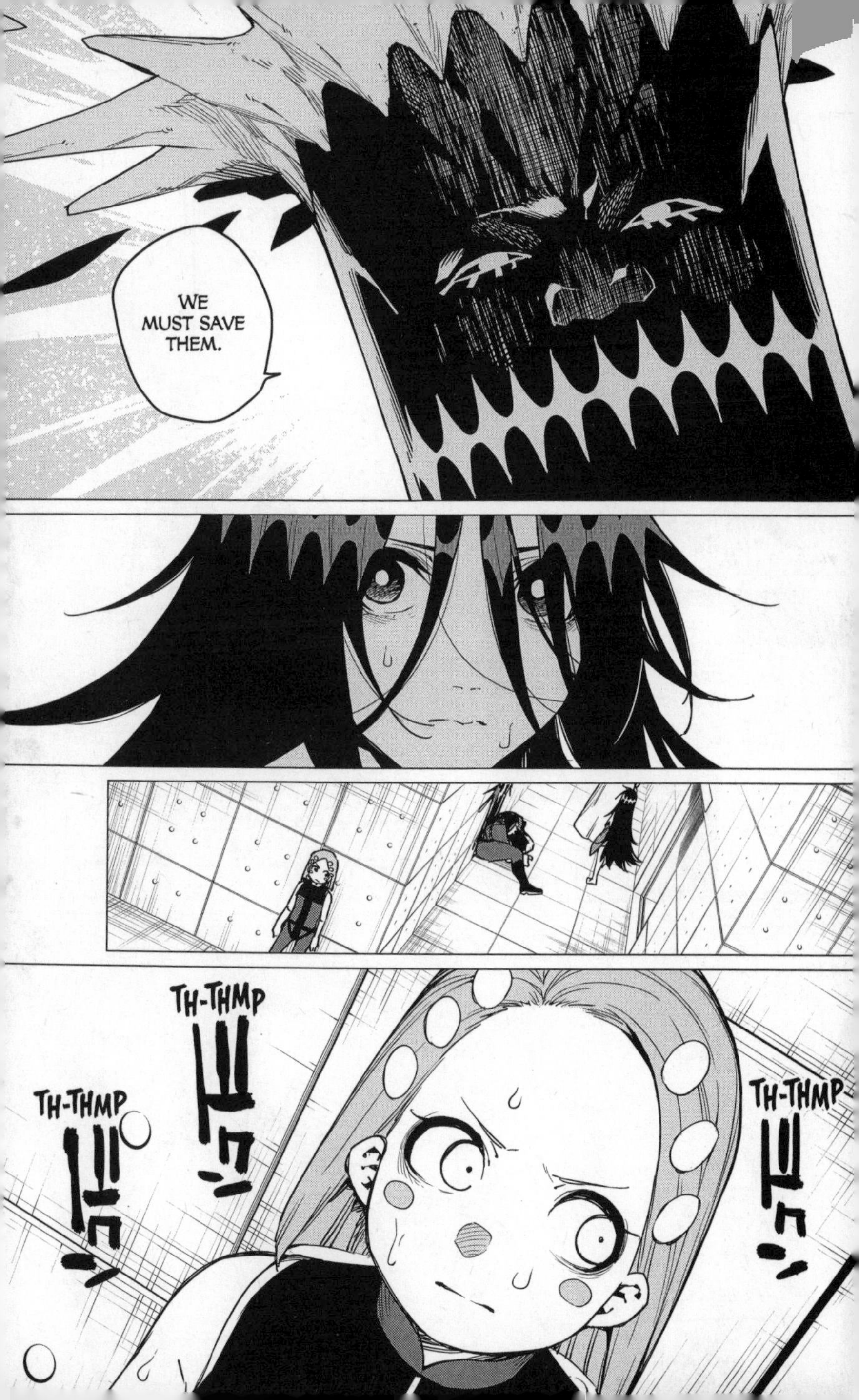
WE MUST SAVE THEM.
TH-THMP
TH-THMP
TH-THMP

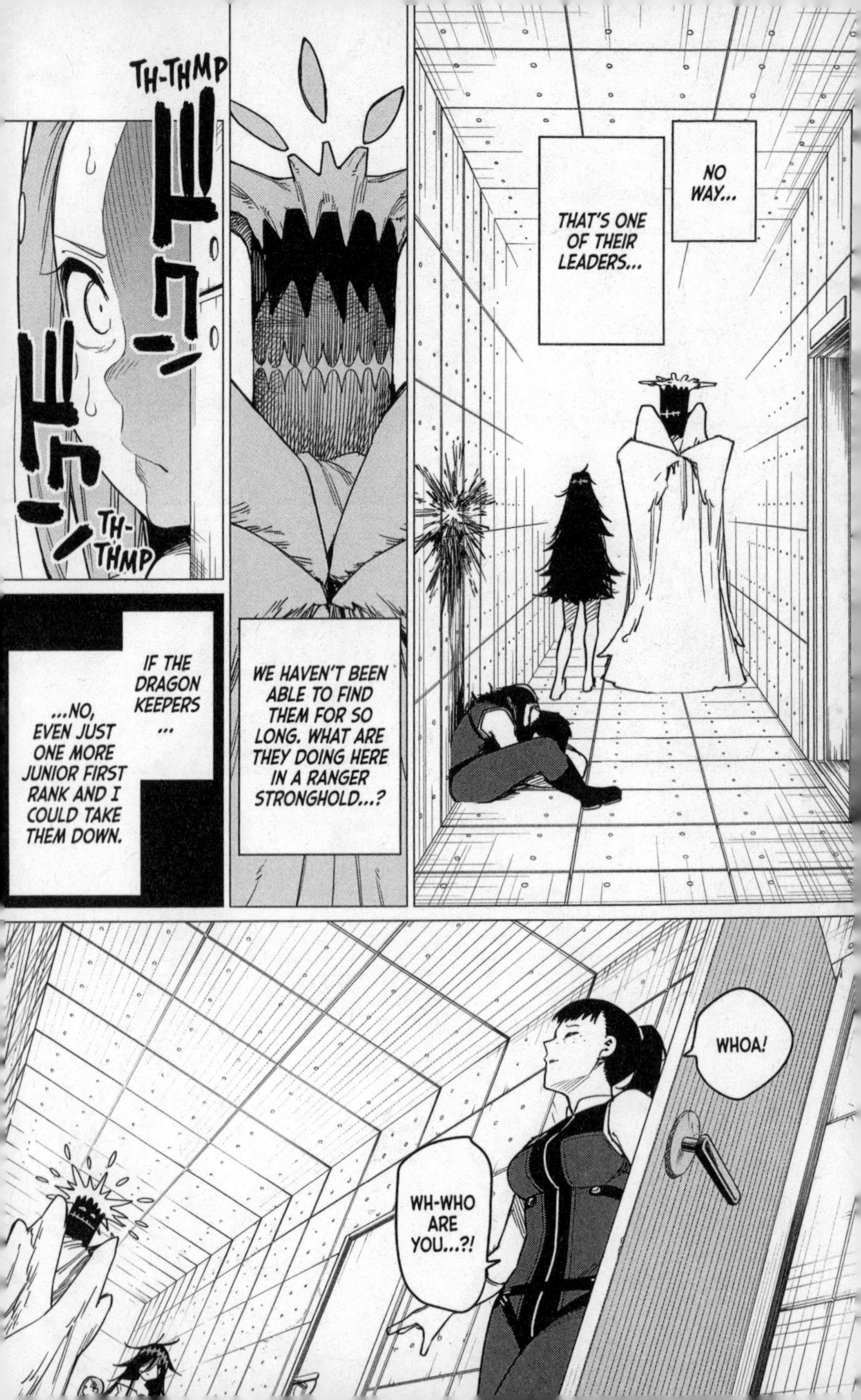
NO WAY...
THAT'S ONE OF THEIR LEADERS...
WE HAVEN'T BEEN ABLE TO FIND THEM FOR SO LONG. WHAT ARE THEY DOING HERE IN A RANGER STRONGHOLD...?
TH-THMP
TH-THMP
IF THE DRAGON KEEPERS...
...NO, EVEN JUST ONE MORE JUNIOR FIRST RANK AND I COULD TAKE THEM DOWN.
WHOA!
WH-WHO ARE YOU...?!

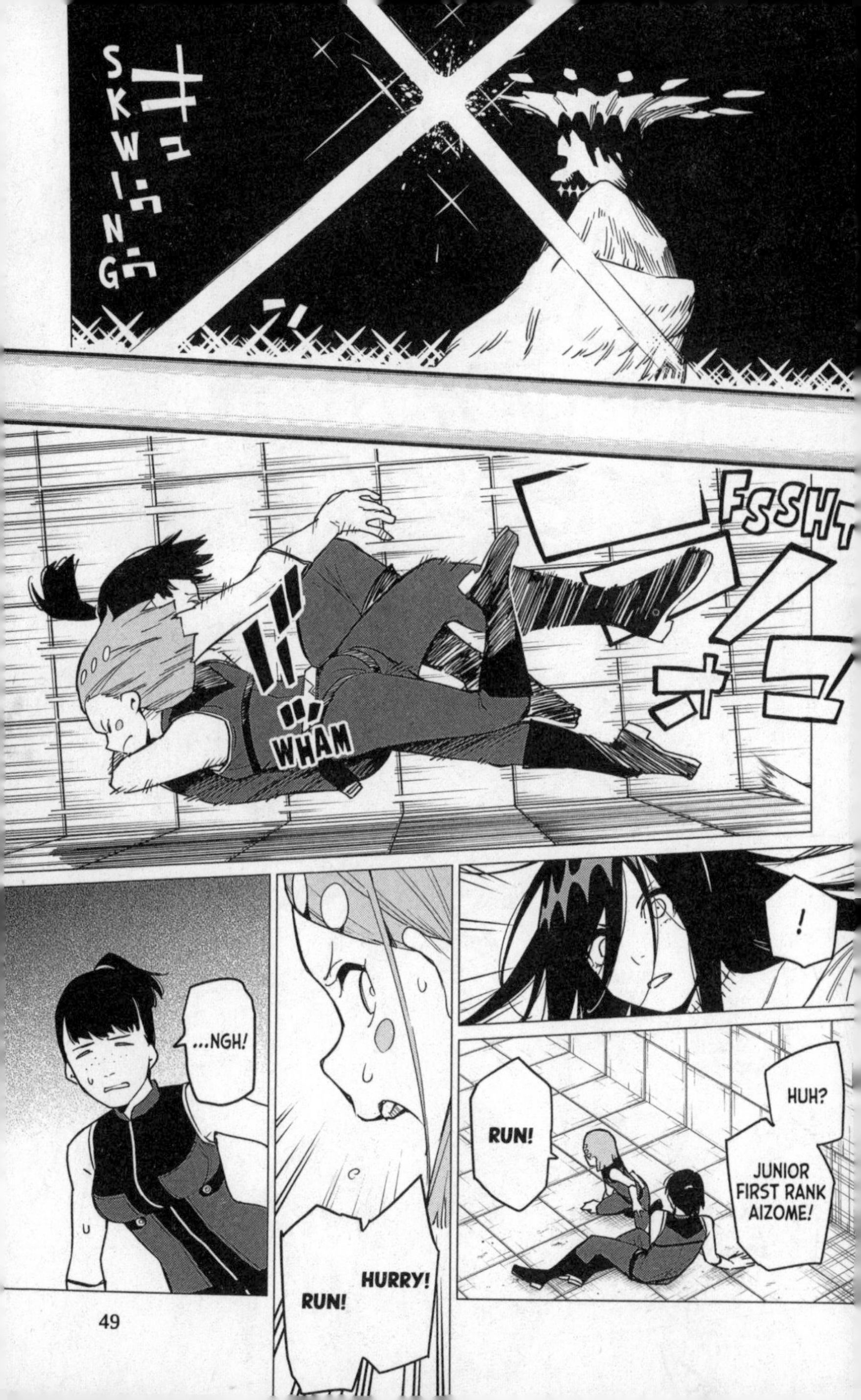
SKWING
FSSHT
WHAM
!
HUH?
JUNIOR FIRST RANK AIZOME!
RUN!
HURRY!
RUN!
...NGH!

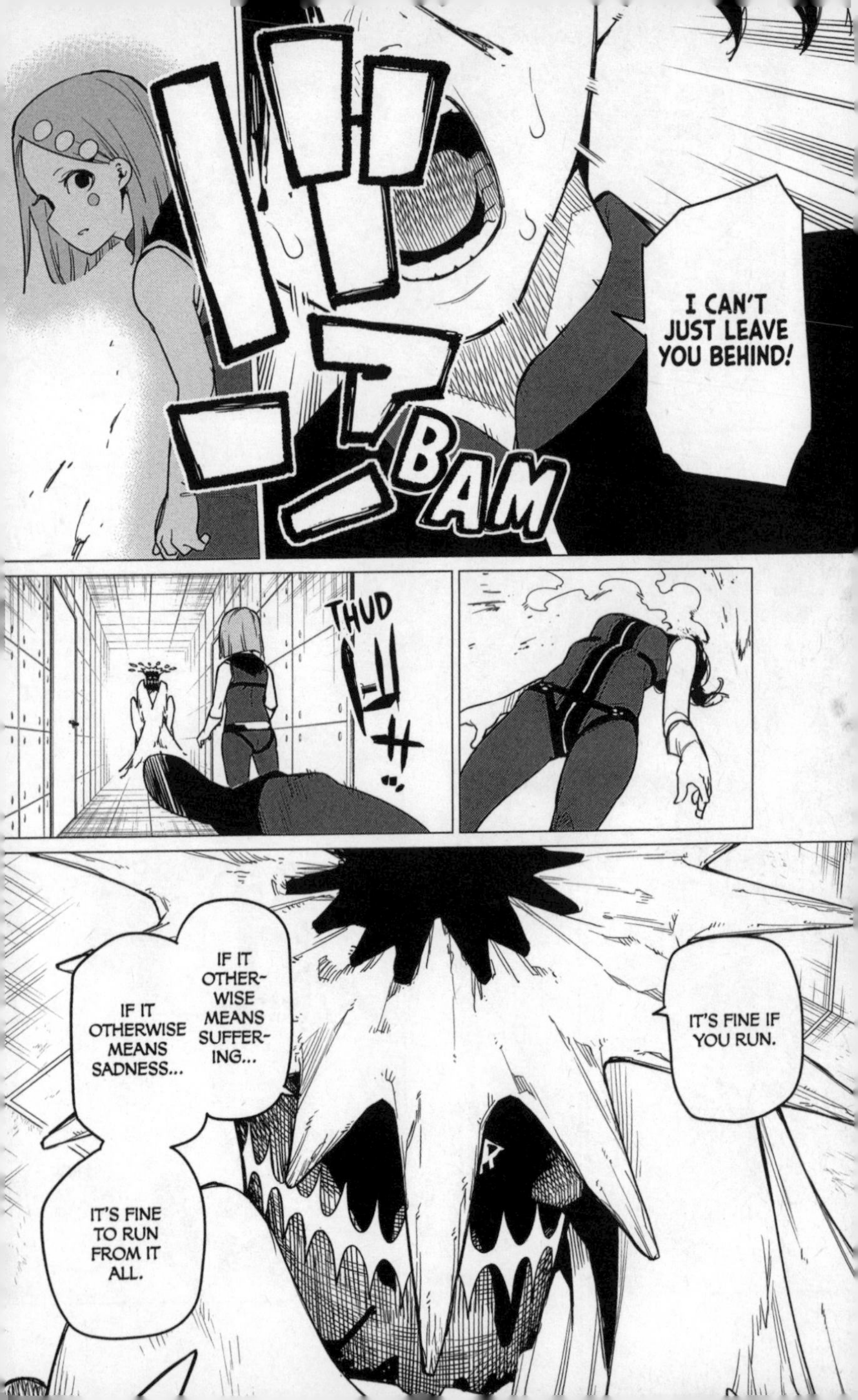
I CAN'T JUST LEAVE YOU BEHIND!
BAM
THUD
IT'S FINE IF YOU RUN.
IF IT OTHER-WISE MEANS SUFFER-ING...
IF IT OTHERWISE MEANS SADNESS...
IT'S FINE TO RUN FROM IT ALL.

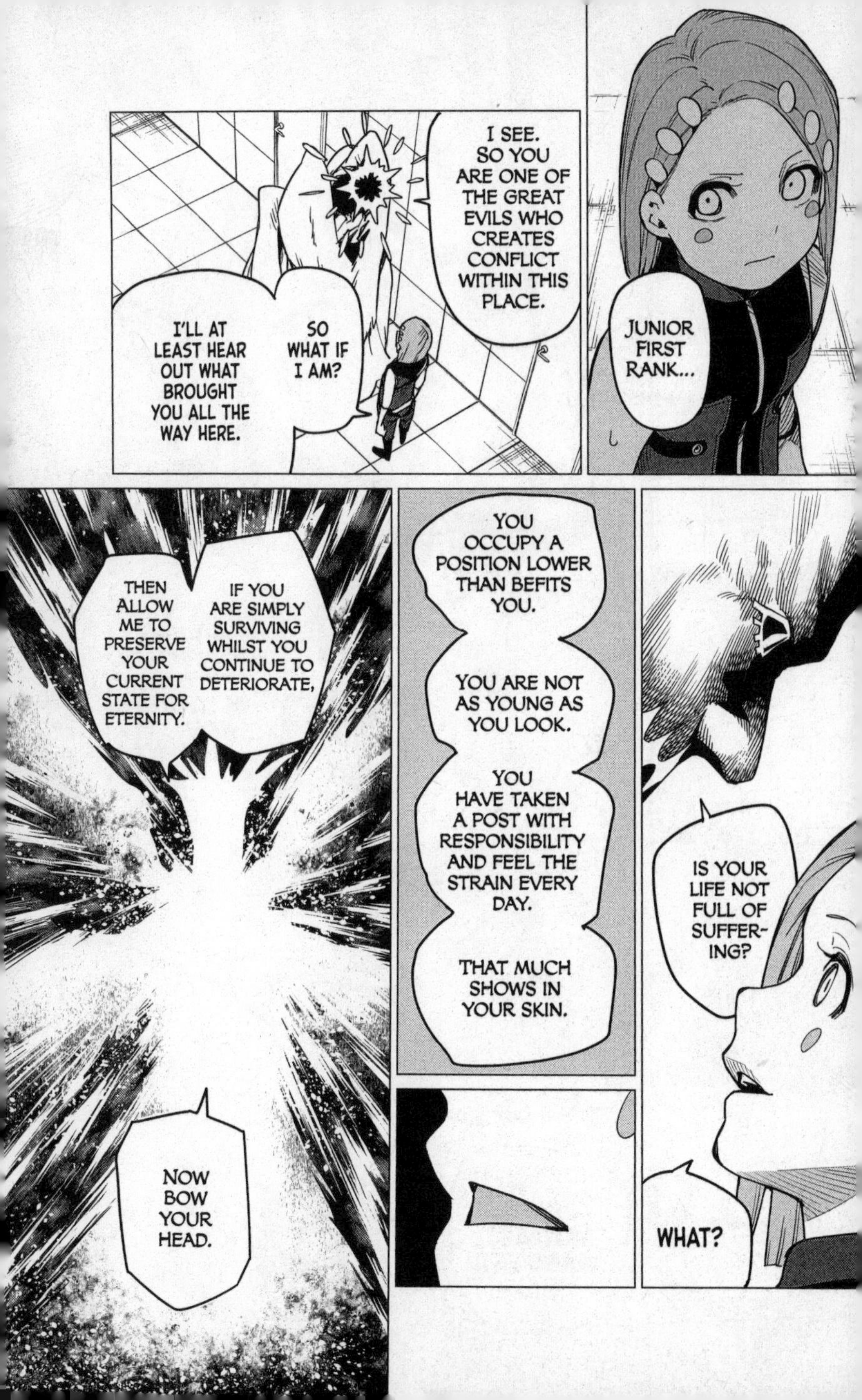
JUNIOR FIRST RANK...
I SEE. SO YOU ARE ONE OF THE GREAT EVILS WHO CREATES CONFLICT WITHIN THIS PLACE.
SO WHAT IF I AM?
I'LL AT LEAST HEAR OUT WHAT BROUGHT YOU ALL THE WAY HERE.
IS YOUR LIFE NOT FULL OF SUFFER-ING?
WHAT?
YOU OCCUPY A POSITION LOWER THAN BEFITS YOU.
YOU ARE NOT AS YOUNG AS YOU LOOK.
YOU HAVE TAKEN A POST WITH RESPONSIBILITY AND FEEL THE STRAIN EVERY DAY.
THAT MUCH SHOWS IN YOUR SKIN.
IF YOU ARE SIMPLY SURVIVING WHILST YOU CONTINUE TO DETERIORATE,
THEN ALLOW ME TO PRESERVE YOUR CURRENT STATE FOR ETERNITY.
NOW BOW YOUR HEAD.

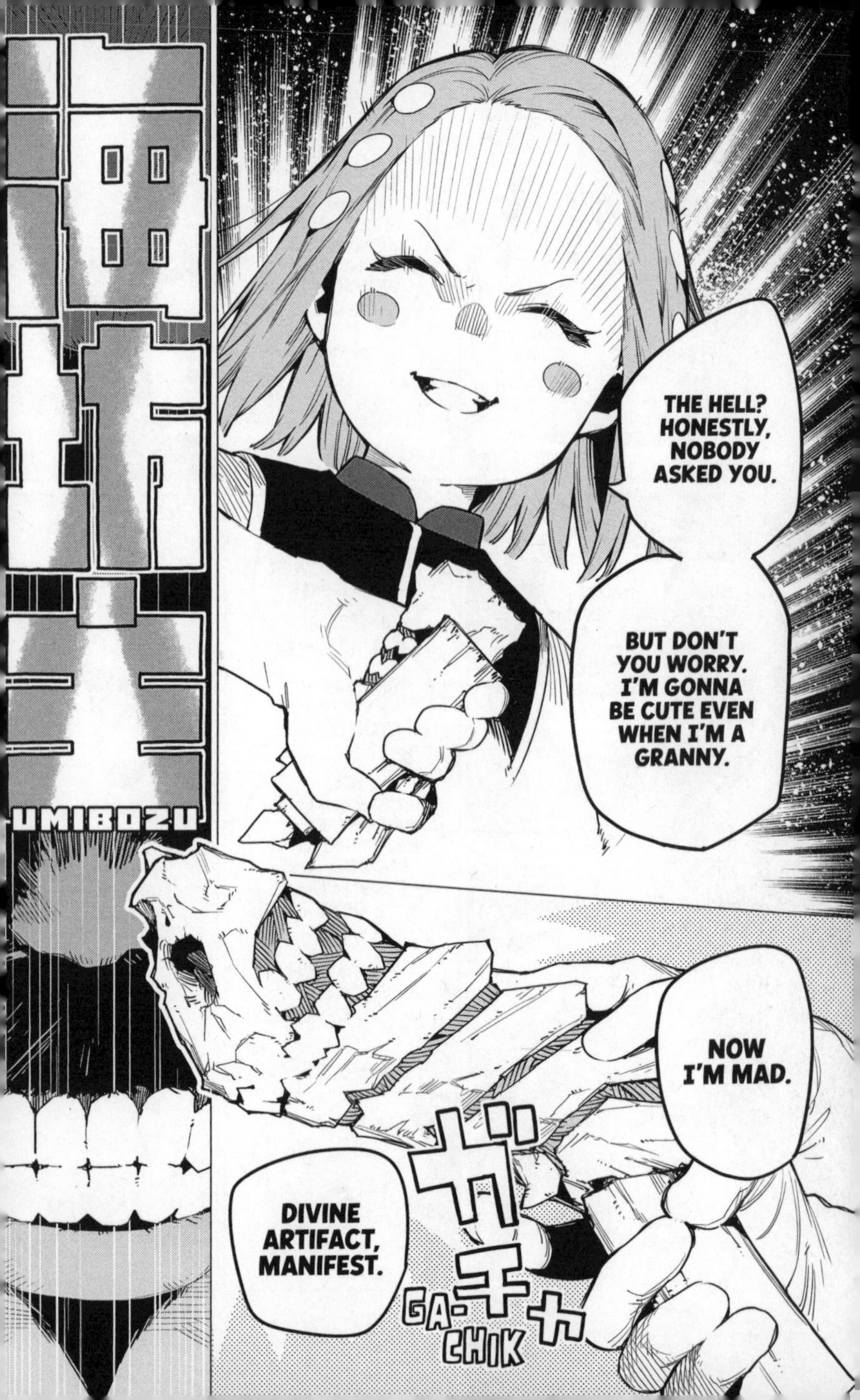
THE HELL? HONESTLY, NOBODY ASKED YOU.
BUT DON'T YOU WORRY. I'M GONNA BE CUTE EVEN WHEN I'M A GRANNY.
NOW I'M MAD.
GA-CHIK
DIVINE ARTIFACT, MANIFEST.
UMIBOZU

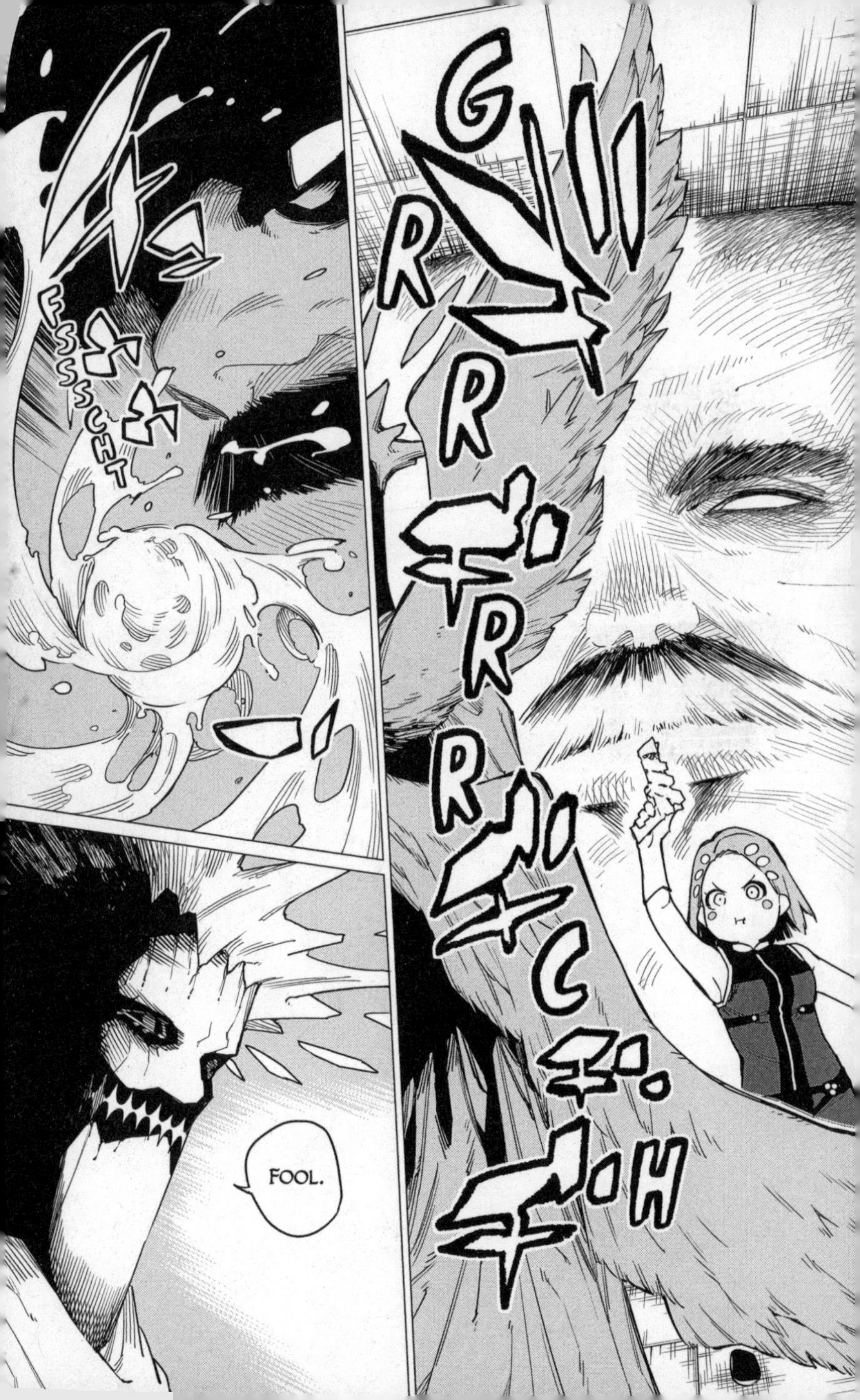
GRRRRRCH
FSSSCHT
FOOL.

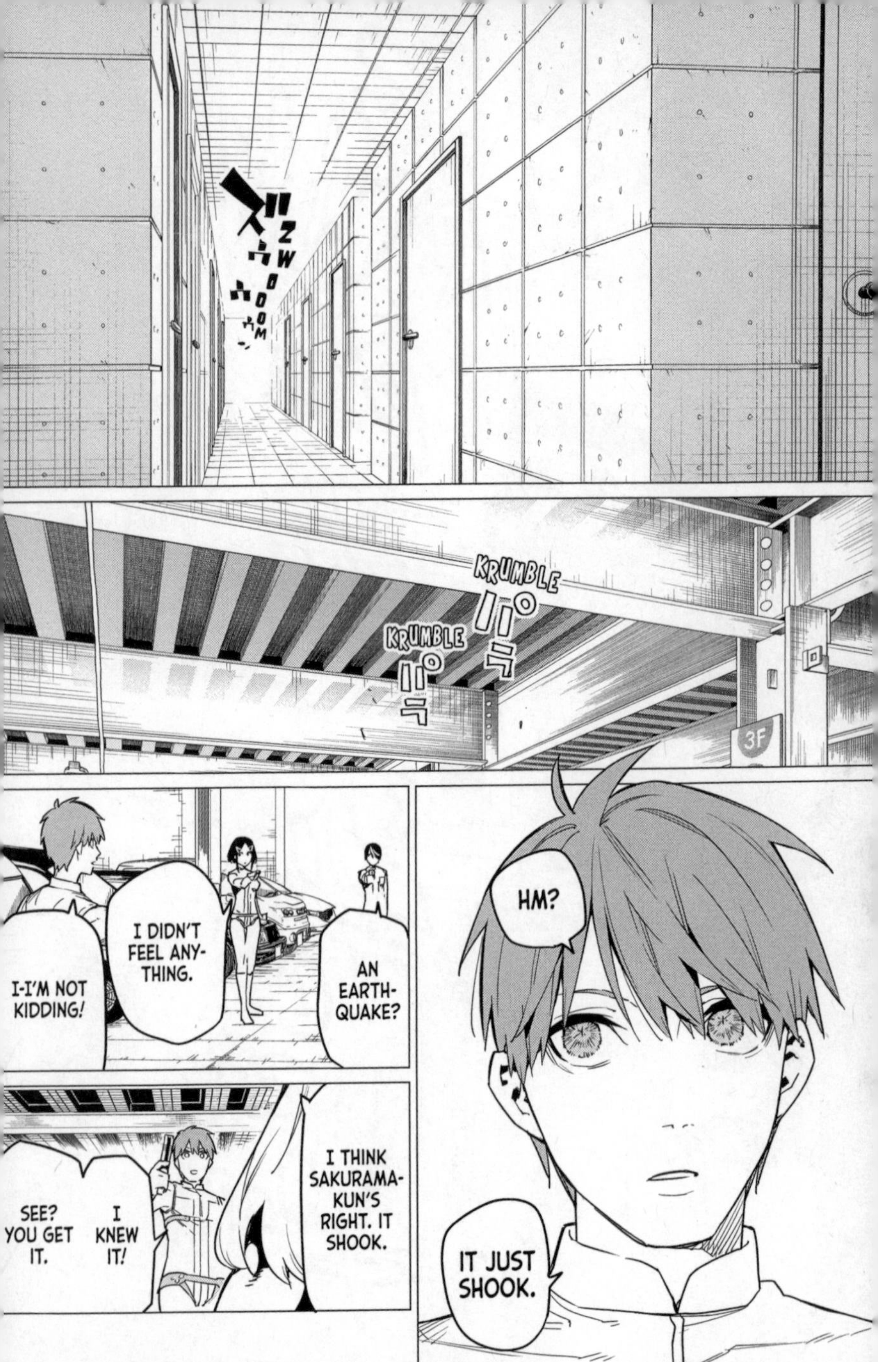
ZWOOOOM
KRUMBLE
KRUMBLE
3F
HM?
IT JUST SHOOK.
AN EARTHQUAKE?
I DIDN'T FEEL ANYTHING.
I-I'M NOT KIDDING!
I THINK SAKURAMA-KUN'S RIGHT. IT SHOOK.
I KNEW IT!
SEE? YOU GET IT.

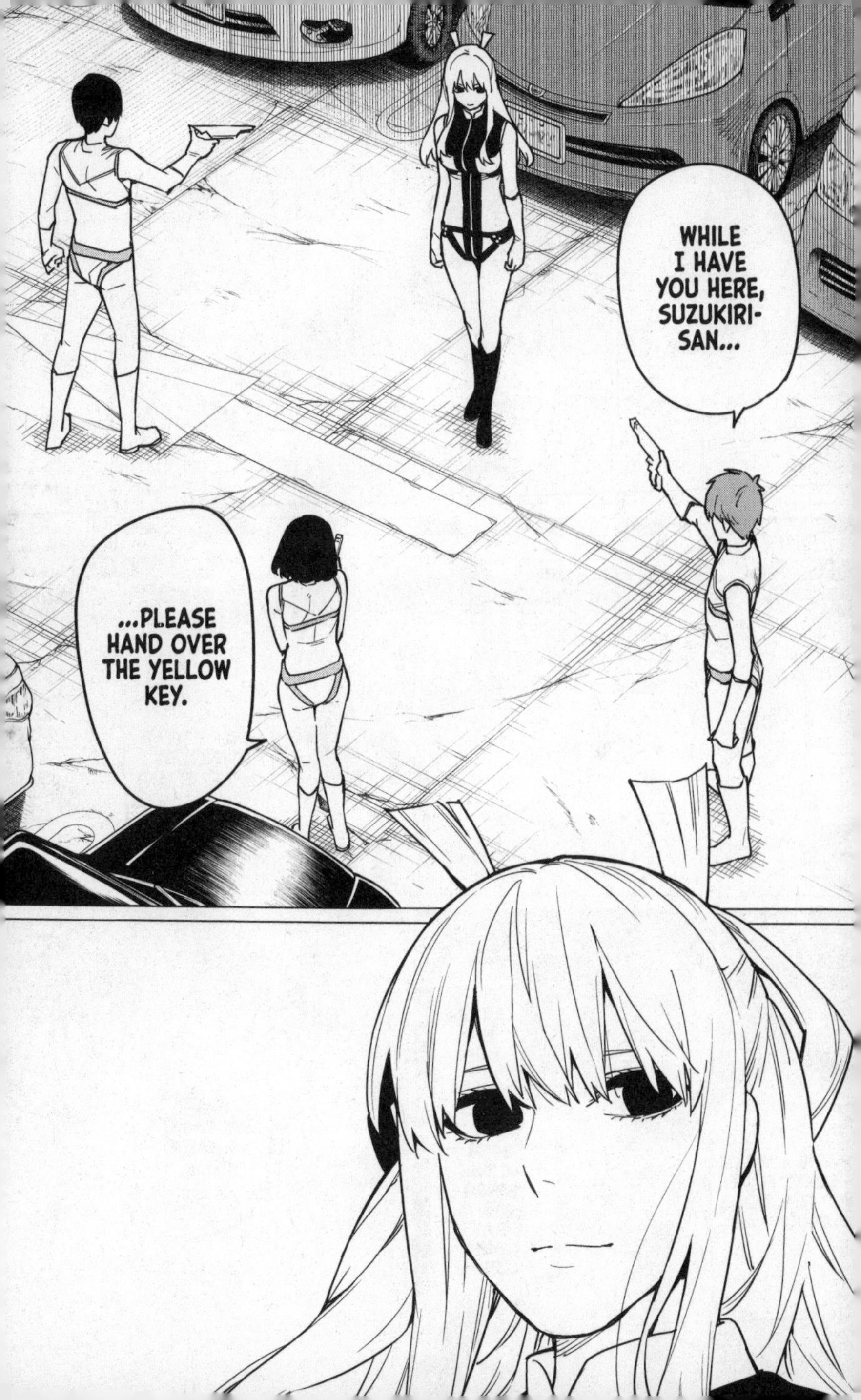
WHILE I HAVE YOU HERE, SUZUKIRI-SAN...
...PLEASE HAND OVER THE YELLOW KEY.

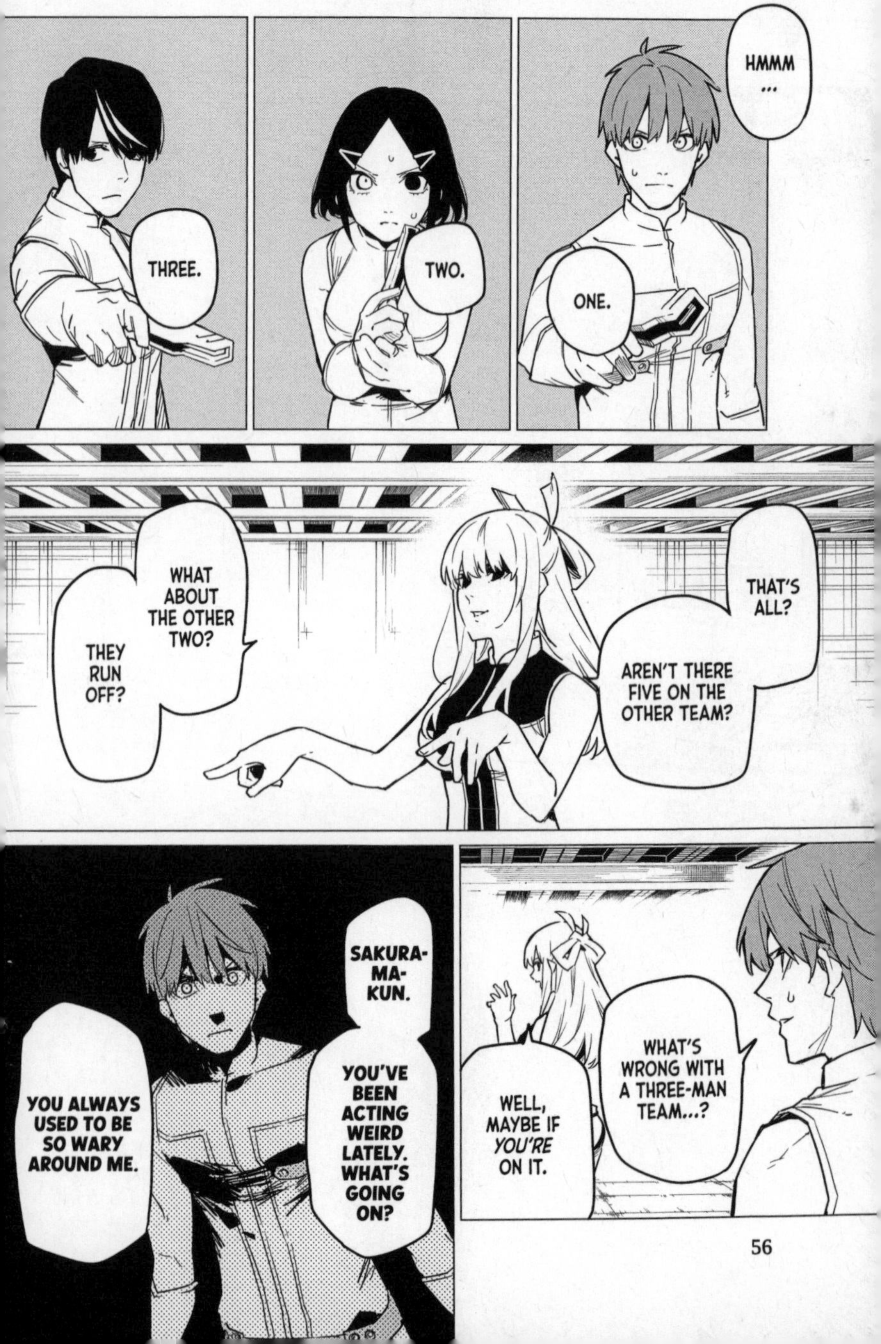
HMMM...
ONE.
TWO.
THREE.
THAT'S ALL?
AREN'T THERE FIVE ON THE OTHER TEAM?
WHAT ABOUT THE OTHER TWO?
THEY RUN OFF?
WHAT'S WRONG WITH A THREE-MAN TEAM...?
WELL, MAYBE IF *YOU'RE* ON IT.
SAKURAMA-KUN.
YOU'VE BEEN ACTING WEIRD LATELY. WHAT'S GOING ON?
YOU ALWAYS USED TO BE SO WARY AROUND ME.

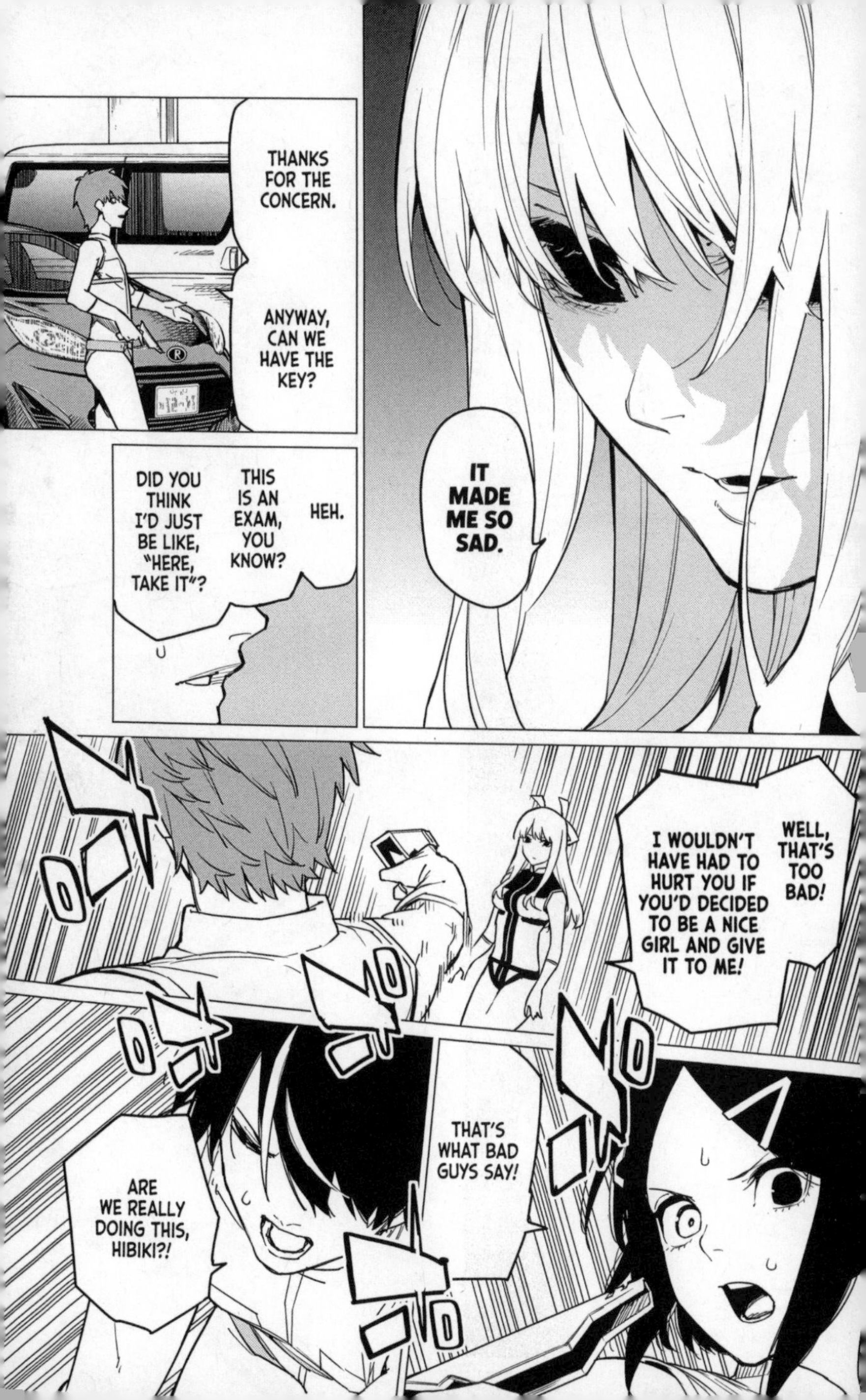
IT MADE ME SO SAD.
THANKS FOR THE CONCERN.
ANYWAY, CAN WE HAVE THE KEY?
HEH.
THIS IS AN EXAM, YOU KNOW?
DID YOU THINK I'D JUST BE LIKE, "HERE, TAKE IT"?
WELL, THAT'S TOO BAD!
I WOULDN'T HAVE HAD TO HURT YOU IF YOU'D DECIDED TO BE A NICE GIRL AND GIVE IT TO ME!
THAT'S WHAT BAD GUYS SAY!
ARE WE REALLY DOING THIS, HIBIKI?!

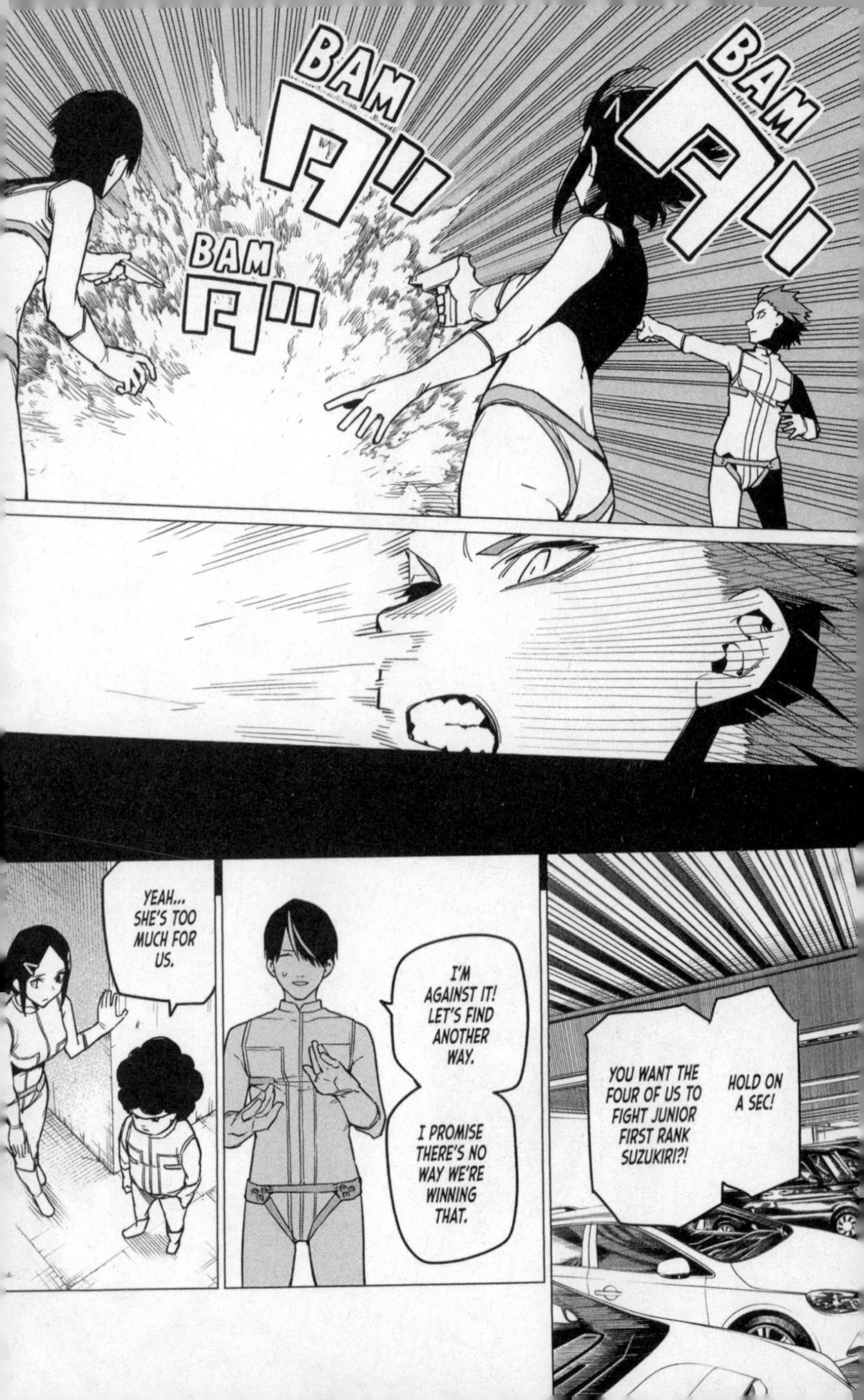
BAM
BAM
BAM
HOLD ON A SEC!
YOU WANT THE FOUR OF US TO FIGHT JUNIOR FIRST RANK SUZUKIRI?!
I'M AGAINST IT! LET'S FIND ANOTHER WAY.
I PROMISE THERE'S NO WAY WE'RE WINNING THAT.
YEAH... SHE'S TOO MUCH FOR US.

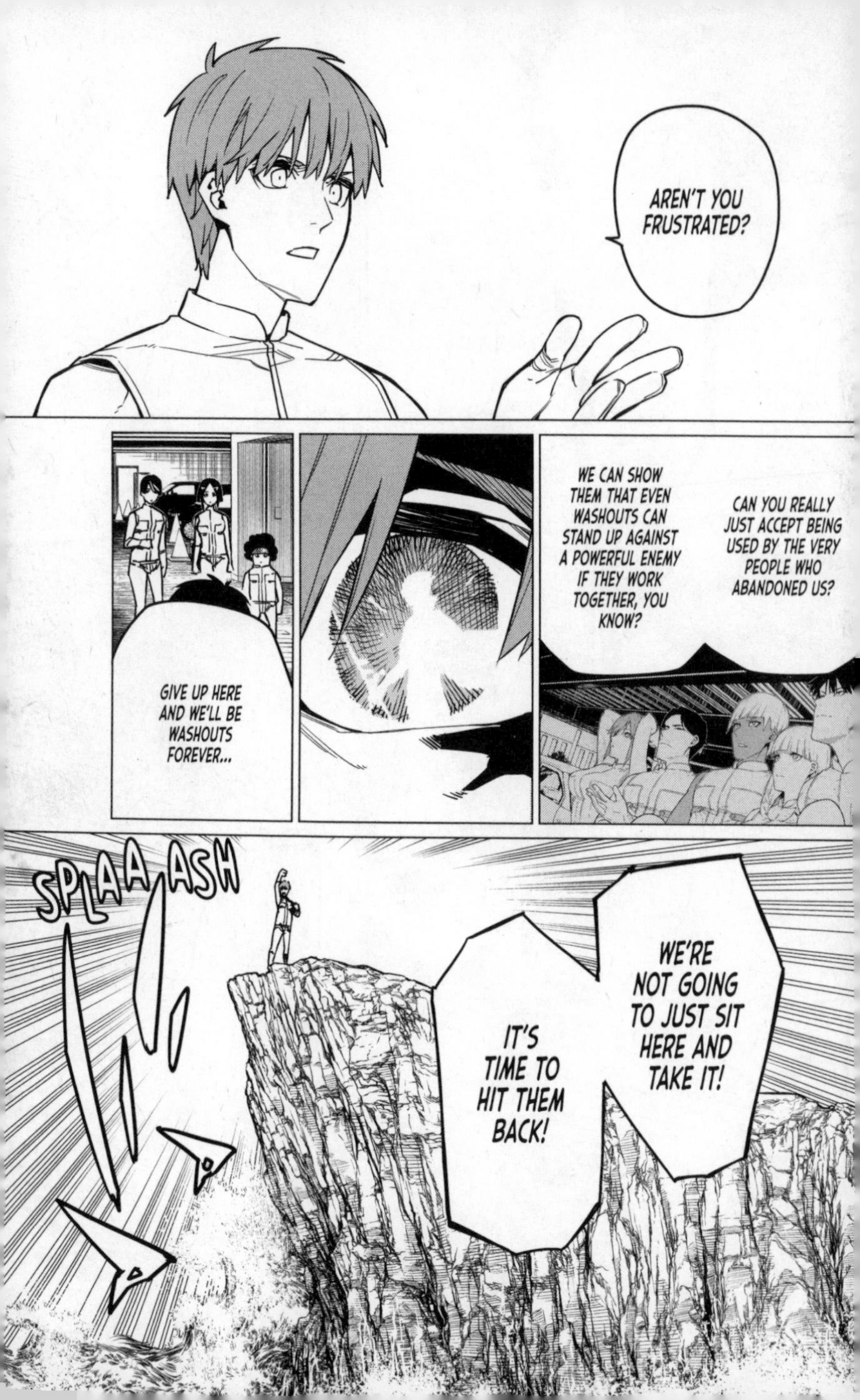
AREN'T YOU FRUSTRATED?
CAN YOU REALLY JUST ACCEPT BEING USED BY THE VERY PEOPLE WHO ABANDONED US?
WE CAN SHOW THEM THAT EVEN WASHOUTS CAN STAND UP AGAINST A POWERFUL ENEMY IF THEY WORK TOGETHER, YOU KNOW?
GIVE UP HERE AND WE'LL BE WASHOUTS FOREVER...
WE'RE NOT GOING TO JUST SIT HERE AND TAKE IT!
IT'S TIME TO HIT THEM BACK!
SPLAAASH

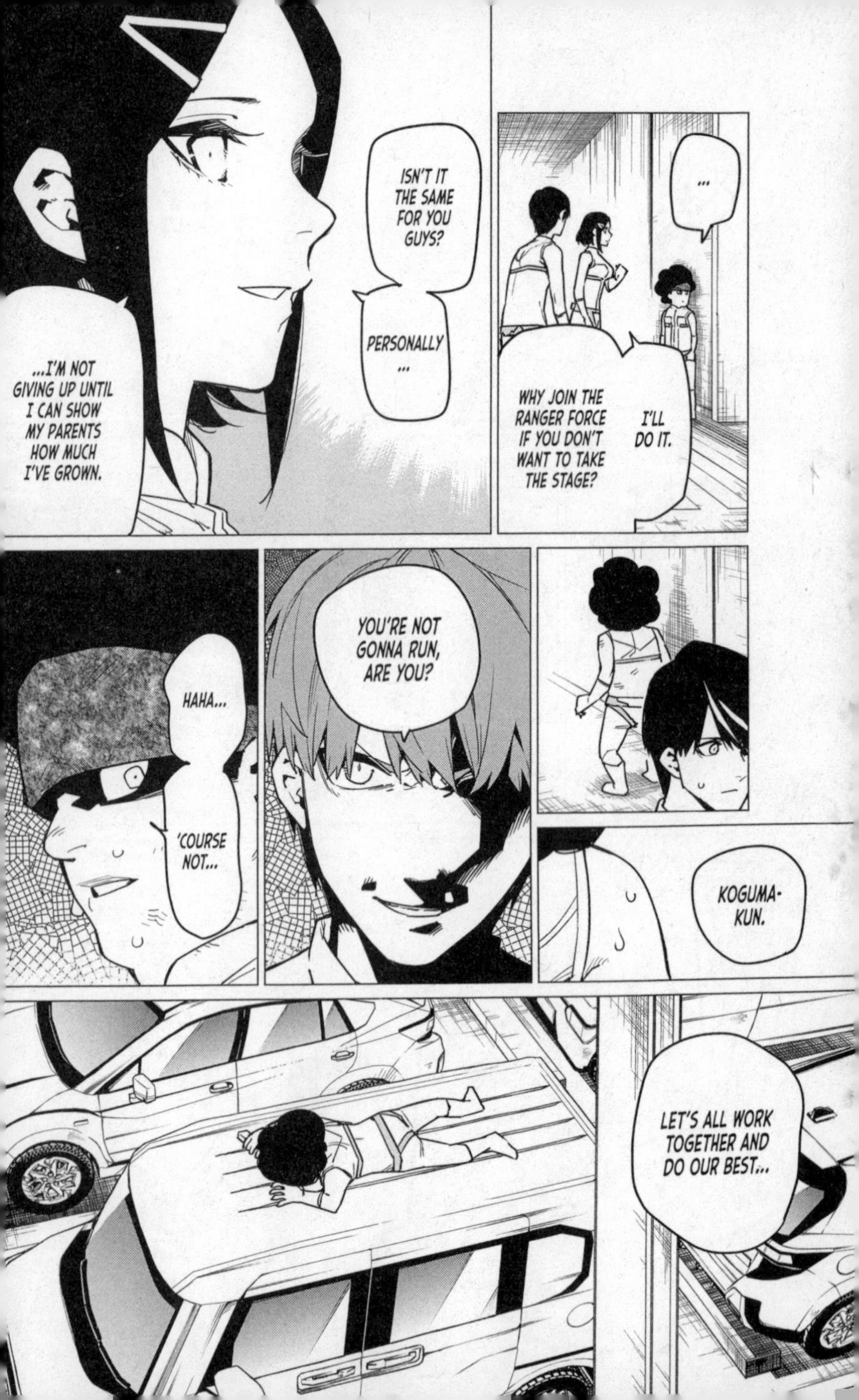
...
I'LL DO IT.
WHY JOIN THE RANGER FORCE IF YOU DON'T WANT TO TAKE THE STAGE?
ISN'T IT THE SAME FOR YOU GUYS?
PERSONALLY...
...I'M NOT GIVING UP UNTIL I CAN SHOW MY PARENTS HOW MUCH I'VE GROWN.
KOGUMA-KUN.
YOU'RE NOT GONNA RUN, ARE YOU?
HAHA...
'COURSE NOT...
LET'S ALL WORK TOGETHER AND DO OUR BEST...

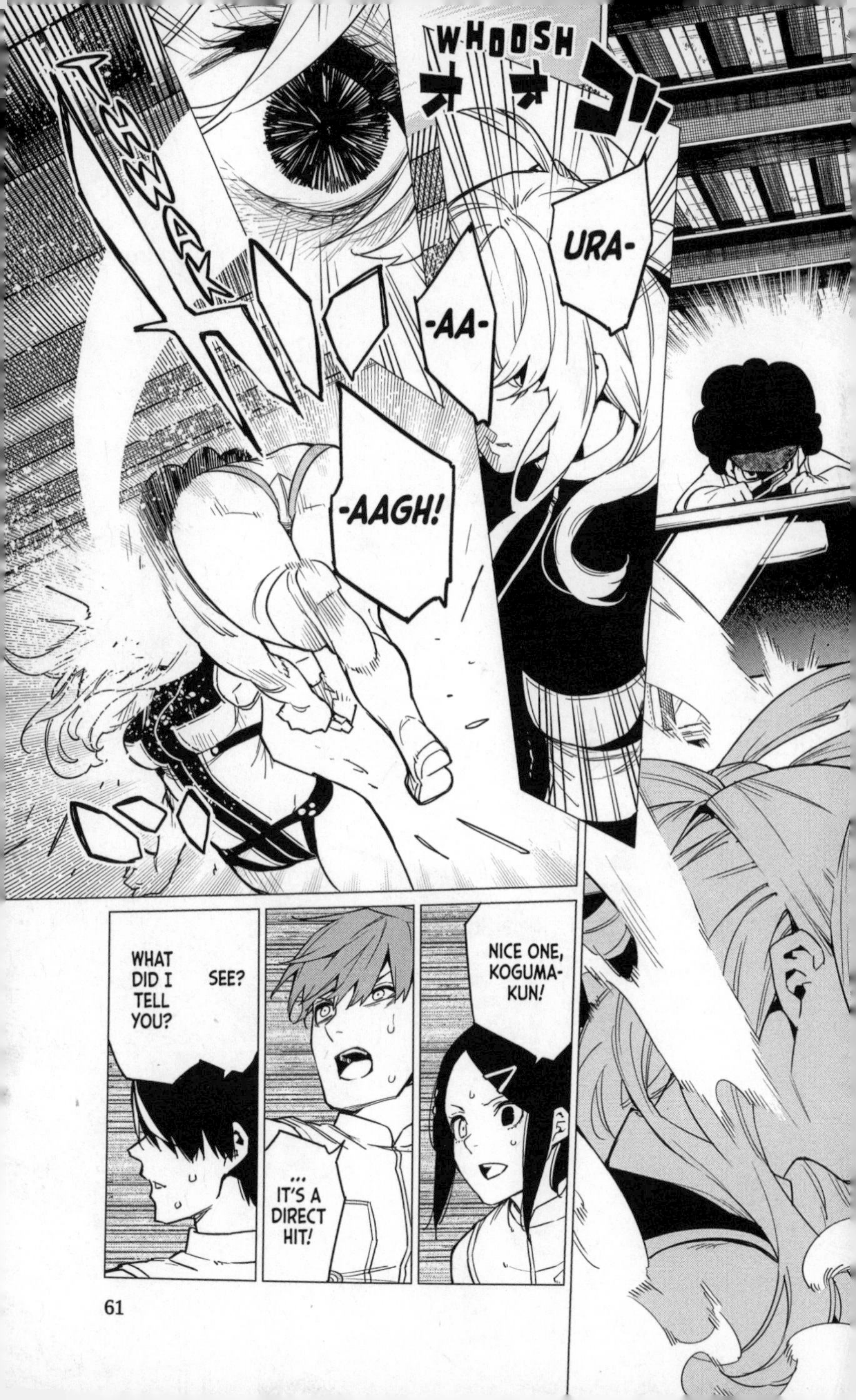
WHOOSH
ゴオオ
URA-
-AA-
-AAGH!
THWAK
NICE ONE, KOGUMA-KUN!
... IT'S A DIRECT HIT!
WHAT DID I TELL YOU?
SEE?

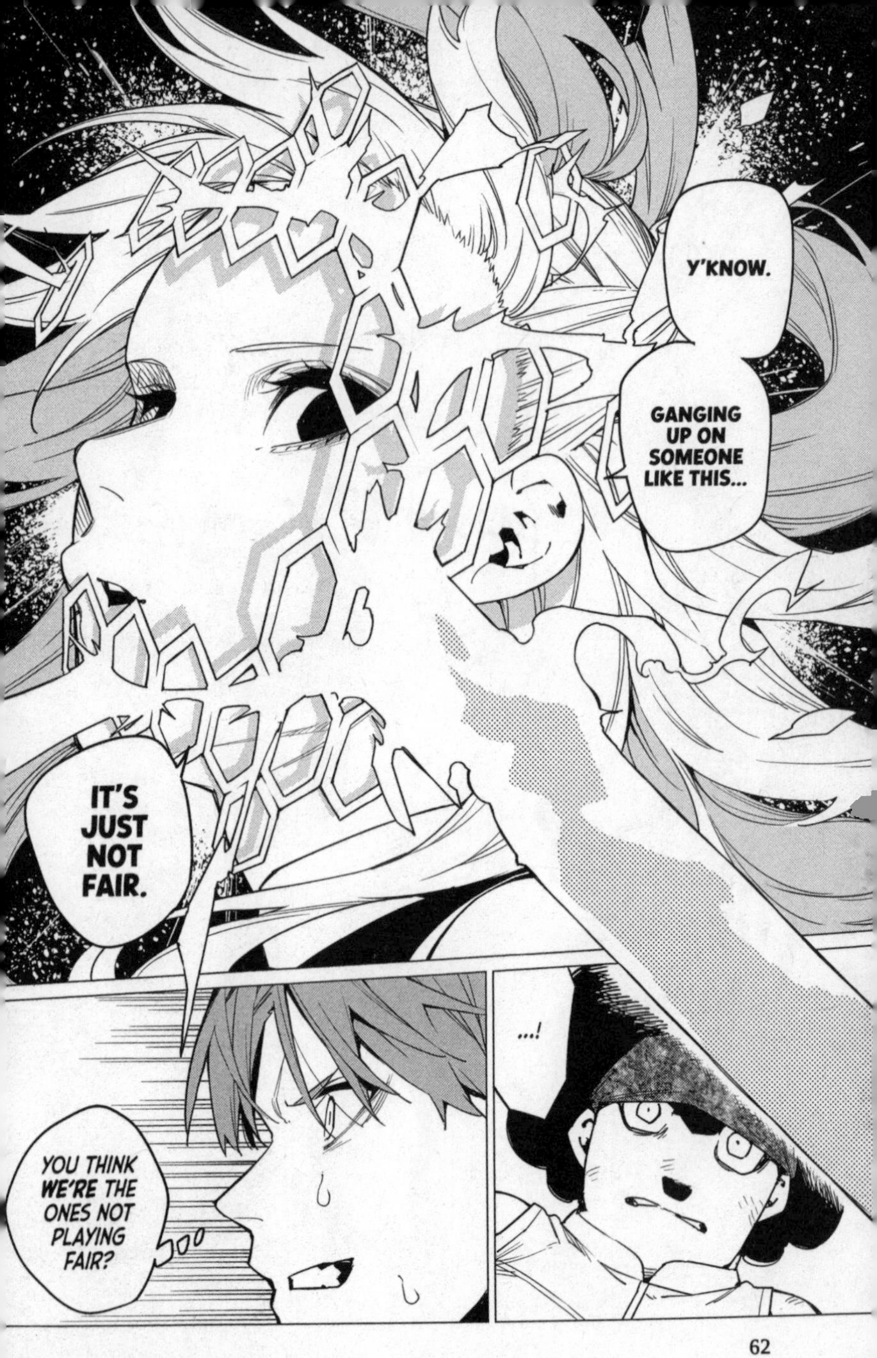
Y'KNOW.
GANGING UP ON SOMEONE LIKE THIS...
IT'S JUST NOT FAIR.
...!
YOU THINK WE'RE THE ONES NOT PLAYING FAIR?

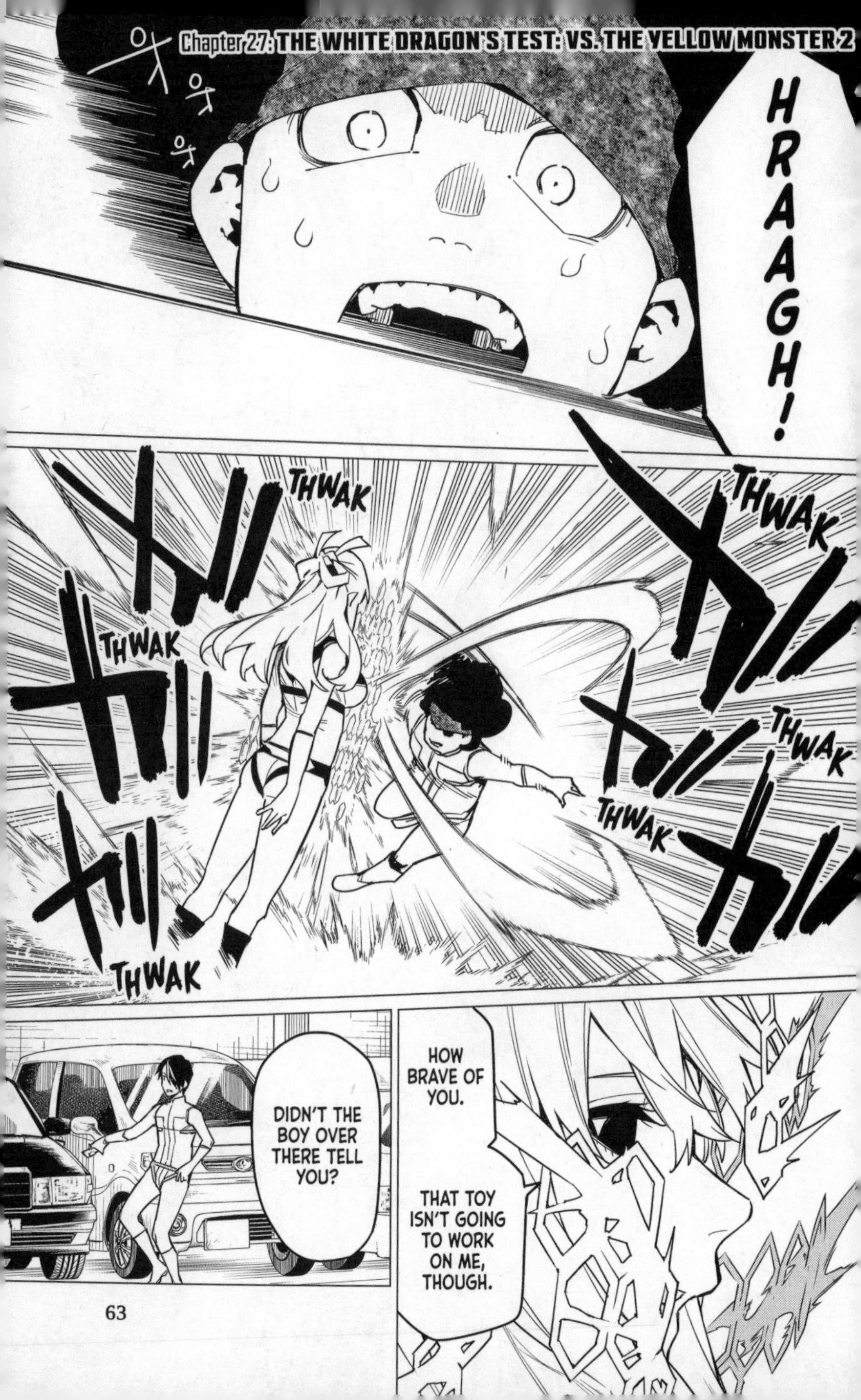
Chapter 27: THE WHITE DRAGON'S TEST: VS. THE YELLOW MONSTER 2
HRAAAGH!
THWAK
THWAK
THWAK
THWAK
THWAK
THWAK
HOW BRAVE OF YOU.
THAT TOY ISN'T GOING TO WORK ON ME, THOUGH.
DIDN'T THE BOY OVER THERE TELL YOU?

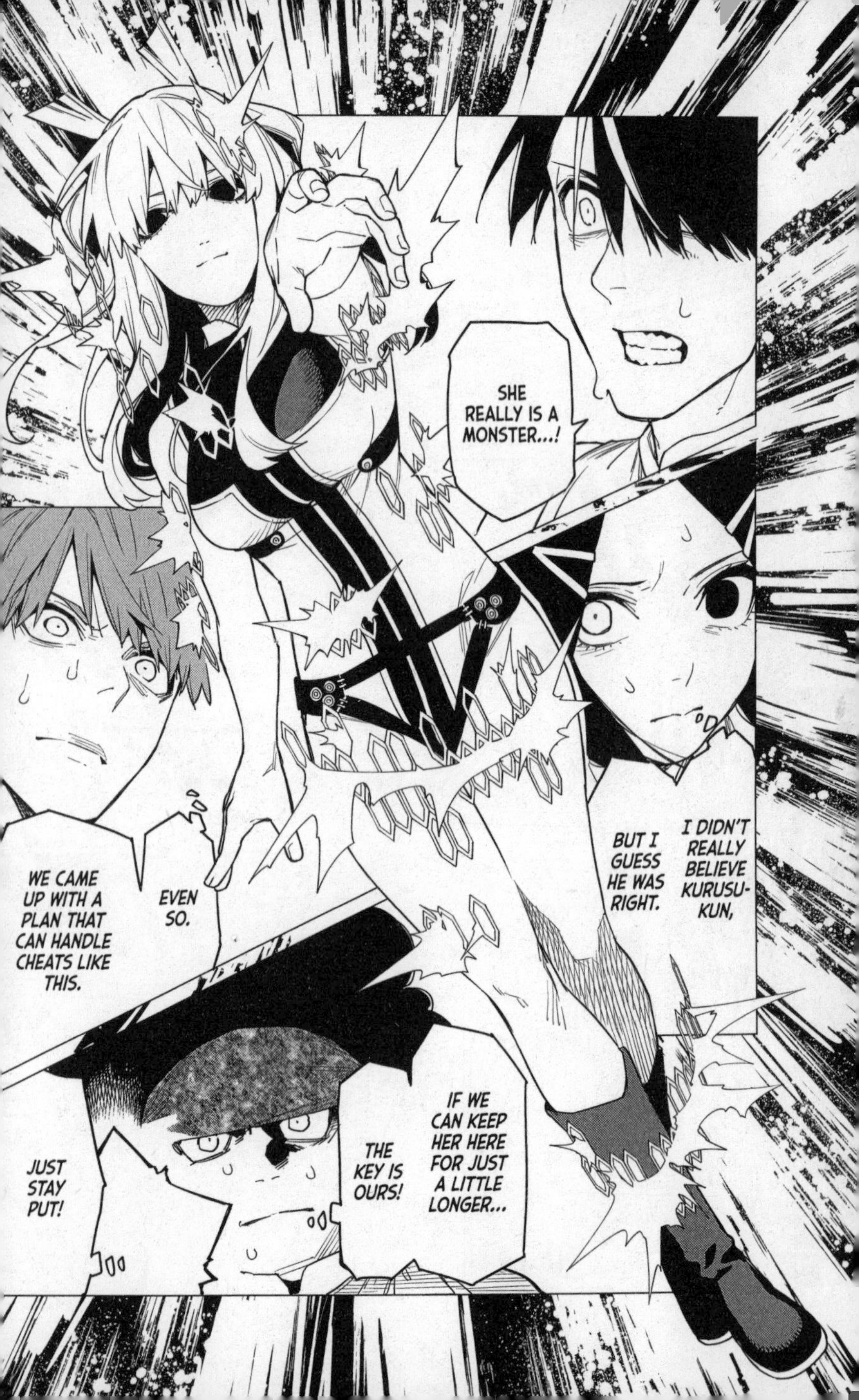
SHE REALLY IS A MONSTER...!
I DIDN'T REALLY BELIEVE KURUSU-KUN,
BUT I GUESS HE WAS RIGHT.
EVEN SO.
WE CAME UP WITH A PLAN THAT CAN HANDLE CHEATS LIKE THIS.
IF WE CAN KEEP HER HERE FOR JUST A LITTLE LONGER...
THE KEY IS OURS!
JUST STAY PUT!

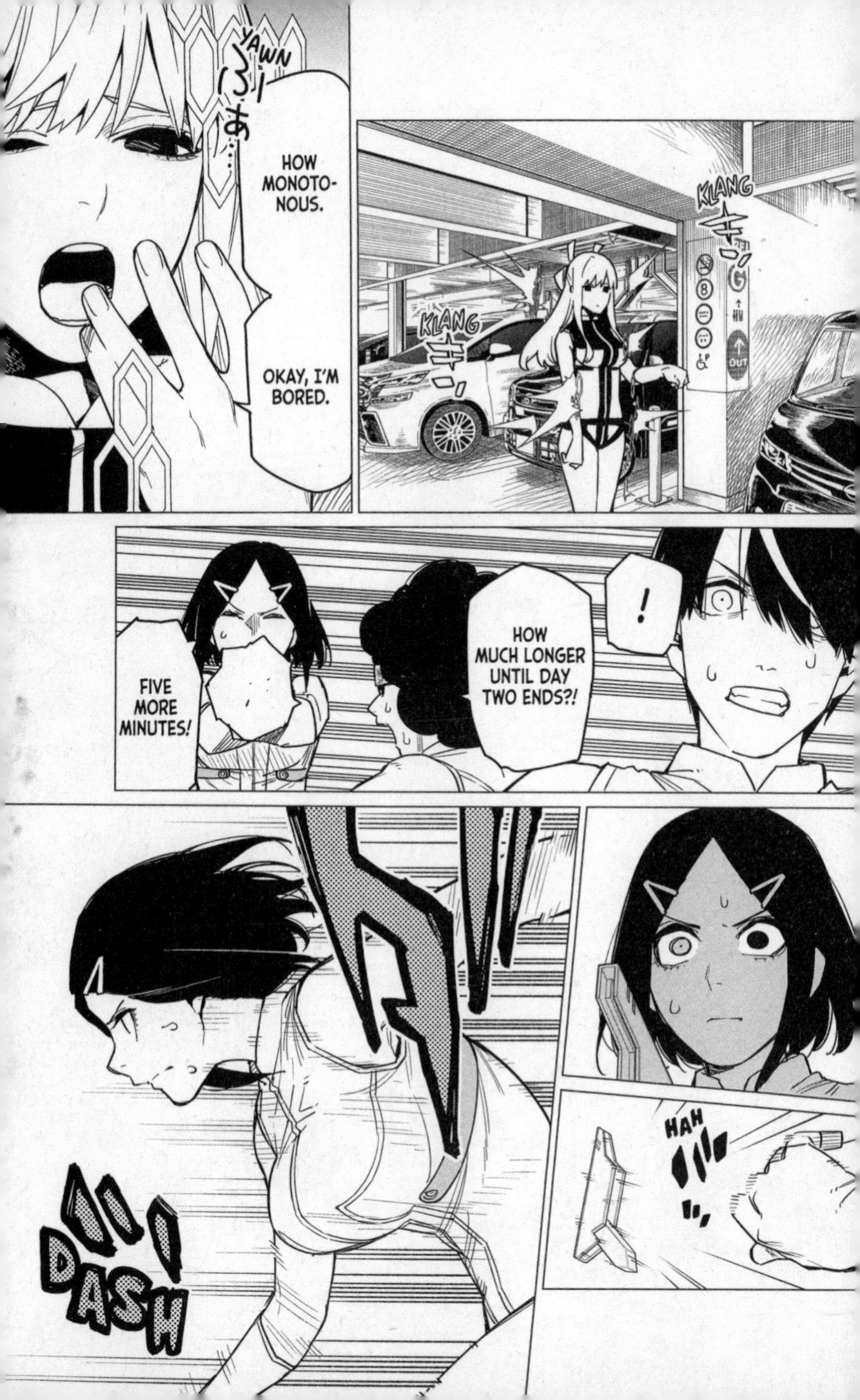
KLANG
キ
KLANG
キ
YAWN
ふぁ
HOW MONOTO-NOUS.
OKAY, I'M BORED.
!
HOW MUCH LONGER UNTIL DAY TWO ENDS?!
FIVE MORE MINUTES!
HAH
DASH

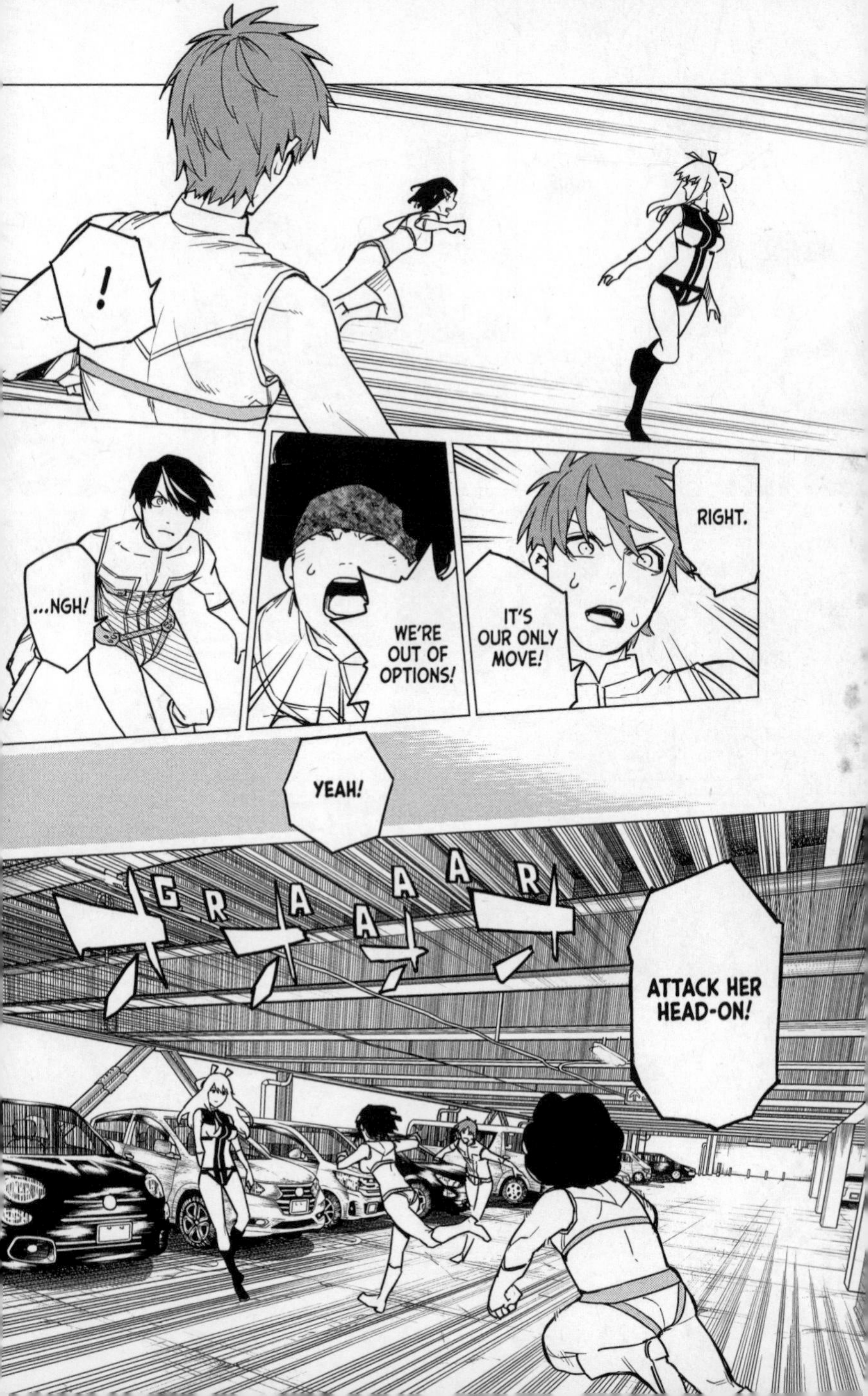
!
RIGHT.
IT'S OUR ONLY MOVE!
WE'RE OUT OF OPTIONS!
...NGH!
YEAH!
ATTACK HER HEAD-ON!
GRAAAAR

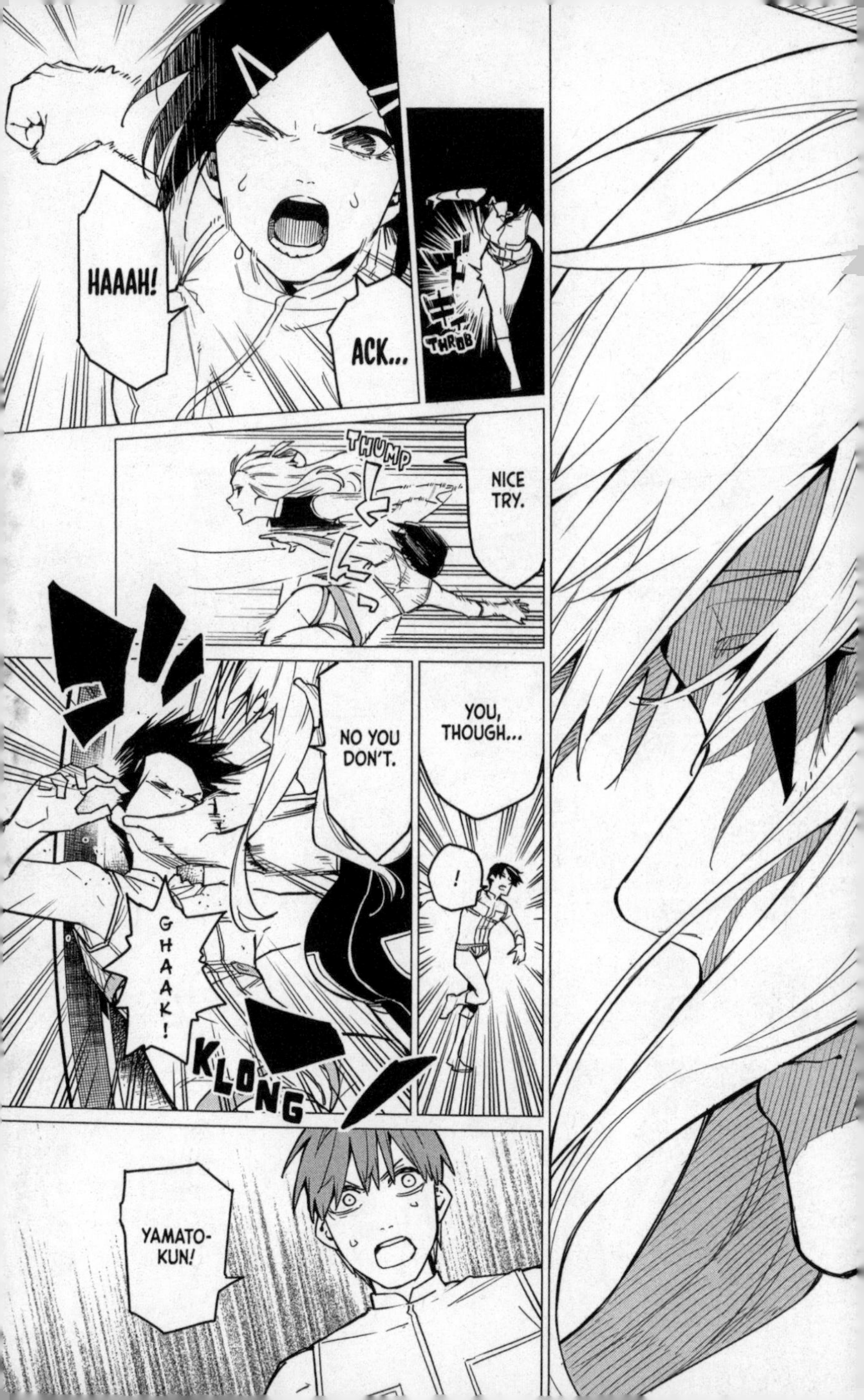
THROB
ACK...
HAAAH!
NICE TRY.
THUMP
YOU, THOUGH...
!
NO YOU DON'T.
GHAAAK!
KLONG
YAMATO-KUN!

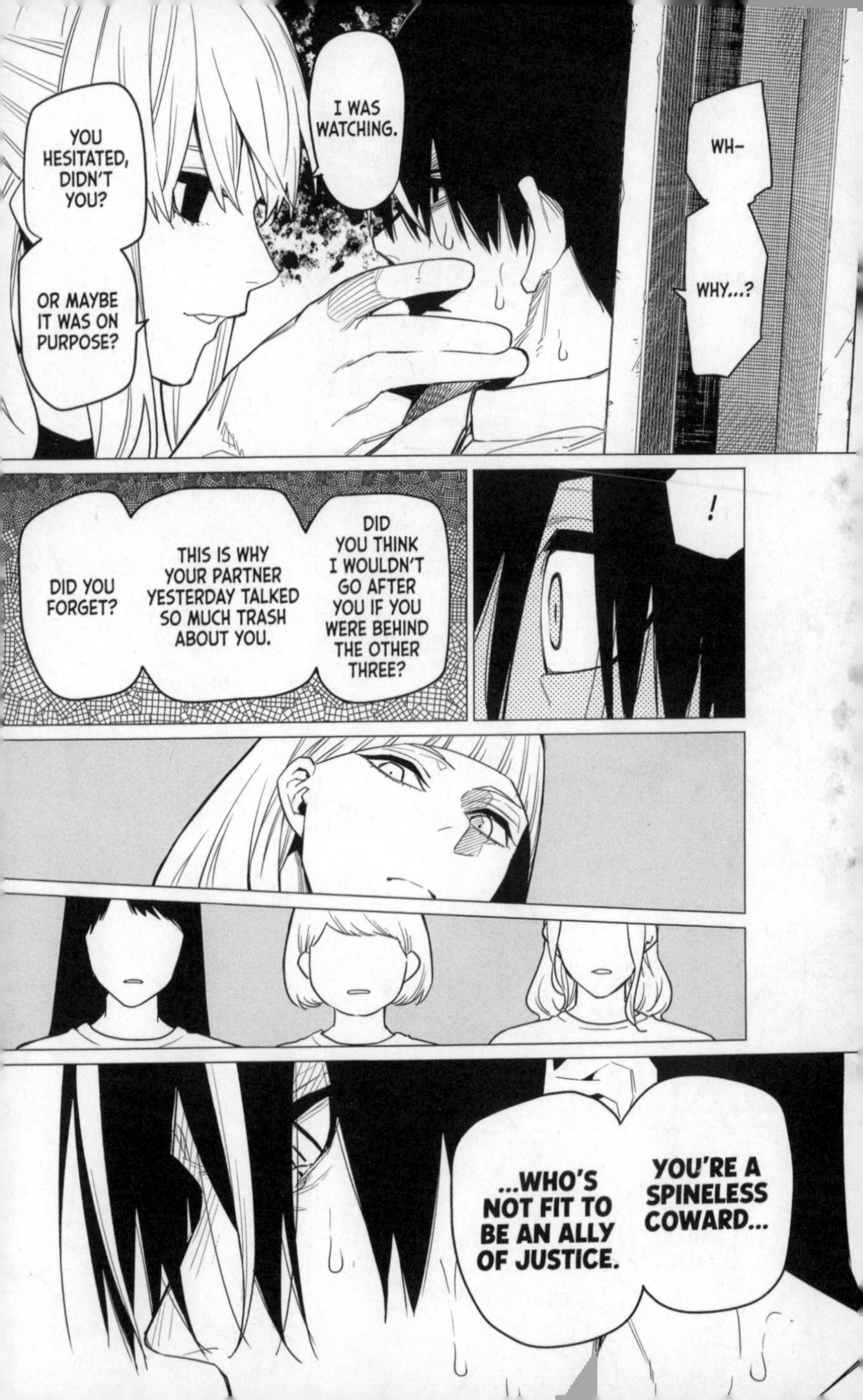
WH–
WHY...?
I WAS WATCHING.
YOU HESITATED, DIDN'T YOU?
OR MAYBE IT WAS ON PURPOSE?
!
DID YOU THINK I WOULDN'T GO AFTER YOU IF YOU WERE BEHIND THE OTHER THREE?
THIS IS WHY YOUR PARTNER YESTERDAY TALKED SO MUCH TRASH ABOUT YOU.
DID YOU FORGET?
YOU'RE A SPINELESS COWARD...
...WHO'S NOT FIT TO BE AN ALLY OF JUSTICE.

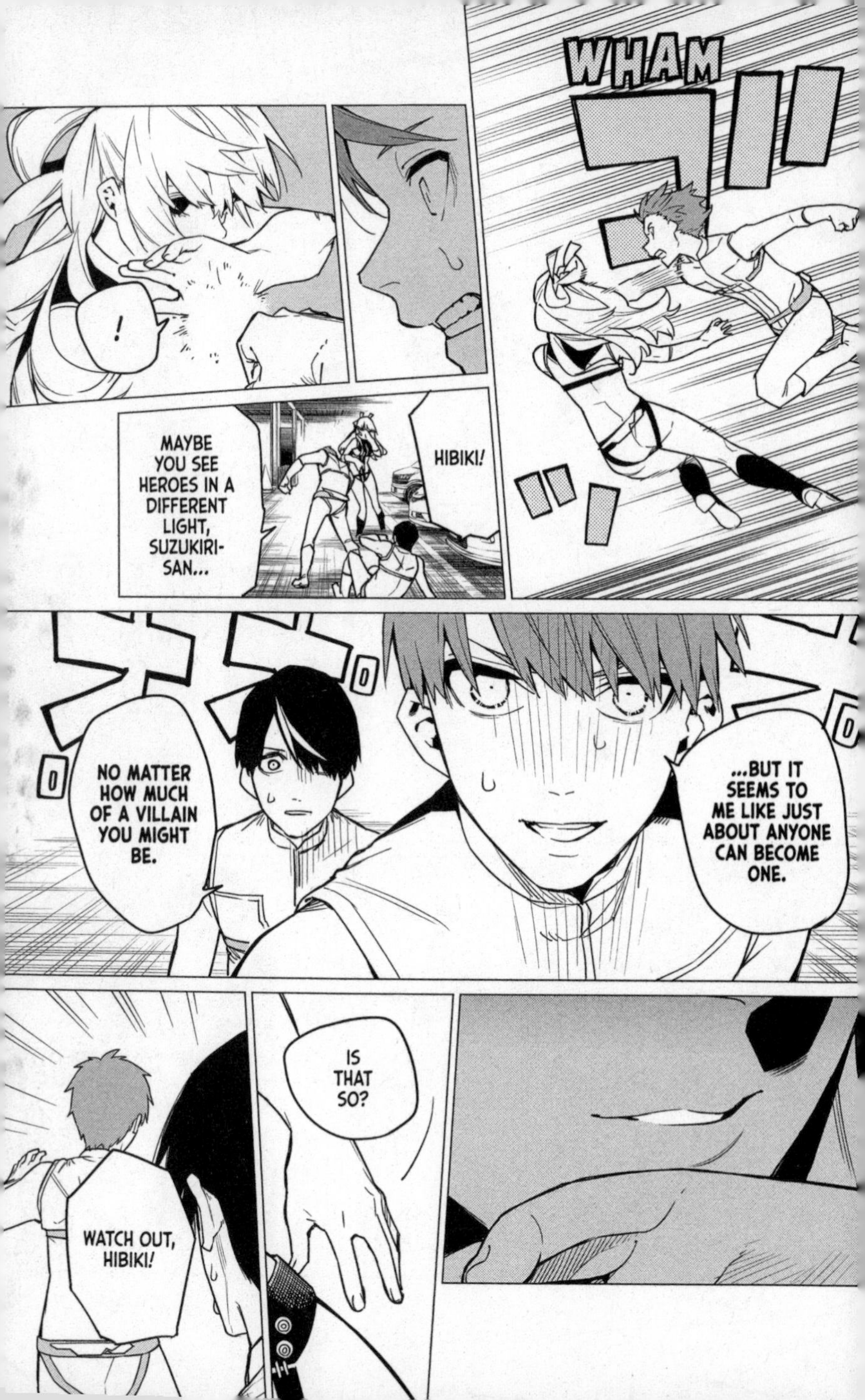
WHAM
!
HIBIKI!
MAYBE YOU SEE HEROES IN A DIFFERENT LIGHT, SUZUKIRI-SAN...
...BUT IT SEEMS TO ME LIKE JUST ABOUT ANYONE CAN BECOME ONE.
NO MATTER HOW MUCH OF A VILLAIN YOU MIGHT BE.
IS THAT SO?
WATCH OUT, HIBIKI!

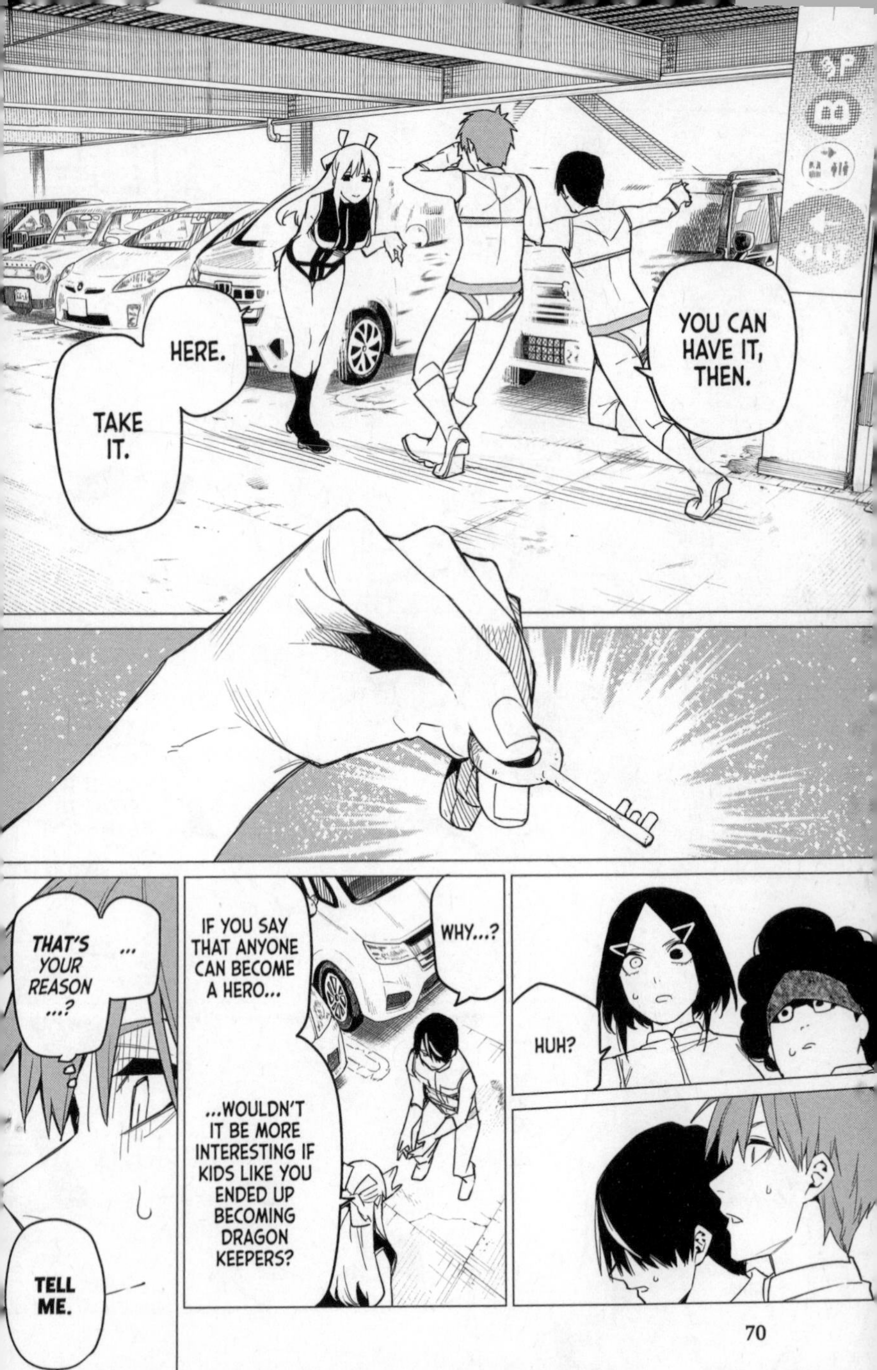
YOU CAN HAVE IT, THEN.
HERE.
TAKE IT.
HUH?
WHY...?
IF YOU SAY THAT ANYONE CAN BECOME A HERO...
...WOULDN'T IT BE MORE INTERESTING IF KIDS LIKE YOU ENDED UP BECOMING DRAGON KEEPERS?
THAT'S YOUR REASON ...?
...
TELL ME.

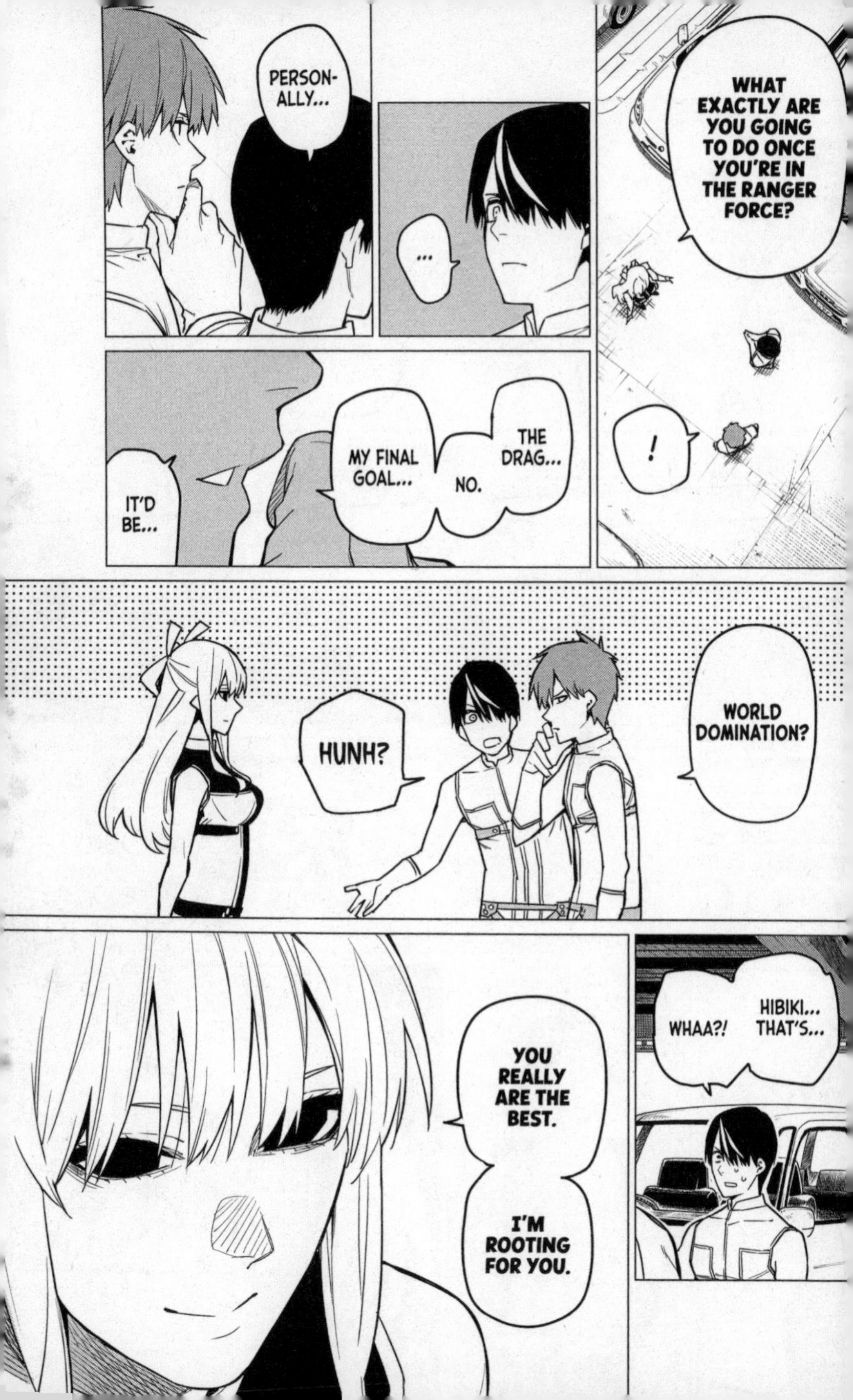
WHAT EXACTLY ARE YOU GOING TO DO ONCE YOU'RE IN THE RANGER FORCE?
!
...
PERSON-ALLY...
THE DRAG...
NO.
MY FINAL GOAL...
IT'D BE...
WORLD DOMINATION?
HUNH?
HIBIKI... THAT'S...
WHAA?!
YOU REALLY ARE THE BEST.
I'M ROOTING FOR YOU.

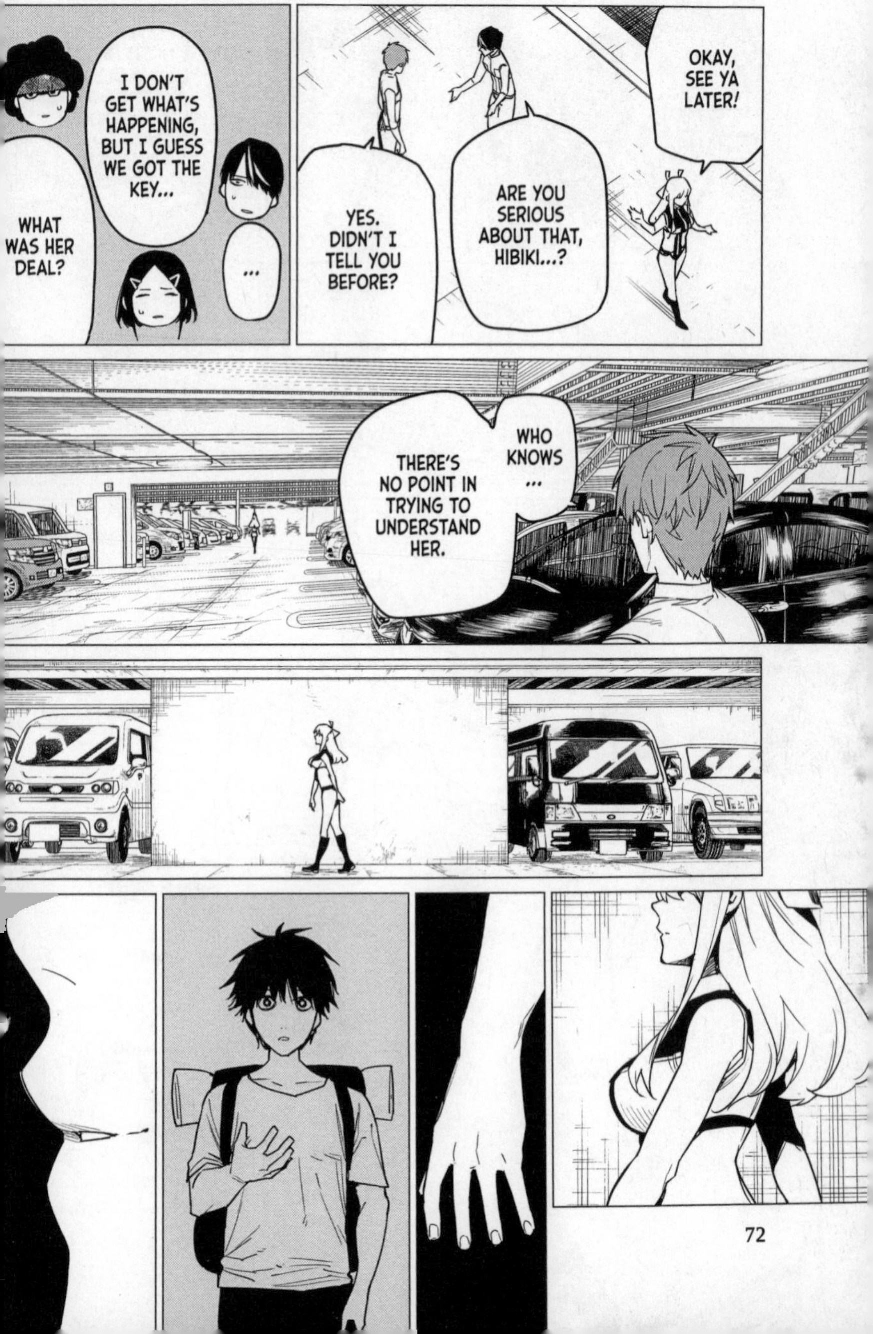
OKAY, SEE YA LATER!
ARE YOU SERIOUS ABOUT THAT, HIBIKI...?
YES. DIDN'T I TELL YOU BEFORE?
I DON'T GET WHAT'S HAPPENING, BUT I GUESS WE GOT THE KEY...
...
WHAT WAS HER DEAL?
WHO KNOWS...
THERE'S NO POINT IN TRYING TO UNDERSTAND HER.

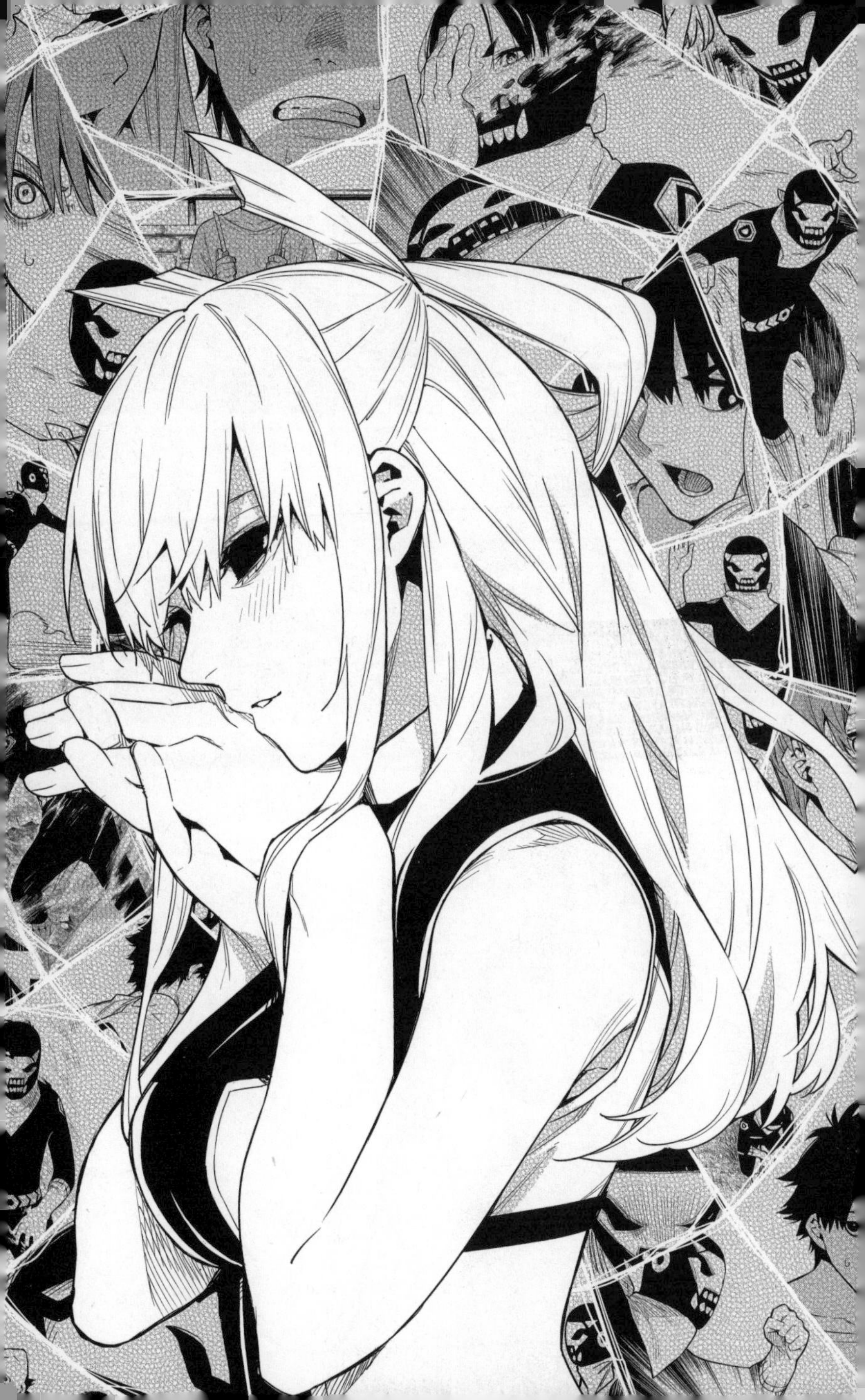

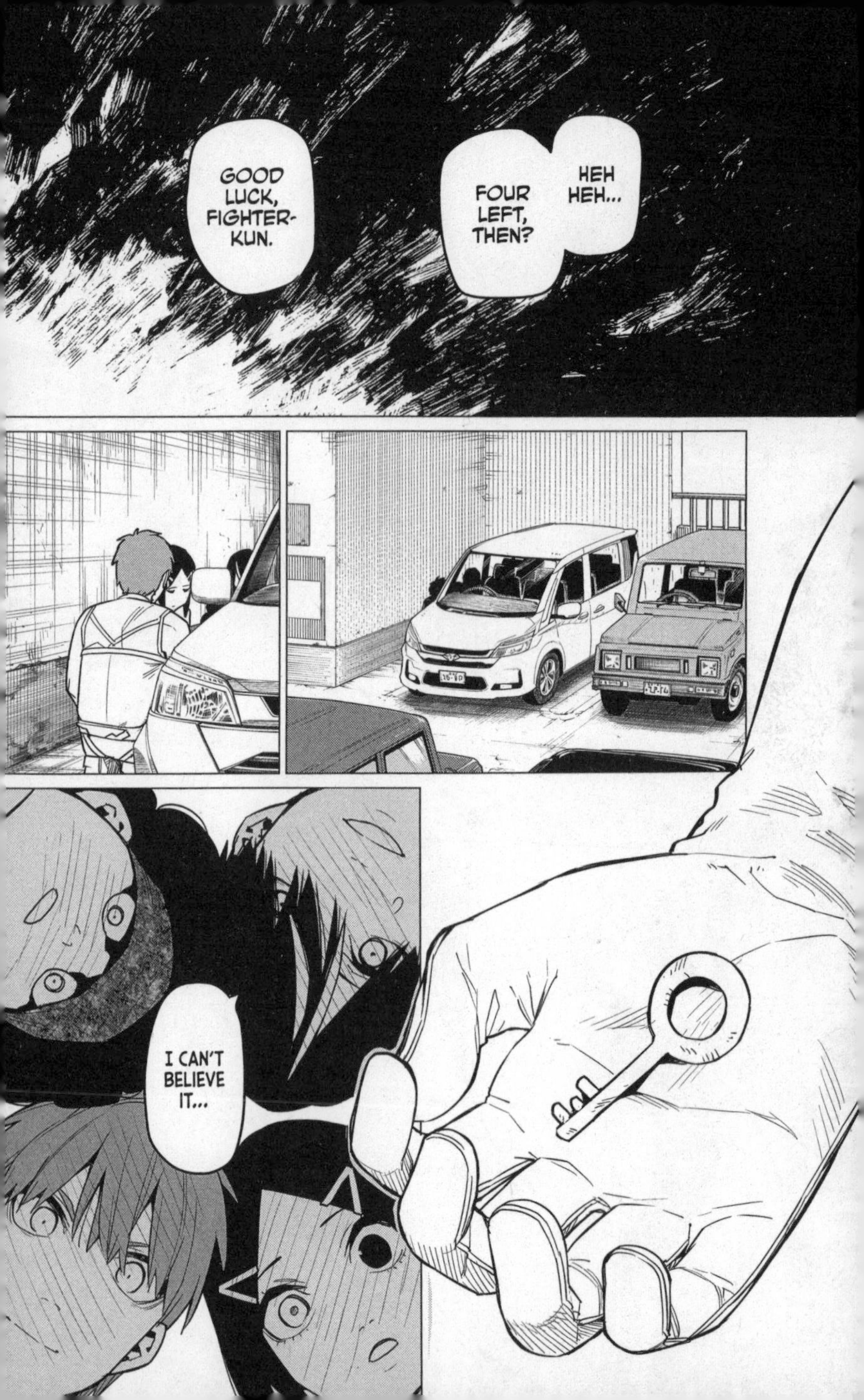
HEH HEH...
FOUR LEFT, THEN?
GOOD LUCK, FIGHTER-KUN.
I CAN'T BELIEVE IT...

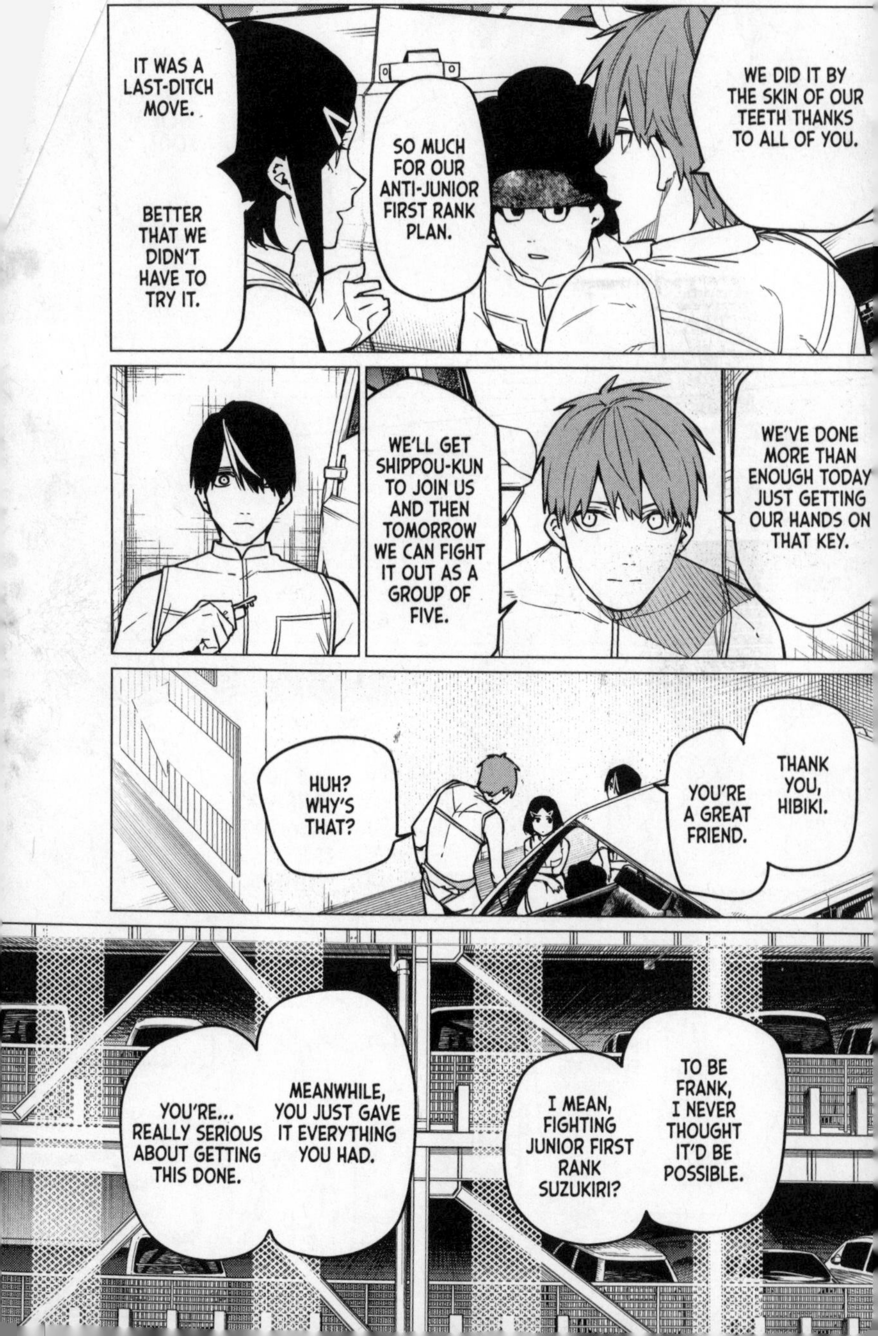
WE DID IT BY THE SKIN OF OUR TEETH THANKS TO ALL OF YOU.
SO MUCH FOR OUR ANTI-JUNIOR FIRST RANK PLAN.
IT WAS A LAST-DITCH MOVE.
BETTER THAT WE DIDN'T HAVE TO TRY IT.
WE'VE DONE MORE THAN ENOUGH TODAY JUST GETTING OUR HANDS ON THAT KEY.
WE'LL GET SHIPPOU-KUN TO JOIN US AND THEN TOMORROW WE CAN FIGHT IT OUT AS A GROUP OF FIVE.
THANK YOU, HIBIKI.
YOU'RE A GREAT FRIEND.
HUH? WHY'S THAT?
TO BE FRANK, I NEVER THOUGHT IT'D BE POSSIBLE.
I MEAN, FIGHTING JUNIOR FIRST RANK SUZUKIRI?
MEANWHILE, YOU JUST GAVE IT EVERYTHING YOU HAD.
YOU'RE... REALLY SERIOUS ABOUT GETTING THIS DONE.

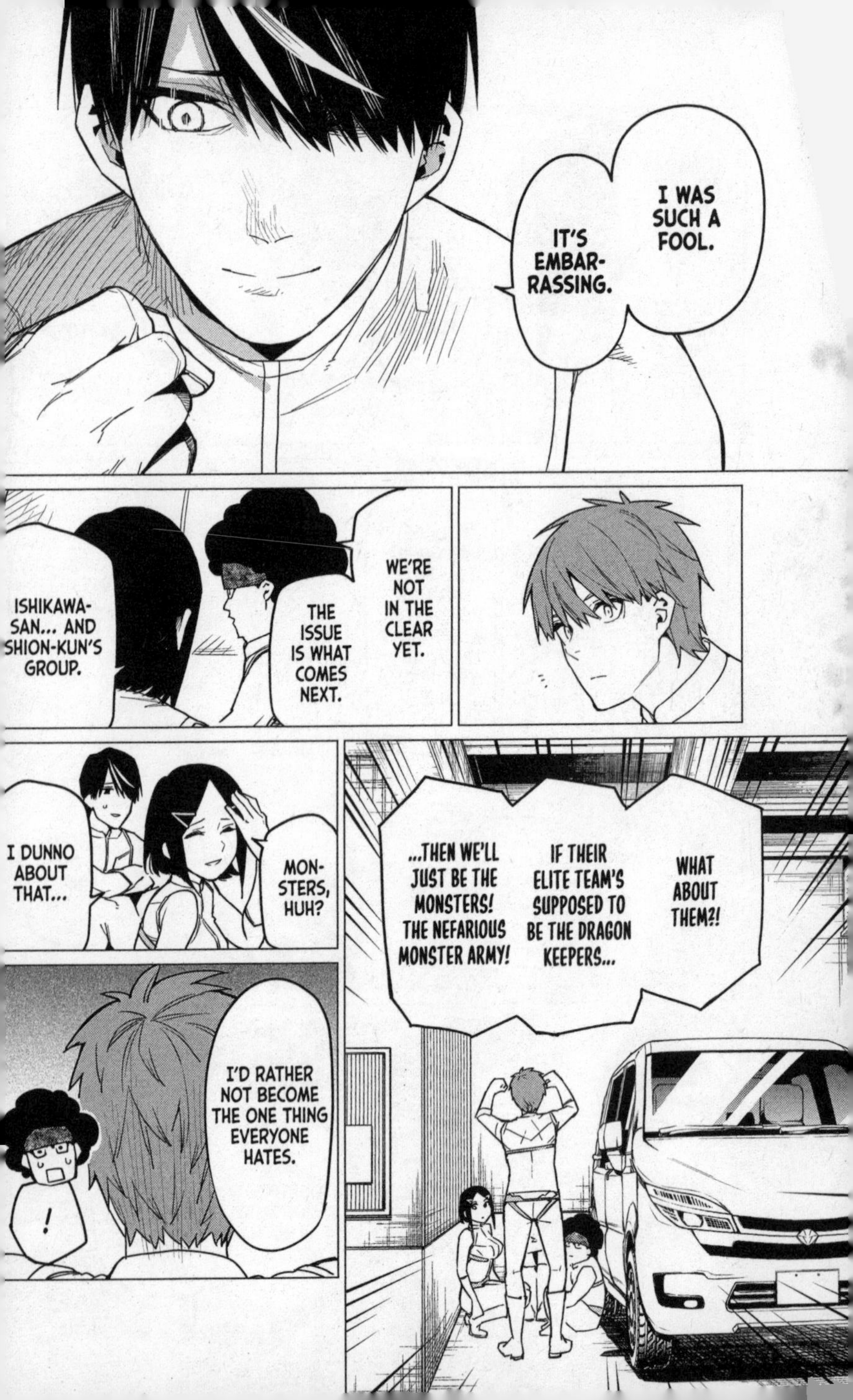
I WAS SUCH A FOOL.
IT'S EMBARRASSING.
WE'RE NOT IN THE CLEAR YET.
THE ISSUE IS WHAT COMES NEXT.
ISHIKAWA-SAN... AND SHION-KUN'S GROUP.
WHAT ABOUT THEM?!
IF THEIR ELITE TEAM'S SUPPOSED TO BE THE DRAGON KEEPERS...
...THEN WE'LL JUST BE THE MONSTERS! THE NEFARIOUS MONSTER ARMY!
MONSTERS, HUH?
I DUNNO ABOUT THAT...
I'D RATHER NOT BECOME THE ONE THING EVERYONE HATES.
!

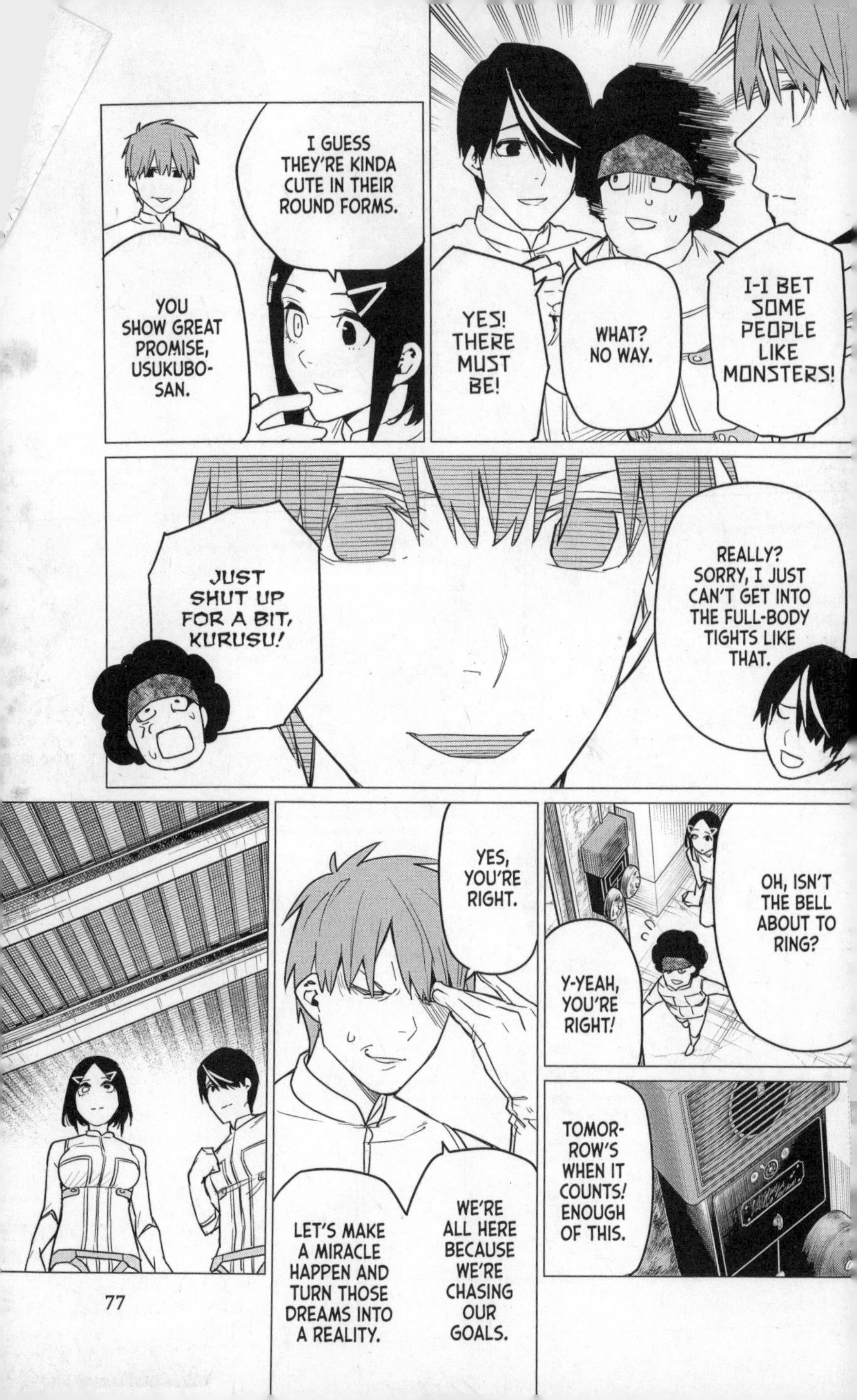
I-I BET SOME PEOPLE LIKE MONSTERS!
WHAT? NO WAY.
YES! THERE MUST BE!
I GUESS THEY'RE KINDA CUTE IN THEIR ROUND FORMS.
YOU SHOW GREAT PROMISE, USUKUBO-SAN.
REALLY? SORRY, I JUST CAN'T GET INTO THE FULL-BODY TIGHTS LIKE THAT.
JUST SHUT UP FOR A BIT, KURUSU!
OH, ISN'T THE BELL ABOUT TO RING?
Y-YEAH, YOU'RE RIGHT!
TOMOR-ROW'S WHEN IT COUNTS! ENOUGH OF THIS.
YES, YOU'RE RIGHT.
WE'RE ALL HERE BECAUSE WE'RE CHASING OUR GOALS.
LET'S MAKE A MIRACLE HAPPEN AND TURN THOSE DREAMS INTO A REALITY.

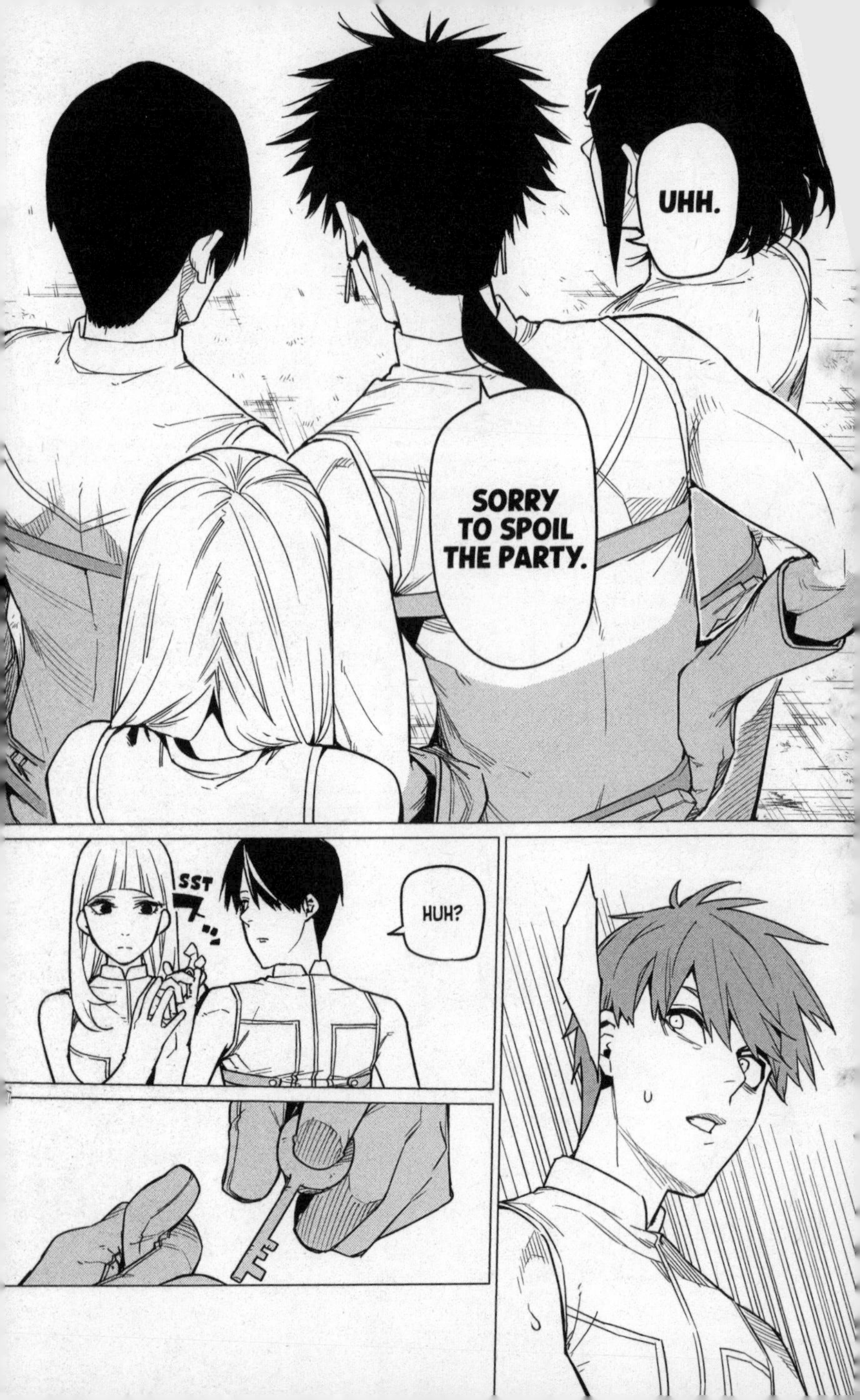
UHH.
SORRY TO SPOIL THE PARTY.
HUH?
SST

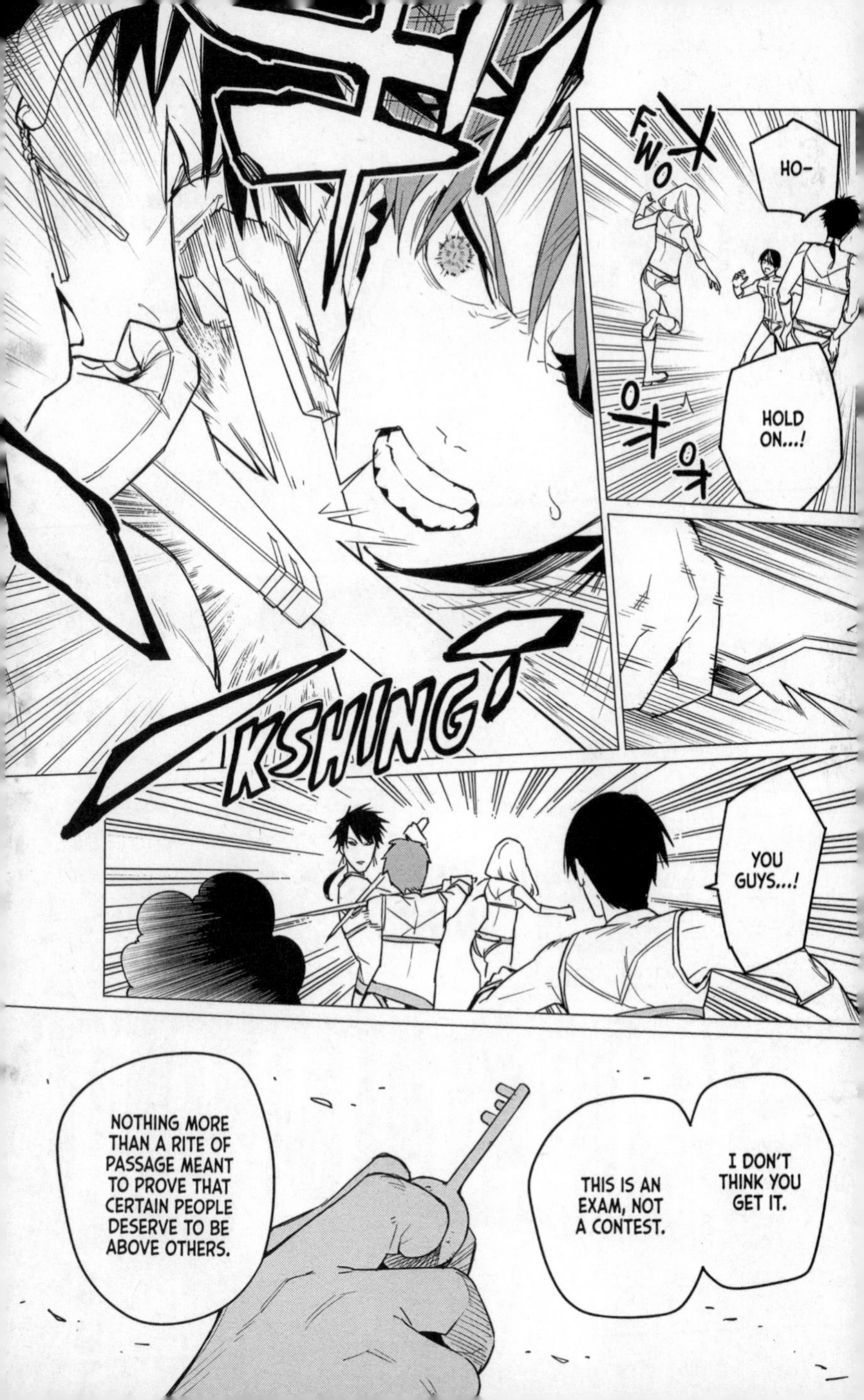
HO-
FWO
HOLD ON...!
KSHING
YOU GUYS...!
I DON'T THINK YOU GET IT.
THIS IS AN EXAM, NOT A CONTEST.
NOTHING MORE THAN A RITE OF PASSAGE MEANT TO PROVE THAT CERTAIN PEOPLE DESERVE TO BE ABOVE OTHERS.

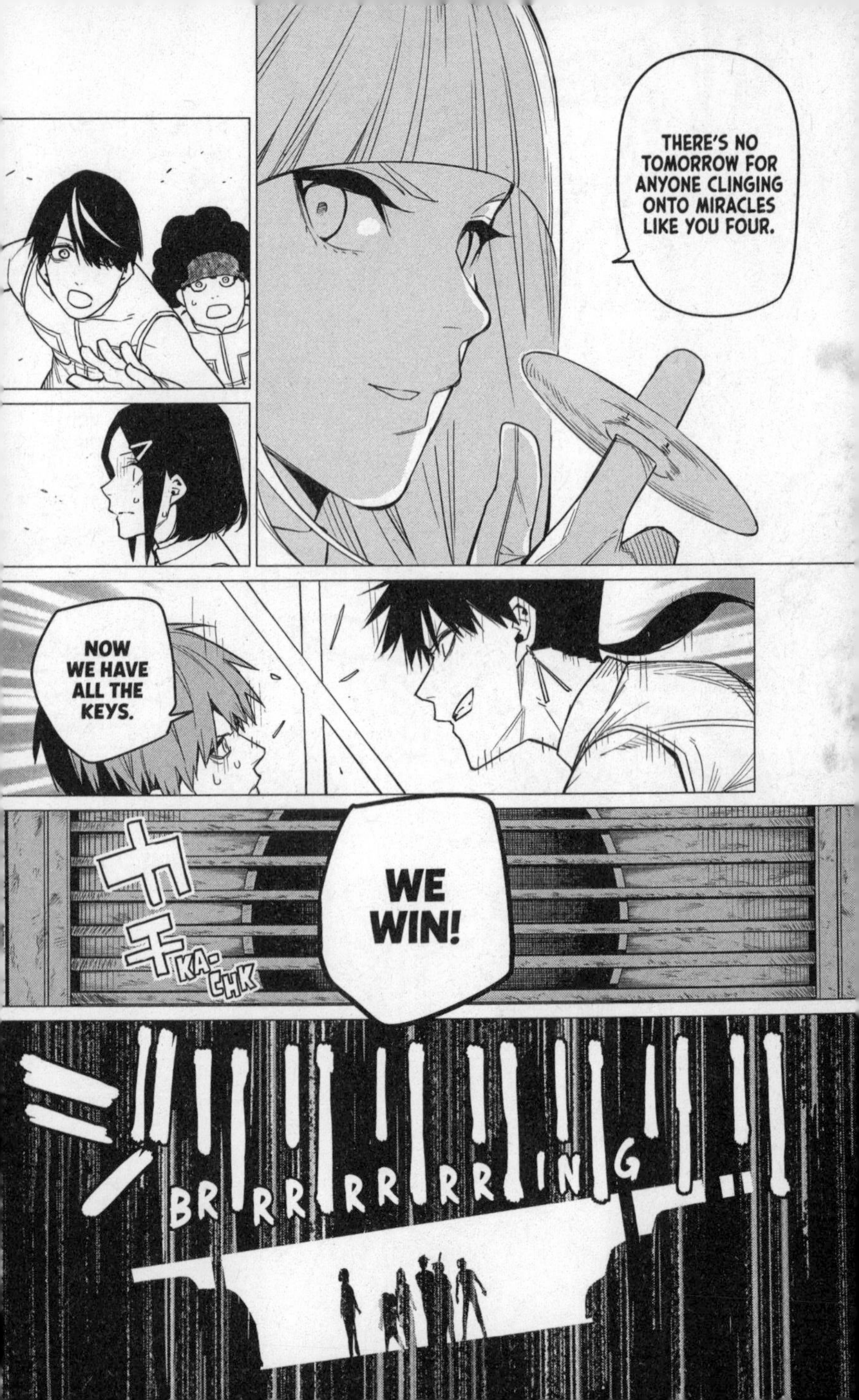
THERE'S NO TOMORROW FOR ANYONE CLINGING ONTO MIRACLES LIKE YOU FOUR.
NOW WE HAVE ALL THE KEYS.
WE WIN!
KA-CHK
BRRRRRRRING...

Chapter 28: **YAMATO KURUSU, AGE 12**

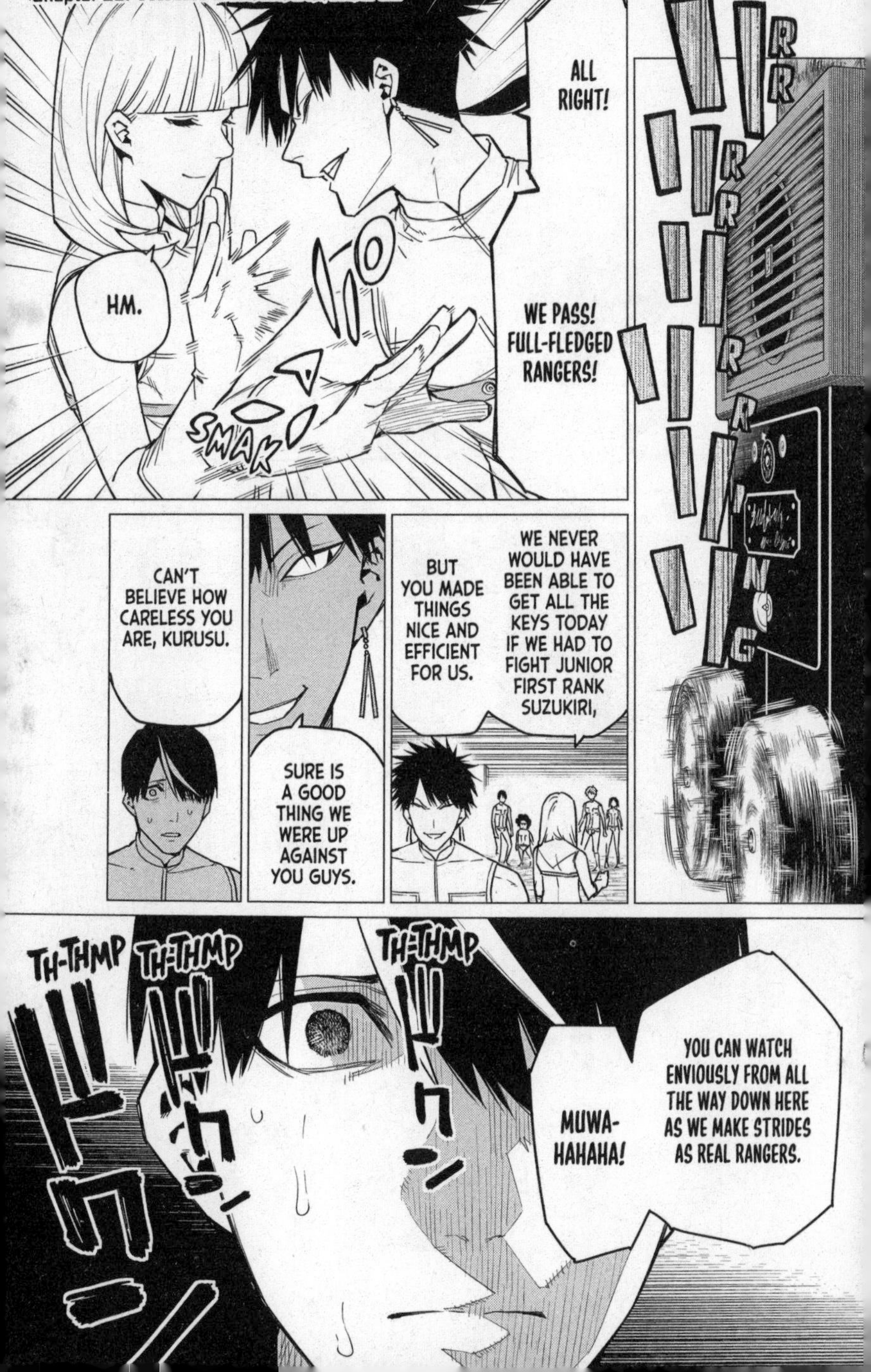
RRRIIIIIIIINNG
ALL RIGHT!
WE PASS! FULL-FLEDGED RANGERS!
SMAK
HM.
WE NEVER WOULD HAVE BEEN ABLE TO GET ALL THE KEYS TODAY IF WE HAD TO FIGHT JUNIOR FIRST RANK SUZUKIRI,
BUT YOU MADE THINGS NICE AND EFFICIENT FOR US.
SURE IS A GOOD THING WE WERE UP AGAINST YOU GUYS.
CAN'T BELIEVE HOW CARELESS YOU ARE, KURUSU.
YOU CAN WATCH ENVIOUSLY FROM ALL THE WAY DOWN HERE AS WE MAKE STRIDES AS REAL RANGERS.
MUWA-HAHAHA!
TH-THMP
TH-THMP
TH-THMP

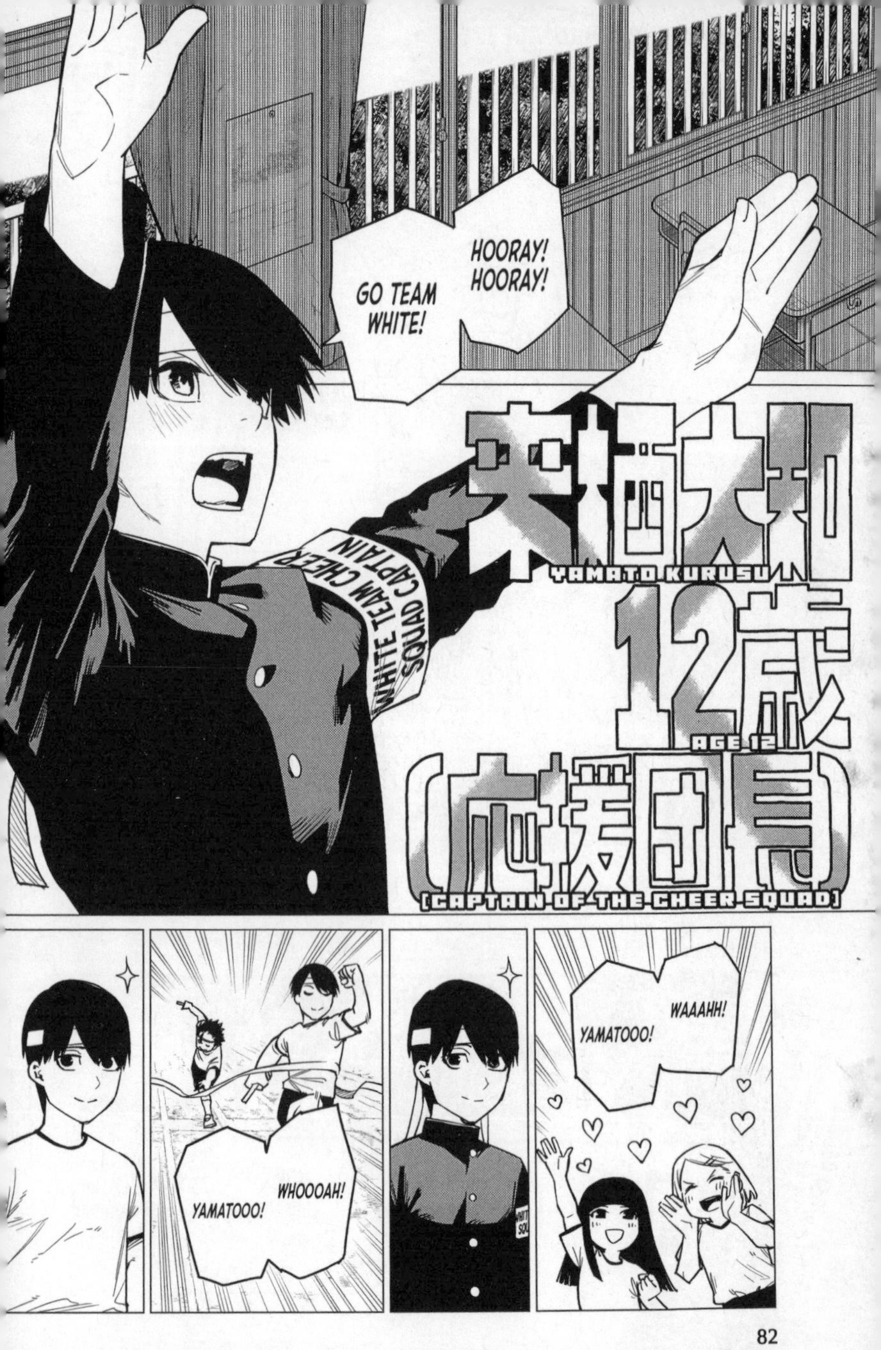
HOORAY! HOORAY!
GO TEAM WHITE!
WHITE TEAM CHEER SQUAD CAPTAIN
来栖大和
YAMATO KURUSU
12歳
AGE 12
(応援団長)
[CAPTAIN OF THE CHEER SQUAD]
WAAAHH!
YAMATOOO!
WHOOOAH!
YAMATOOO!

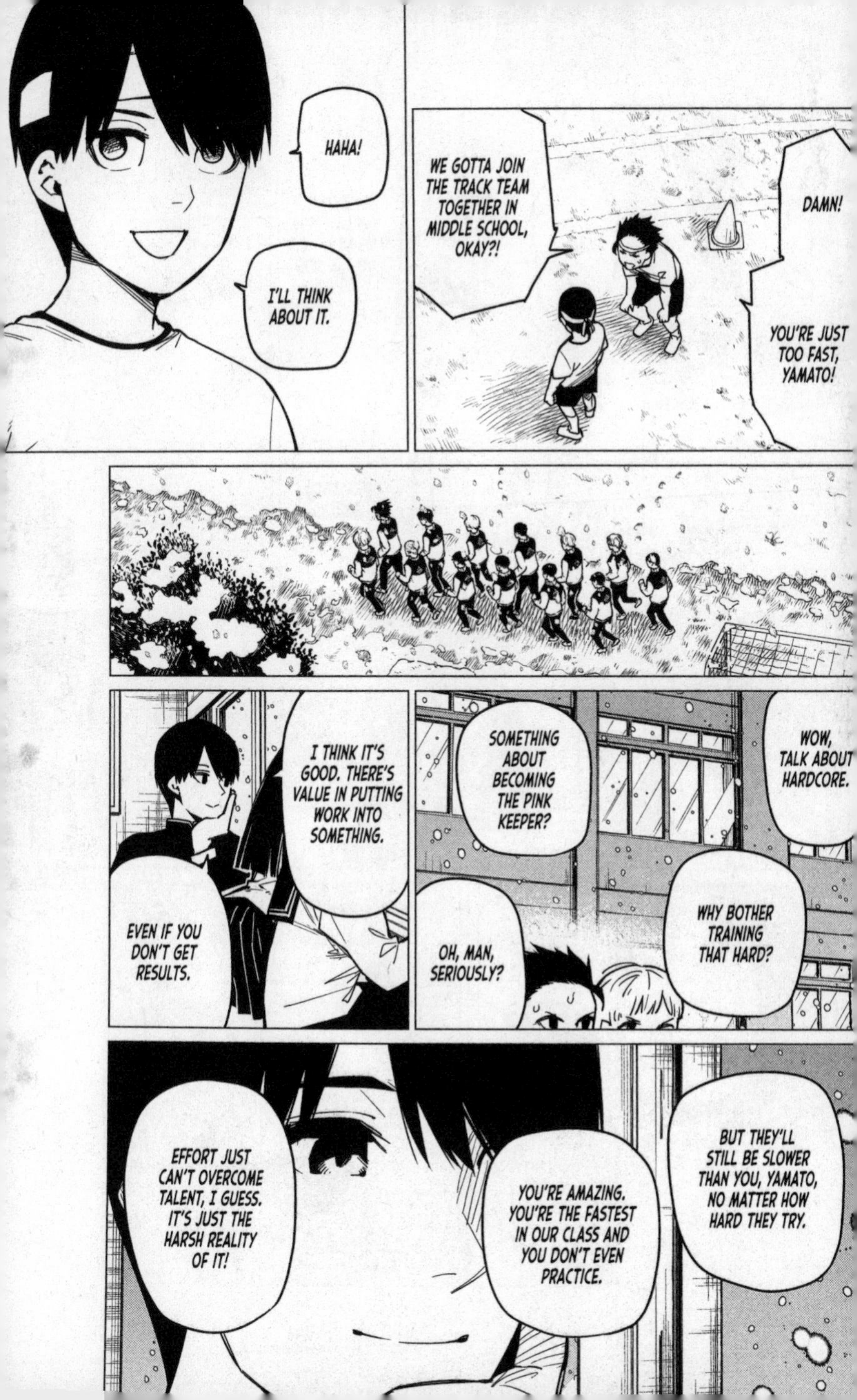
DAMN!
YOU'RE JUST TOO FAST, YAMATO!
WE GOTTA JOIN THE TRACK TEAM TOGETHER IN MIDDLE SCHOOL, OKAY?!
HAHA!
I'LL THINK ABOUT IT.
WOW, TALK ABOUT HARDCORE.
SOMETHING ABOUT BECOMING THE PINK KEEPER?
WHY BOTHER TRAINING THAT HARD?
OH, MAN, SERIOUSLY?
I THINK IT'S GOOD. THERE'S VALUE IN PUTTING WORK INTO SOMETHING.
EVEN IF YOU DON'T GET RESULTS.
BUT THEY'LL STILL BE SLOWER THAN YOU, YAMATO, NO MATTER HOW HARD THEY TRY.
YOU'RE AMAZING. YOU'RE THE FASTEST IN OUR CLASS AND YOU DON'T EVEN PRACTICE.
EFFORT JUST CAN'T OVERCOME TALENT, I GUESS. IT'S JUST THE HARSH REALITY OF IT!

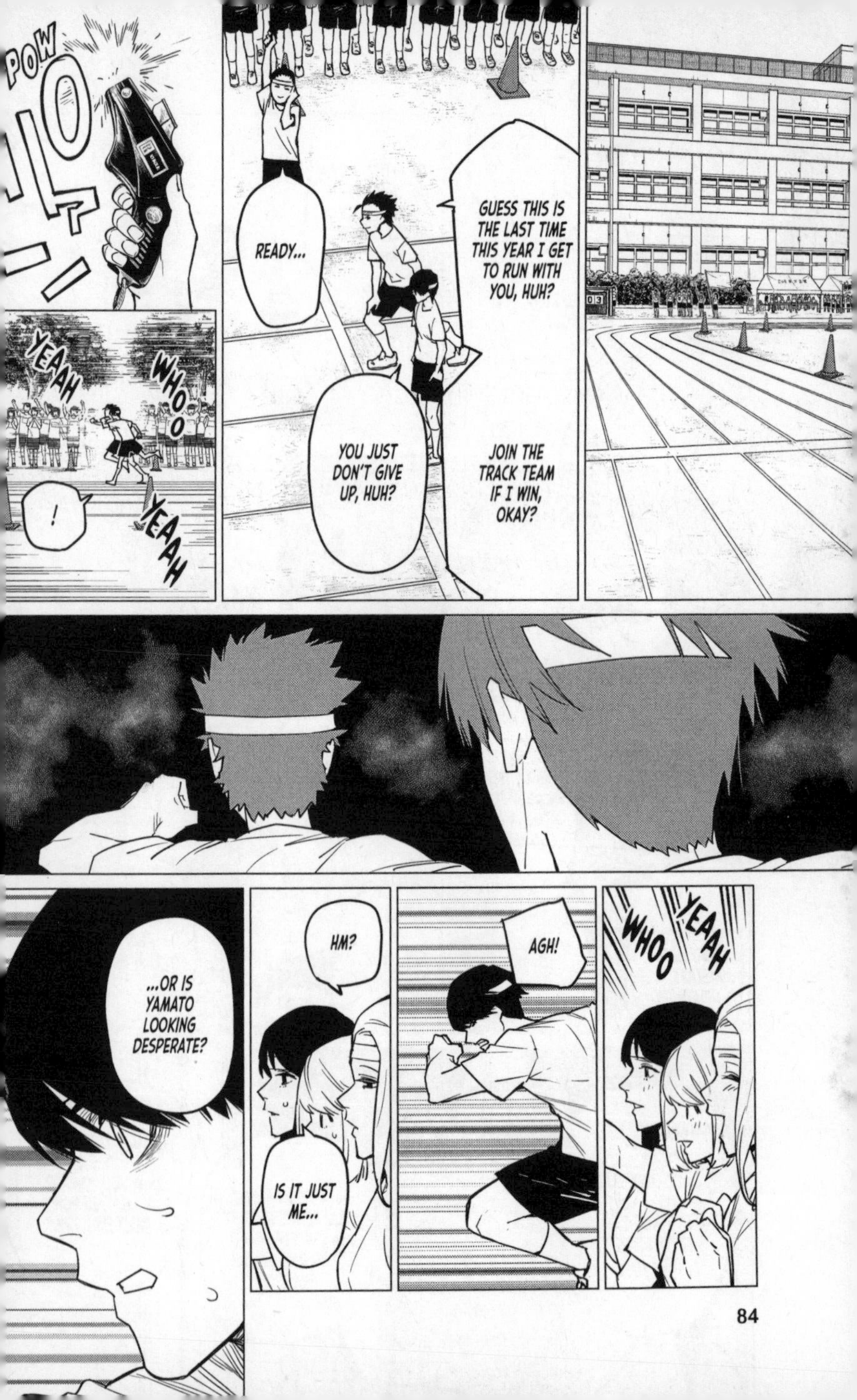
GUESS THIS IS THE LAST TIME THIS YEAR I GET TO RUN WITH YOU, HUH?
JOIN THE TRACK TEAM IF I WIN, OKAY?
YOU JUST DON'T GIVE UP, HUH?
READY...
POW
YEAAH
WHOO
YEAAH
!
WHOO
YEAAH
AGH!
HM?
IS IT JUST ME...
...OR IS YAMATO LOOKING DESPERATE?

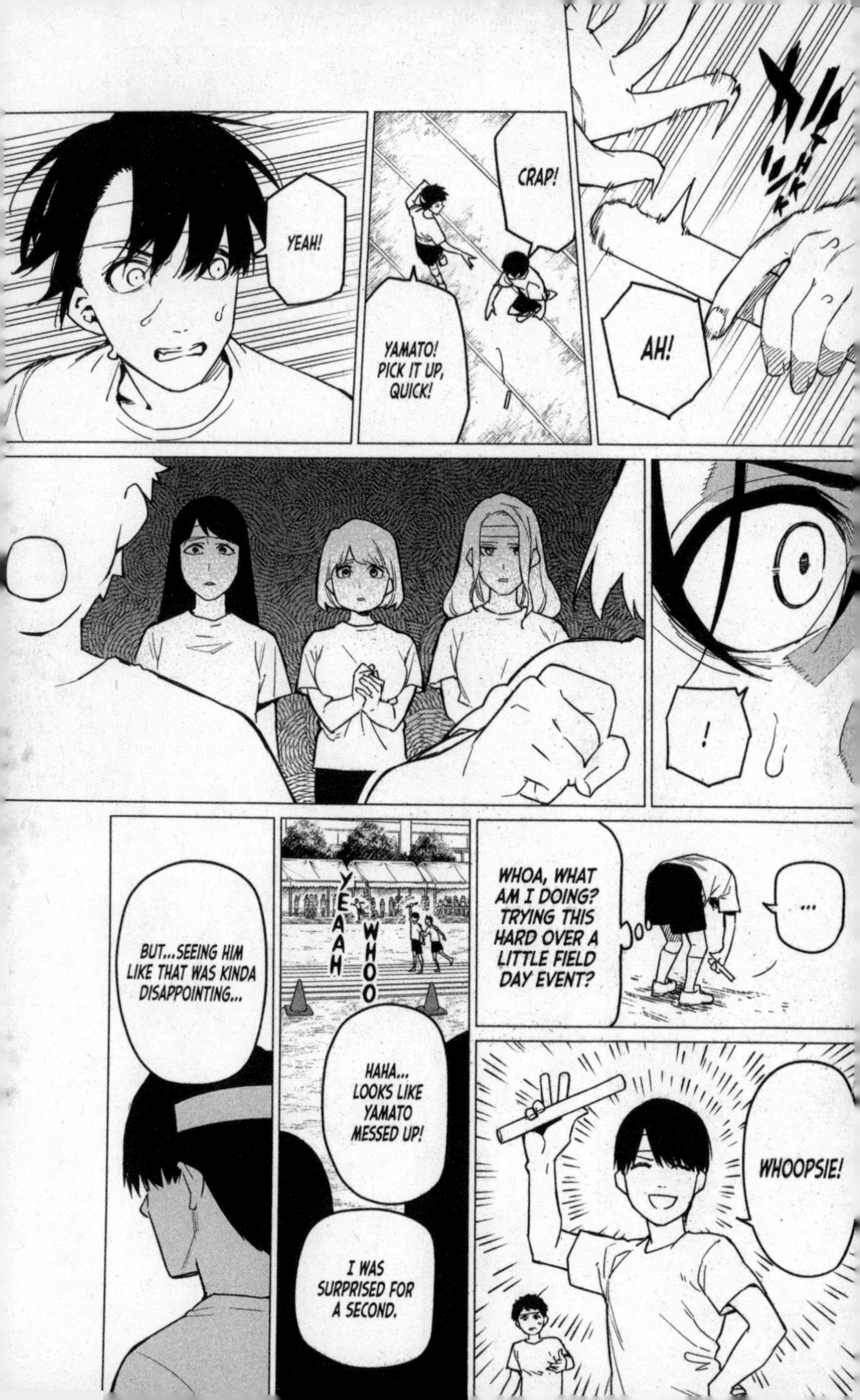
THKK
AH!
CRAP!
YAMATO! PICK IT UP, QUICK!
YEAH!
!
...
WHOA, WHAT AM I DOING? TRYING THIS HARD OVER A LITTLE FIELD DAY EVENT?
WHOOPSIE!
YEAAH
WHOO
HAHA... LOOKS LIKE YAMATO MESSED UP!
I WAS SURPRISED FOR A SECOND.
BUT...SEEING HIM LIKE THAT WAS KINDA DISAPPOINTING...

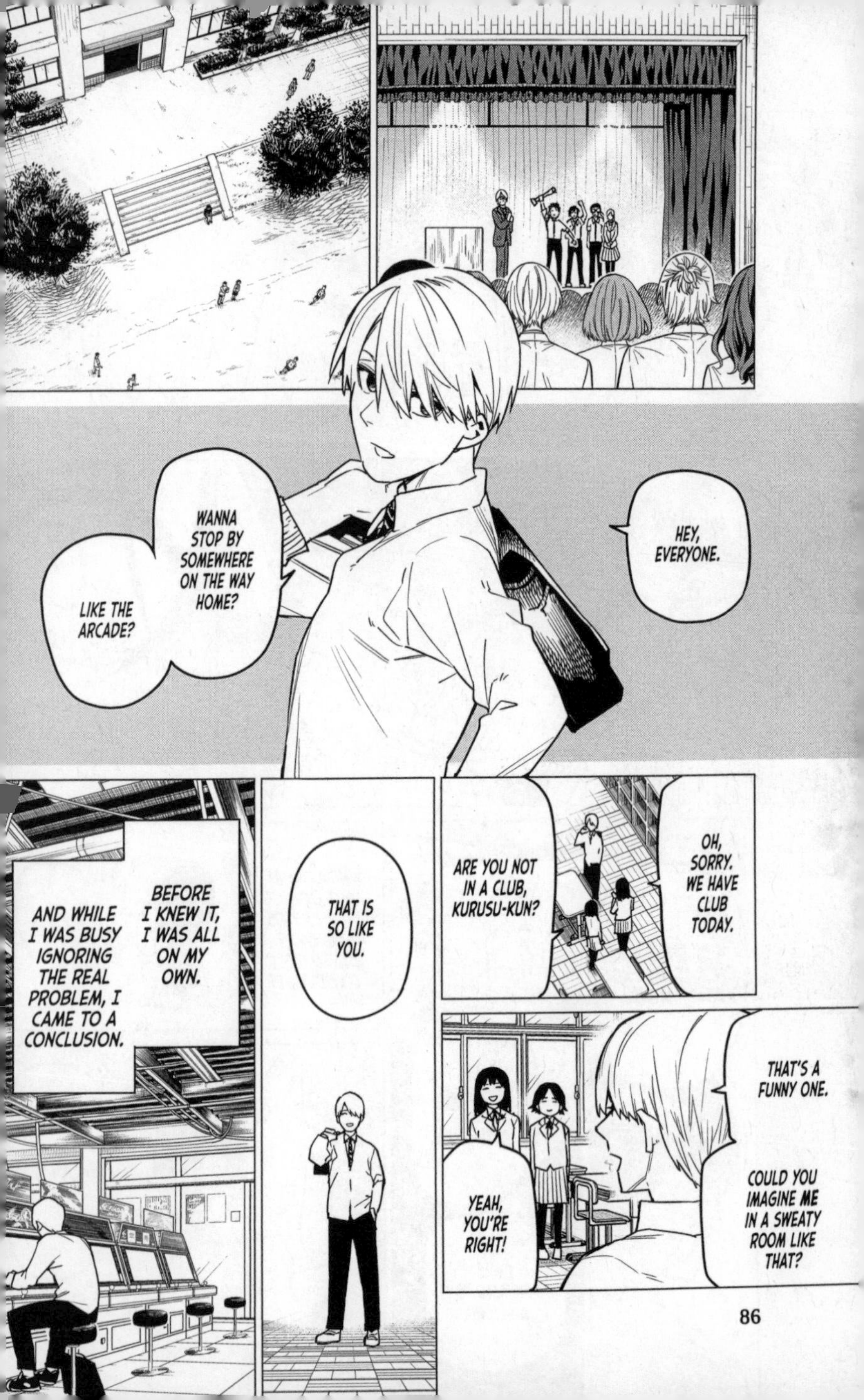

HEY, EVERYONE.
WANNA STOP BY SOMEWHERE ON THE WAY HOME?
LIKE THE ARCADE?
OH, SORRY. WE HAVE CLUB TODAY.
ARE YOU NOT IN A CLUB, KURUSU-KUN?
THAT'S A FUNNY ONE.
COULD YOU IMAGINE ME IN A SWEATY ROOM LIKE THAT?
YEAH, YOU'RE RIGHT!
THAT IS SO LIKE YOU.
BEFORE I KNEW IT, I WAS ALL ON MY OWN.
AND WHILE I WAS BUSY IGNORING THE REAL PROBLEM, I CAME TO A CONCLUSION.

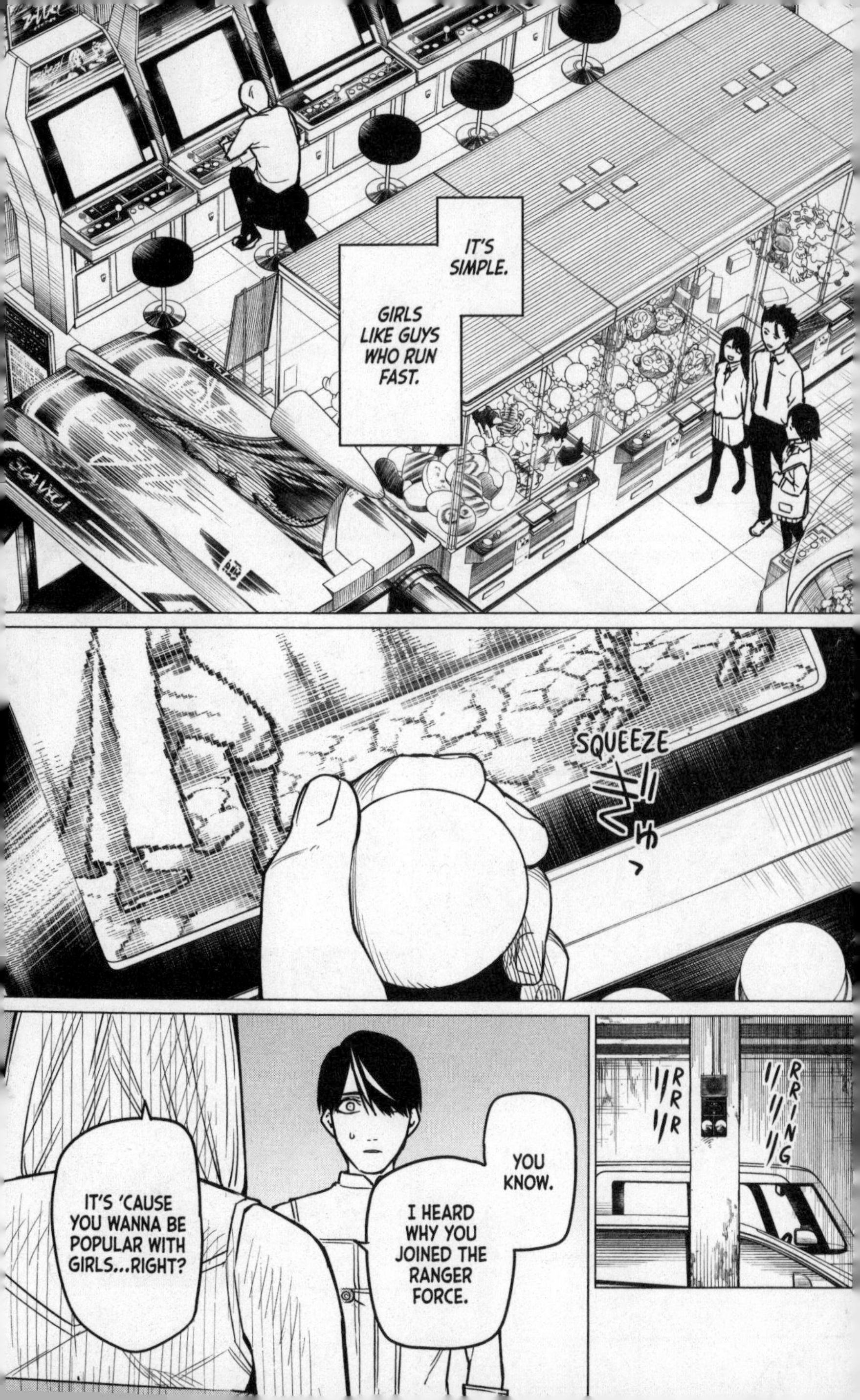
IT'S SIMPLE.
GIRLS LIKE GUYS WHO RUN FAST.
SQUEEZE
RRING
RRR
YOU KNOW.
I HEARD WHY YOU JOINED THE RANGER FORCE.
IT'S 'CAUSE YOU WANNA BE POPULAR WITH GIRLS...RIGHT?

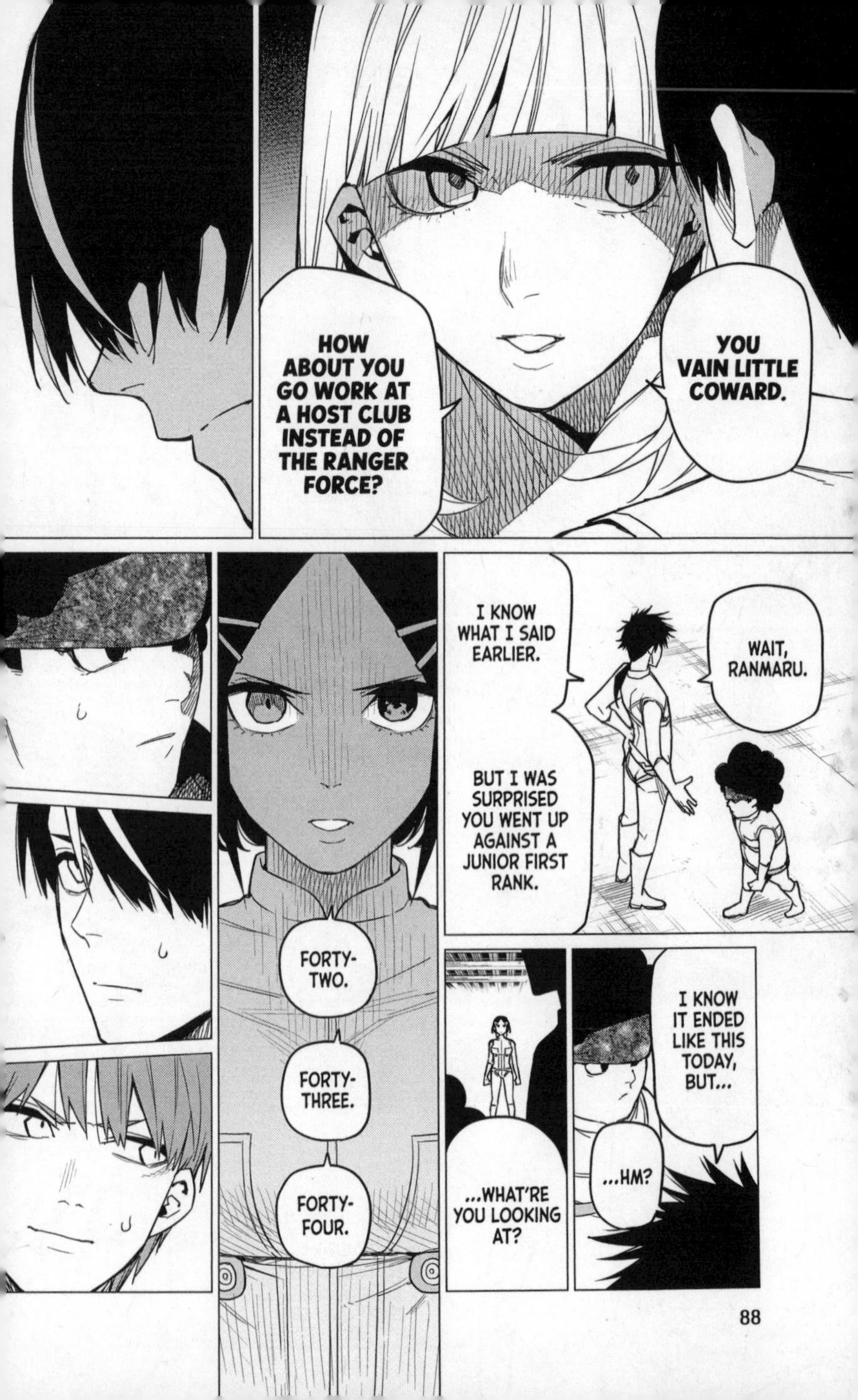
YOU VAIN LITTLE COWARD.
HOW ABOUT YOU GO WORK AT A HOST CLUB INSTEAD OF THE RANGER FORCE?
WAIT, RANMARU.
I KNOW WHAT I SAID EARLIER.
BUT I WAS SURPRISED YOU WENT UP AGAINST A JUNIOR FIRST RANK.
I KNOW IT ENDED LIKE THIS TODAY, BUT...
...HM?
...WHAT'RE YOU LOOKING AT?
FORTY-TWO.
FORTY-THREE.
FORTY-FOUR.

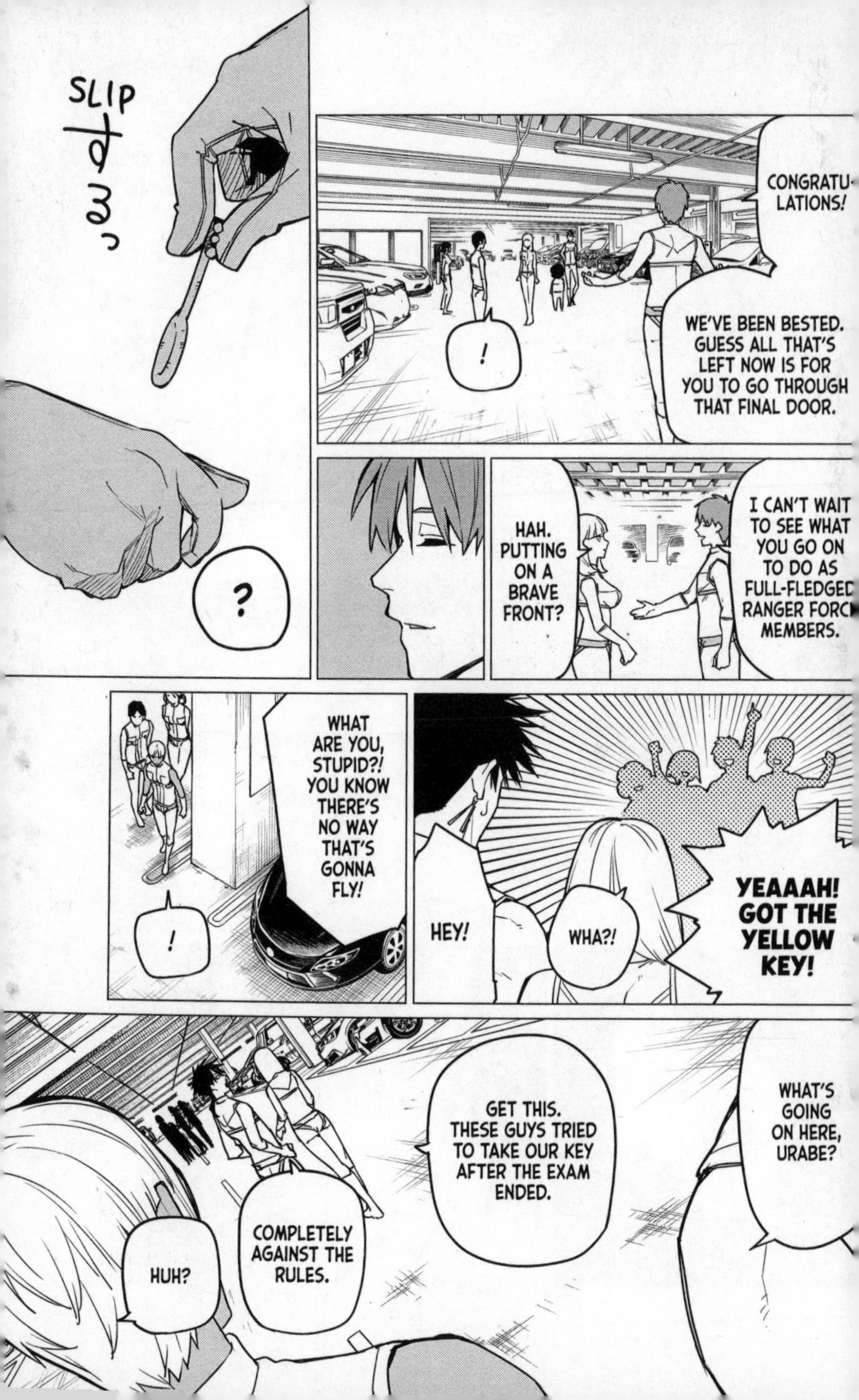
CONGRATULATIONS!
WE'VE BEEN BESTED. GUESS ALL THAT'S LEFT NOW IS FOR YOU TO GO THROUGH THAT FINAL DOOR.
!
I CAN'T WAIT TO SEE WHAT YOU GO ON TO DO AS FULL-FLEDGED RANGER FORCE MEMBERS.
HAH. PUTTING ON A BRAVE FRONT?
SLIP
すっ
?
YEAAAH! GOT THE YELLOW KEY!
WHA?!
HEY!
WHAT ARE YOU, STUPID?! YOU KNOW THERE'S NO WAY THAT'S GONNA FLY!
!
WHAT'S GOING ON HERE, URABE?
GET THIS. THESE GUYS TRIED TO TAKE OUR KEY AFTER THE EXAM ENDED.
COMPLETELY AGAINST THE RULES.
HUH?

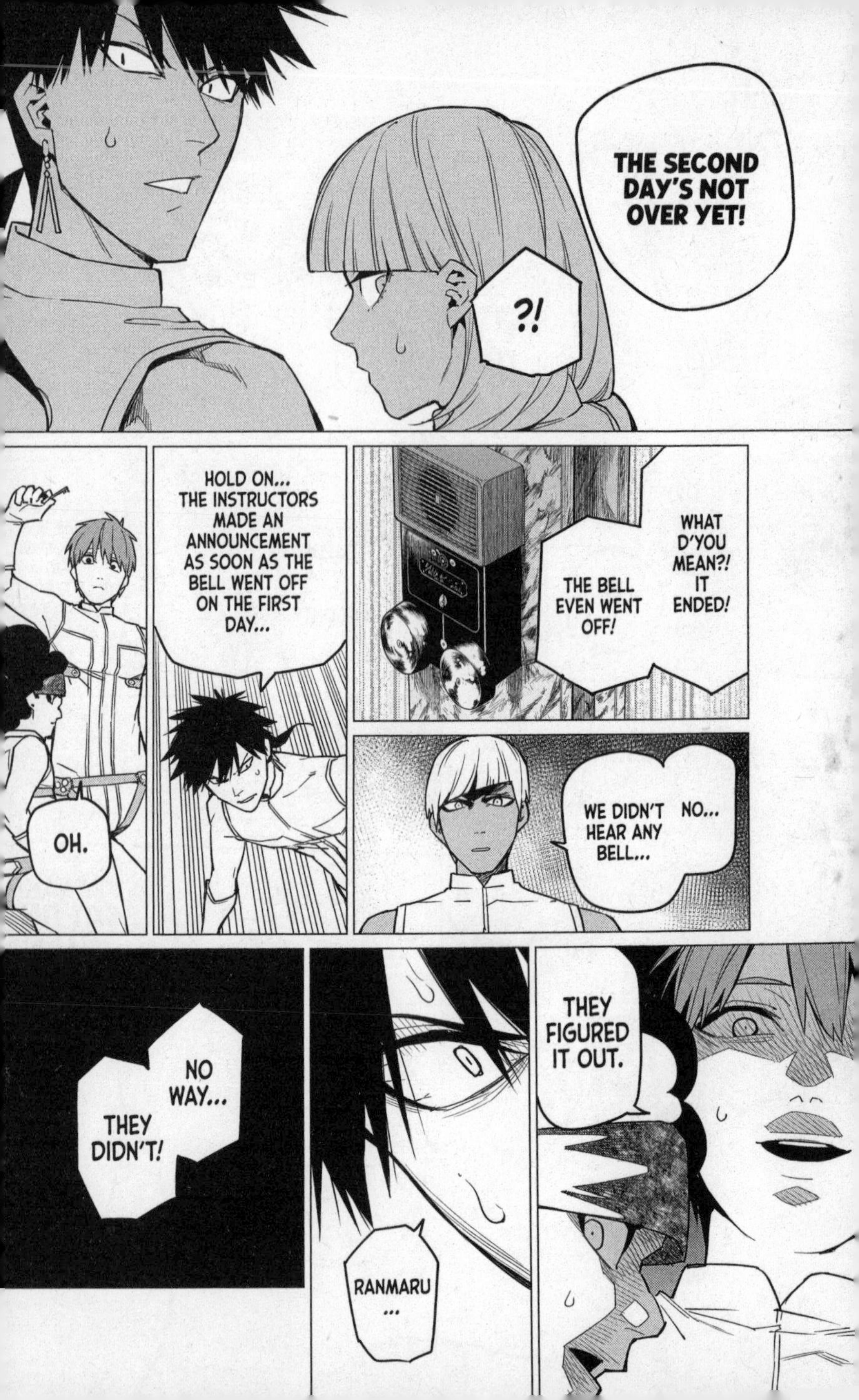
THE SECOND DAY'S NOT OVER YET!
?!
WHAT D'YOU MEAN?! IT ENDED!
THE BELL EVEN WENT OFF!
NO...
WE DIDN'T HEAR ANY BELL...
HOLD ON... THE INSTRUCTORS MADE AN ANNOUNCEMENT AS SOON AS THE BELL WENT OFF ON THE FIRST DAY...
OH.
THEY FIGURED IT OUT.
RANMARU ...
NO WAY...
THEY DIDN'T!

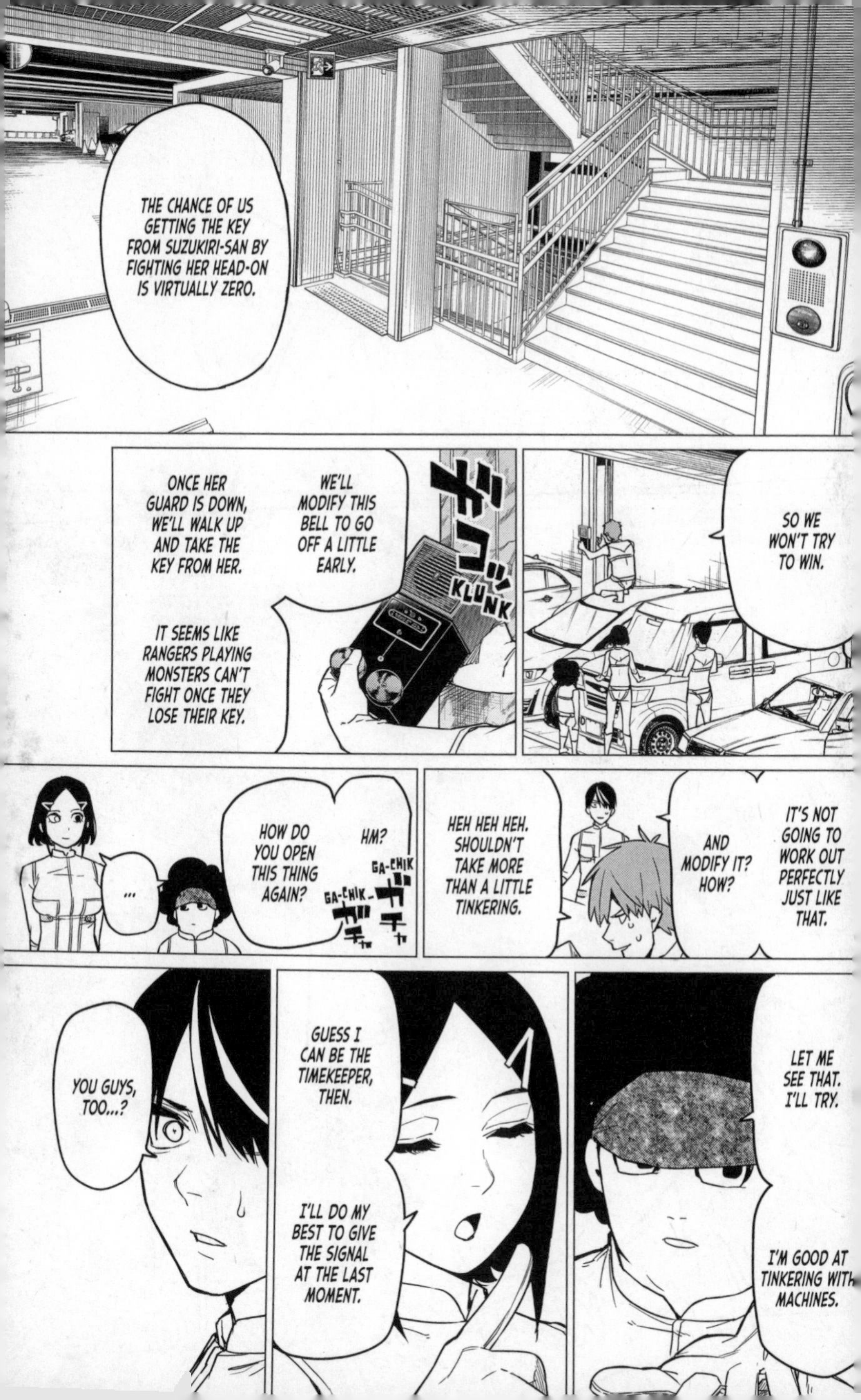

THE CHANCE OF US GETTING THE KEY FROM SUZUKIRI-SAN BY FIGHTING HER HEAD-ON IS VIRTUALLY ZERO.
SO WE WON'T TRY TO WIN.
KLUNK
WE'LL MODIFY THIS BELL TO GO OFF A LITTLE EARLY.
ONCE HER GUARD IS DOWN, WE'LL WALK UP AND TAKE THE KEY FROM HER.
IT SEEMS LIKE RANGERS PLAYING MONSTERS CAN'T FIGHT ONCE THEY LOSE THEIR KEY.
IT'S NOT GOING TO WORK OUT PERFECTLY JUST LIKE THAT.
AND MODIFY IT? HOW?
HEH HEH HEH. SHOULDN'T TAKE MORE THAN A LITTLE TINKERING.
HM?
GA-CHIK
GA-CHIK
HOW DO YOU OPEN THIS THING AGAIN?
...
LET ME SEE THAT. I'LL TRY.
I'M GOOD AT TINKERING WITH MACHINES.
GUESS I CAN BE THE TIMEKEEPER, THEN.
I'LL DO MY BEST TO GIVE THE SIGNAL AT THE LAST MOMENT.
YOU GUYS, TOO...?

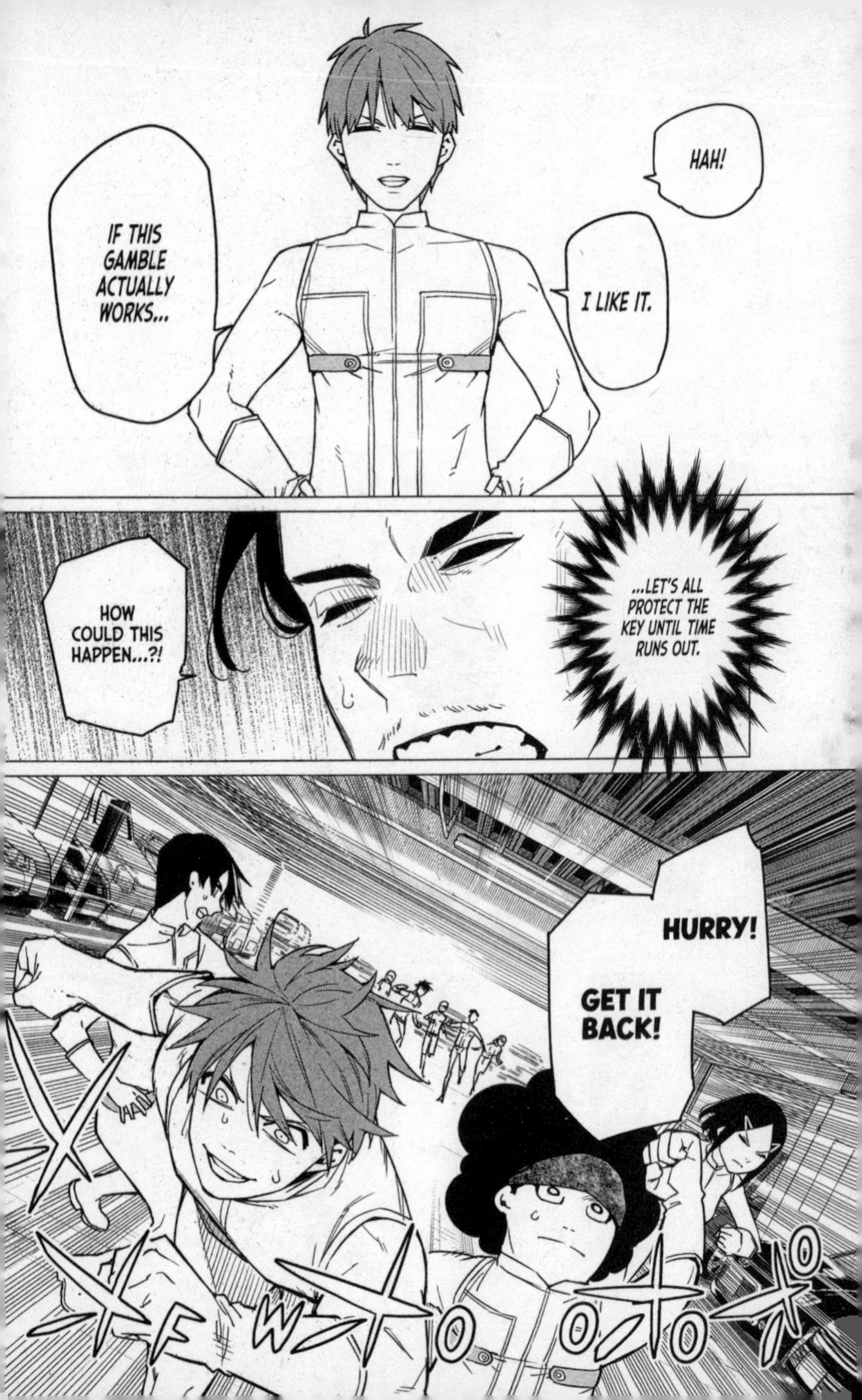
HAH!
I LIKE IT.
IF THIS GAMBLE ACTUALLY WORKS...
...LET'S ALL PROTECT THE KEY UNTIL TIME RUNS OUT.
HOW COULD THIS HAPPEN...?!
HURRY!
GET IT BACK!
FWOOO

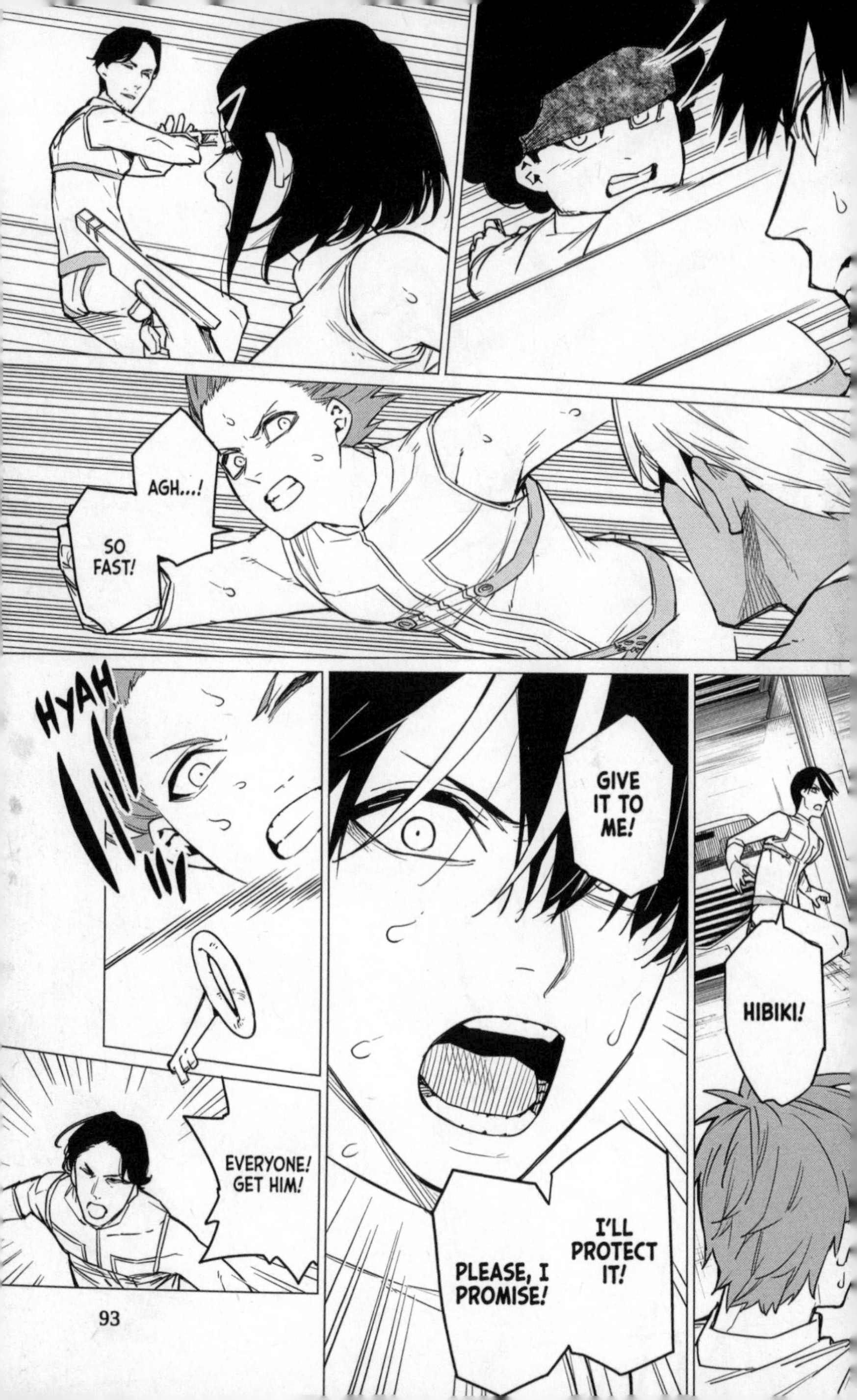
AGH...!
SO FAST!
HIBIKI!
GIVE IT TO ME!
I'LL PROTECT IT!
PLEASE, I PROMISE!
HYAH
EVERYONE! GET HIM!

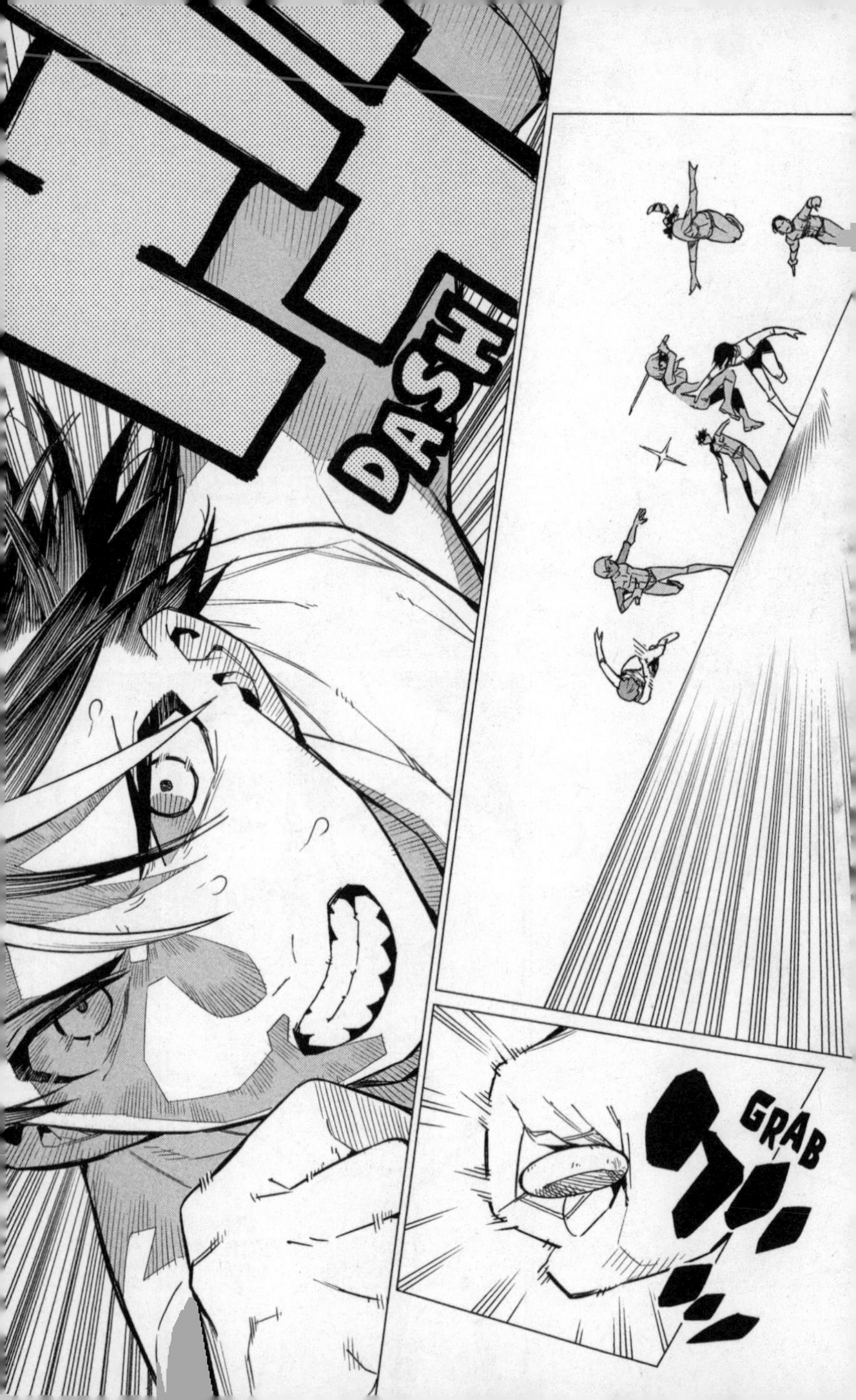
DASH
GRAB

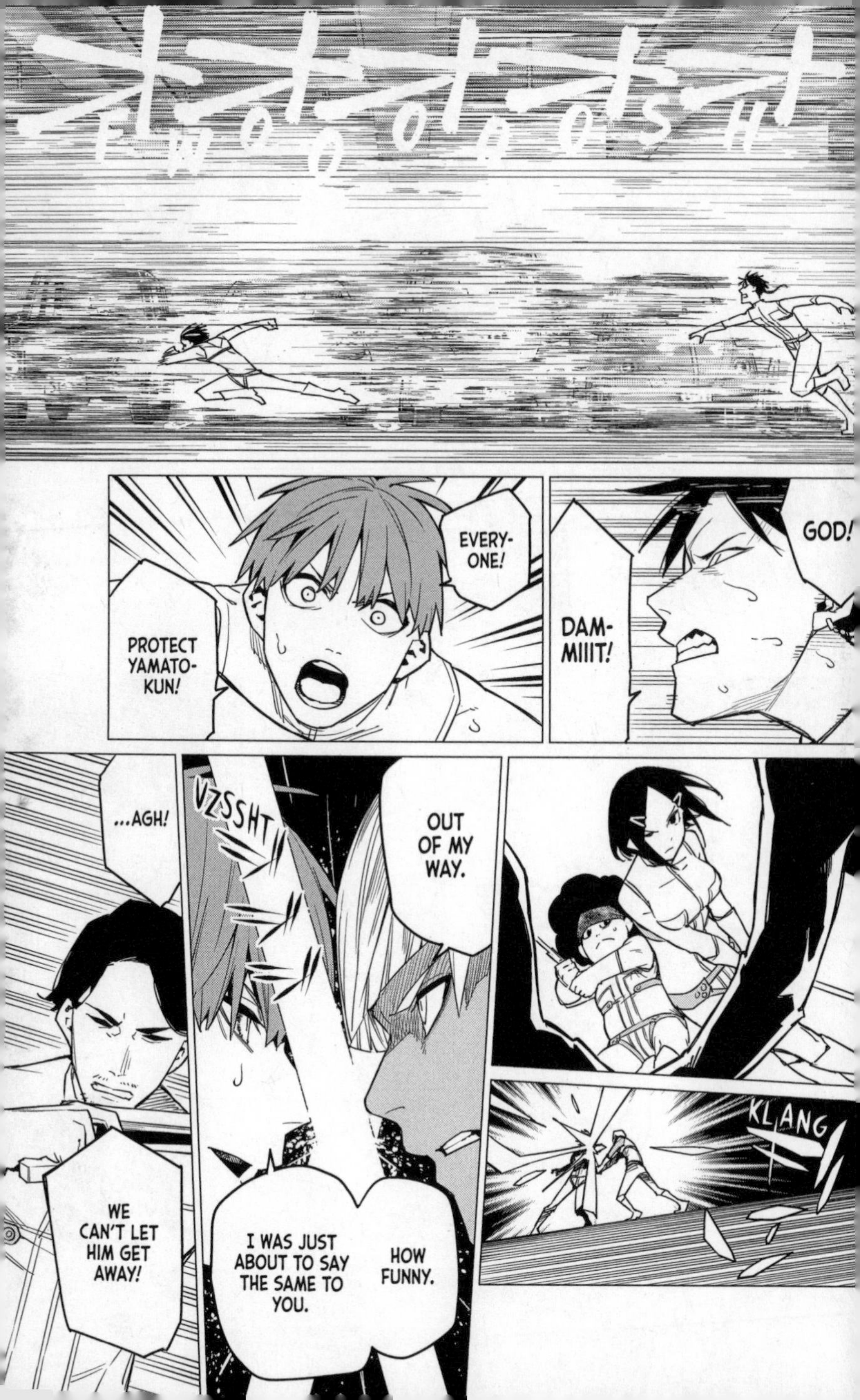
FWOOOOOSH
GOD!
DAM-MIIIT!
EVERY-ONE!
PROTECT YAMATO-KUN!
KLANG
VZSSHT
OUT OF MY WAY.
HOW FUNNY.
I WAS JUST ABOUT TO SAY THE SAME TO YOU.
...AGH!
WE CAN'T LET HIM GET AWAY!

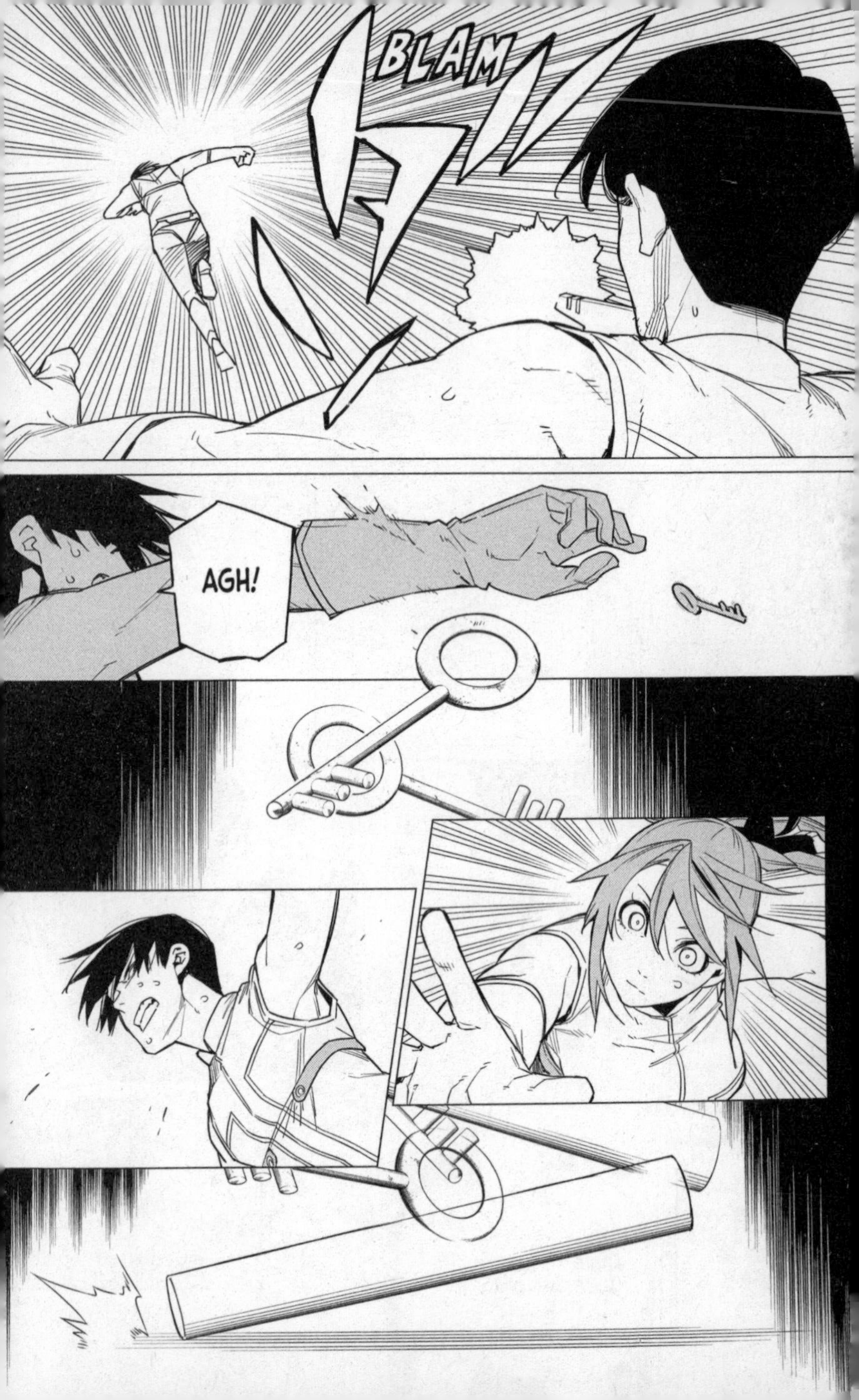
BLAM
AGH!

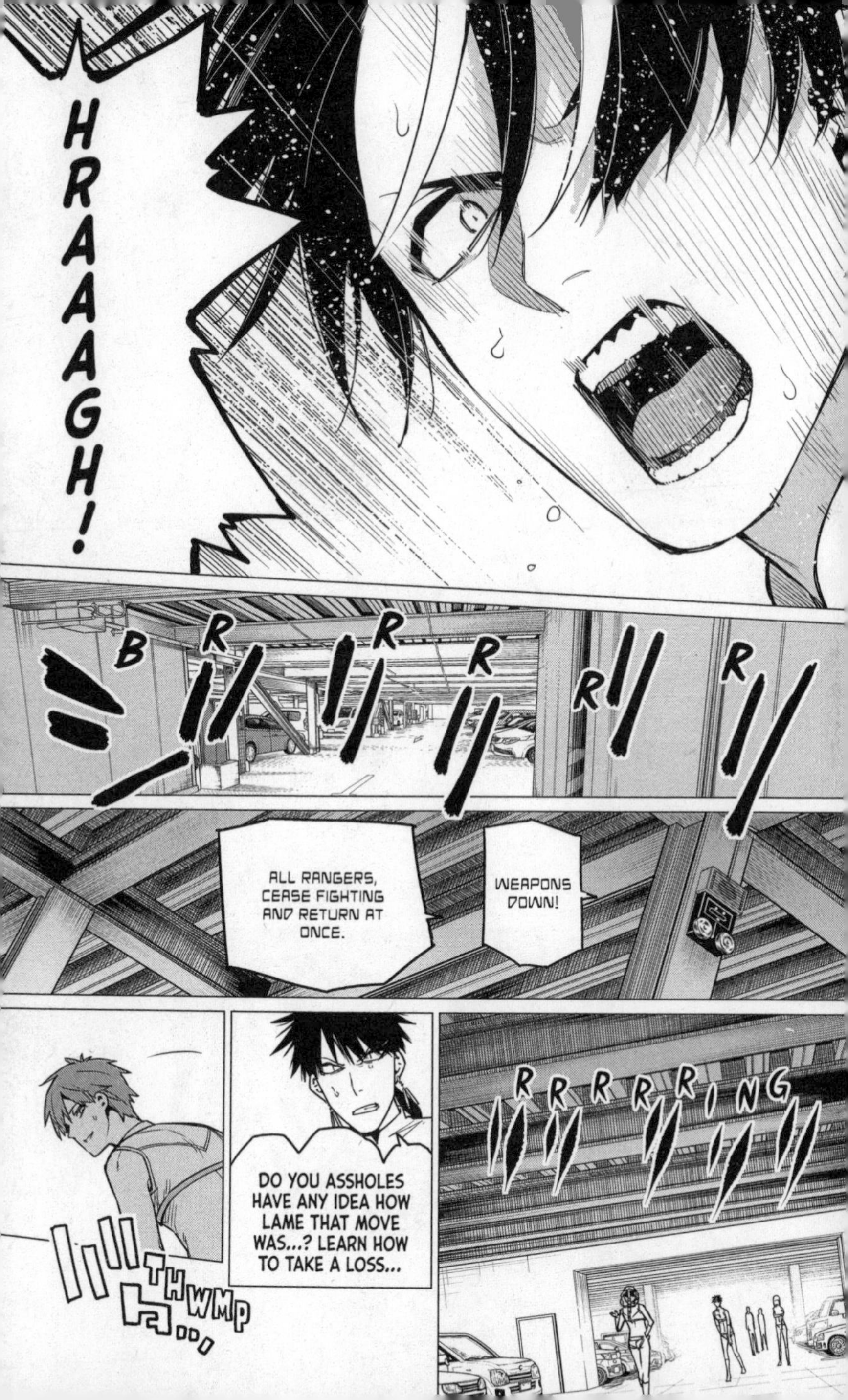
HRAAAGH!
BRRRRR
WEAPONS DOWN!
ALL RANGERS, CEASE FIGHTING AND RETURN AT ONCE.
RRRRRING
DO YOU ASSHOLES HAVE ANY IDEA HOW LAME THAT MOVE WAS...? LEARN HOW TO TAKE A LOSS...
THWMP

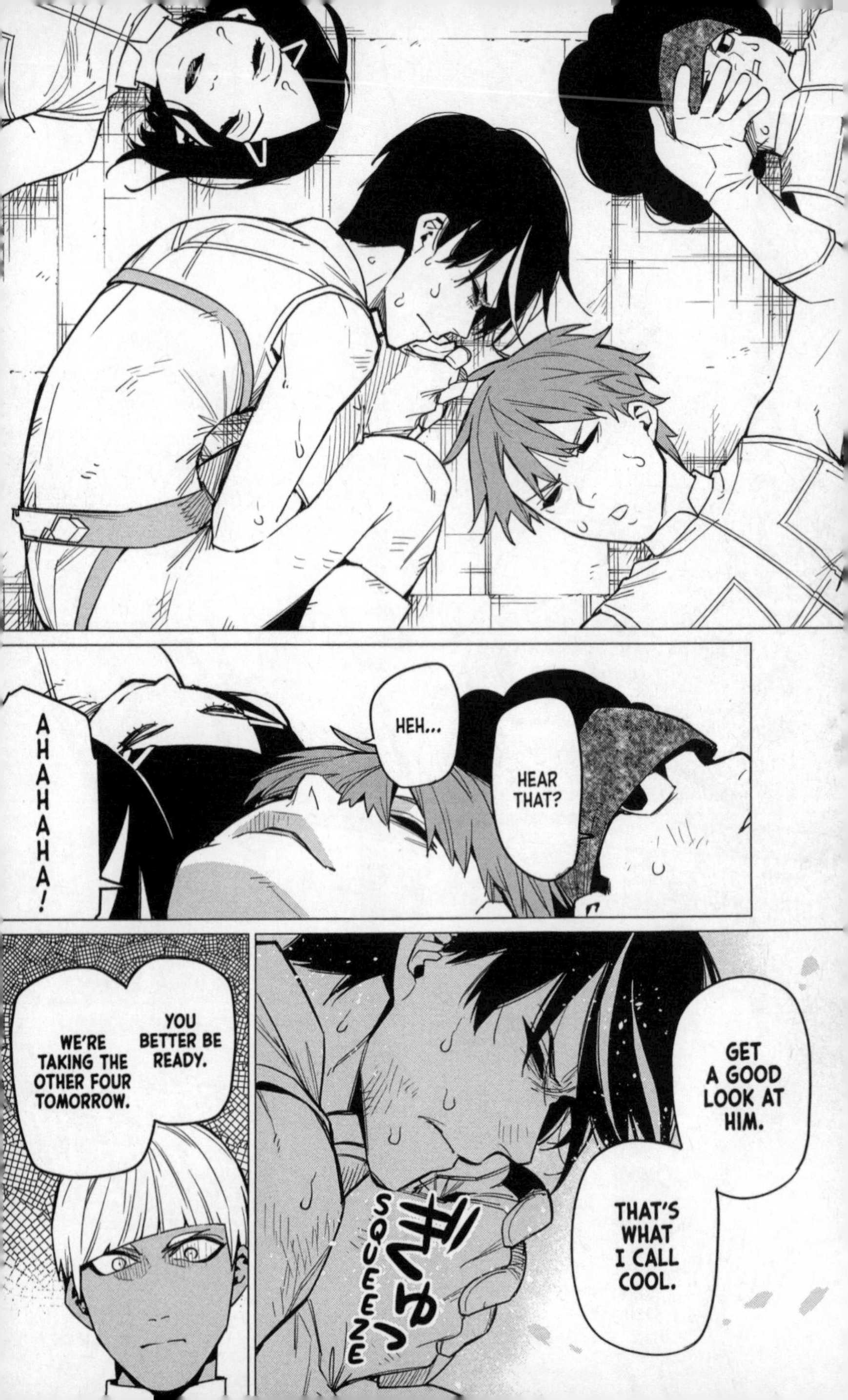
HEH...
HEAR THAT?
AHAHAHAHA!
GET A GOOD LOOK AT HIM.
THAT'S WHAT I CALL COOL.
SQUEEZE
YOU BETTER BE READY.
WE'RE TAKING THE OTHER FOUR TOMORROW.

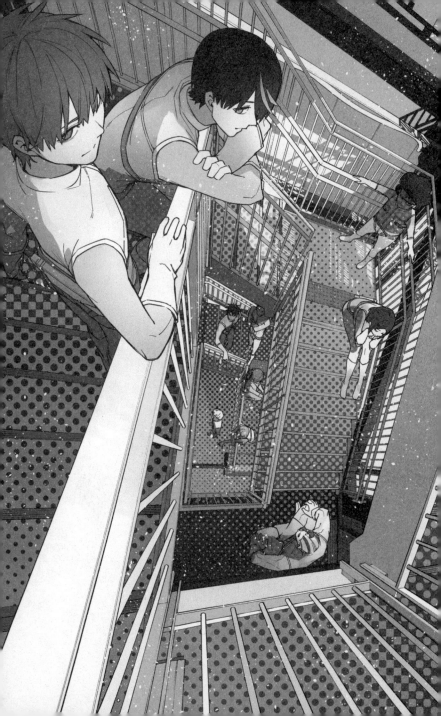

GO! GO!
LOSER RANGER!

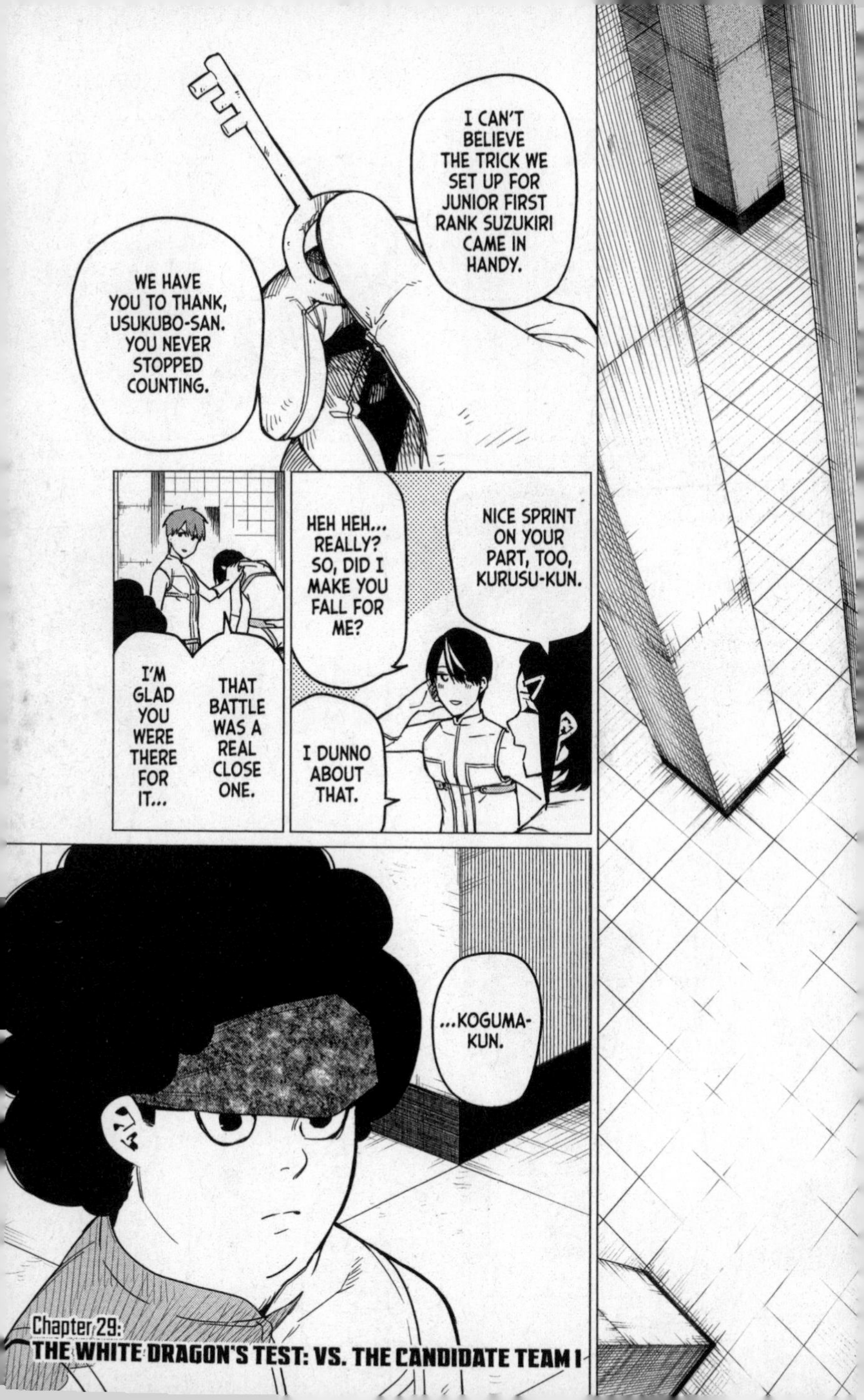
I CAN'T BELIEVE THE TRICK WE SET UP FOR JUNIOR FIRST RANK SUZUKIRI CAME IN HANDY.
WE HAVE YOU TO THANK, USUKUBO-SAN. YOU NEVER STOPPED COUNTING.
NICE SPRINT ON YOUR PART, TOO, KURUSU-KUN.
HEH HEH... REALLY? SO, DID I MAKE YOU FALL FOR ME?
I DUNNO ABOUT THAT.
THAT BATTLE WAS A REAL CLOSE ONE.
I'M GLAD YOU WERE THERE FOR IT...
...KOGUMA-KUN.

Chapter 29:
THE WHITE DRAGON'S TEST: VS. THE CANDIDATE TEAM 1

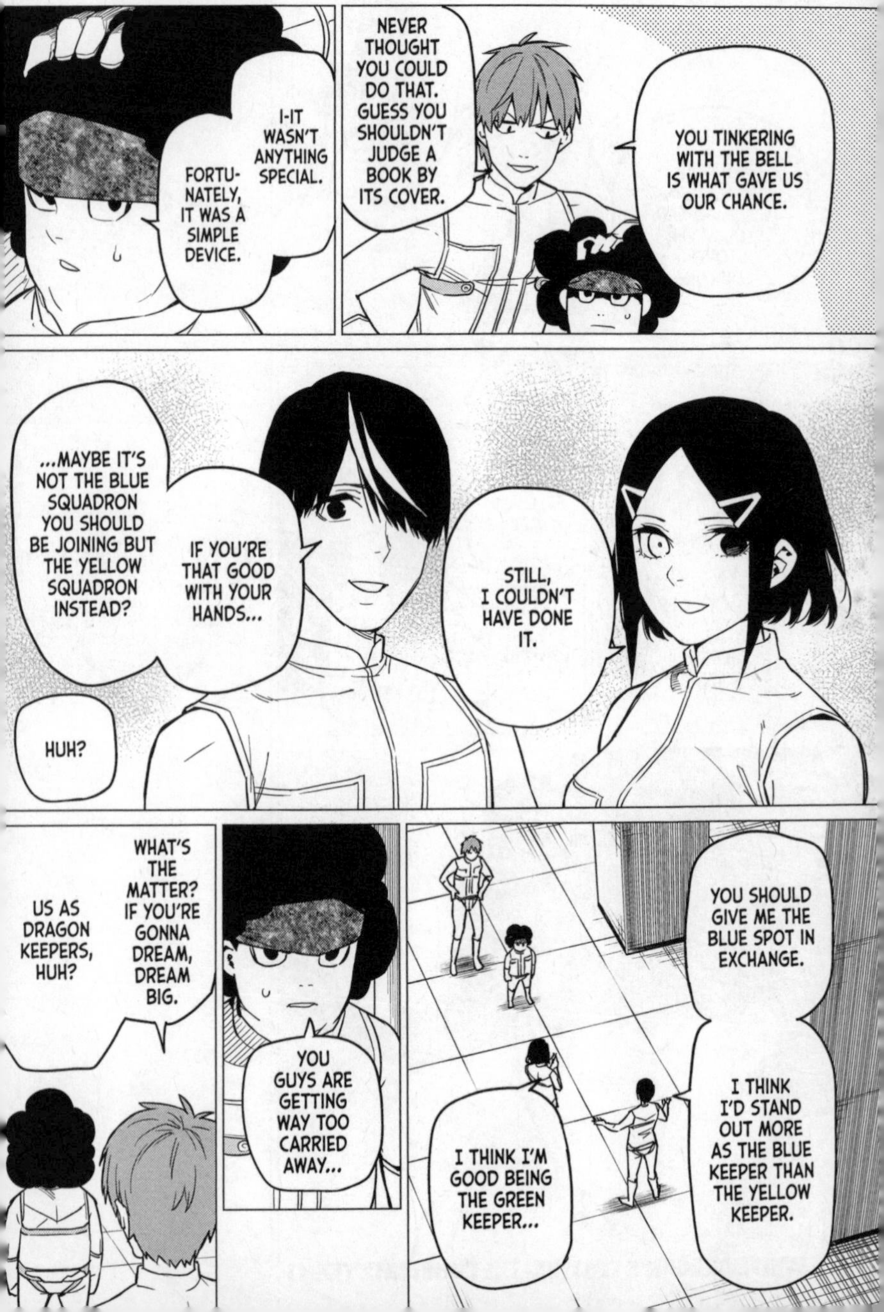
YOU TINKERING WITH THE BELL IS WHAT GAVE US OUR CHANCE.
NEVER THOUGHT YOU COULD DO THAT. GUESS YOU SHOULDN'T JUDGE A BOOK BY ITS COVER.
I-IT WASN'T ANYTHING SPECIAL.
FORTU-NATELY, IT WAS A SIMPLE DEVICE.
STILL, I COULDN'T HAVE DONE IT.
IF YOU'RE THAT GOOD WITH YOUR HANDS...
...MAYBE IT'S NOT THE BLUE SQUADRON YOU SHOULD BE JOINING BUT THE YELLOW SQUADRON INSTEAD?
HUH?
YOU SHOULD GIVE ME THE BLUE SPOT IN EXCHANGE.
I THINK I'D STAND OUT MORE AS THE BLUE KEEPER THAN THE YELLOW KEEPER.
I THINK I'M GOOD BEING THE GREEN KEEPER...
YOU GUYS ARE GETTING WAY TOO CARRIED AWAY...
WHAT'S THE MATTER? IF YOU'RE GONNA DREAM, DREAM BIG.
US AS DRAGON KEEPERS, HUH?

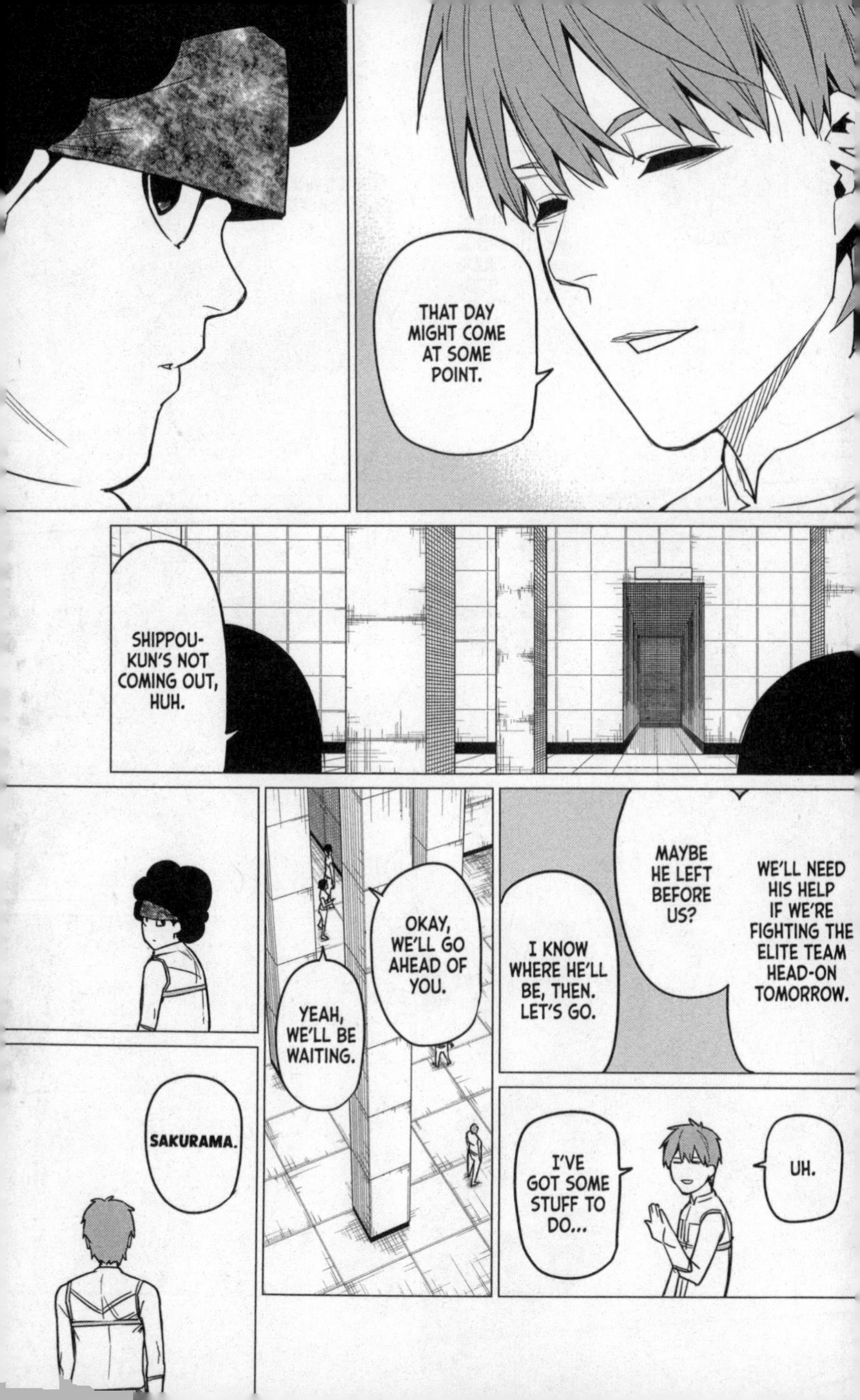
THAT DAY MIGHT COME AT SOME POINT.
SHIPPOU-KUN'S NOT COMING OUT, HUH.
WE'LL NEED HIS HELP IF WE'RE FIGHTING THE ELITE TEAM HEAD-ON TOMORROW.
MAYBE HE LEFT BEFORE US?
I KNOW WHERE HE'LL BE, THEN. LET'S GO.
UH.
I'VE GOT SOME STUFF TO DO...
OKAY, WE'LL GO AHEAD OF YOU.
YEAH, WE'LL BE WAITING.
SAKURAMA.

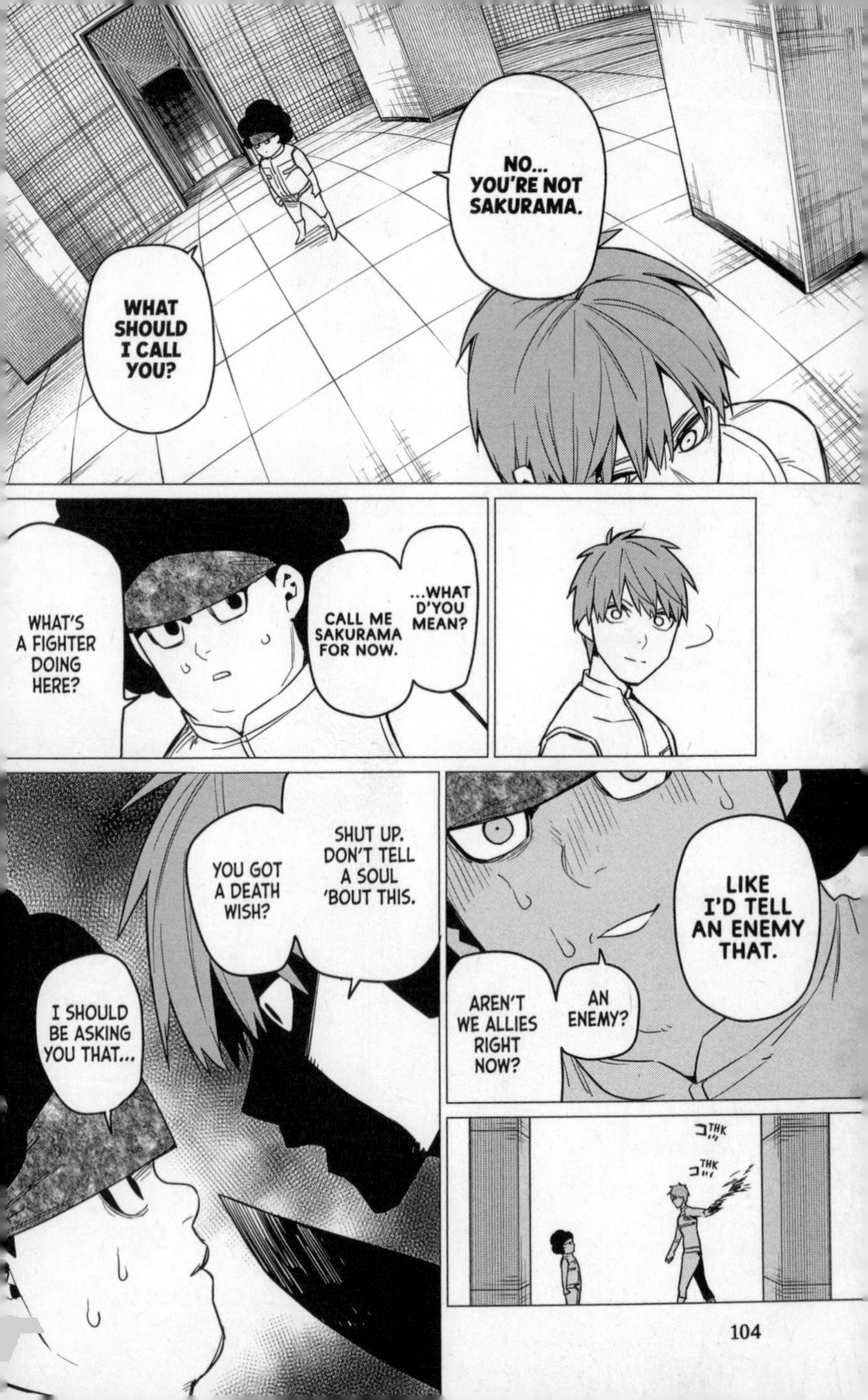
NO... YOU'RE NOT SAKURAMA.
WHAT SHOULD I CALL YOU?
...WHAT D'YOU MEAN?
CALL ME SAKURAMA FOR NOW.
WHAT'S A FIGHTER DOING HERE?
LIKE I'D TELL AN ENEMY THAT.
AN ENEMY?
AREN'T WE ALLIES RIGHT NOW?
THK
THK
SHUT UP. DON'T TELL A SOUL 'BOUT THIS.
YOU GOT A DEATH WISH?
I SHOULD BE ASKING YOU THAT...

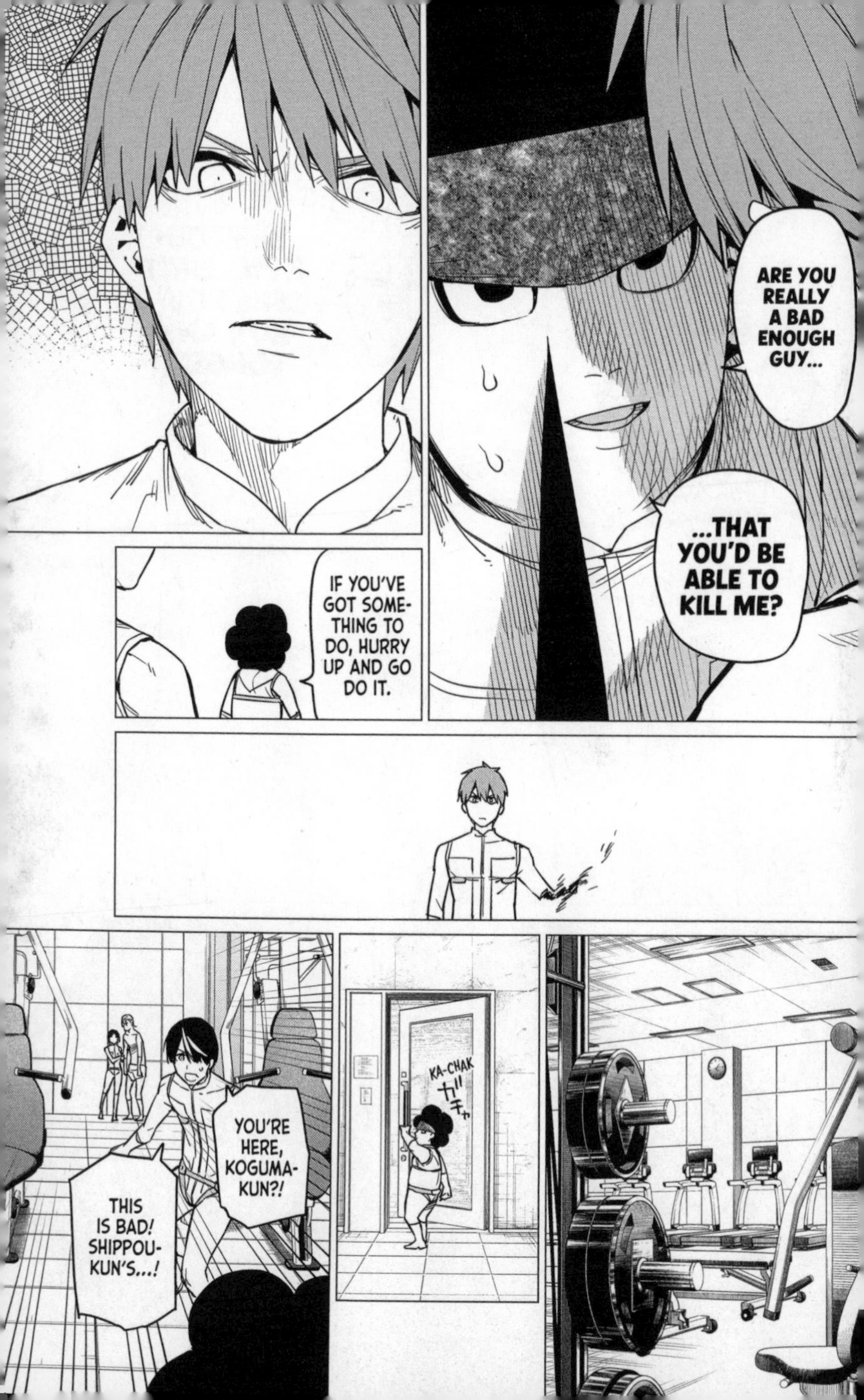
ARE YOU REALLY A BAD ENOUGH GUY...
...THAT YOU'D BE ABLE TO KILL ME?
IF YOU'VE GOT SOME-THING TO DO, HURRY UP AND GO DO IT.
KA-CHAK
YOU'RE HERE, KOGUMA-KUN?!
THIS IS BAD! SHIPPOU-KUN'S...!

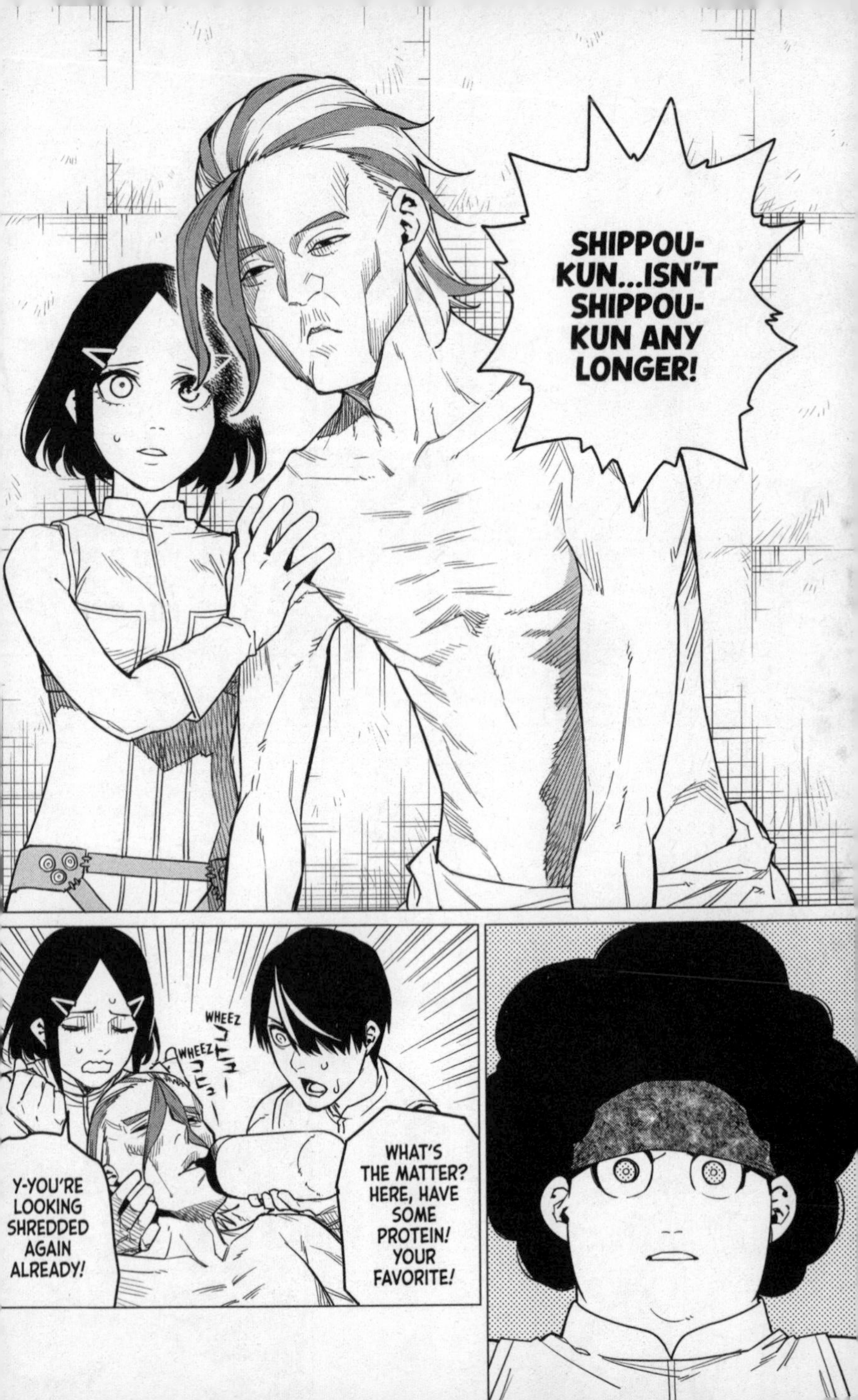
SHIPPOU-KUN...ISN'T SHIPPOU-KUN ANY LONGER!
WHEEZ
WHEEZ
WHAT'S THE MATTER? HERE, HAVE SOME PROTEIN! YOUR FAVORITE!
Y-YOU'RE LOOKING SHREDDED AGAIN ALREADY!

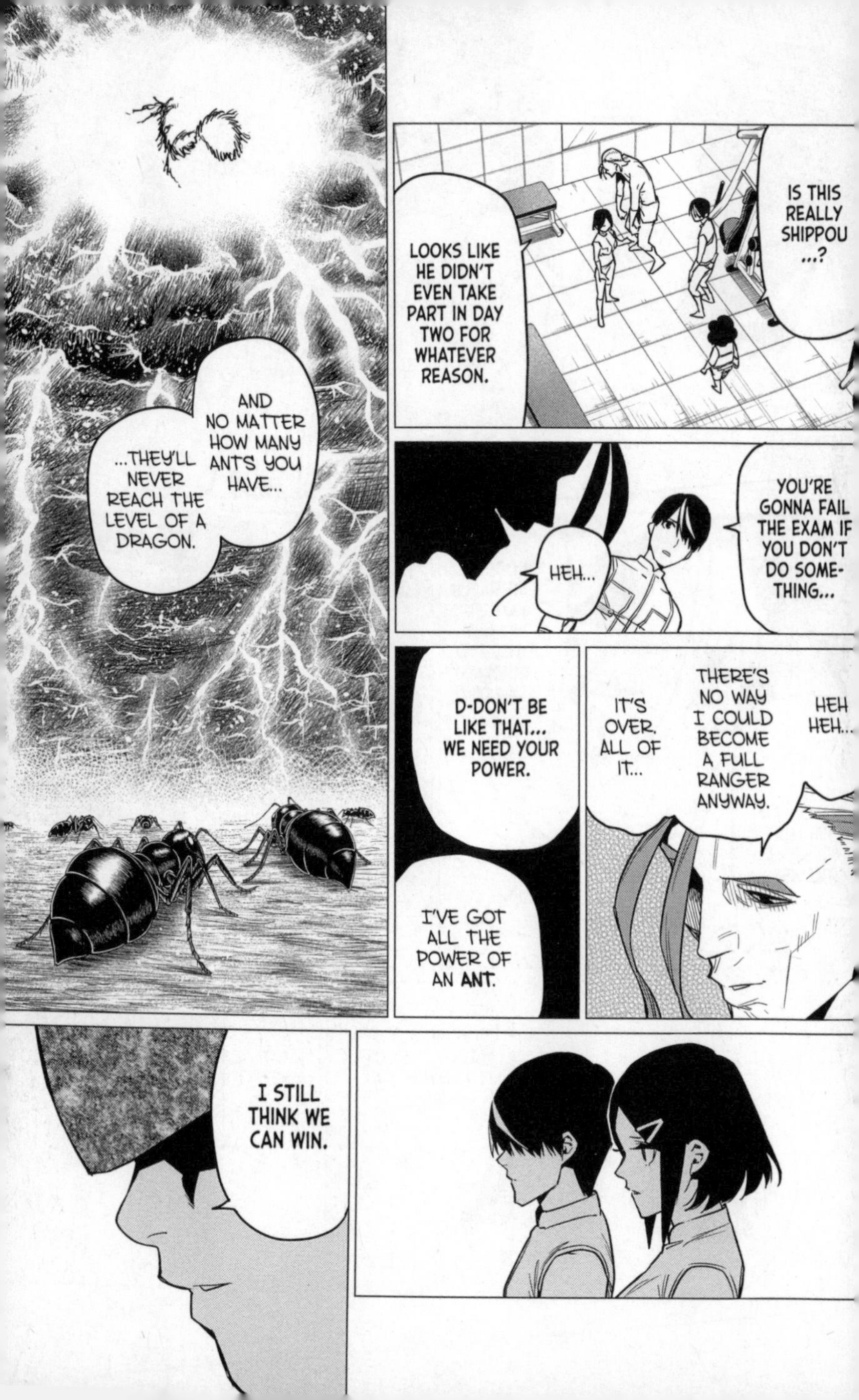
IS THIS REALLY SHIPPOU ...?
LOOKS LIKE HE DIDN'T EVEN TAKE PART IN DAY TWO FOR WHATEVER REASON.
YOU'RE GONNA FAIL THE EXAM IF YOU DON'T DO SOME-THING...
HEH...
HEH HEH...
THERE'S NO WAY I COULD BECOME A FULL RANGER ANYWAY.
IT'S OVER. ALL OF IT...
D-DON'T BE LIKE THAT... WE NEED YOUR POWER.
I'VE GOT ALL THE POWER OF AN ANT.
AND NO MATTER HOW MANY ANTS YOU HAVE...
...THEY'LL NEVER REACH THE LEVEL OF A DRAGON.
I STILL THINK WE CAN WIN.

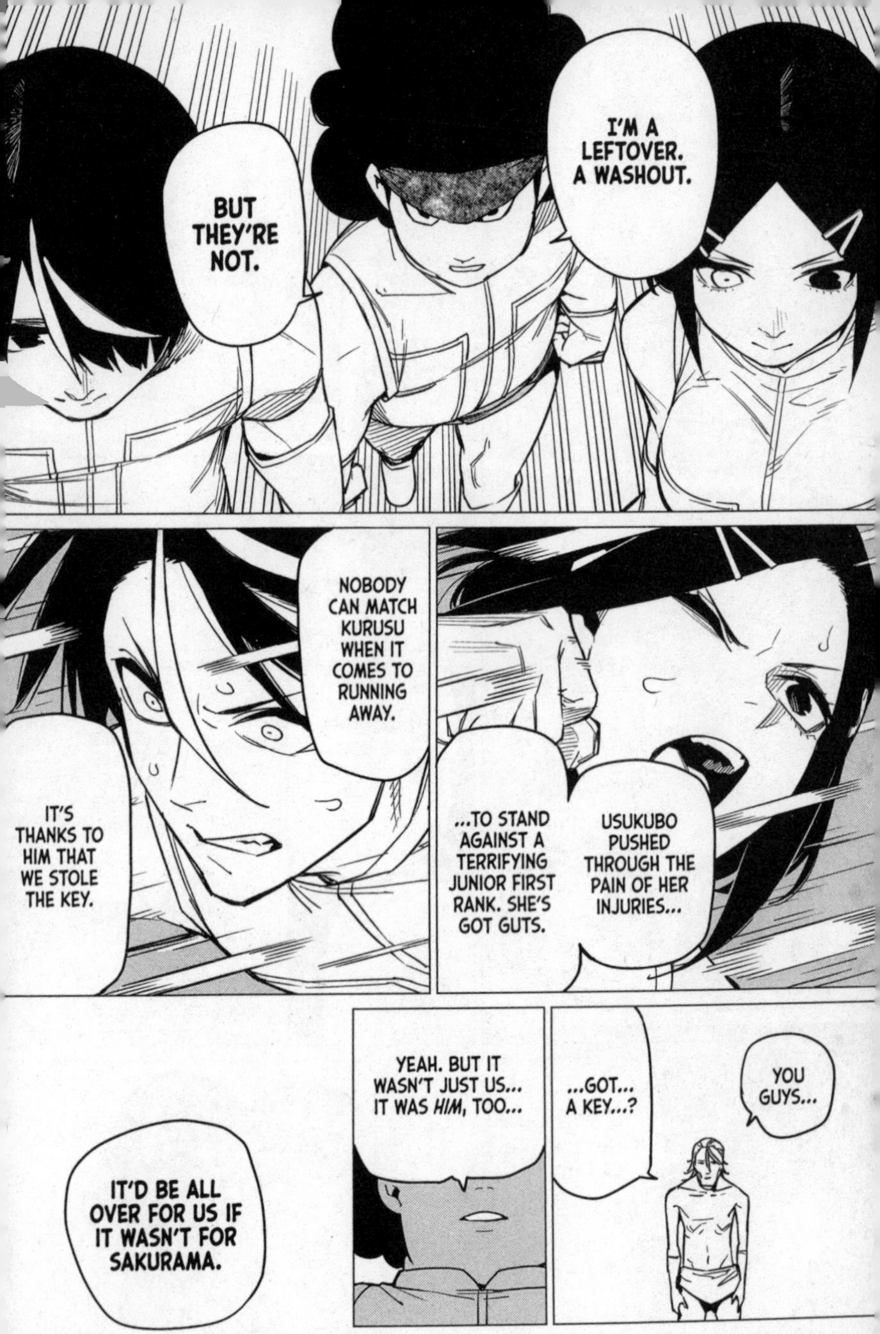
I'M A LEFTOVER. A WASHOUT.
BUT THEY'RE NOT.
USUKUBO PUSHED THROUGH THE PAIN OF HER INJURIES...
...TO STAND AGAINST A TERRIFYING JUNIOR FIRST RANK. SHE'S GOT GUTS.
NOBODY CAN MATCH KURUSU WHEN IT COMES TO RUNNING AWAY.
IT'S THANKS TO HIM THAT WE STOLE THE KEY.
YOU GUYS...
...GOT... A KEY...?
YEAH. BUT IT WASN'T JUST US... IT WAS *HIM*, TOO...
IT'D BE ALL OVER FOR US IF IT WASN'T FOR SAKURAMA.

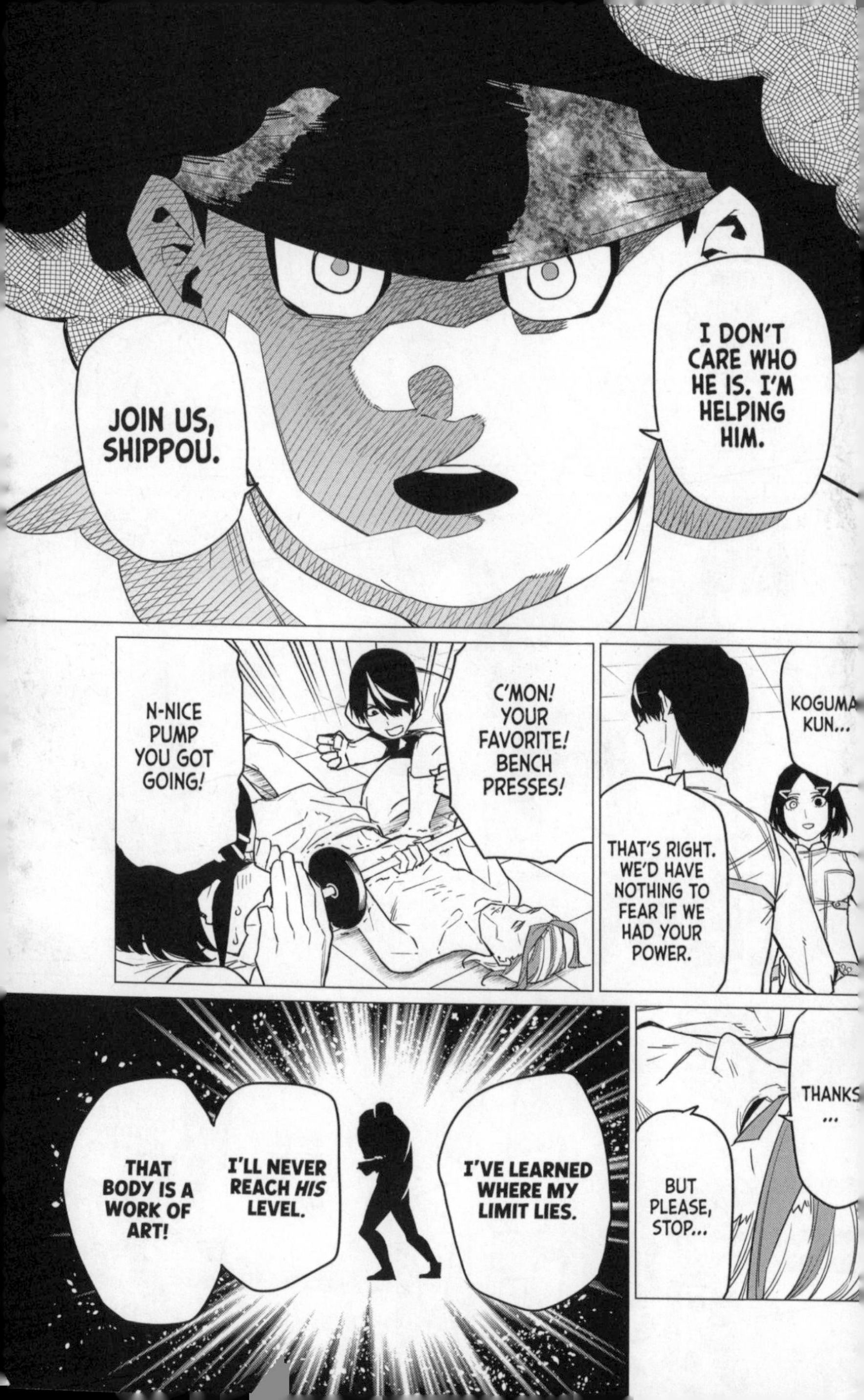
I DON'T CARE WHO HE IS. I'M HELPING HIM.
JOIN US, SHIPPOU.
KOGUMA KUN...
THAT'S RIGHT. WE'D HAVE NOTHING TO FEAR IF WE HAD YOUR POWER.
C'MON! YOUR FAVORITE! BENCH PRESSES!
N-NICE PUMP YOU GOT GOING!
THANKS...
BUT PLEASE, STOP...
I'VE LEARNED WHERE MY LIMIT LIES.
I'LL NEVER REACH *HIS* LEVEL.
THAT BODY IS A WORK OF ART!

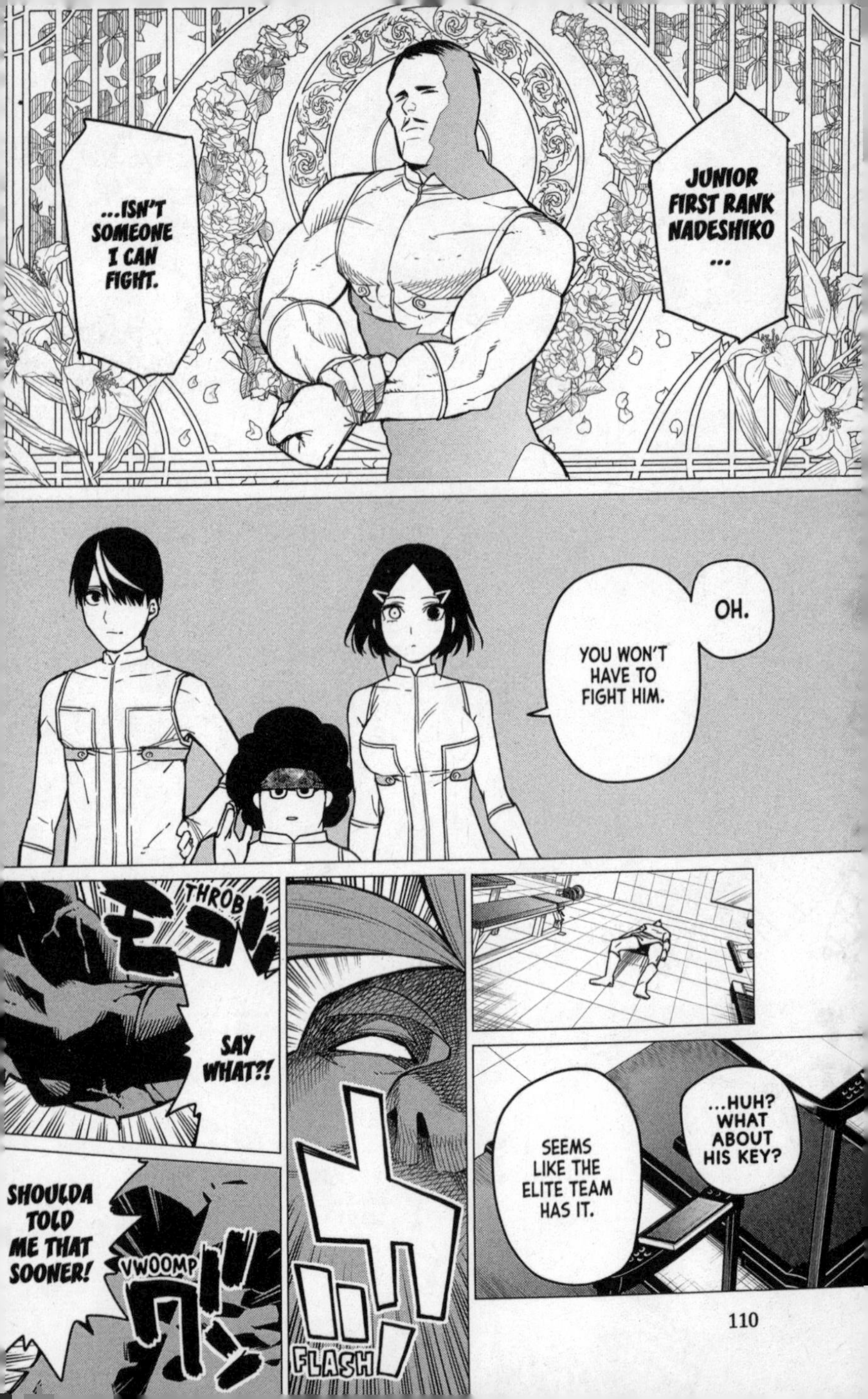

JUNIOR FIRST RANK NADESHIKO ...
...ISN'T SOMEONE I CAN FIGHT.
OH.
YOU WON'T HAVE TO FIGHT HIM.
...HUH? WHAT ABOUT HIS KEY?
SEEMS LIKE THE ELITE TEAM HAS IT.
FLASH
THROB
SAY WHAT?!
SHOULDA TOLD ME THAT SOONER!
VWOOMP

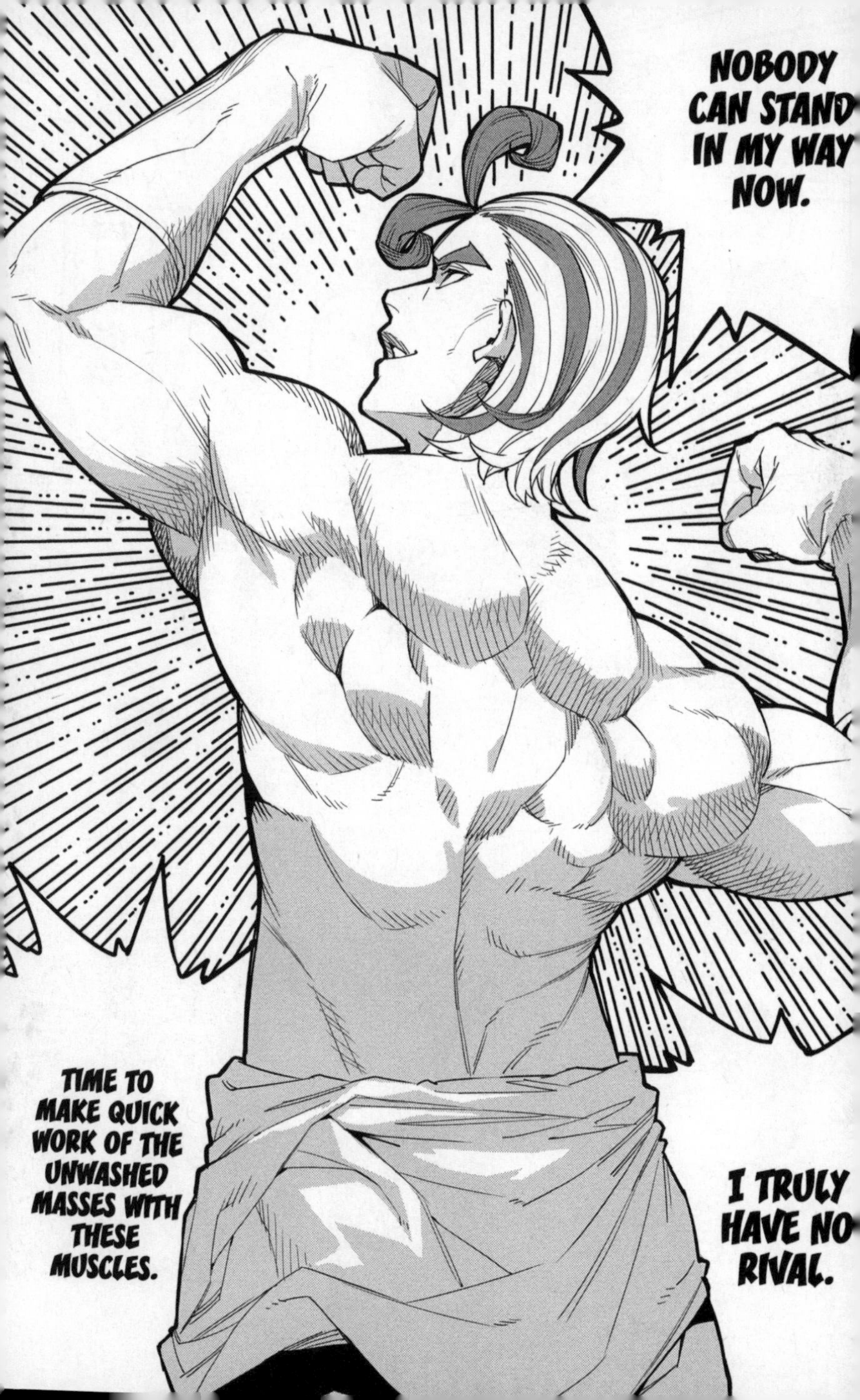
NOBODY CAN STAND IN MY WAY NOW.
I TRULY HAVE NO RIVAL.
TIME TO MAKE QUICK WORK OF THE UNWASHED MASSES WITH THESE MUSCLES.

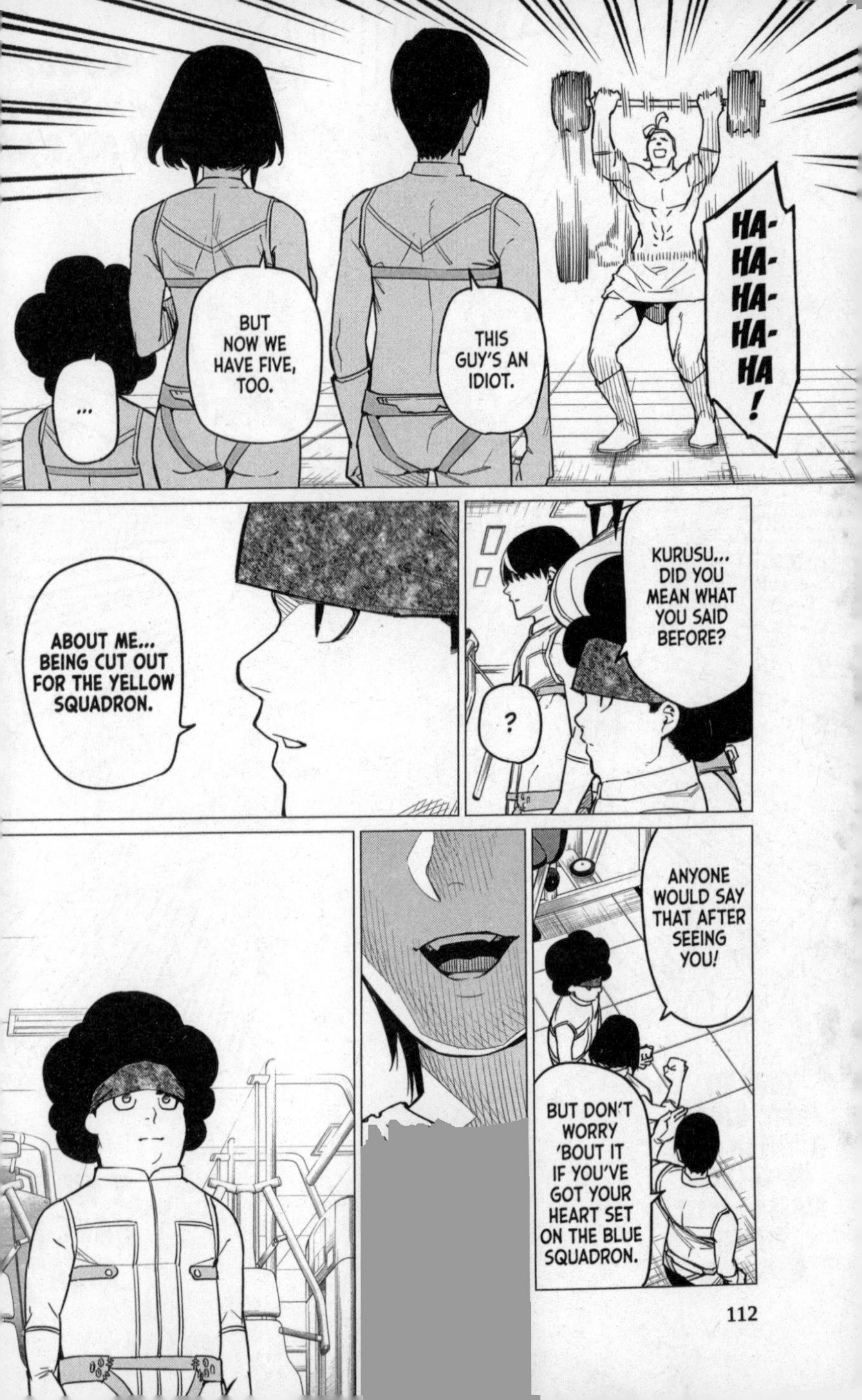
HA-HA-HA-HA-HA!
THIS GUY'S AN IDIOT.
BUT NOW WE HAVE FIVE, TOO.
...
KURUSU... DID YOU MEAN WHAT YOU SAID BEFORE?
?
ABOUT ME... BEING CUT OUT FOR THE YELLOW SQUADRON.
ANYONE WOULD SAY THAT AFTER SEEING YOU!
BUT DON'T WORRY 'BOUT IT IF YOU'VE GOT YOUR HEART SET ON THE BLUE SQUADRON.

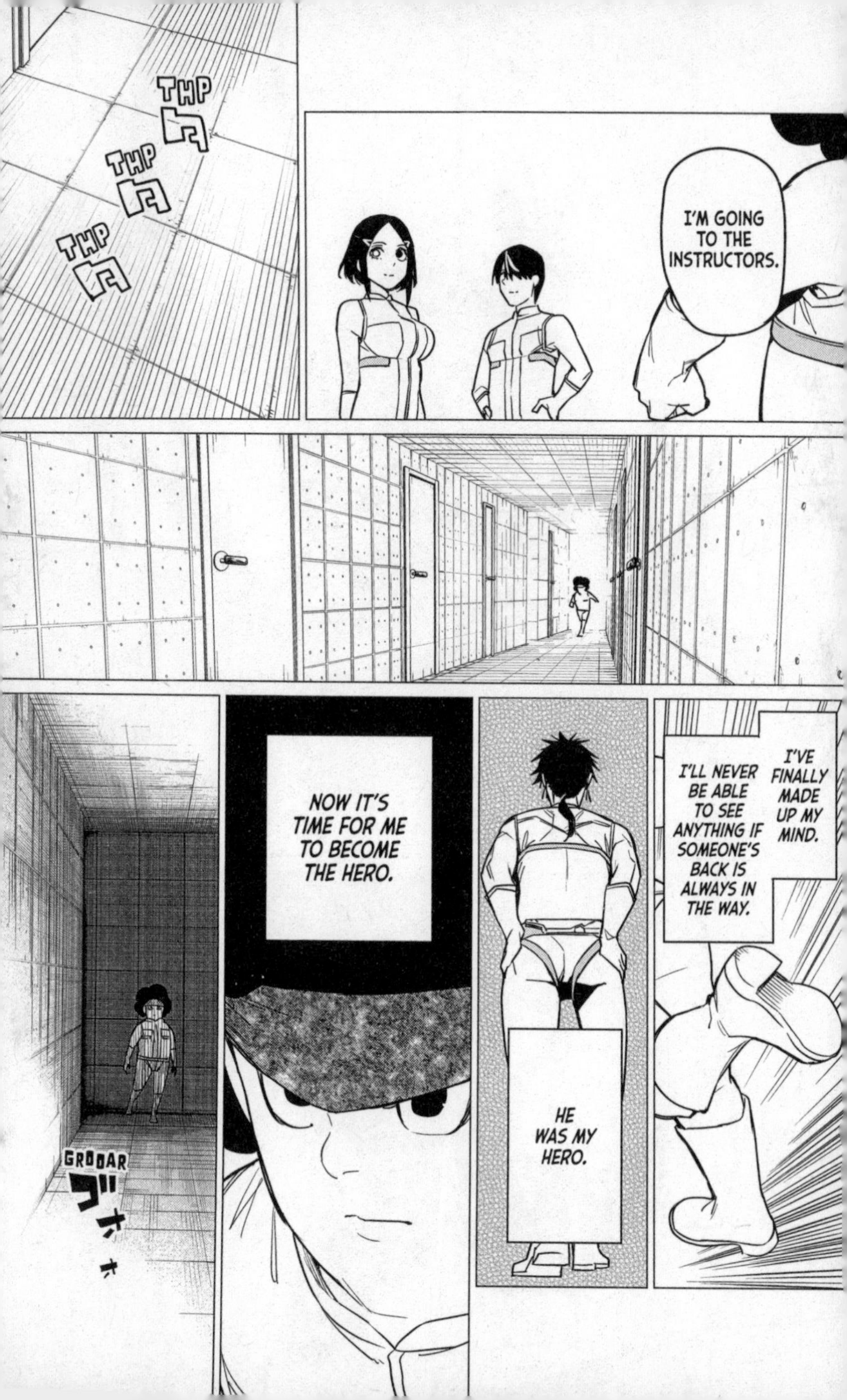
I'M GOING TO THE INSTRUCTORS.
THP
THP
THP
I'VE FINALLY MADE UP MY MIND.
I'LL NEVER BE ABLE TO SEE ANYTHING IF SOMEONE'S BACK IS ALWAYS IN THE WAY.
HE WAS MY HERO.
NOW IT'S TIME FOR ME TO BECOME THE HERO.
GROOAR

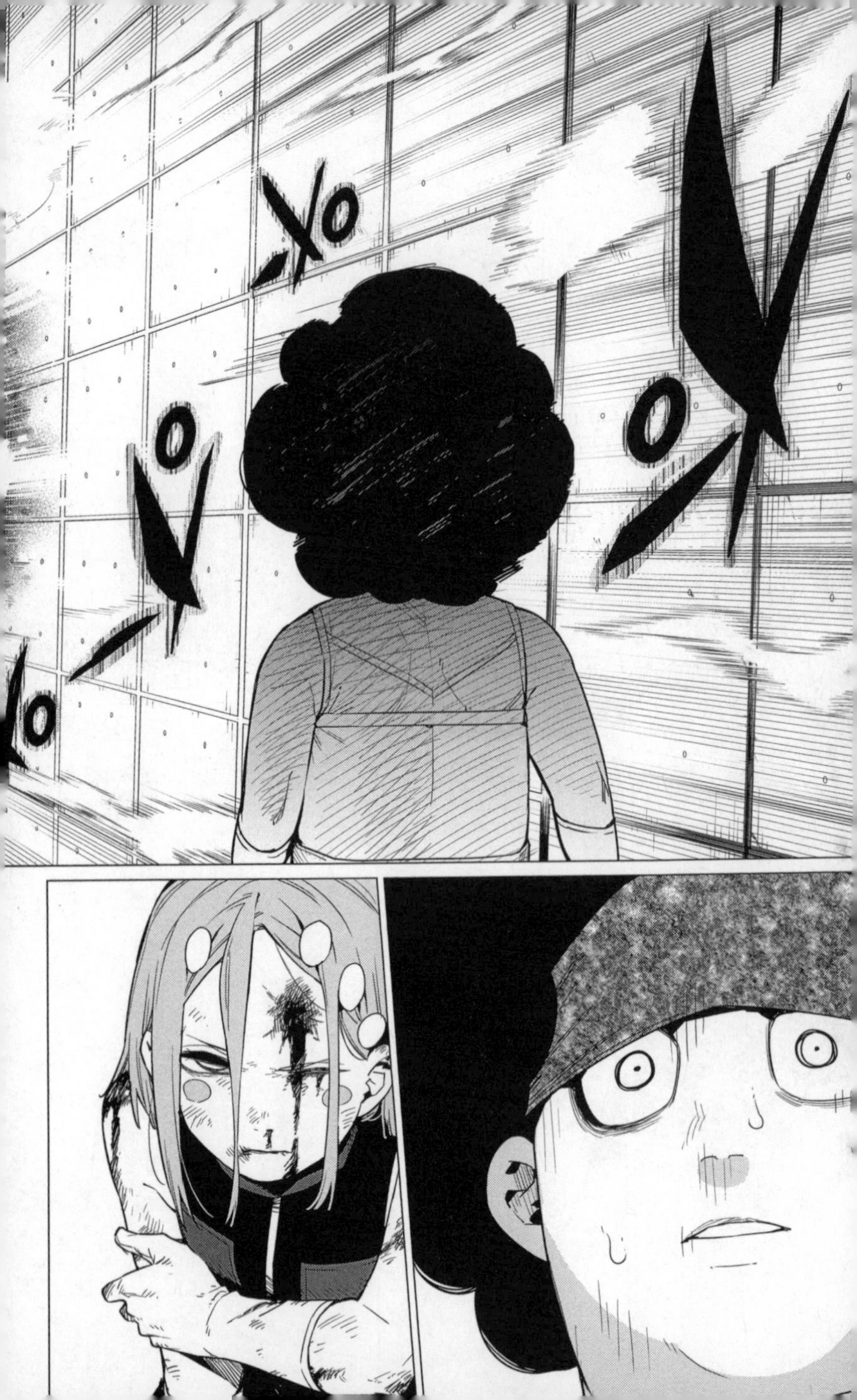

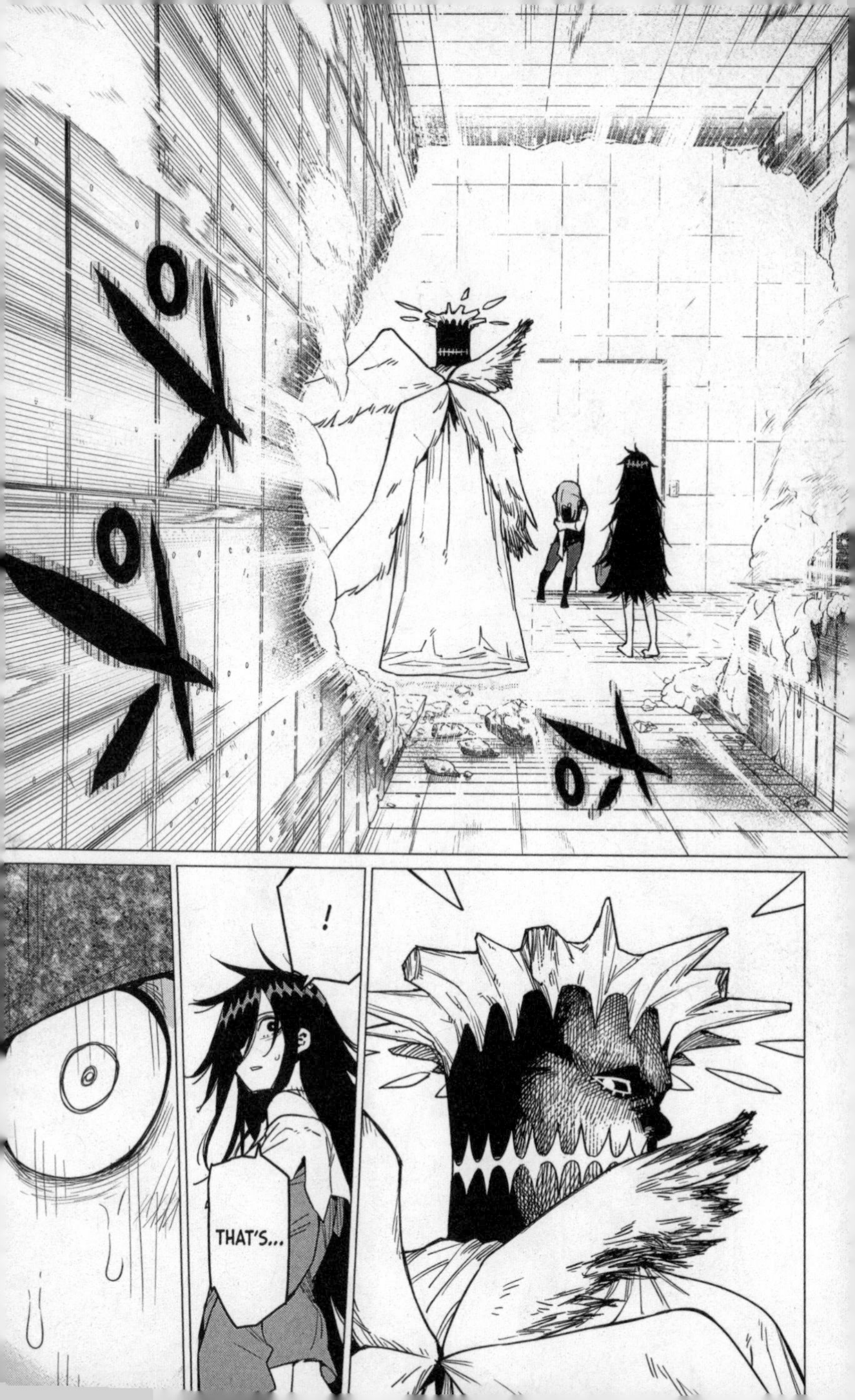
!
THAT'S...

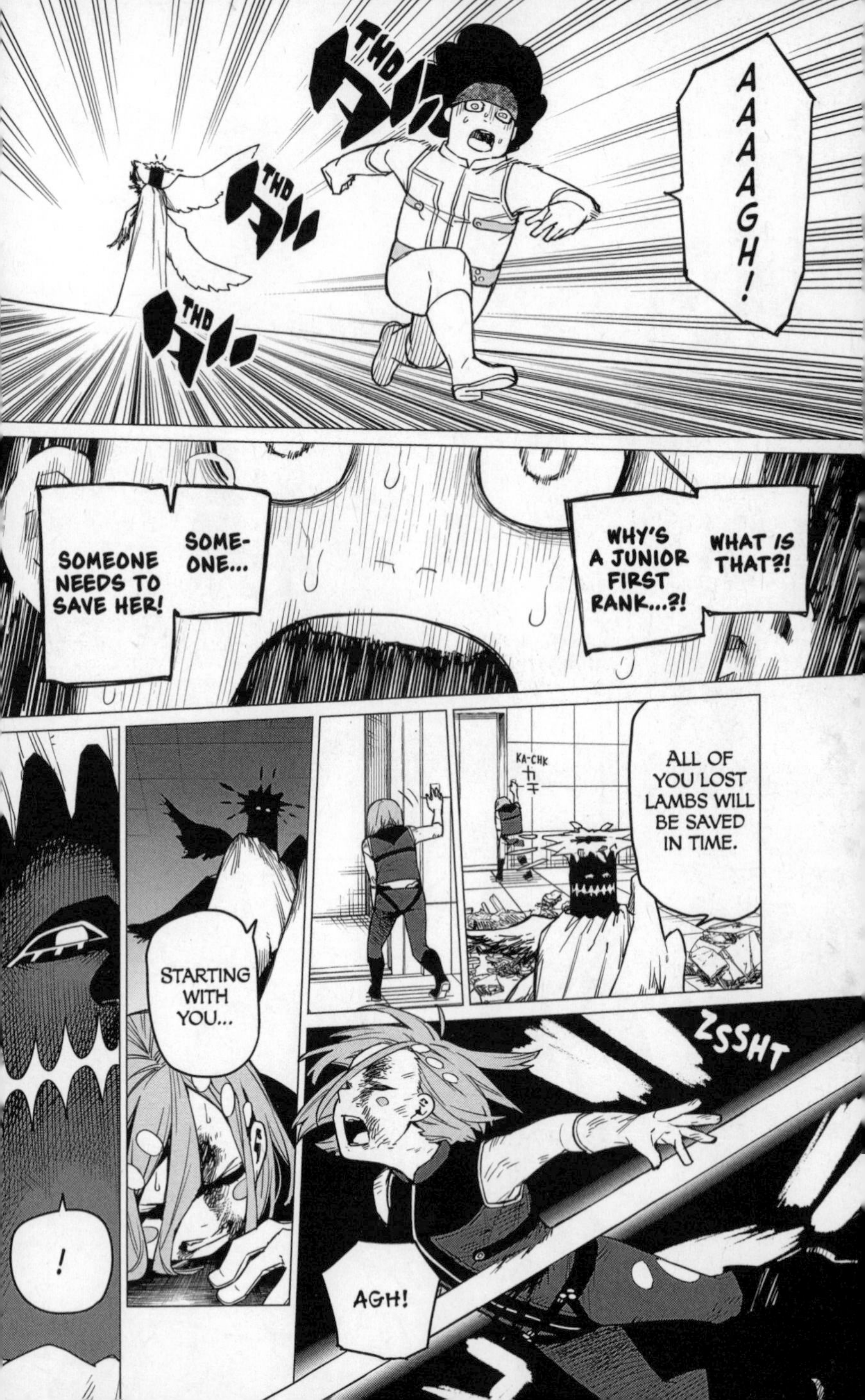
AAAAAGH!
THD
THD
THD
WHAT IS THAT?!
WHY'S A JUNIOR FIRST RANK...?!
SOME-ONE...
SOMEONE NEEDS TO SAVE HER!
ALL OF YOU LOST LAMBS WILL BE SAVED IN TIME.
KA-CHK
ZSSHT
AGH!
STARTING WITH YOU...
!

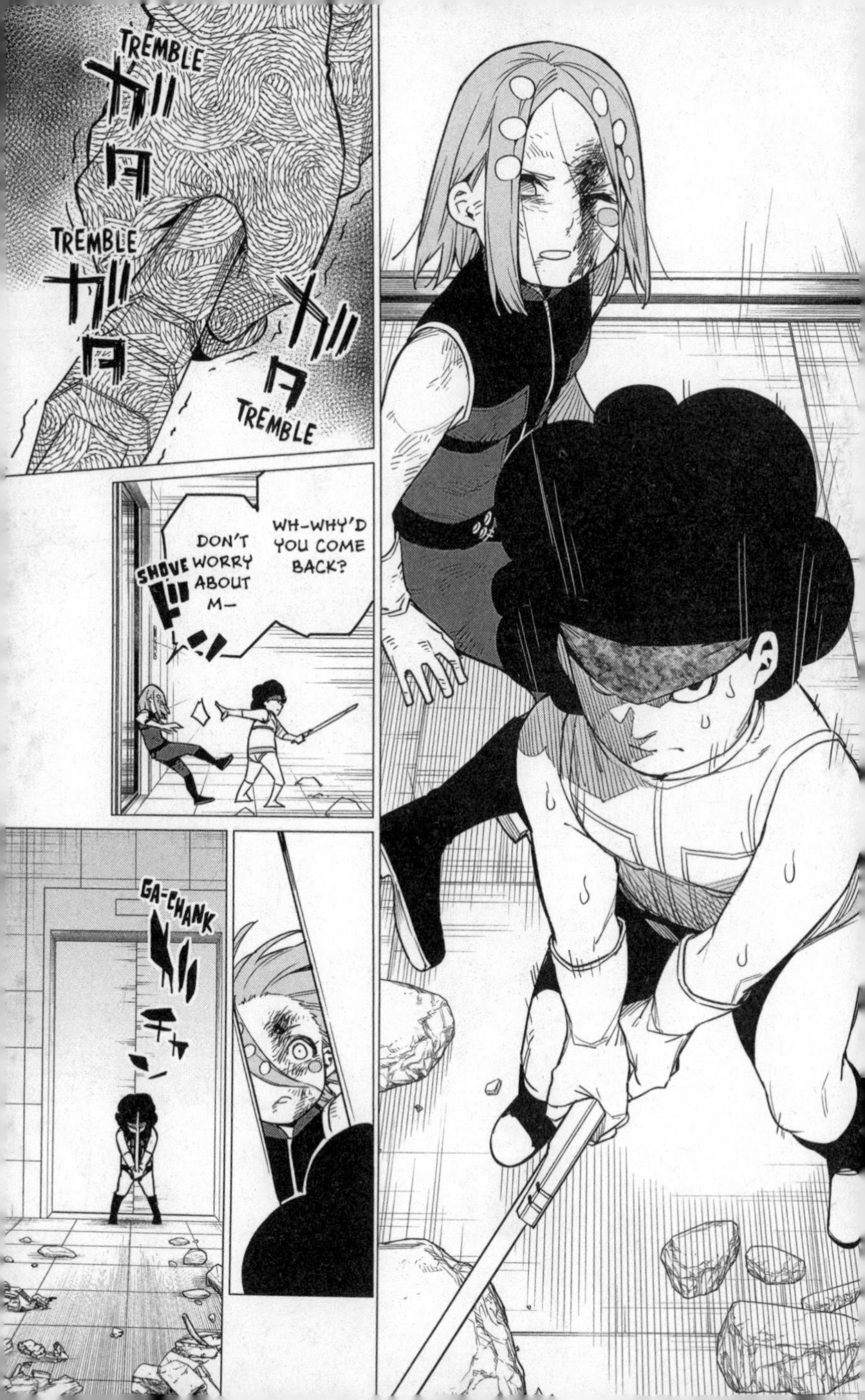
TREMBLE
TREMBLE
TREMBLE
WH-WHY'D YOU COME BACK?
DON'T WORRY ABOUT M-
SHOVE
GA-CHANK

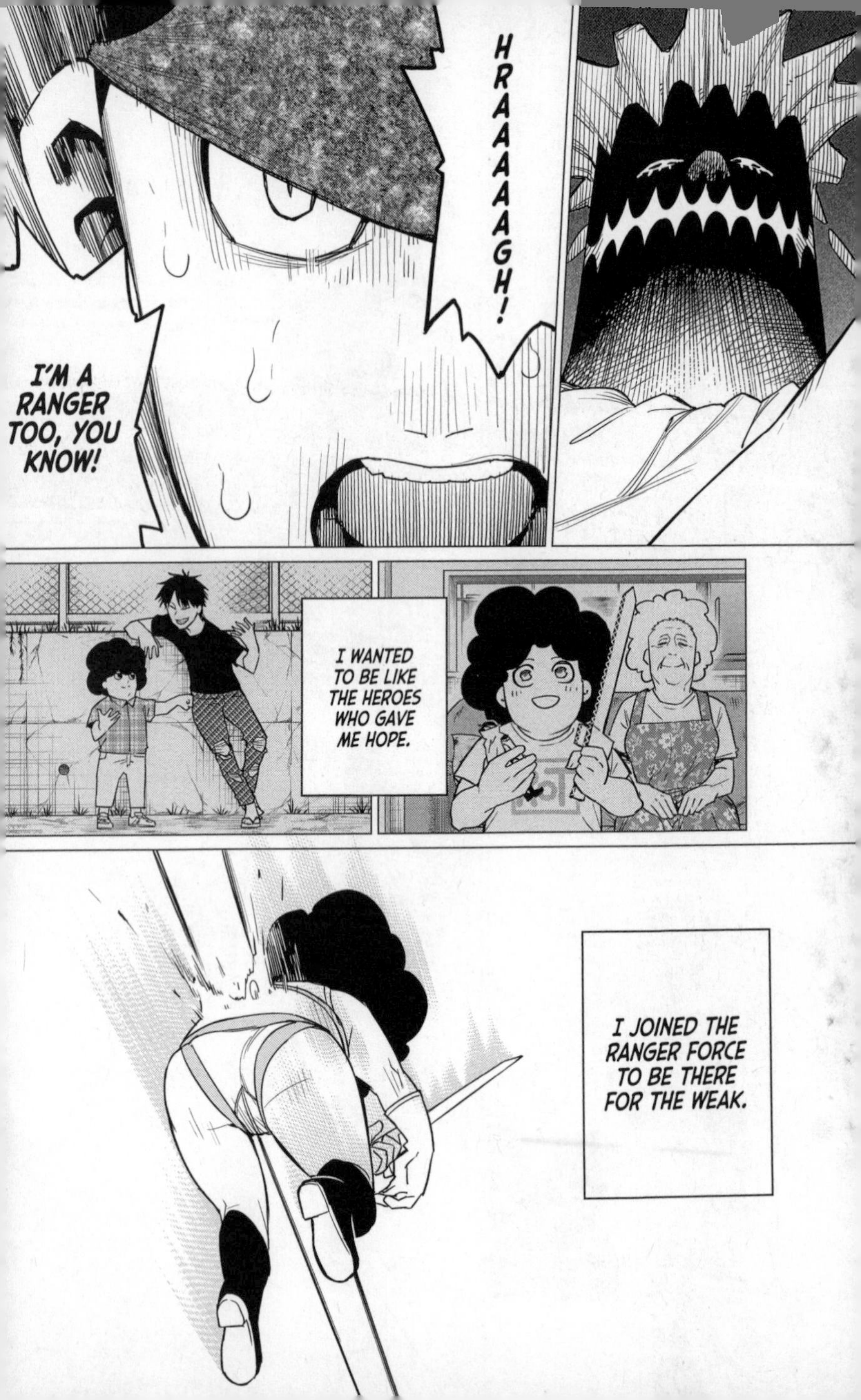
HRAAAAAAGH!
I'M A RANGER TOO, YOU KNOW!
I WANTED TO BE LIKE THE HEROES WHO GAVE ME HOPE.
I JOINED THE RANGER FORCE TO BE THERE FOR THE WEAK.

Chapter 30: THE WHITE DRAGON'S TEST: VS. THE CANDIDATE TEAM 2

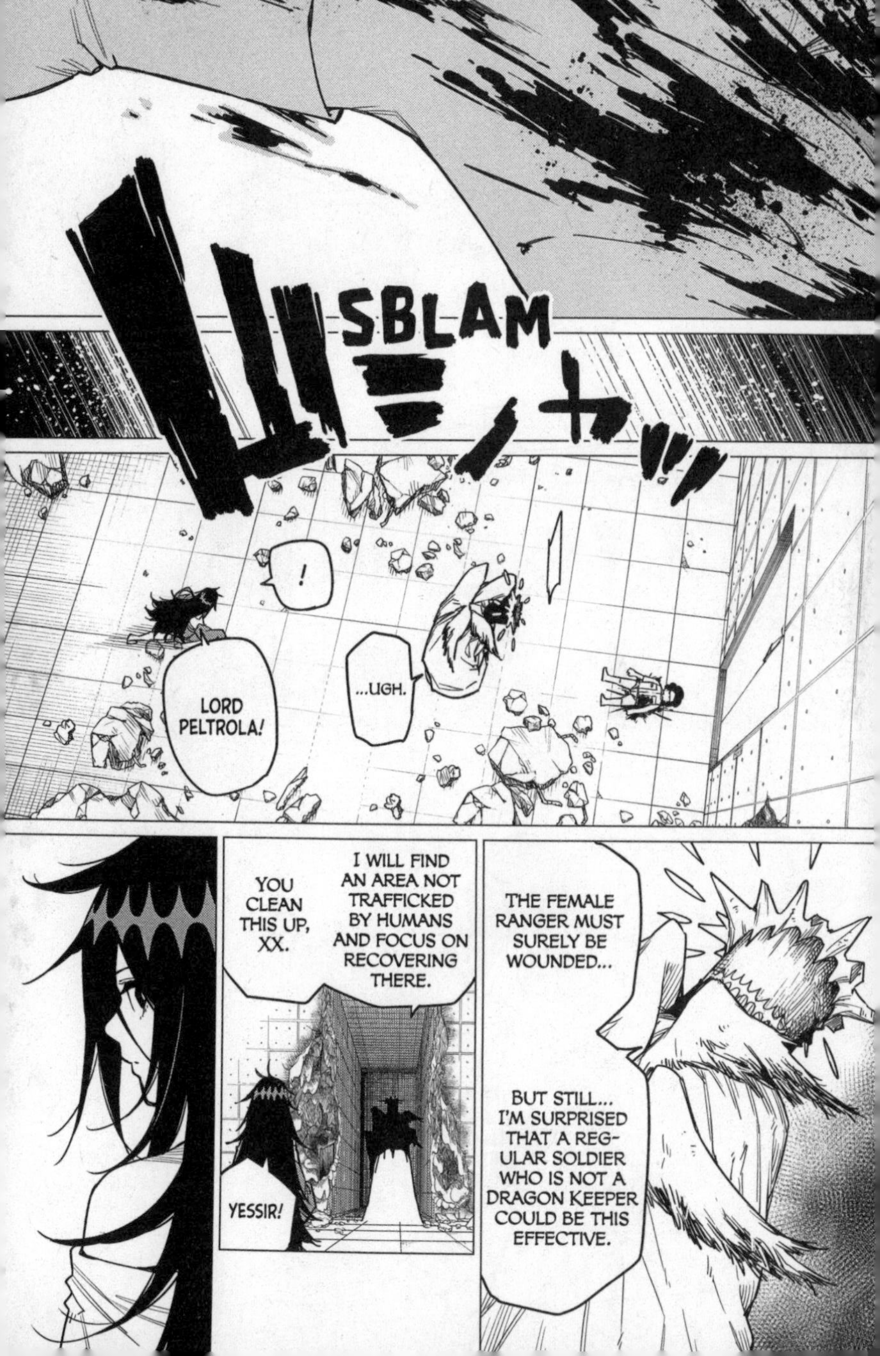
SBLAM
!
...UGH.
LORD PELTROLA!
THE FEMALE RANGER MUST SURELY BE WOUNDED...
BUT STILL... I'M SURPRISED THAT A REG-ULAR SOLDIER WHO IS NOT A DRAGON KEEPER COULD BE THIS EFFECTIVE.
I WILL FIND AN AREA NOT TRAFFICKED BY HUMANS AND FOCUS ON RECOVERING THERE.
YOU CLEAN THIS UP, XX.
YESSIR!

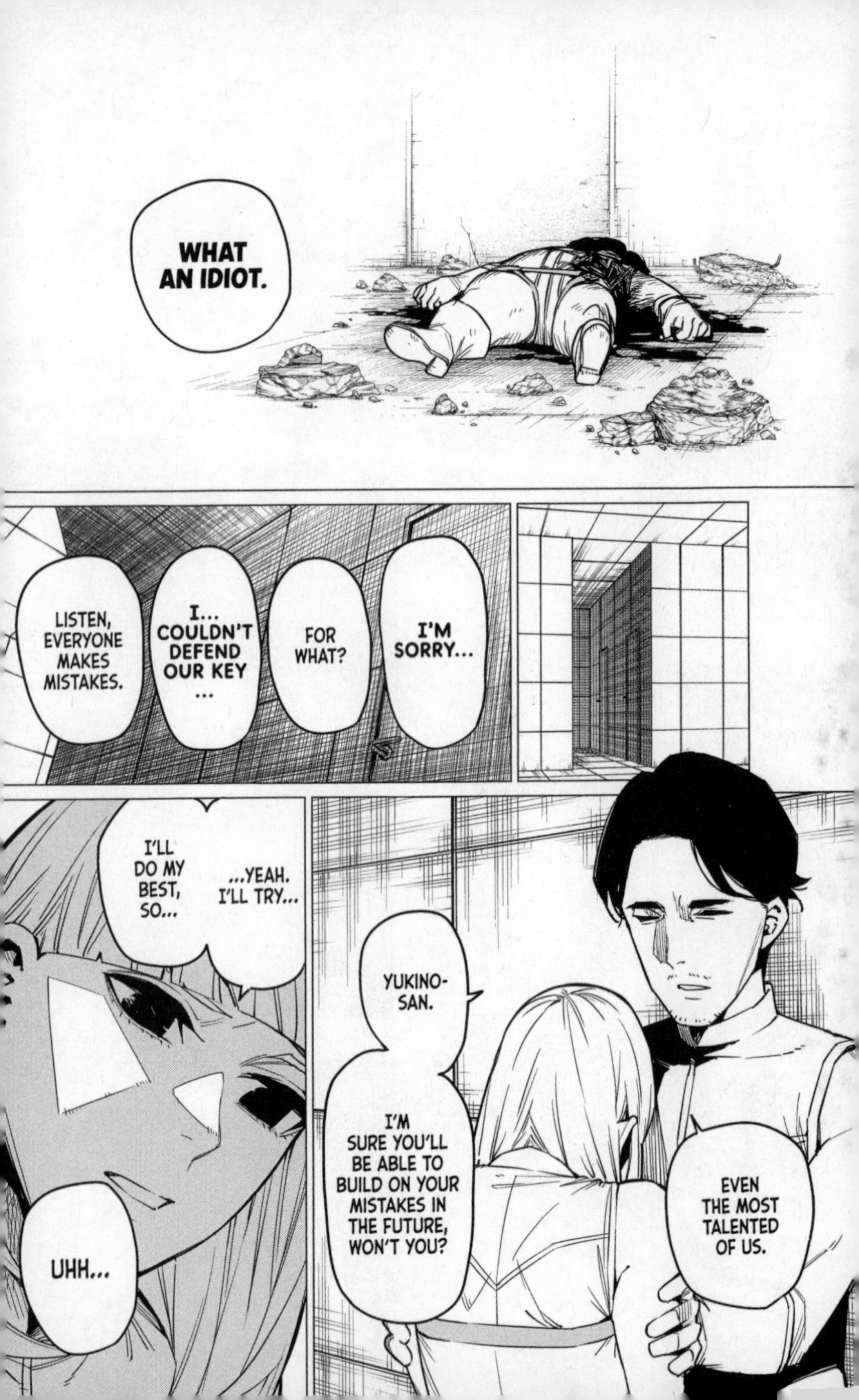
WHAT AN IDIOT.
I'M SORRY...
FOR WHAT?
I... COULDN'T DEFEND OUR KEY ...
LISTEN, EVERYONE MAKES MISTAKES.
EVEN THE MOST TALENTED OF US.
YUKINO-SAN.
I'M SURE YOU'LL BE ABLE TO BUILD ON YOUR MISTAKES IN THE FUTURE, WON'T YOU?
...YEAH. I'LL TRY...
I'LL DO MY BEST, SO...
UHH...

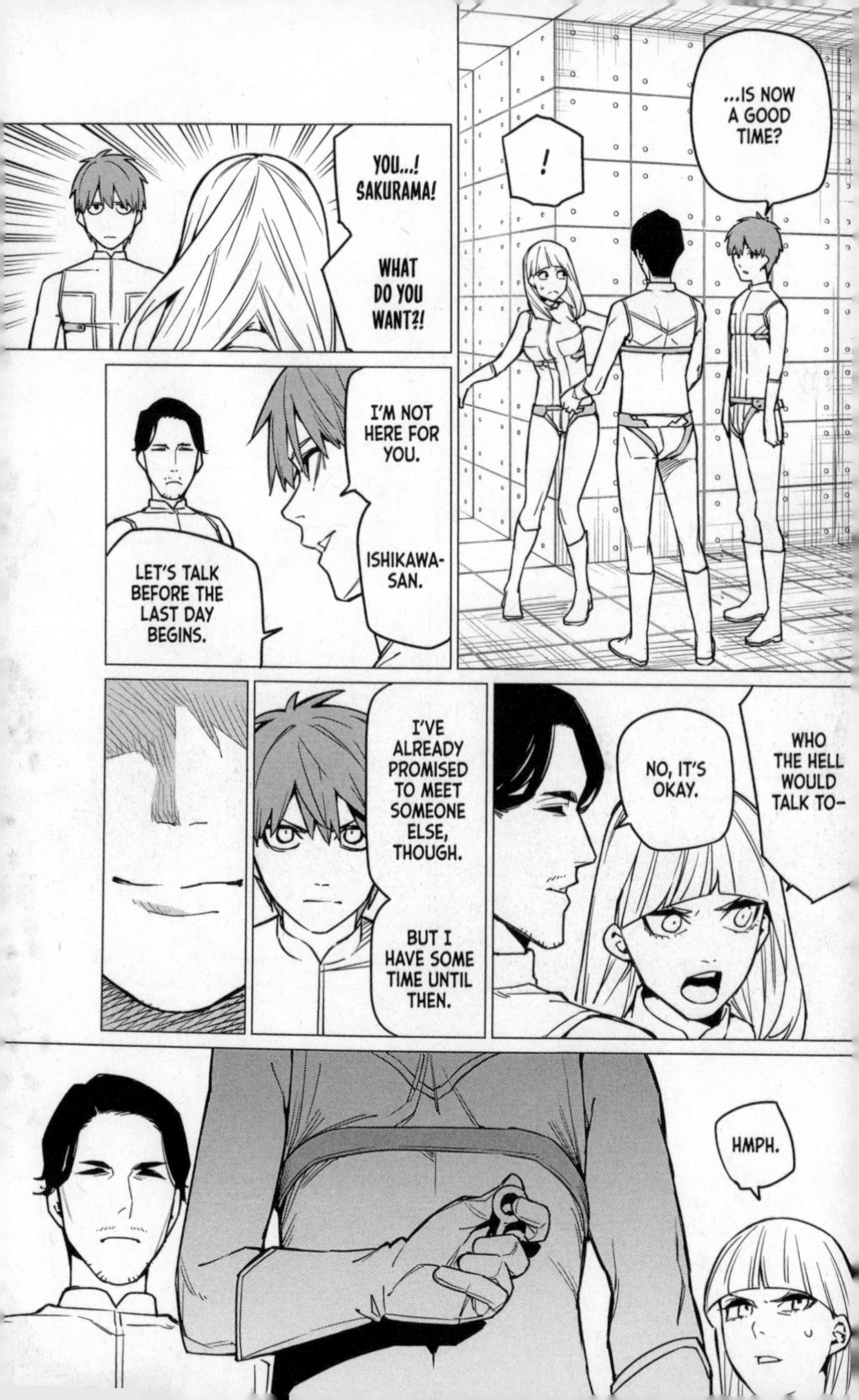
...IS NOW A GOOD TIME?
!
YOU...! SAKURAMA!
WHAT DO YOU WANT?!
I'M NOT HERE FOR YOU.
ISHIKAWA-SAN.
LET'S TALK BEFORE THE LAST DAY BEGINS.
WHO THE HELL WOULD TALK TO-
NO, IT'S OKAY.
I'VE ALREADY PROMISED TO MEET SOMEONE ELSE, THOUGH.
BUT I HAVE SOME TIME UNTIL THEN.
HMPH.

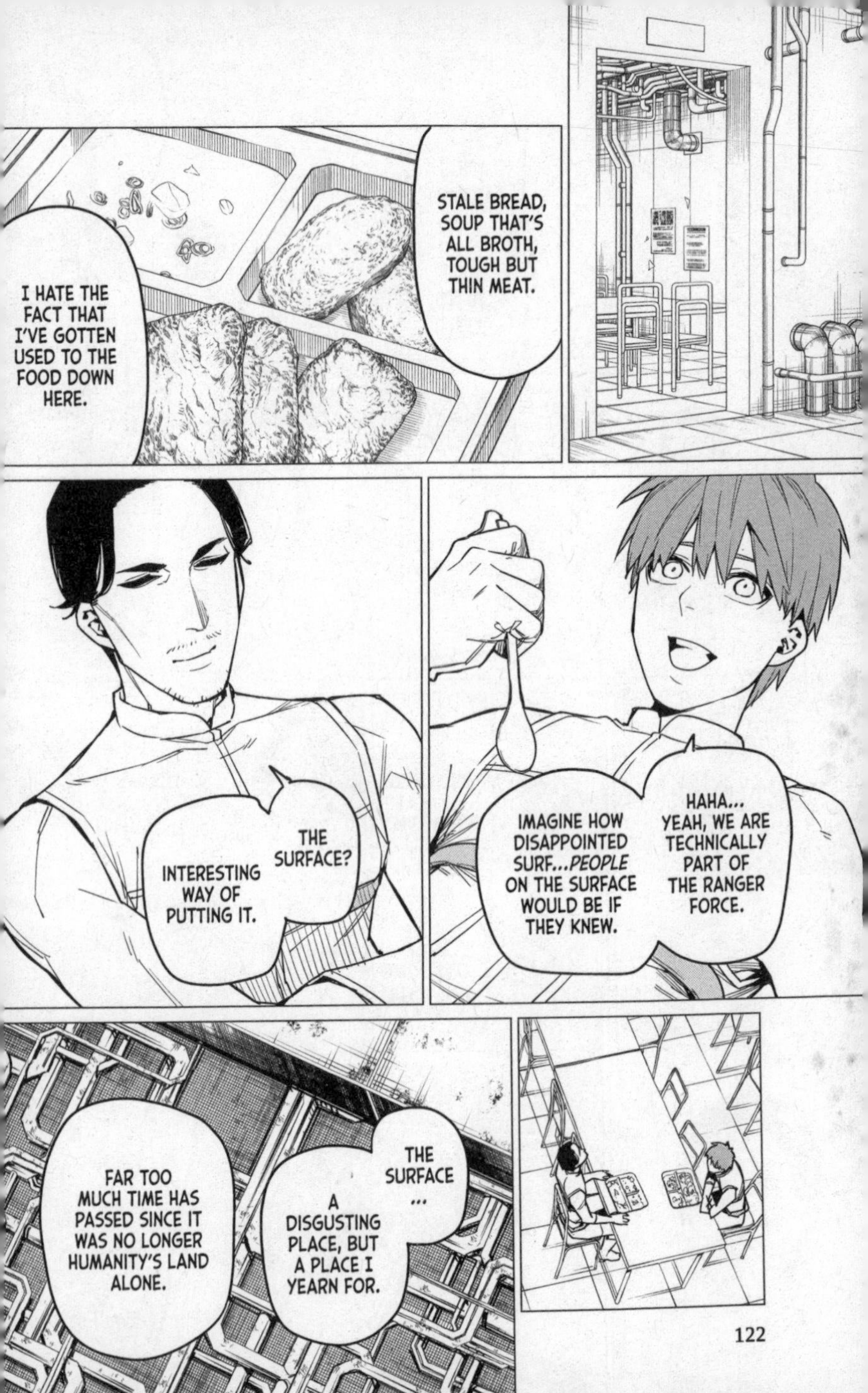

STALE BREAD, SOUP THAT'S ALL BROTH, TOUGH BUT THIN MEAT.
I HATE THE FACT THAT I'VE GOTTEN USED TO THE FOOD DOWN HERE.
HAHA... YEAH, WE ARE TECHNICALLY PART OF THE RANGER FORCE.
IMAGINE HOW DISAPPOINTED SURF...*PEOPLE* ON THE SURFACE WOULD BE IF THEY KNEW.
THE SURFACE?
INTERESTING WAY OF PUTTING IT.
THE SURFACE ...
A DISGUSTING PLACE, BUT A PLACE I YEARN FOR.
FAR TOO MUCH TIME HAS PASSED SINCE IT WAS NO LONGER HUMANITY'S LAND ALONE.

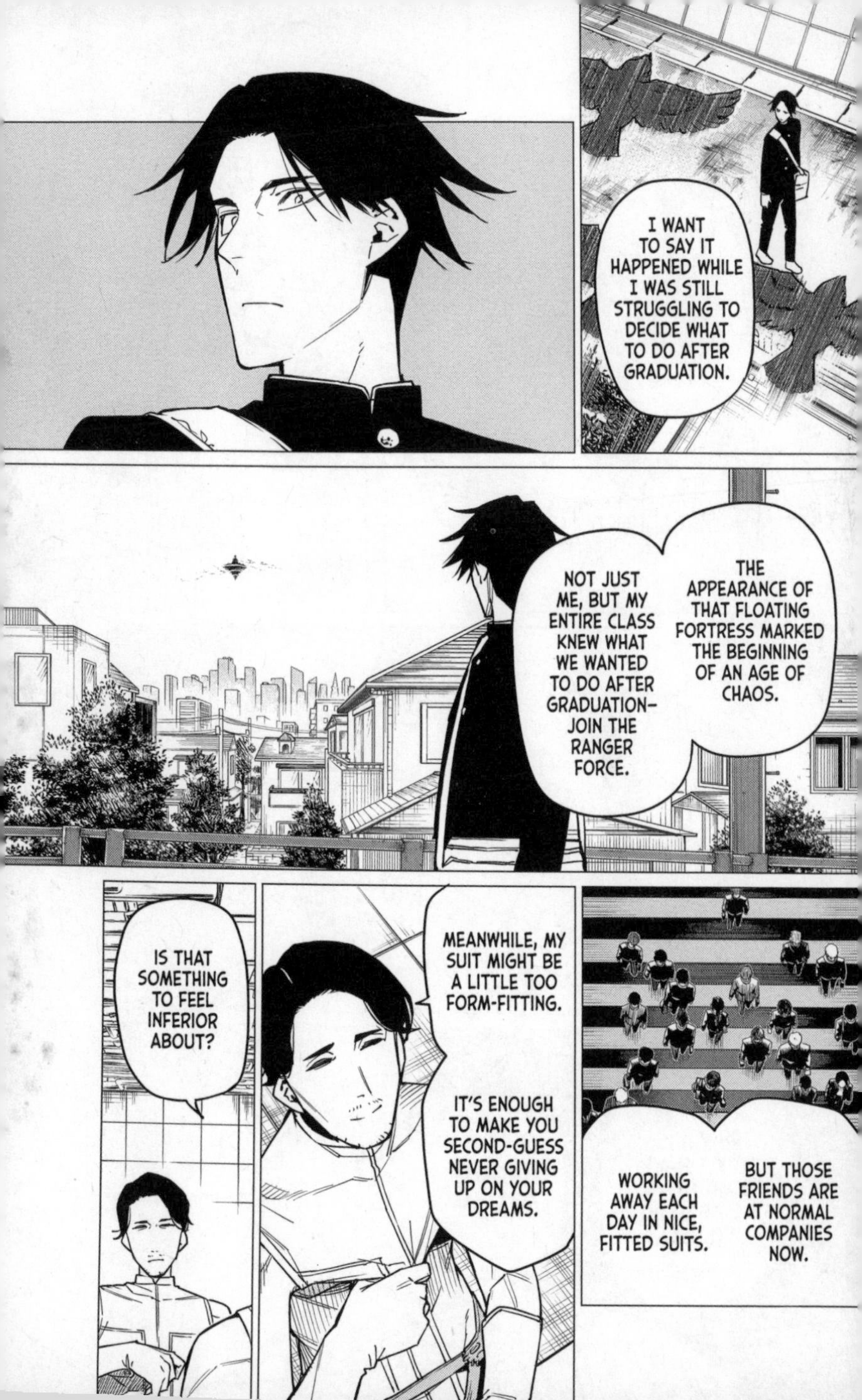
I WANT TO SAY IT HAPPENED WHILE I WAS STILL STRUGGLING TO DECIDE WHAT TO DO AFTER GRADUATION.
THE APPEARANCE OF THAT FLOATING FORTRESS MARKED THE BEGINNING OF AN AGE OF CHAOS.
NOT JUST ME, BUT MY ENTIRE CLASS KNEW WHAT WE WANTED TO DO AFTER GRADUATION– JOIN THE RANGER FORCE.
BUT THOSE FRIENDS ARE AT NORMAL COMPANIES NOW.
WORKING AWAY EACH DAY IN NICE, FITTED SUITS.
MEANWHILE, MY SUIT MIGHT BE A LITTLE TOO FORM-FITTING.
IT'S ENOUGH TO MAKE YOU SECOND-GUESS NEVER GIVING UP ON YOUR DREAMS.
IS THAT SOMETHING TO FEEL INFERIOR ABOUT?

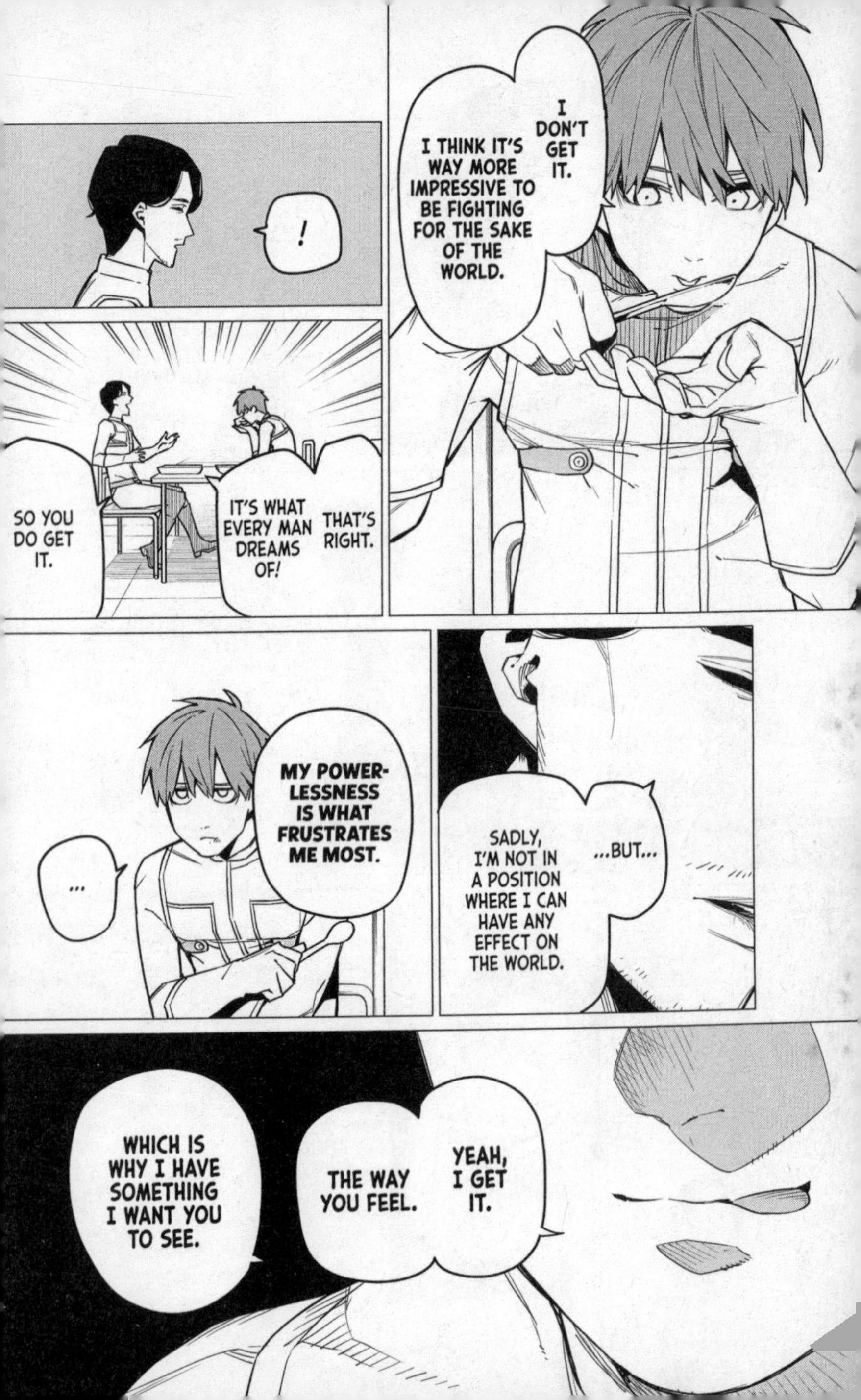
I DON'T GET IT.
I THINK IT'S WAY MORE IMPRESSIVE TO BE FIGHTING FOR THE SAKE OF THE WORLD.
!
THAT'S RIGHT.
IT'S WHAT EVERY MAN DREAMS OF!
SO YOU DO GET IT.
...BUT...
SADLY, I'M NOT IN A POSITION WHERE I CAN HAVE ANY EFFECT ON THE WORLD.
MY POWER-LESSNESS IS WHAT FRUSTRATES ME MOST.
...
YEAH, I GET IT.
THE WAY YOU FEEL.
WHICH IS WHY I HAVE SOMETHING I WANT YOU TO SEE.

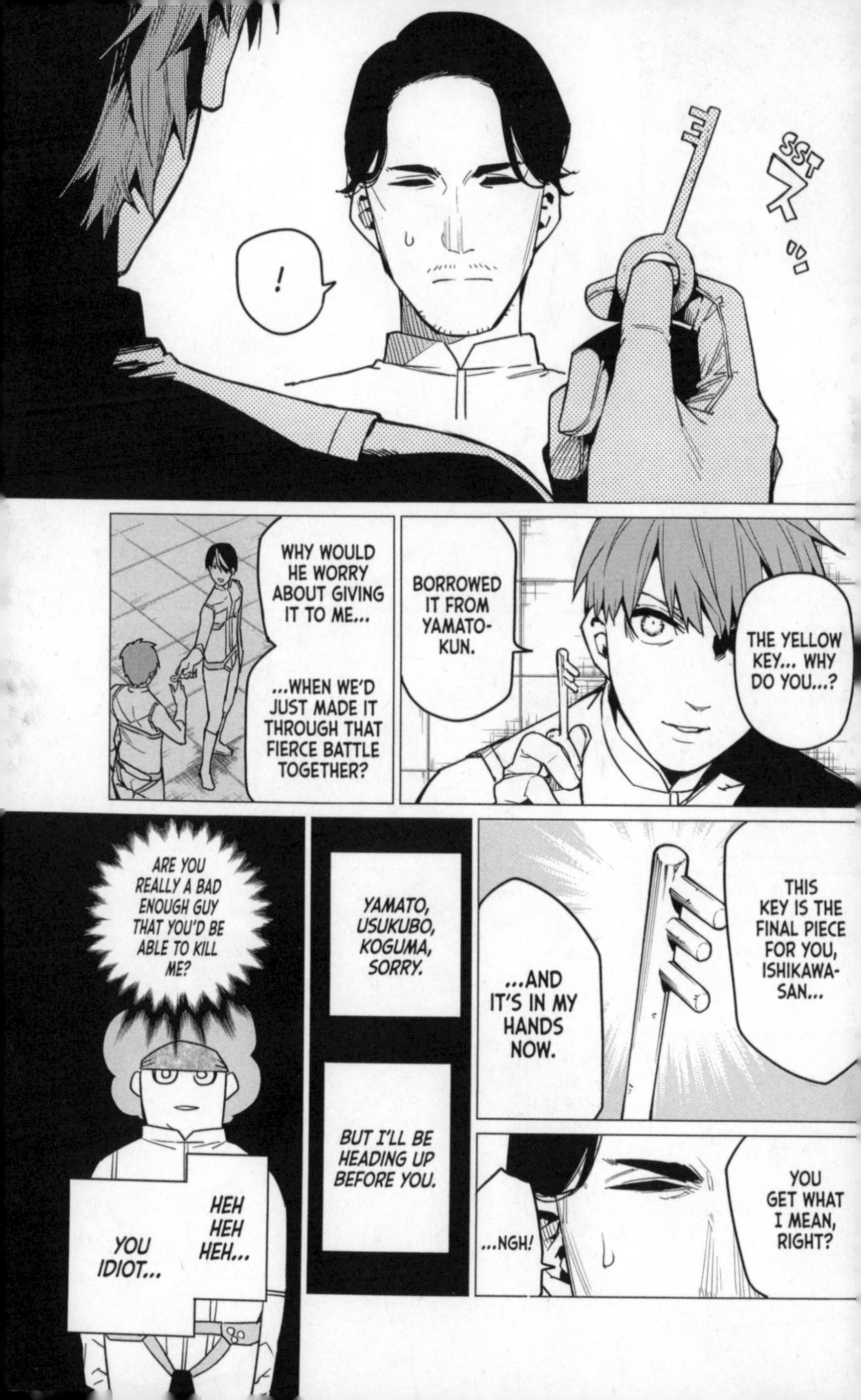
SST
!
THE YELLOW KEY... WHY DO YOU...?
BORROWED IT FROM YAMATO-KUN.
WHY WOULD HE WORRY ABOUT GIVING IT TO ME...
...WHEN WE'D JUST MADE IT THROUGH THAT FIERCE BATTLE TOGETHER?
THIS KEY IS THE FINAL PIECE FOR YOU, ISHIKAWA-SAN...
...AND IT'S IN MY HANDS NOW.
YOU GET WHAT I MEAN, RIGHT?
...NGH!
YAMATO, USUKUBO, KOGUMA, SORRY.
BUT I'LL BE HEADING UP BEFORE YOU.
ARE YOU REALLY A BAD ENOUGH GUY THAT YOU'D BE ABLE TO KILL ME?
HEH HEH HEH...
YOU IDIOT...

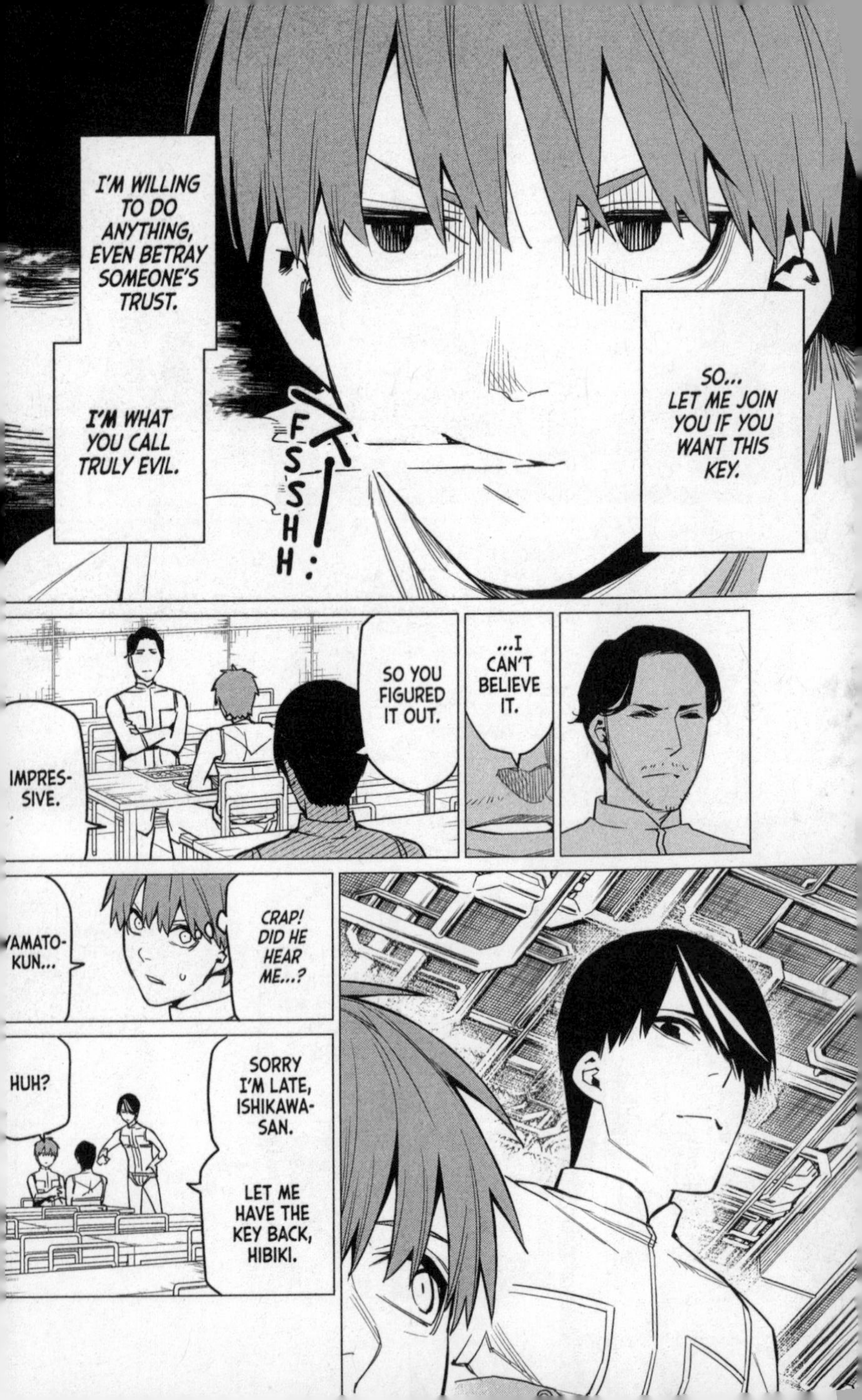
I'M WILLING TO DO ANYTHING, EVEN BETRAY SOMEONE'S TRUST.
I'M WHAT YOU CALL TRULY EVIL.
FSSHH
SO... LET ME JOIN YOU IF YOU WANT THIS KEY.
...I CAN'T BELIEVE IT.
SO YOU FIGURED IT OUT.
IMPRESSIVE.
CRAP! DID HE HEAR ME...?
YAMATO-KUN...
SORRY I'M LATE, ISHIKAWA-SAN.
LET ME HAVE THE KEY BACK, HIBIKI.
HUH?

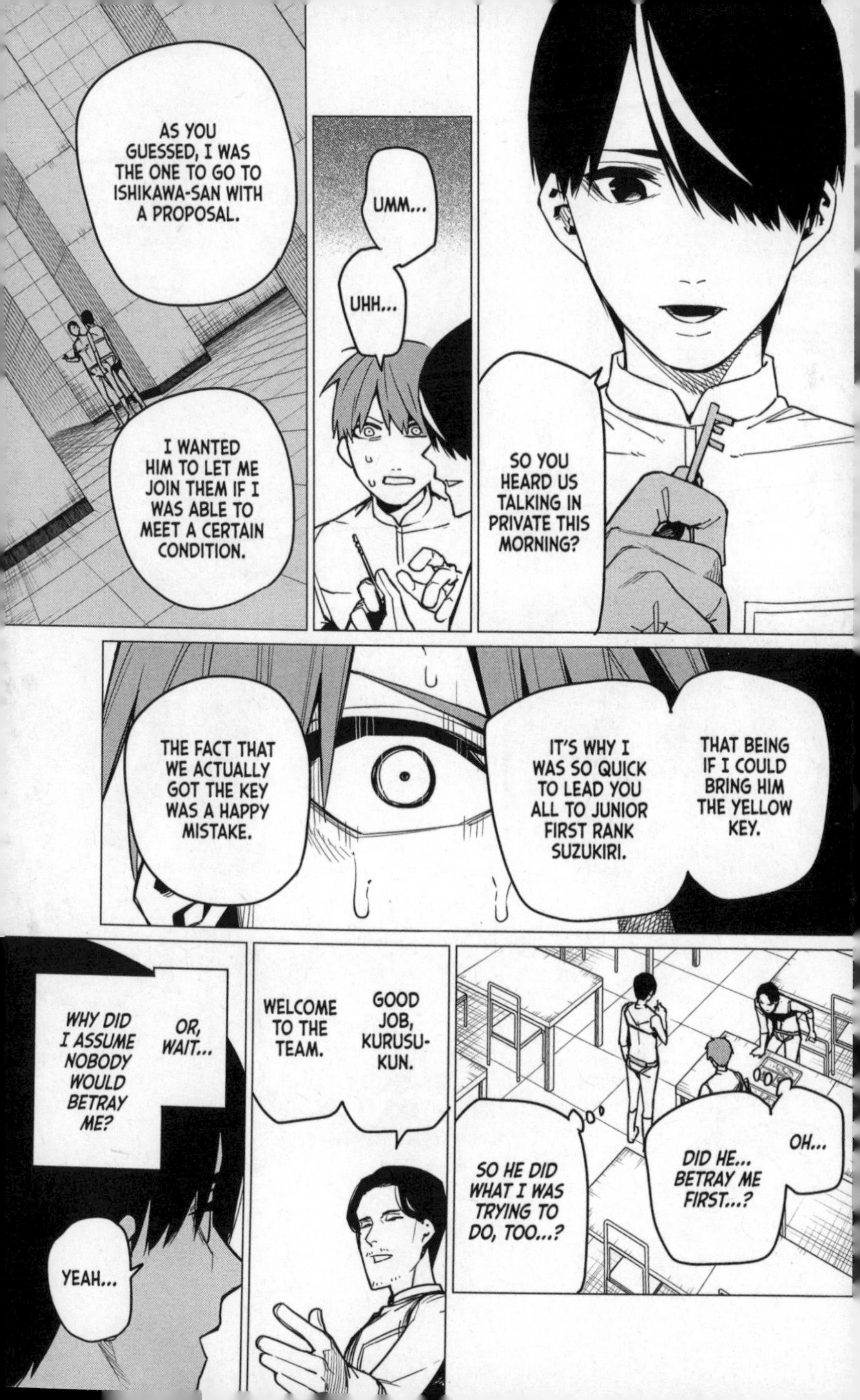
SO YOU HEARD US TALKING IN PRIVATE THIS MORNING?
UMM...
UHH...
AS YOU GUESSED, I WAS THE ONE TO GO TO ISHIKAWA-SAN WITH A PROPOSAL.
I WANTED HIM TO LET ME JOIN THEM IF I WAS ABLE TO MEET A CERTAIN CONDITION.
THAT BEING IF I COULD BRING HIM THE YELLOW KEY.
IT'S WHY I WAS SO QUICK TO LEAD YOU ALL TO JUNIOR FIRST RANK SUZUKIRI.
THE FACT THAT WE ACTUALLY GOT THE KEY WAS A HAPPY MISTAKE.
OH...
DID HE... BETRAY ME FIRST...?
SO HE DID WHAT I WAS TRYING TO DO, TOO...?
GOOD JOB, KURUSU-KUN.
WELCOME TO THE TEAM.
OR, WAIT...
WHY DID I ASSUME NOBODY WOULD BETRAY ME?
YEAH...

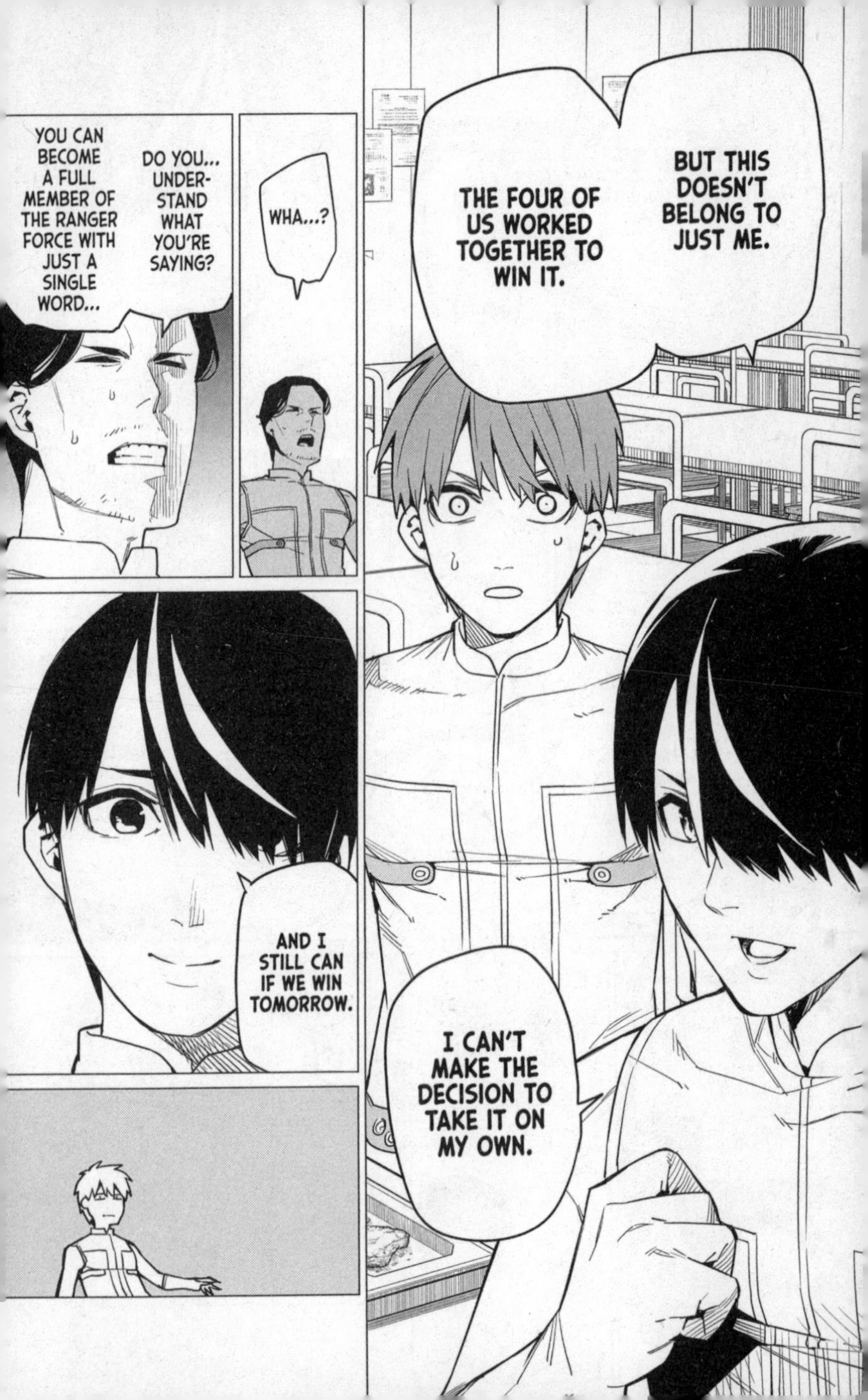
BUT THIS DOESN'T BELONG TO JUST ME.
THE FOUR OF US WORKED TOGETHER TO WIN IT.
I CAN'T MAKE THE DECISION TO TAKE IT ON MY OWN.
WHA...?
DO YOU... UNDER-STAND WHAT YOU'RE SAYING?
YOU CAN BECOME A FULL MEMBER OF THE RANGER FORCE WITH JUST A SINGLE WORD...
AND I STILL CAN IF WE WIN TOMORROW.

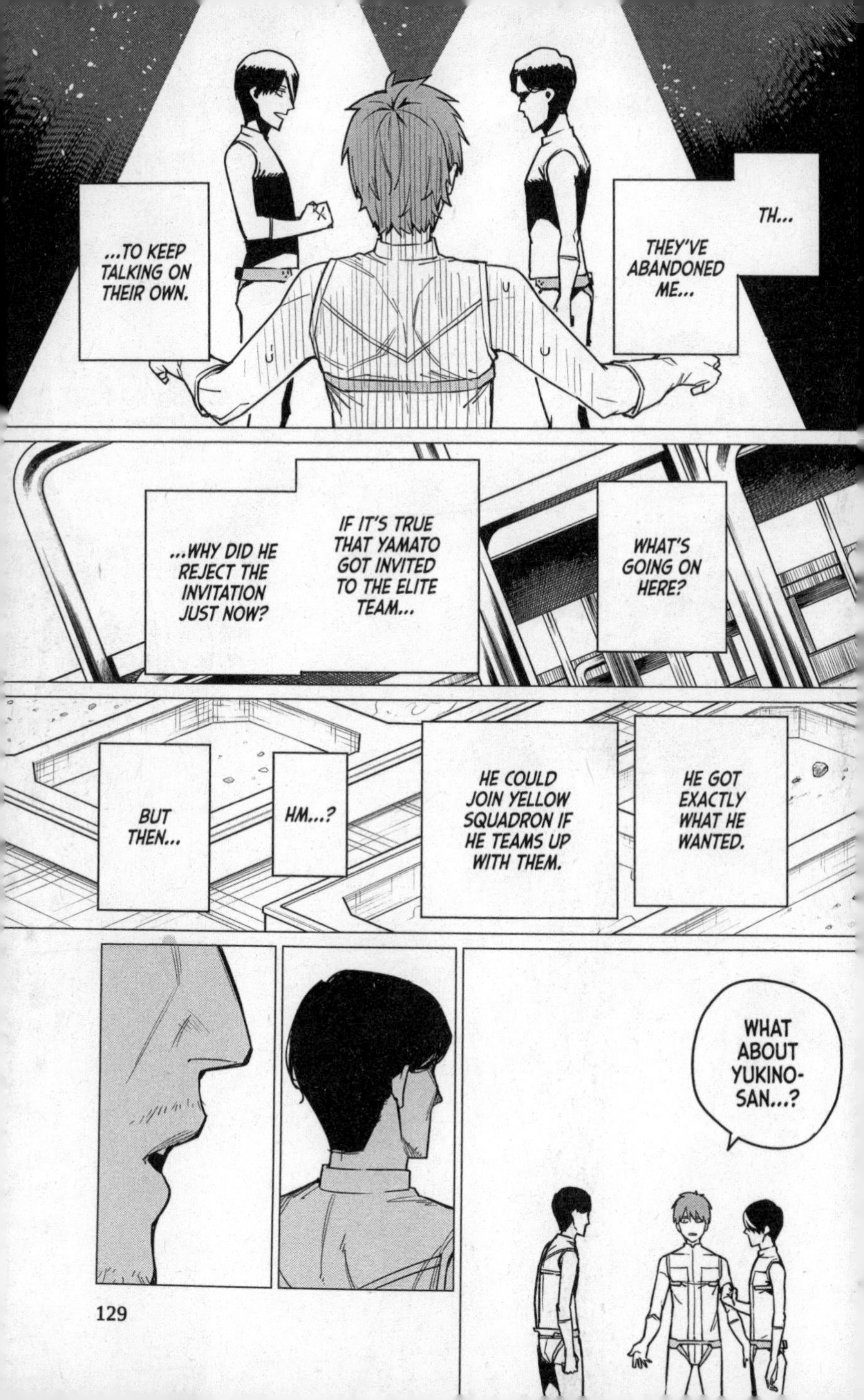
TH...
THEY'VE ABANDONED ME...
...TO KEEP TALKING ON THEIR OWN.
WHAT'S GOING ON HERE?
IF IT'S TRUE THAT YAMATO GOT INVITED TO THE ELITE TEAM...
...WHY DID HE REJECT THE INVITATION JUST NOW?
HE GOT EXACTLY WHAT HE WANTED.
HE COULD JOIN YELLOW SQUADRON IF HE TEAMS UP WITH THEM.
HM...?
BUT THEN...
WHAT ABOUT YUKINO-SAN...?

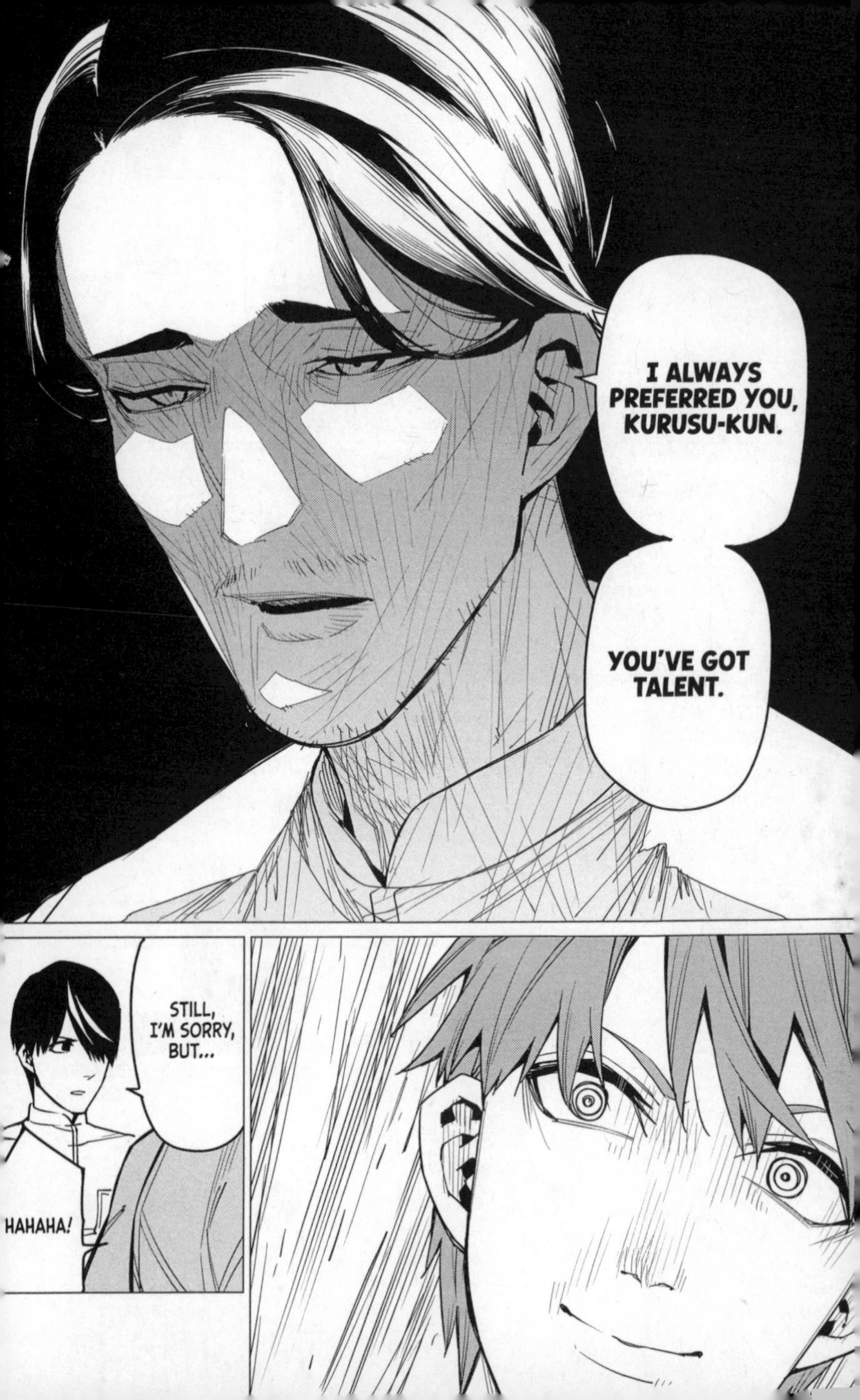
I ALWAYS PREFERRED YOU, KURUSU-KUN.
YOU'VE GOT TALENT.
STILL, I'M SORRY, BUT...
HAHAHA!

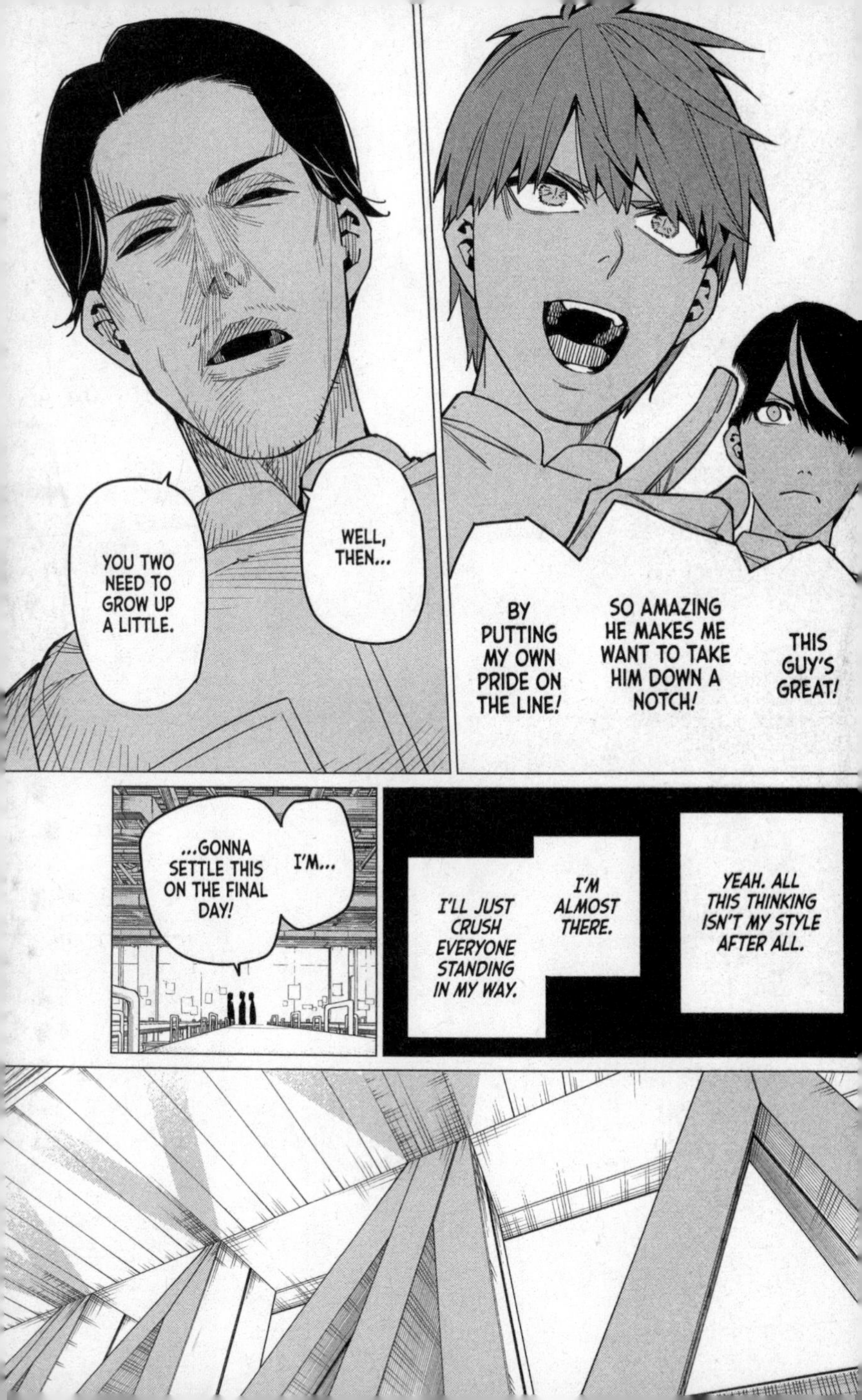
THIS GUY'S GREAT!
SO AMAZING HE MAKES ME WANT TO TAKE HIM DOWN A NOTCH!
BY PUTTING MY OWN PRIDE ON THE LINE!
WELL, THEN...
YOU TWO NEED TO GROW UP A LITTLE.
YEAH. ALL THIS THINKING ISN'T MY STYLE AFTER ALL.
I'M ALMOST THERE.
I'LL JUST CRUSH EVERYONE STANDING IN MY WAY.
I'M...
...GONNA SETTLE THIS ON THE FINAL DAY!

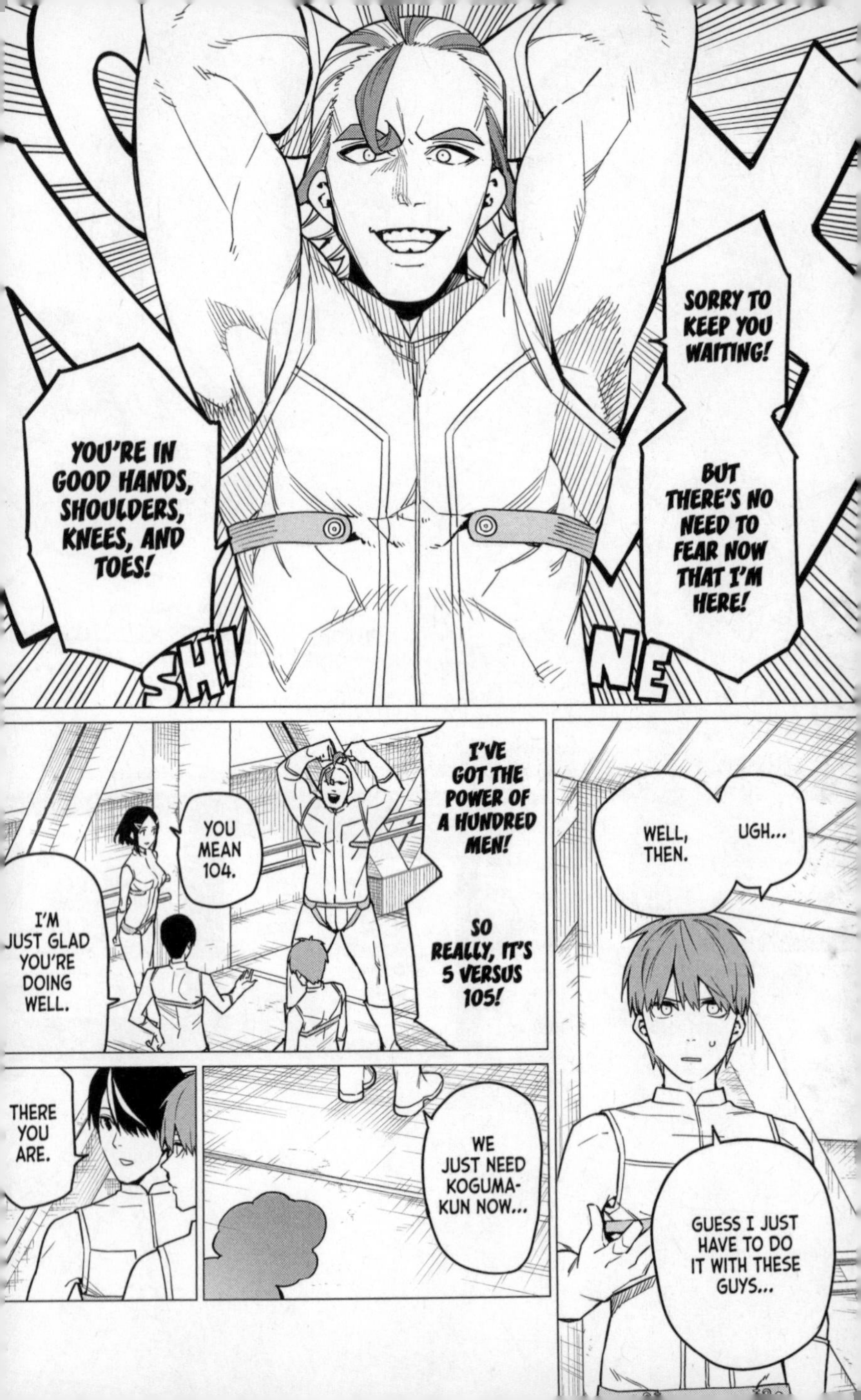
SORRY TO KEEP YOU WAITING!
BUT THERE'S NO NEED TO FEAR NOW THAT I'M HERE!
YOU'RE IN GOOD HANDS, SHOULDERS, KNEES, AND TOES!
SHI
NE
UGH...
WELL, THEN.
GUESS I JUST HAVE TO DO IT WITH THESE GUYS...
I'VE GOT THE POWER OF A HUNDRED MEN!
SO REALLY, IT'S 5 VERSUS 105!
YOU MEAN 104.
I'M JUST GLAD YOU'RE DOING WELL.
WE JUST NEED KOGUMA-KUN NOW...
THERE YOU ARE.

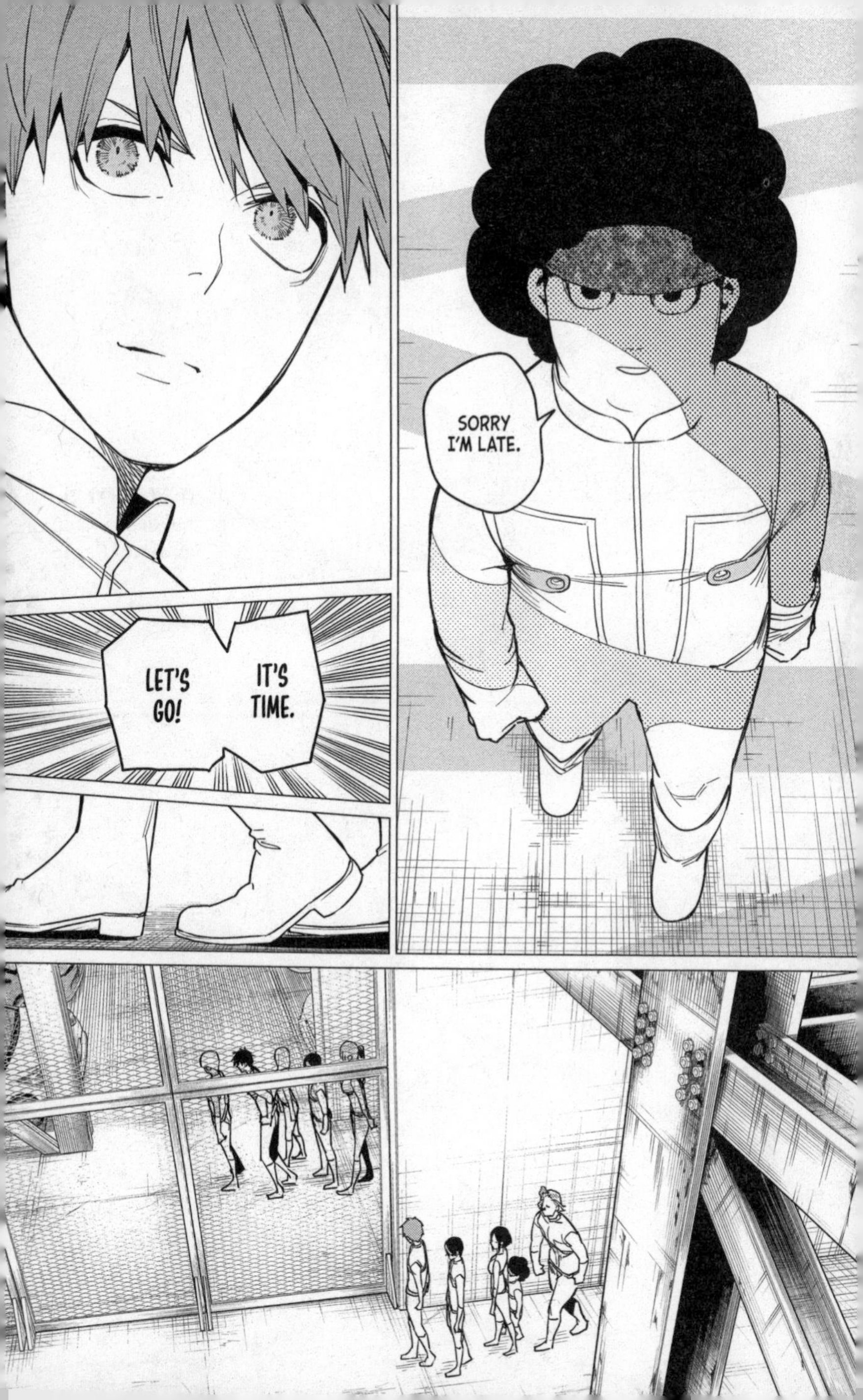
SORRY I'M LATE.
IT'S TIME.
LET'S GO!

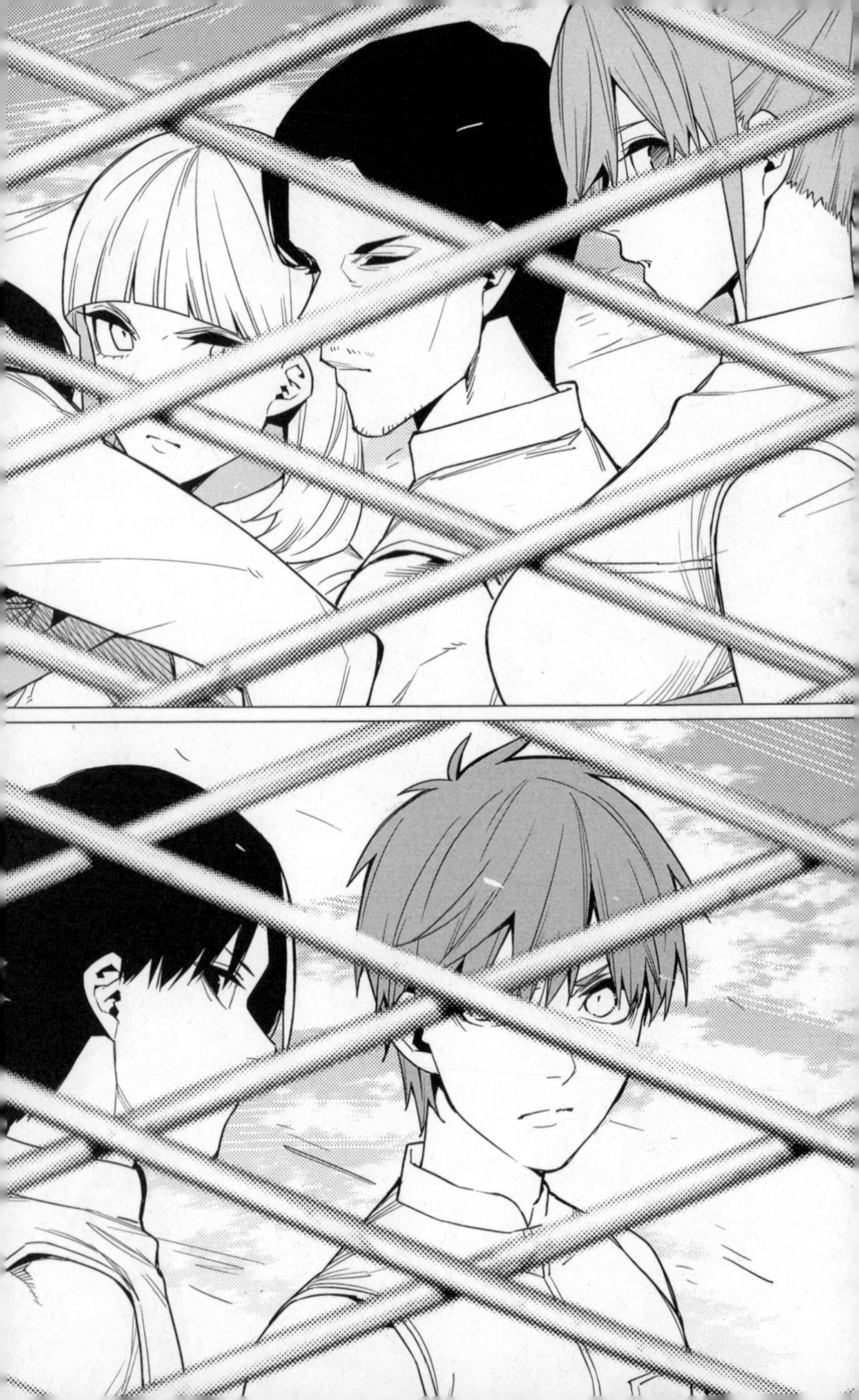

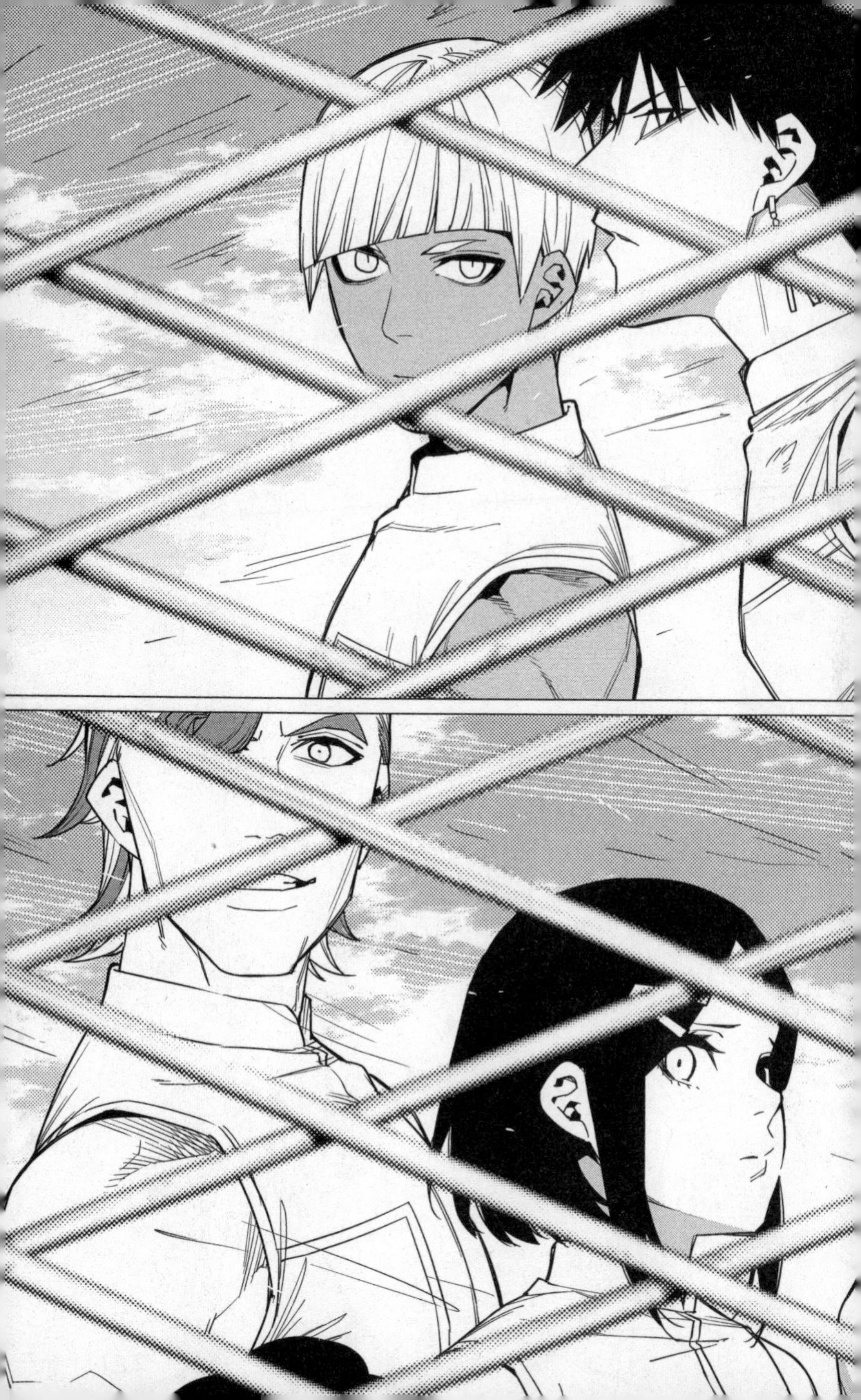

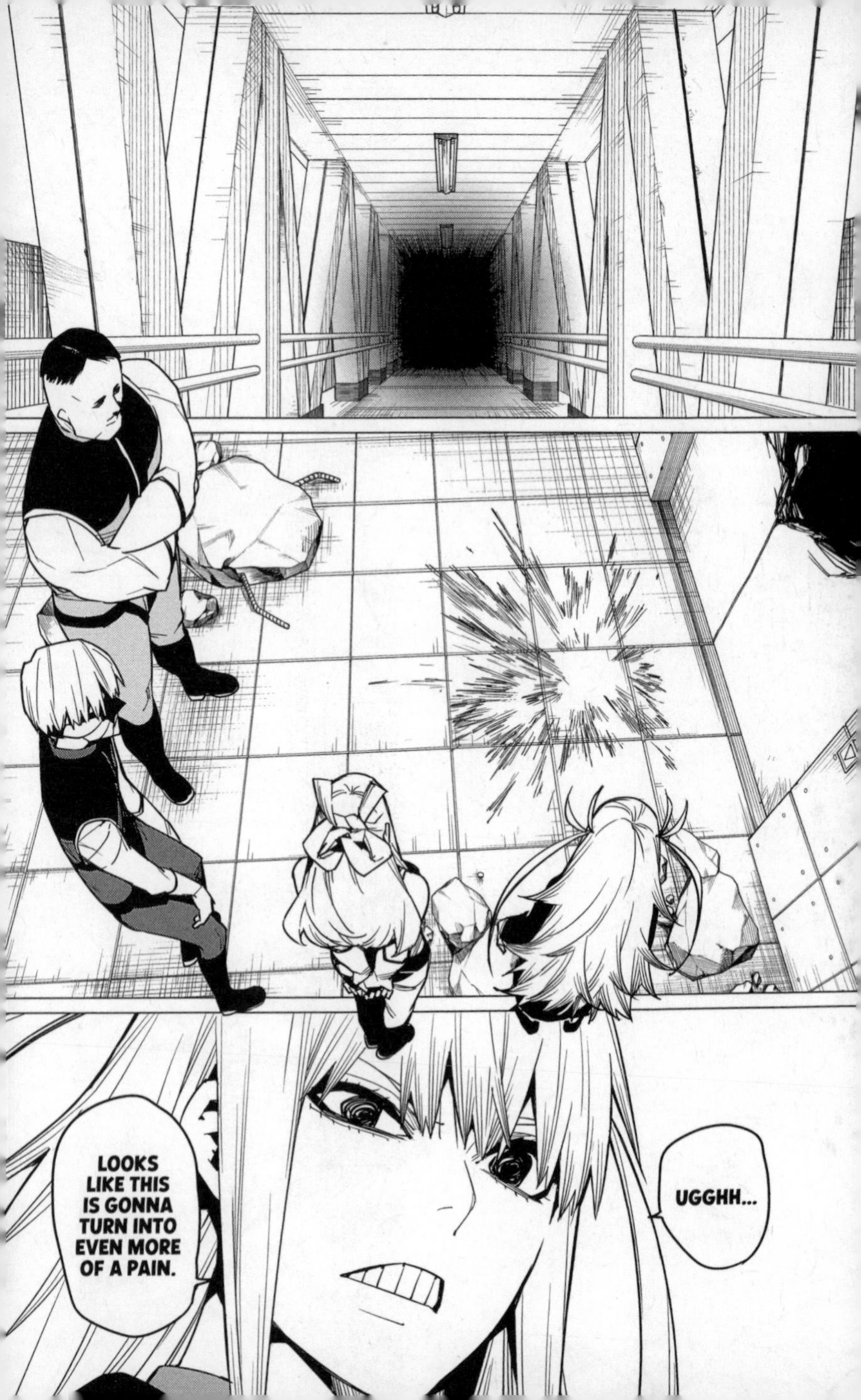
UGGHH...
LOOKS LIKE THIS IS GONNA TURN INTO EVEN MORE OF A PAIN.

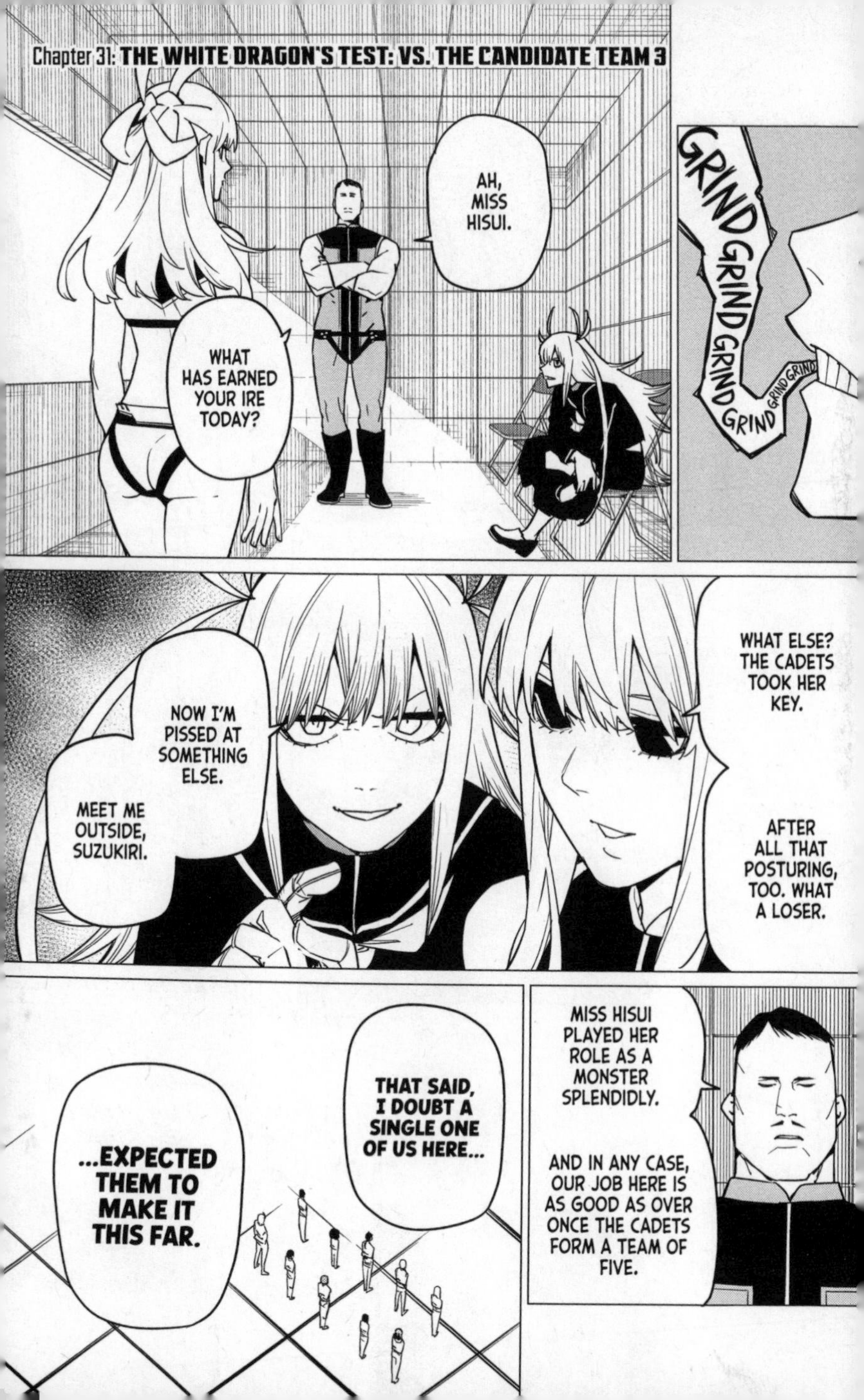
Chapter 31: THE WHITE DRAGON'S TEST: VS. THE CANDIDATE TEAM 3
GRIND GRIND GRIND GRIND GRIND GRIND
AH, MISS HISUI.
WHAT HAS EARNED YOUR IRE TODAY?
WHAT ELSE? THE CADETS TOOK HER KEY.
AFTER ALL THAT POSTURING, TOO. WHAT A LOSER.
NOW I'M PISSED AT SOMETHING ELSE.
MEET ME OUTSIDE, SUZUKIRI.
MISS HISUI PLAYED HER ROLE AS A MONSTER SPLENDIDLY.
AND IN ANY CASE, OUR JOB HERE IS AS GOOD AS OVER ONCE THE CADETS FORM A TEAM OF FIVE.
THAT SAID, I DOUBT A SINGLE ONE OF US HERE...
...EXPECTED THEM TO MAKE IT THIS FAR.

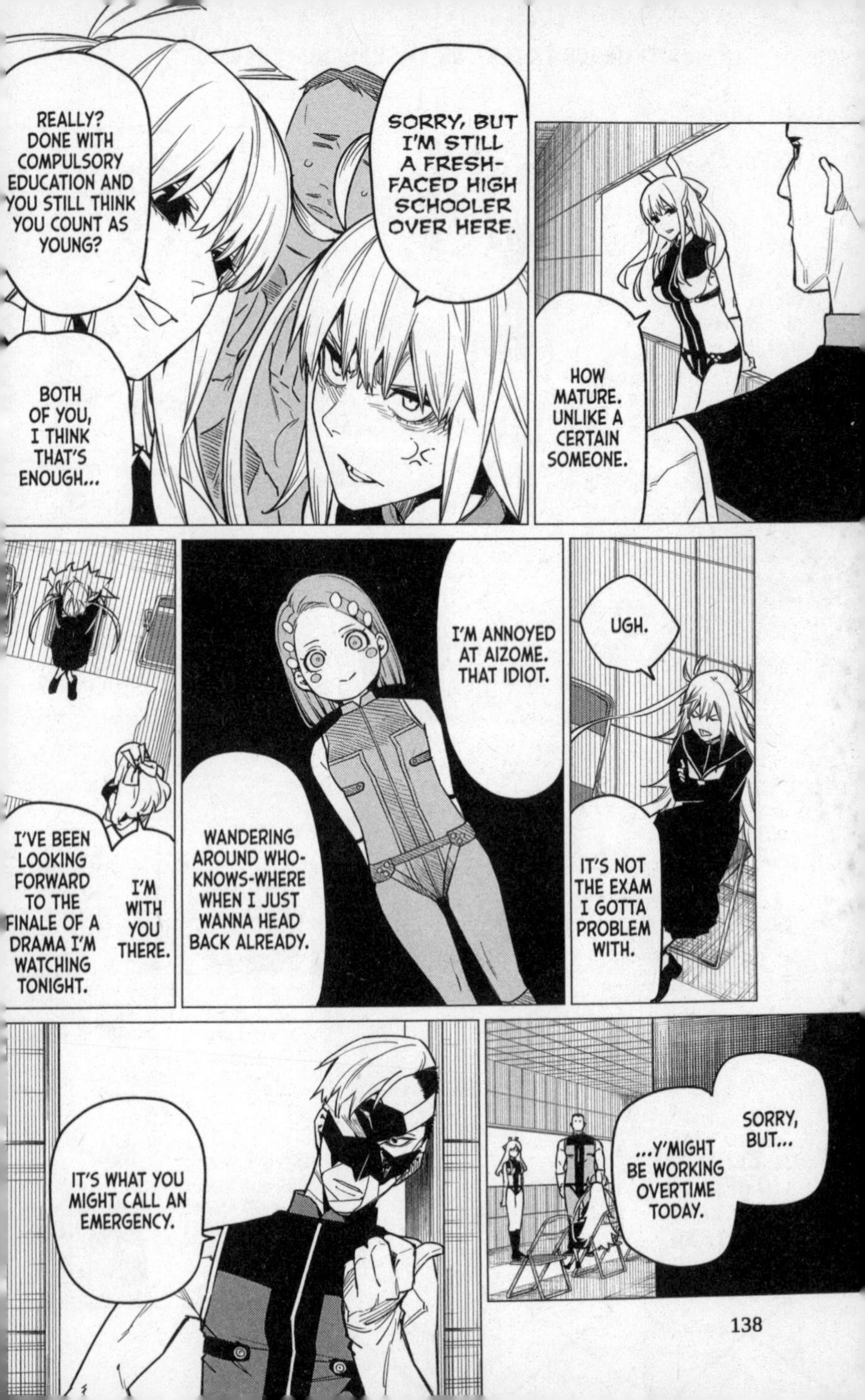
HOW MATURE. UNLIKE A CERTAIN SOMEONE.
SORRY, BUT I'M STILL A FRESH-FACED HIGH SCHOOLER OVER HERE.
REALLY? DONE WITH COMPULSORY EDUCATION AND YOU STILL THINK YOU COUNT AS YOUNG?
BOTH OF YOU, I THINK THAT'S ENOUGH...
UGH.
IT'S NOT THE EXAM I GOTTA PROBLEM WITH.
I'M ANNOYED AT AIZOME. THAT IDIOT.
WANDERING AROUND WHO-KNOWS-WHERE WHEN I JUST WANNA HEAD BACK ALREADY.
I'M WITH YOU THERE.
I'VE BEEN LOOKING FORWARD TO THE FINALE OF A DRAMA I'M WATCHING TONIGHT.
SORRY, BUT...
...Y'MIGHT BE WORKING OVERTIME TODAY.
IT'S WHAT YOU MIGHT CALL AN EMERGENCY.

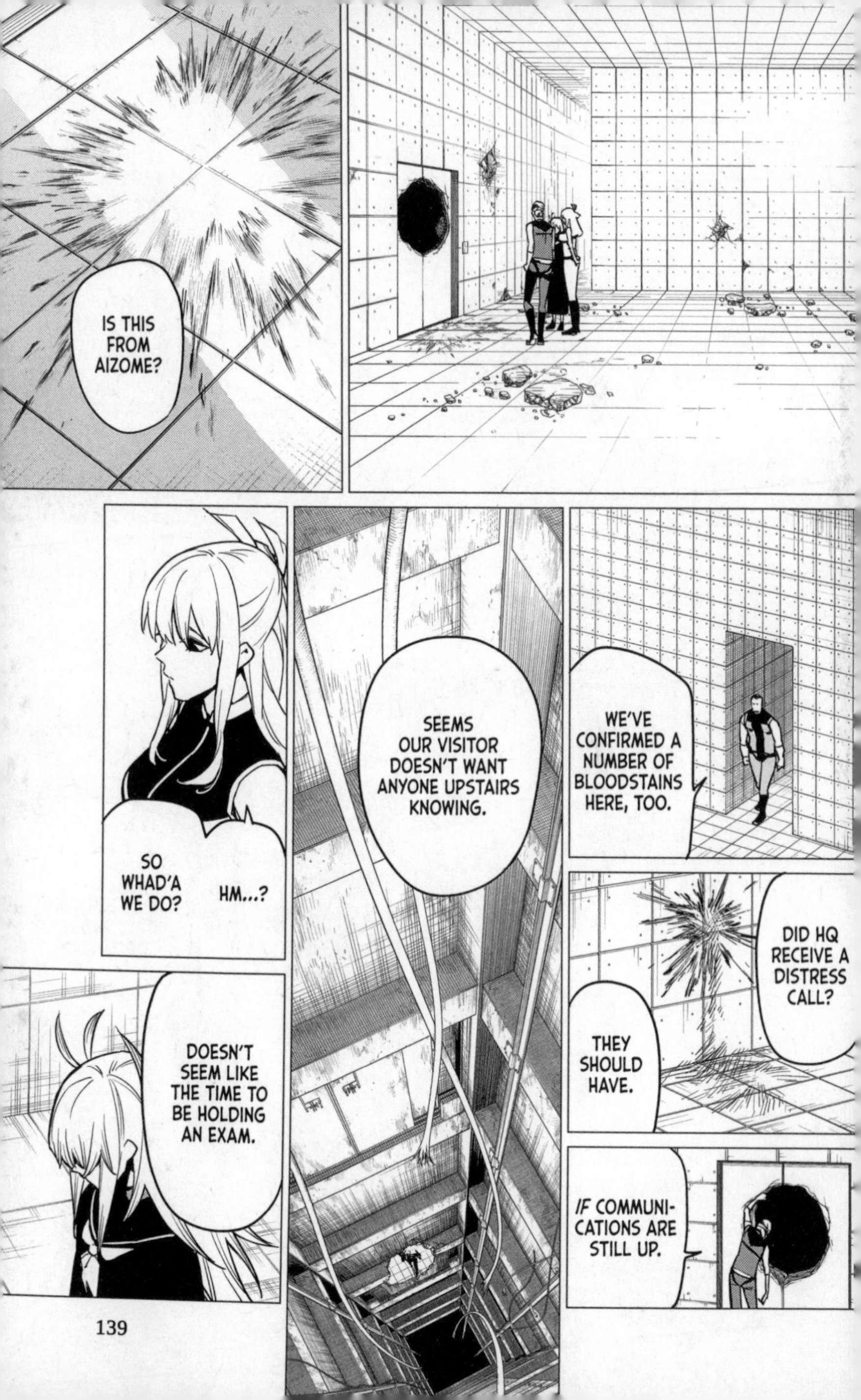
IS THIS FROM AIZOME?
WE'VE CONFIRMED A NUMBER OF BLOODSTAINS HERE, TOO.
DID HQ RECEIVE A DISTRESS CALL?
THEY SHOULD HAVE.
IF COMMUNICATIONS ARE STILL UP.
SEEMS OUR VISITOR DOESN'T WANT ANYONE UPSTAIRS KNOWING.
HM...?
SO WHAD'A WE DO?
DOESN'T SEEM LIKE THE TIME TO BE HOLDING AN EXAM.

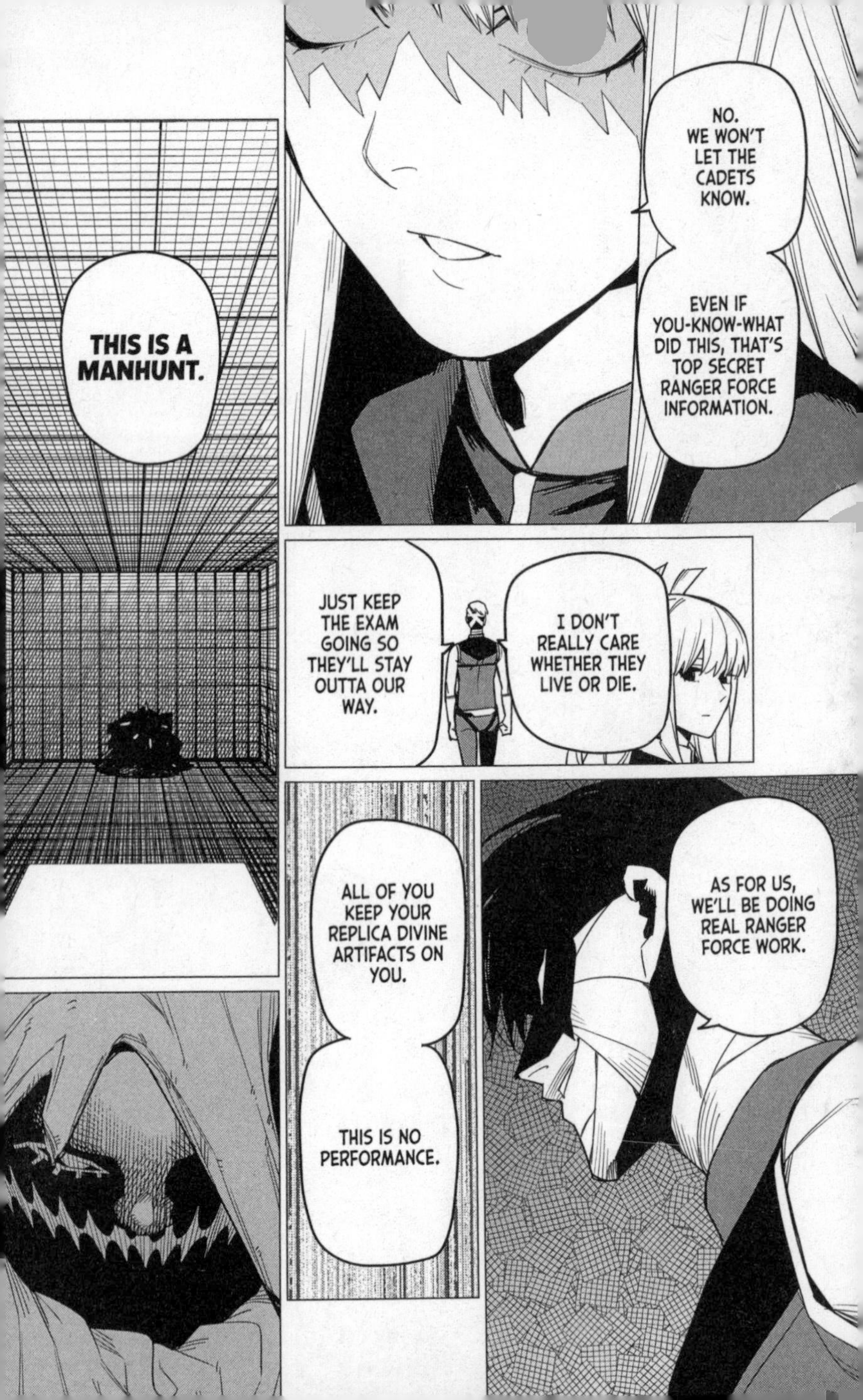
NO. WE WON'T LET THE CADETS KNOW.
EVEN IF YOU-KNOW-WHAT DID THIS, THAT'S TOP SECRET RANGER FORCE INFORMATION.
I DON'T REALLY CARE WHETHER THEY LIVE OR DIE.
JUST KEEP THE EXAM GOING SO THEY'LL STAY OUTTA OUR WAY.
THIS IS A MANHUNT.
AS FOR US, WE'LL BE DOING REAL RANGER FORCE WORK.
ALL OF YOU KEEP YOUR REPLICA DIVINE ARTIFACTS ON YOU.
THIS IS NO PERFORMANCE.

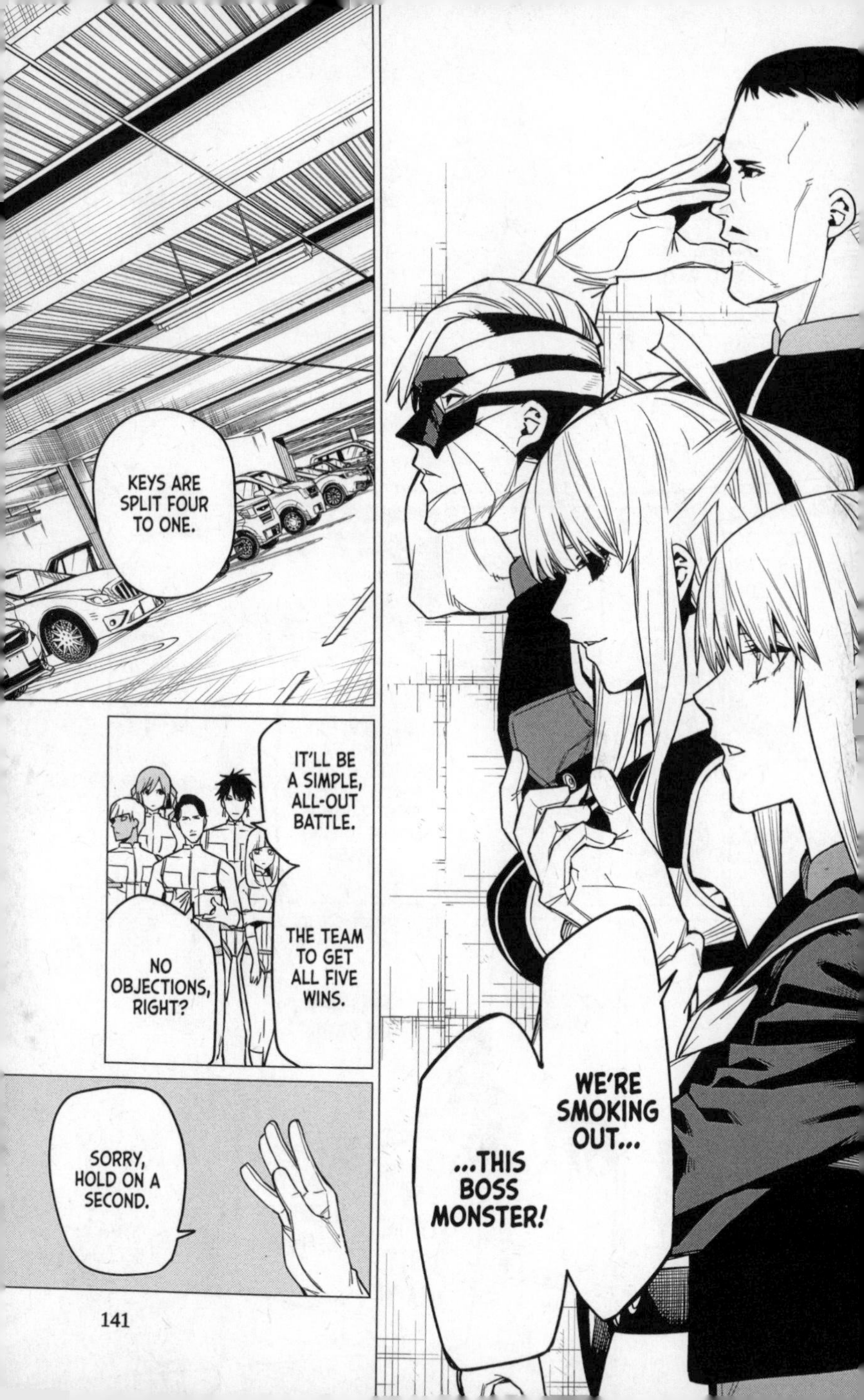
WE'RE SMOKING OUT...
...THIS BOSS MONSTER!
KEYS ARE SPLIT FOUR TO ONE.
IT'LL BE A SIMPLE, ALL-OUT BATTLE.
THE TEAM TO GET ALL FIVE WINS.
NO OBJECTIONS, RIGHT?
SORRY, HOLD ON A SECOND.

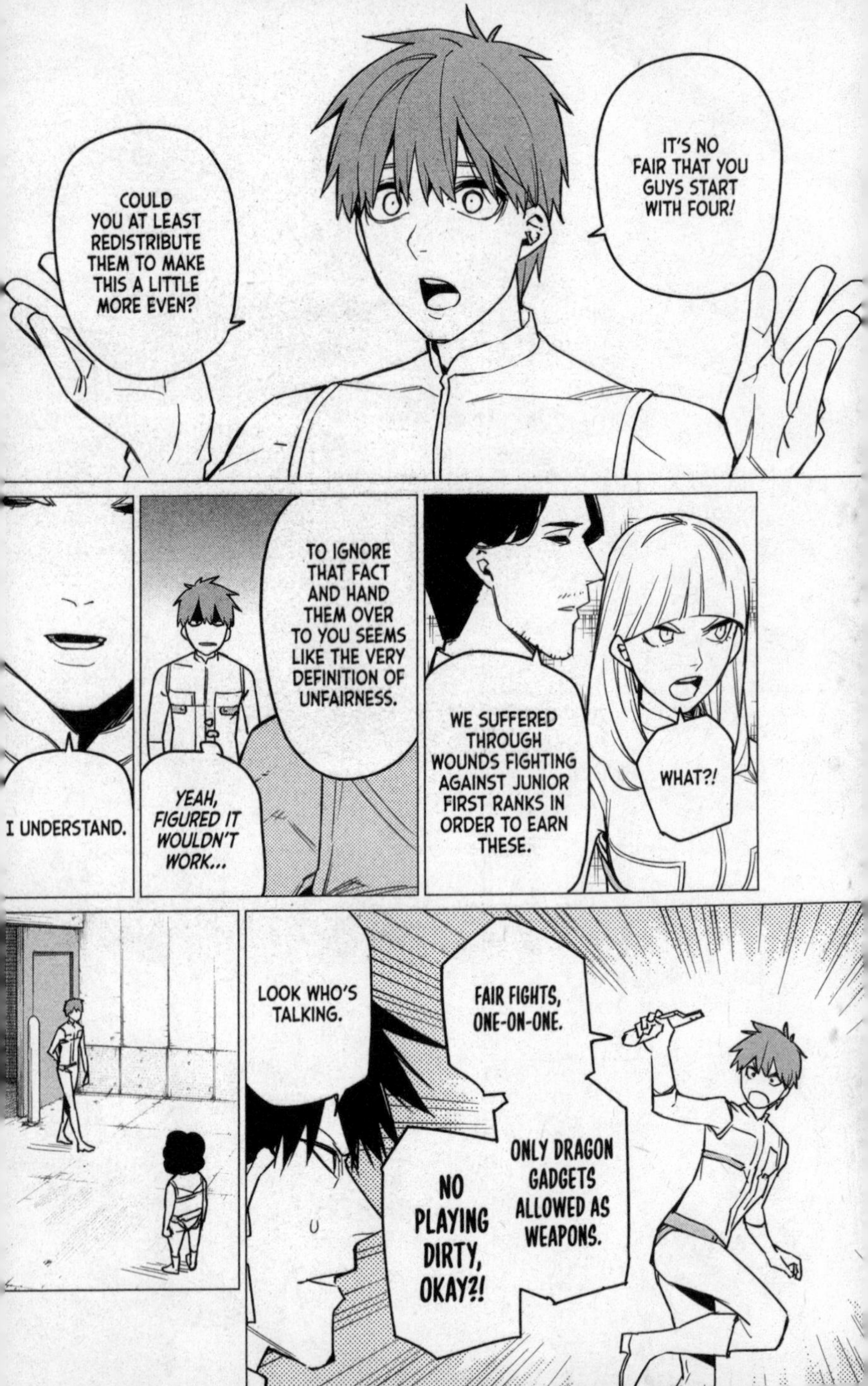
IT'S NO FAIR THAT YOU GUYS START WITH FOUR!
COULD YOU AT LEAST REDISTRIBUTE THEM TO MAKE THIS A LITTLE MORE EVEN?
WHAT?!
WE SUFFERED THROUGH WOUNDS FIGHTING AGAINST JUNIOR FIRST RANKS IN ORDER TO EARN THESE.
TO IGNORE THAT FACT AND HAND THEM OVER TO YOU SEEMS LIKE THE VERY DEFINITION OF UNFAIRNESS.
YEAH, FIGURED IT WOULDN'T WORK...
I UNDERSTAND.
FAIR FIGHTS, ONE-ON-ONE.
ONLY DRAGON GADGETS ALLOWED AS WEAPONS.
NO PLAYING DIRTY, OKAY?!
LOOK WHO'S TALKING.

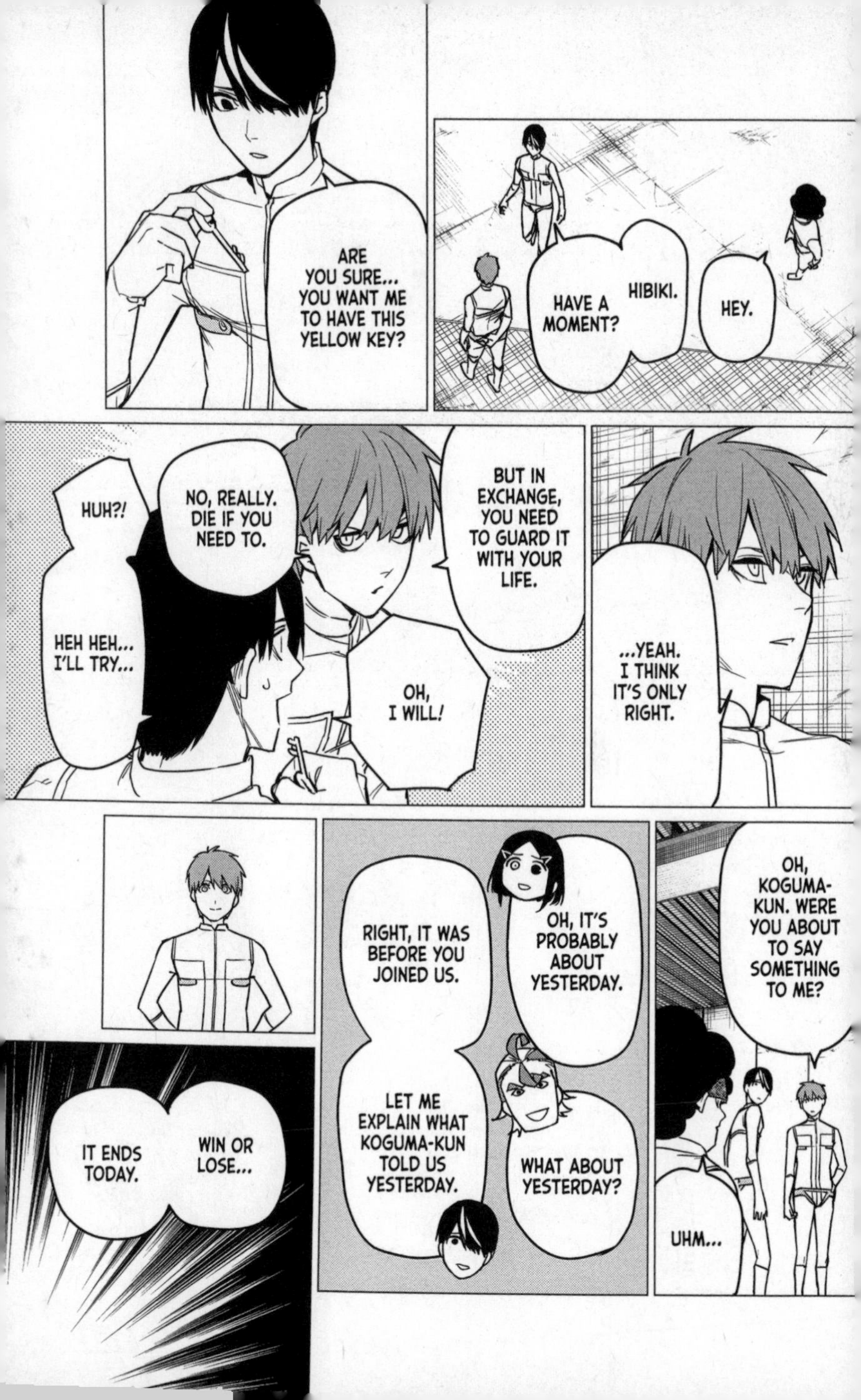
HEY.
HIBIKI.
HAVE A MOMENT?
ARE YOU SURE... YOU WANT ME TO HAVE THIS YELLOW KEY?
...YEAH. I THINK IT'S ONLY RIGHT.
BUT IN EXCHANGE, YOU NEED TO GUARD IT WITH YOUR LIFE.
OH, I WILL!
NO, REALLY. DIE IF YOU NEED TO.
HUH?!
HEH HEH... I'LL TRY...
OH, KOGUMA-KUN. WERE YOU ABOUT TO SAY SOMETHING TO ME?
UHM...
OH, IT'S PROBABLY ABOUT YESTERDAY.
WHAT ABOUT YESTERDAY?
RIGHT, IT WAS BEFORE YOU JOINED US.
LET ME EXPLAIN WHAT KOGUMA-KUN TOLD US YESTERDAY.
WIN OR LOSE...
IT ENDS TODAY.

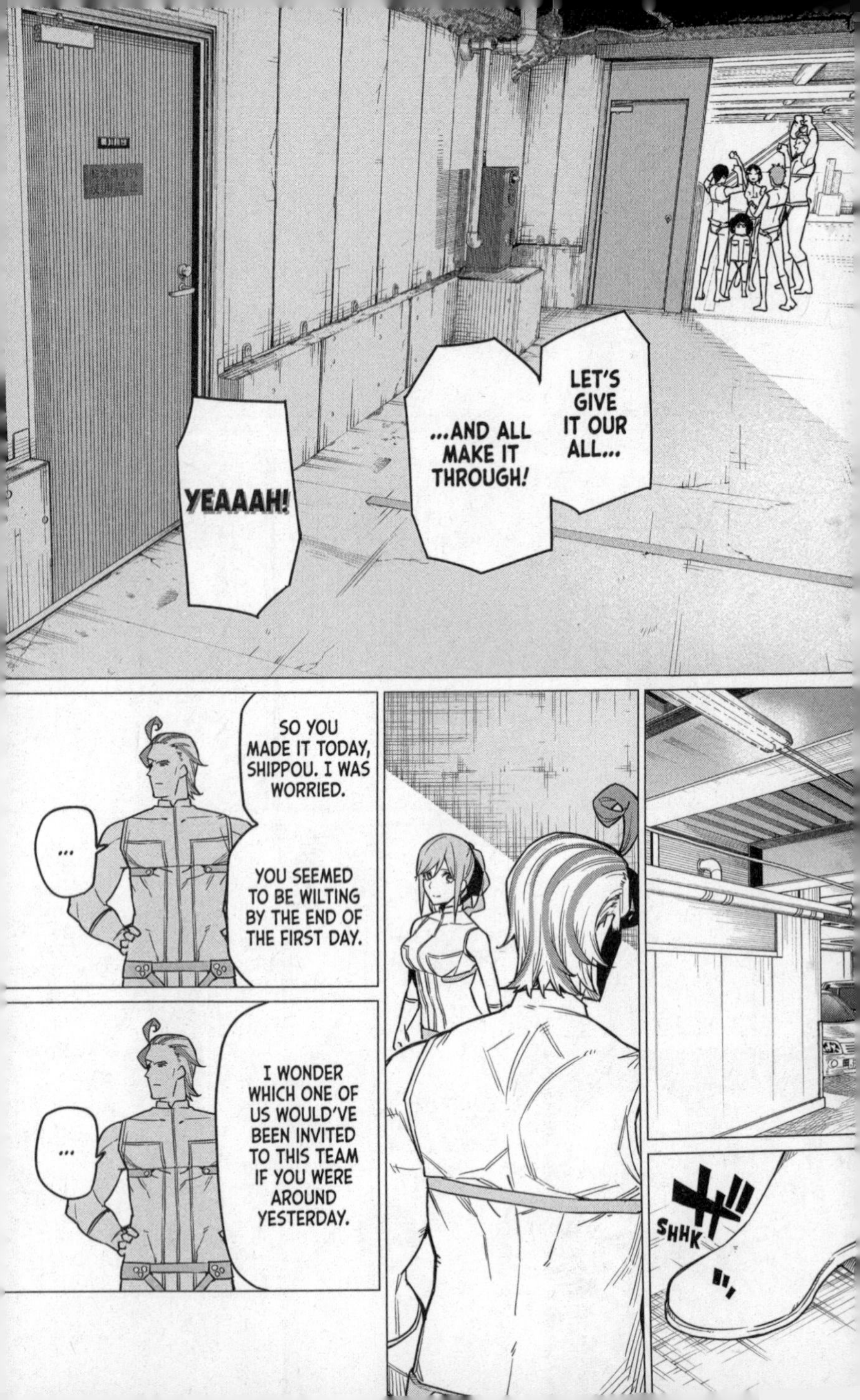

LET'S GIVE IT OUR ALL...
...AND ALL MAKE IT THROUGH!
YEAAAH!
SHHK
SO YOU MADE IT TODAY, SHIPPOU. I WAS WORRIED.
YOU SEEMED TO BE WILTING BY THE END OF THE FIRST DAY.
...
I WONDER WHICH ONE OF US WOULD'VE BEEN INVITED TO THIS TEAM IF YOU WERE AROUND YESTERDAY.
...

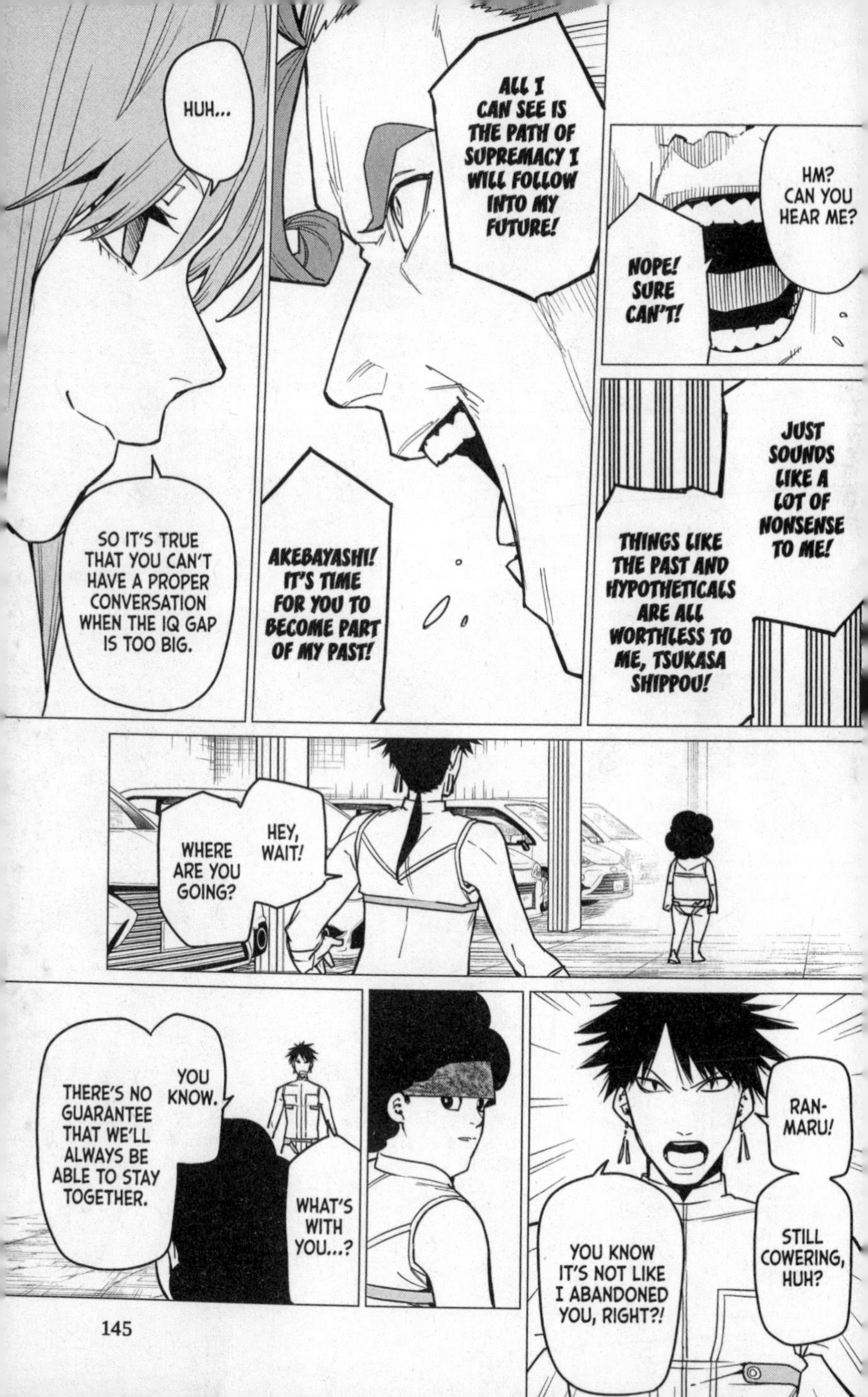
HM? CAN YOU HEAR ME?
NOPE! SURE CAN'T!
JUST SOUNDS LIKE A LOT OF NONSENSE TO ME!
THINGS LIKE THE PAST AND HYPOTHETICALS ARE ALL WORTHLESS TO ME, TSUKASA SHIPPOU!
ALL I CAN SEE IS THE PATH OF SUPREMACY I WILL FOLLOW INTO MY FUTURE!
AKEBAYASHI! IT'S TIME FOR YOU TO BECOME PART OF MY PAST!
HUH...
SO IT'S TRUE THAT YOU CAN'T HAVE A PROPER CONVERSATION WHEN THE IQ GAP IS TOO BIG.
HEY, WAIT!
WHERE ARE YOU GOING?
RAN-MARU!
STILL COWERING, HUH?
YOU KNOW IT'S NOT LIKE I ABANDONED YOU, RIGHT?!
YOU KNOW.
THERE'S NO GUARANTEE THAT WE'LL ALWAYS BE ABLE TO STAY TOGETHER.
WHAT'S WITH YOU...?

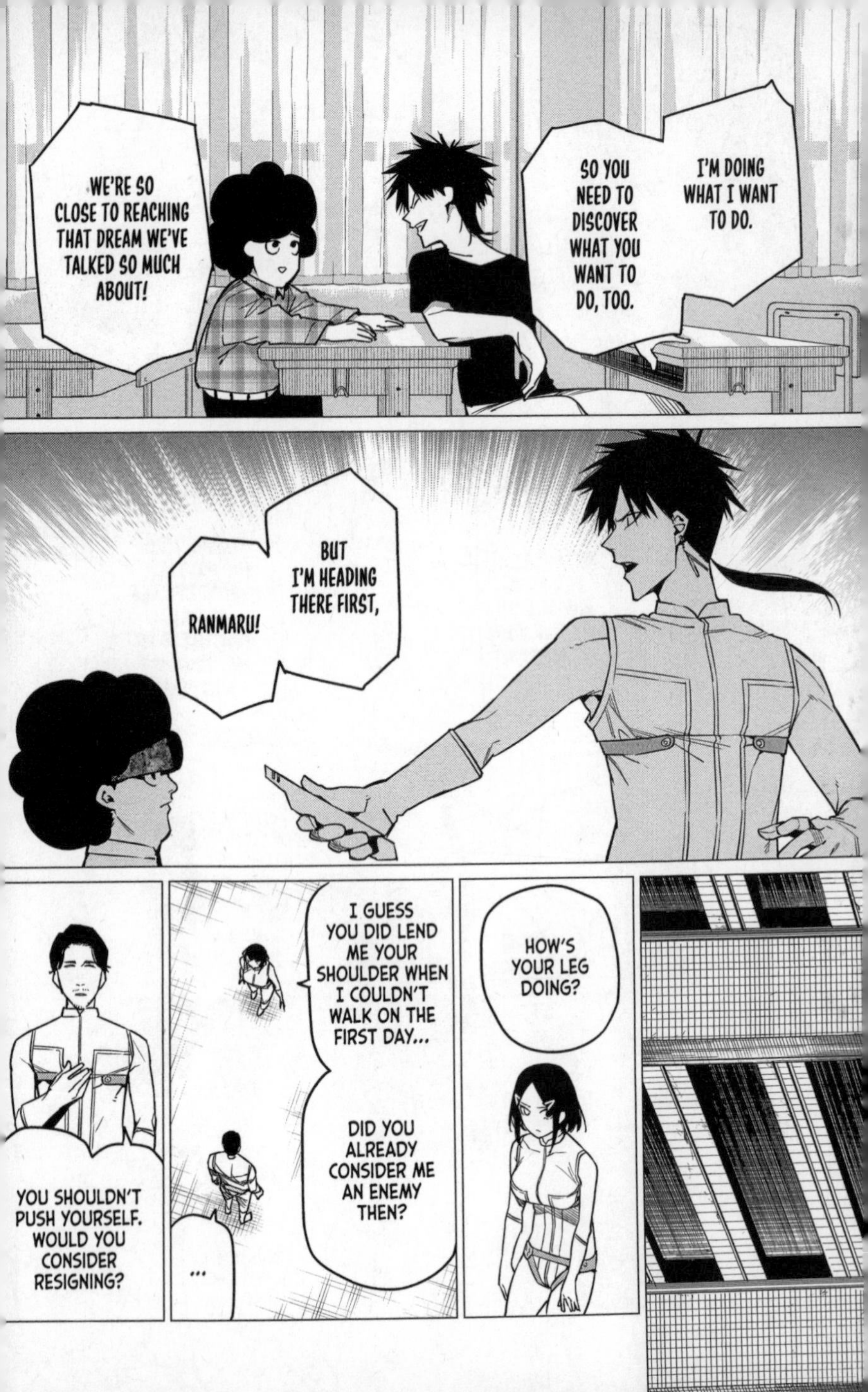
I'M DOING WHAT I WANT TO DO.
SO YOU NEED TO DISCOVER WHAT YOU WANT TO DO, TOO.
WE'RE SO CLOSE TO REACHING THAT DREAM WE'VE TALKED SO MUCH ABOUT!
BUT I'M HEADING THERE FIRST,
RANMARU!
HOW'S YOUR LEG DOING?
I GUESS YOU DID LEND ME YOUR SHOULDER WHEN I COULDN'T WALK ON THE FIRST DAY...
DID YOU ALREADY CONSIDER ME AN ENEMY THEN?
...
YOU SHOULDN'T PUSH YOURSELF. WOULD YOU CONSIDER RESIGNING?

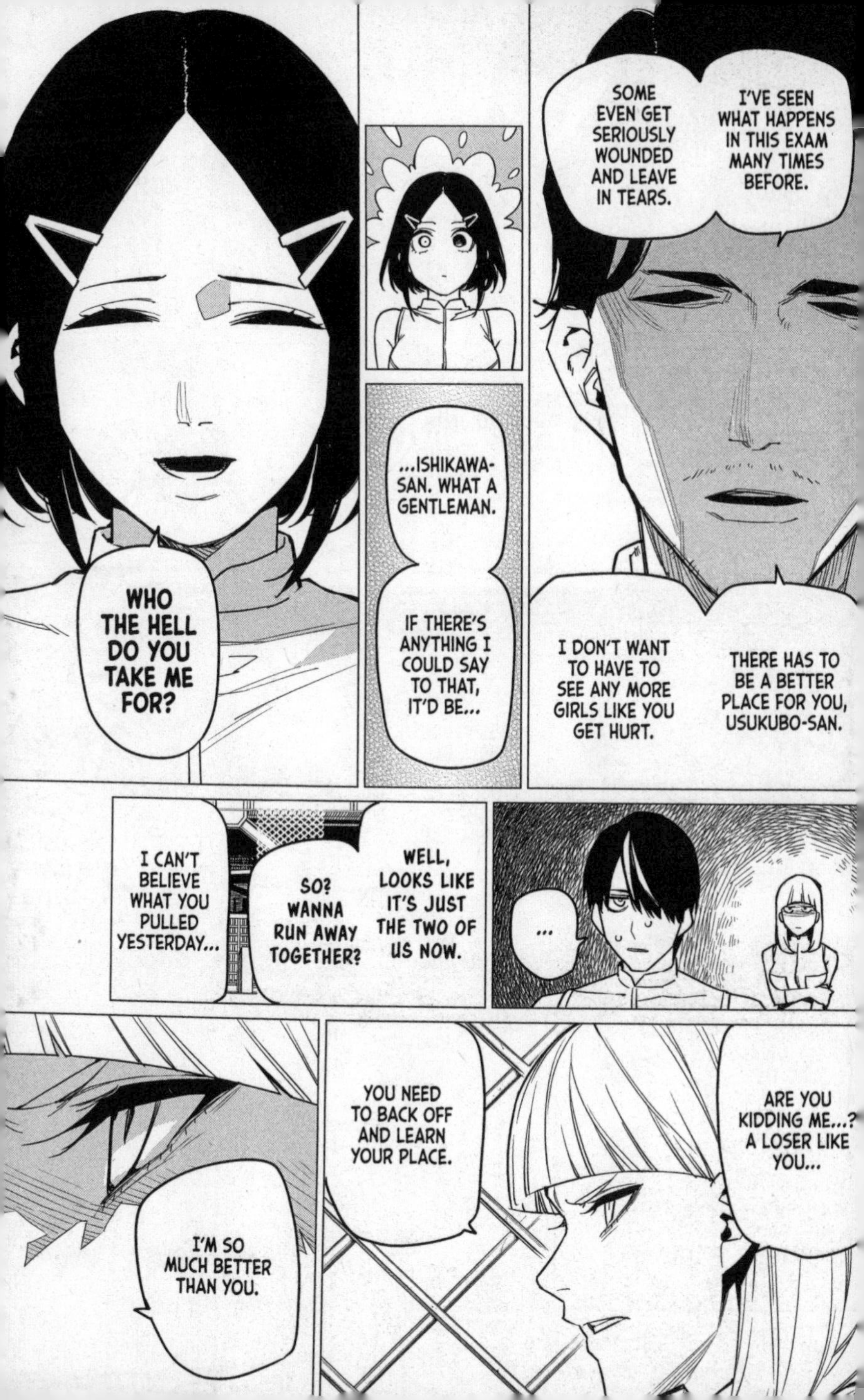
I'VE SEEN WHAT HAPPENS IN THIS EXAM MANY TIMES BEFORE.
SOME EVEN GET SERIOUSLY WOUNDED AND LEAVE IN TEARS.
THERE HAS TO BE A BETTER PLACE FOR YOU, USUKUBO-SAN.
I DON'T WANT TO HAVE TO SEE ANY MORE GIRLS LIKE YOU GET HURT.
...ISHIKAWA-SAN. WHAT A GENTLEMAN.
IF THERE'S ANYTHING I COULD SAY TO THAT, IT'D BE...
WHO THE HELL DO YOU TAKE ME FOR?
...
WELL, LOOKS LIKE IT'S JUST THE TWO OF US NOW.
SO? WANNA RUN AWAY TOGETHER?
I CAN'T BELIEVE WHAT YOU PULLED YESTERDAY...
ARE YOU KIDDING ME...? A LOSER LIKE YOU...
YOU NEED TO BACK OFF AND LEARN YOUR PLACE.
I'M SO MUCH BETTER THAN YOU.

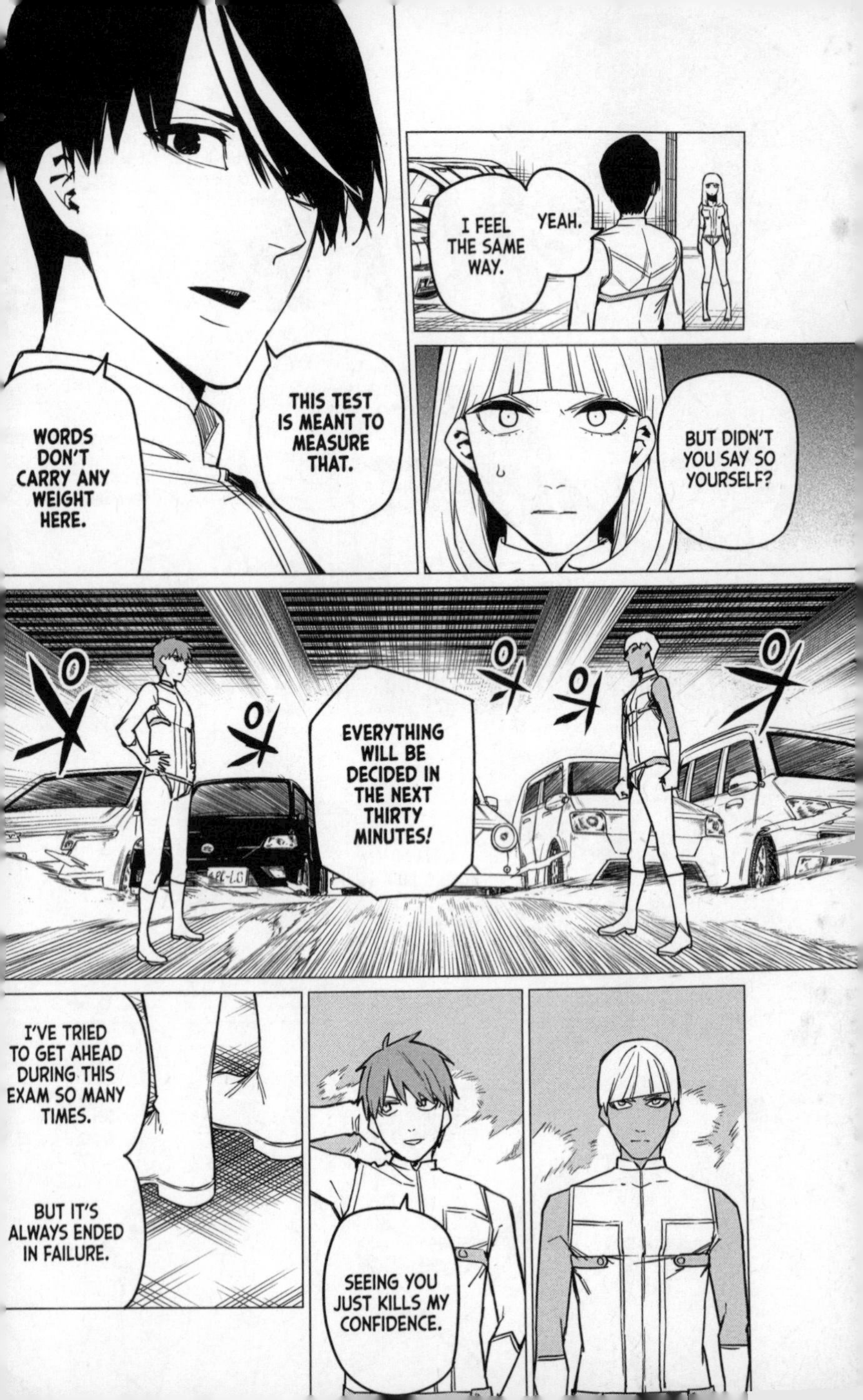
YEAH.
I FEEL THE SAME WAY.
BUT DIDN'T YOU SAY SO YOURSELF?
THIS TEST IS MEANT TO MEASURE THAT.
WORDS DON'T CARRY ANY WEIGHT HERE.
EVERYTHING WILL BE DECIDED IN THE NEXT THIRTY MINUTES!
SEEING YOU JUST KILLS MY CONFIDENCE.
I'VE TRIED TO GET AHEAD DURING THIS EXAM SO MANY TIMES.
BUT IT'S ALWAYS ENDED IN FAILURE.

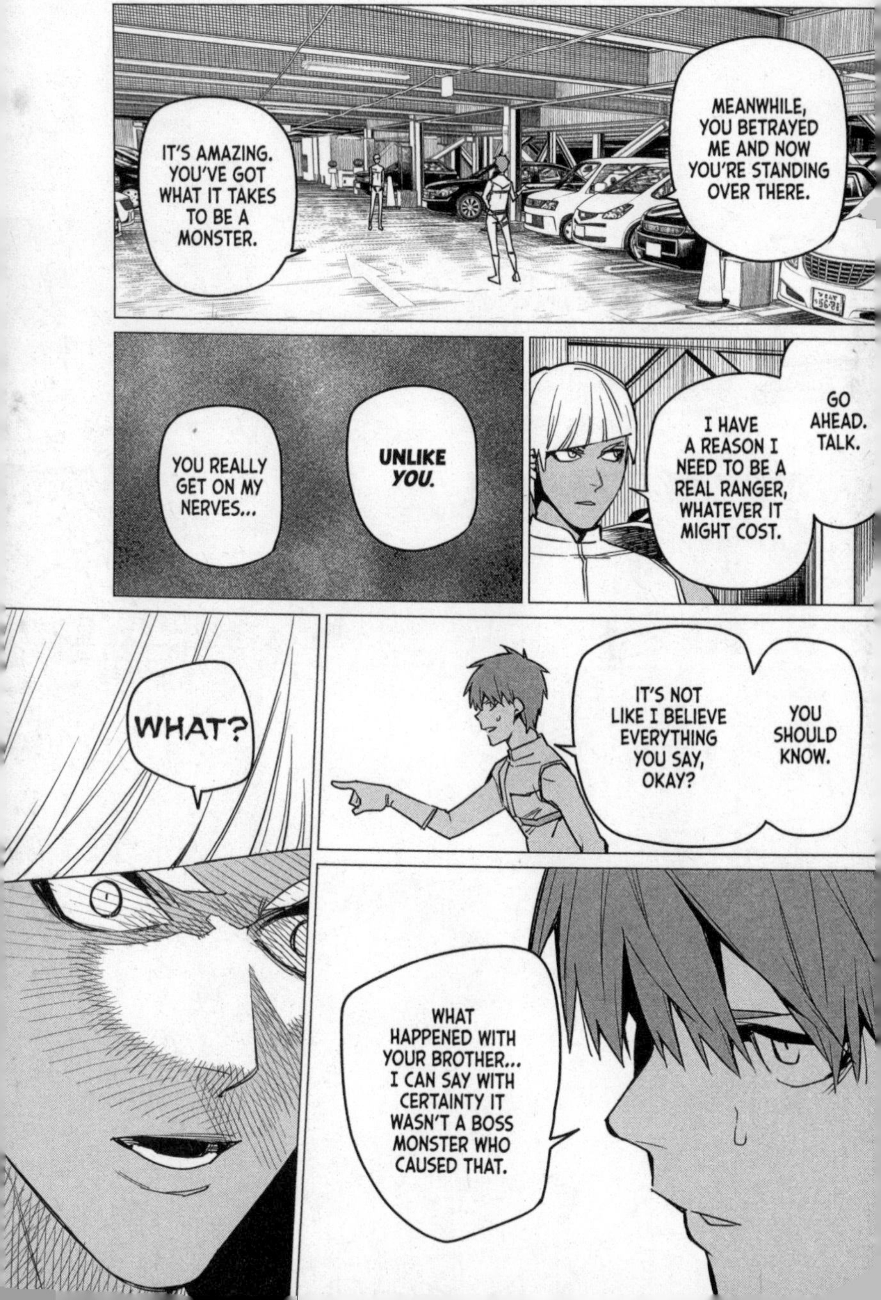
MEANWHILE, YOU BETRAYED ME AND NOW YOU'RE STANDING OVER THERE.
IT'S AMAZING. YOU'VE GOT WHAT IT TAKES TO BE A MONSTER.
GO AHEAD. TALK.
I HAVE A REASON I NEED TO BE A REAL RANGER, WHATEVER IT MIGHT COST.
UNLIKE *YOU.*
YOU REALLY GET ON MY NERVES...
YOU SHOULD KNOW.
IT'S NOT LIKE I BELIEVE EVERYTHING YOU SAY, OKAY?
WHAT?
WHAT HAPPENED WITH YOUR BROTHER... I CAN SAY WITH CERTAINTY IT WASN'T A BOSS MONSTER WHO CAUSED THAT.

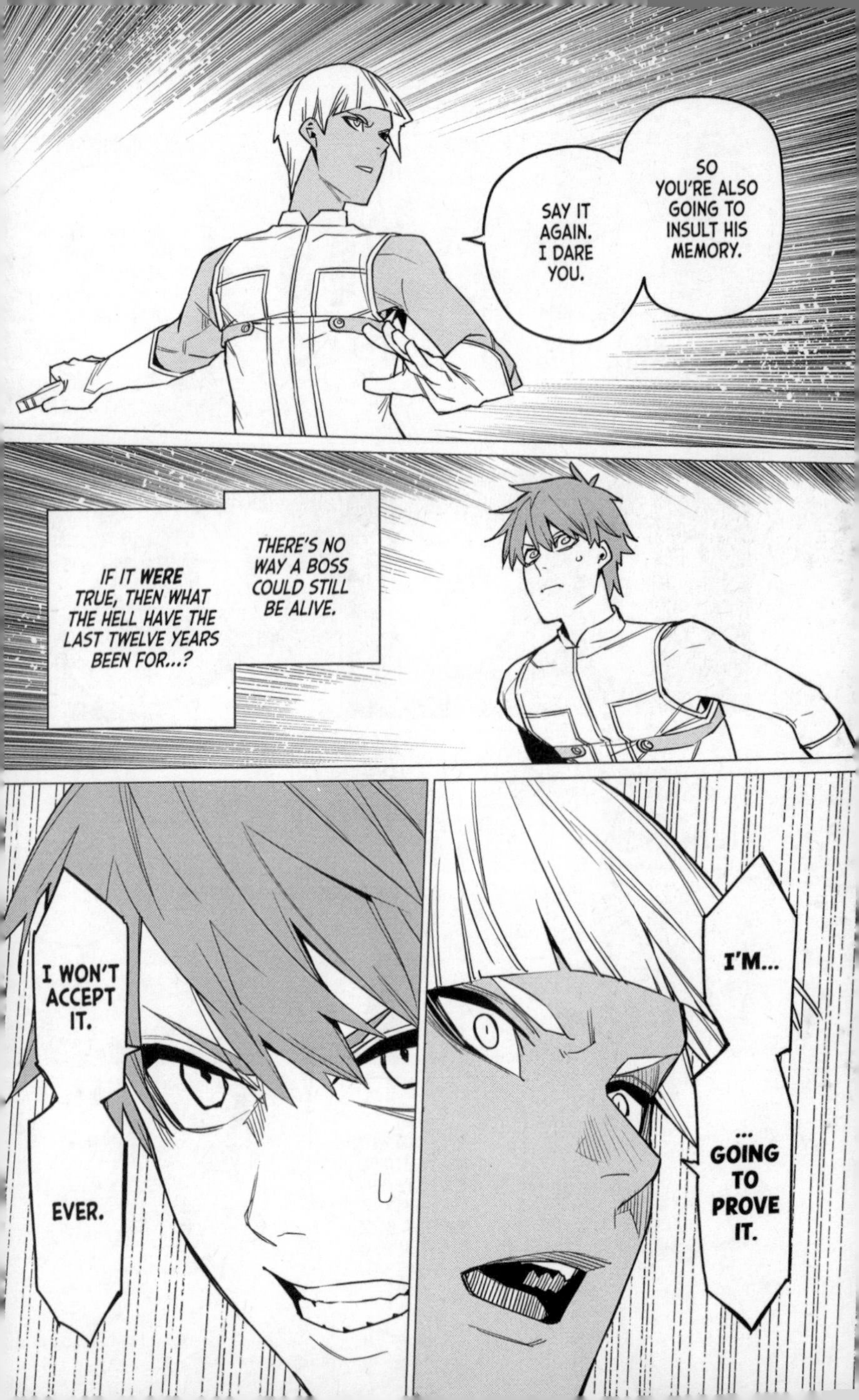
SO YOU'RE ALSO GOING TO INSULT HIS MEMORY.
SAY IT AGAIN. I DARE YOU.
THERE'S NO WAY A BOSS COULD STILL BE ALIVE.
IF IT WERE TRUE, THEN WHAT THE HELL HAVE THE LAST TWELVE YEARS BEEN FOR...?
I'M...
...GOING TO PROVE IT.
I WON'T ACCEPT IT.
EVER.

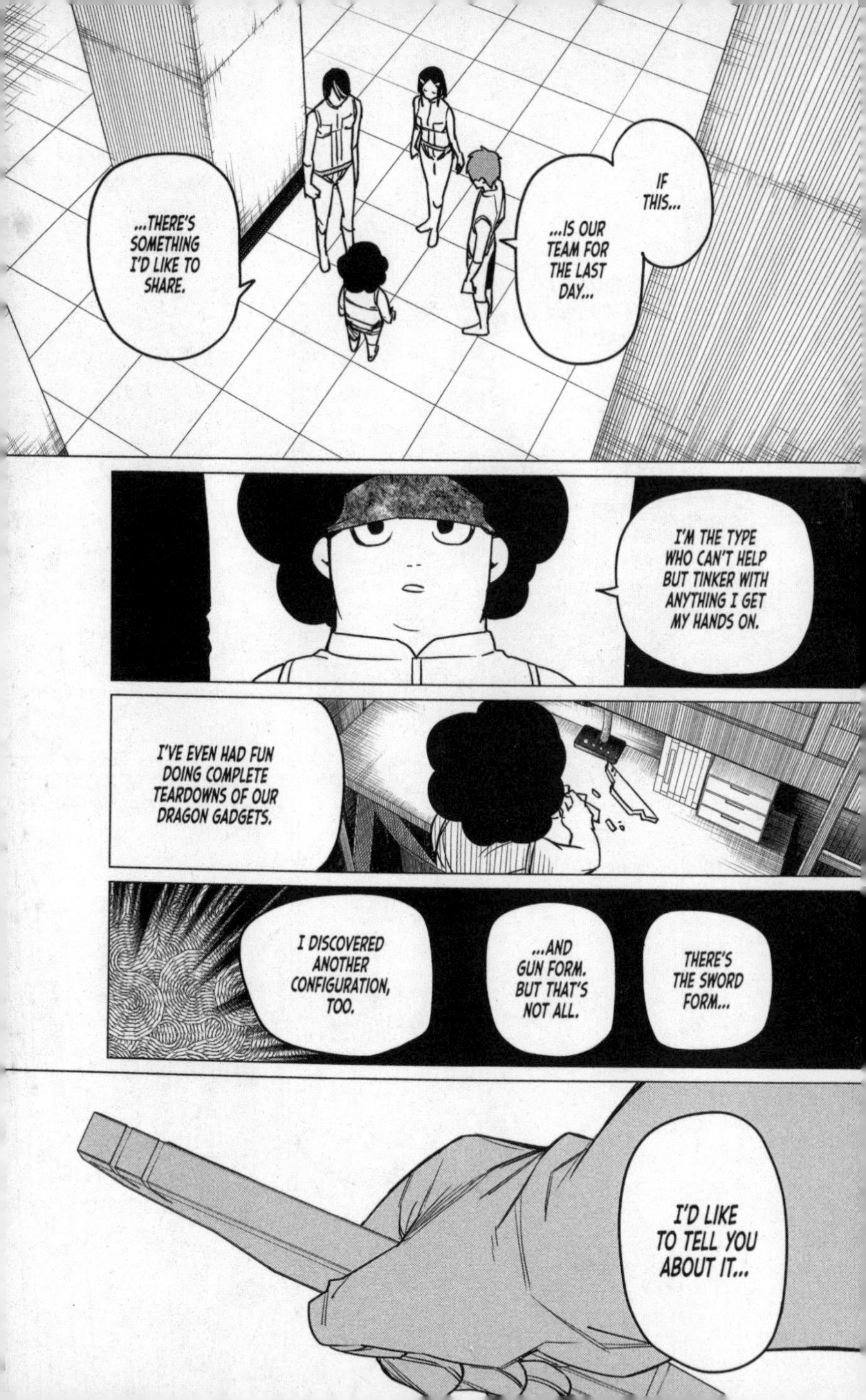
IF THIS...
...IS OUR TEAM FOR THE LAST DAY...
...THERE'S SOMETHING I'D LIKE TO SHARE.
I'M THE TYPE WHO CAN'T HELP BUT TINKER WITH ANYTHING I GET MY HANDS ON.
I'VE EVEN HAD FUN DOING COMPLETE TEARDOWNS OF OUR DRAGON GADGETS.
THERE'S THE SWORD FORM...
...AND GUN FORM. BUT THAT'S NOT ALL.
I DISCOVERED ANOTHER CONFIGURATION, TOO.
I'D LIKE TO TELL YOU ABOUT IT...

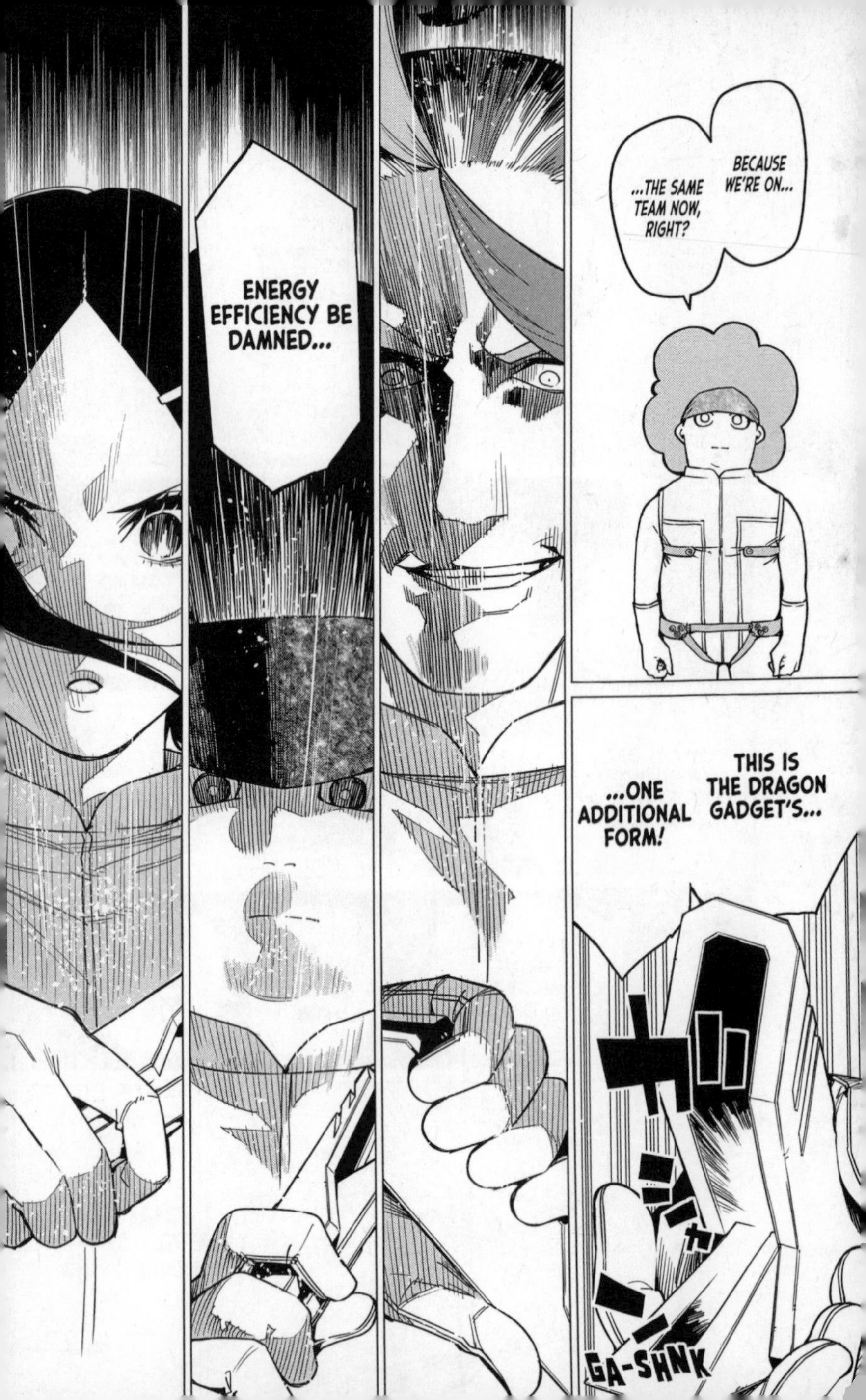
BECAUSE WE'RE ON...
...THE SAME TEAM NOW, RIGHT?
THIS IS THE DRAGON GADGET'S...
...ONE ADDITIONAL FORM!
GA-SHNK
ENERGY EFFICIENCY BE DAMNED...

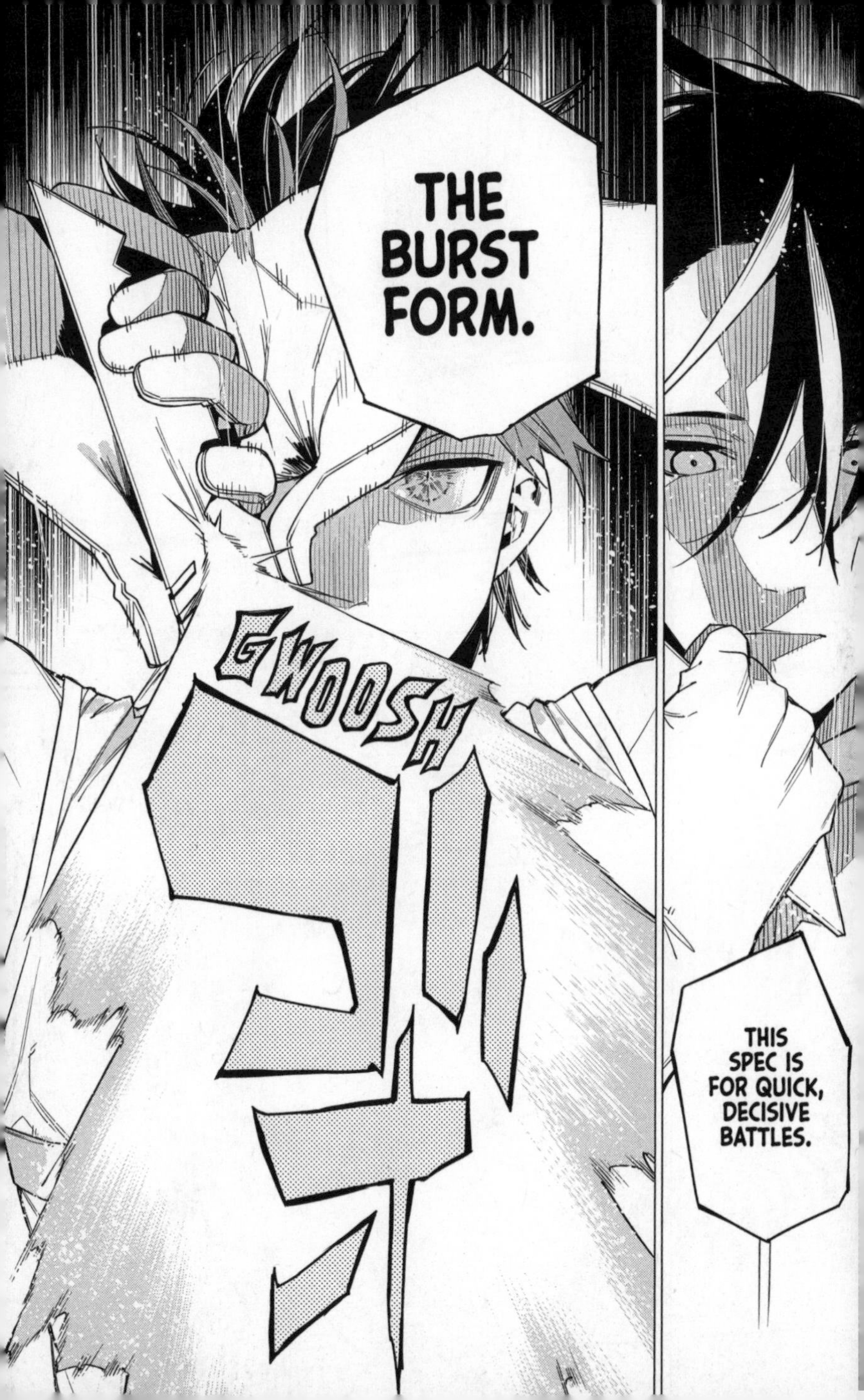
THIS SPEC IS FOR QUICK, DECISIVE BATTLES.
THE BURST FORM.
GWOOSH

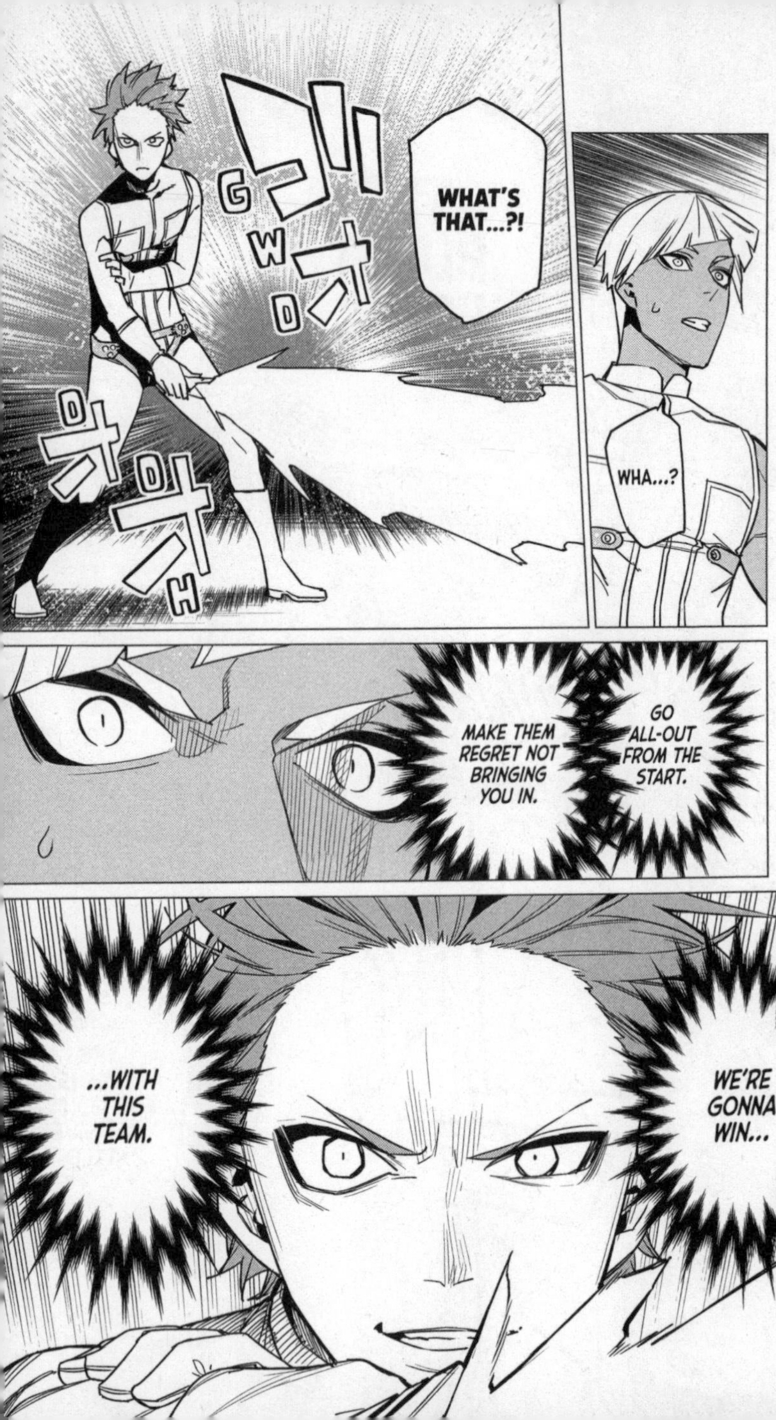
WHA...?
WHAT'S THAT...?!
GWOOOH
GO ALL-OUT FROM THE START.
MAKE THEM REGRET NOT BRINGING YOU IN.
WE'RE GONNA WIN...
...WITH THIS TEAM.

Chapter 32: **THE WHITE DRAGON'S TEST: VS. THE CANDIDATE TEAM 4**

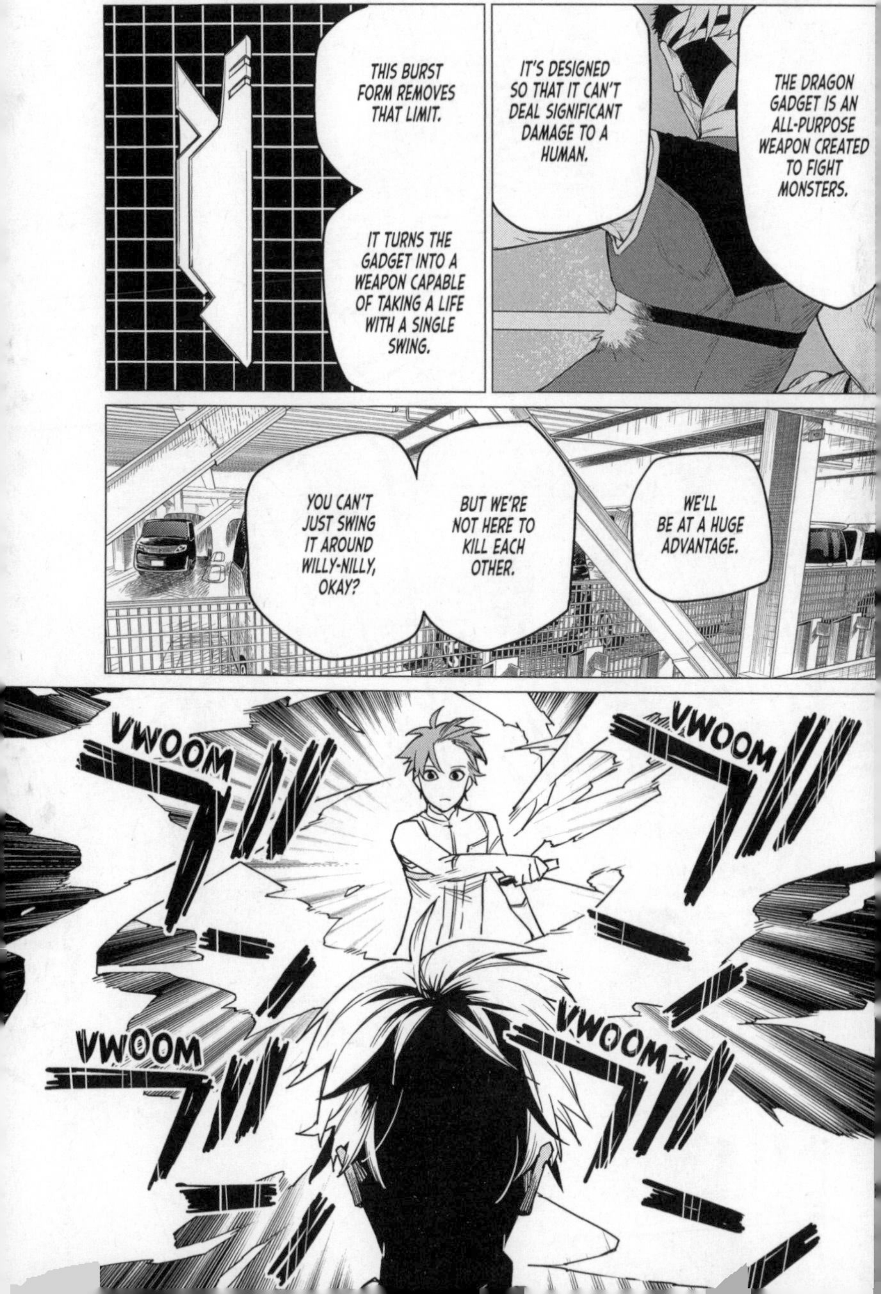
THE DRAGON GADGET IS AN ALL-PURPOSE WEAPON CREATED TO FIGHT MONSTERS.
IT'S DESIGNED SO THAT IT CAN'T DEAL SIGNIFICANT DAMAGE TO A HUMAN.
THIS BURST FORM REMOVES THAT LIMIT.
IT TURNS THE GADGET INTO A WEAPON CAPABLE OF TAKING A LIFE WITH A SINGLE SWING.
WE'LL BE AT A HUGE ADVANTAGE.
BUT WE'RE NOT HERE TO KILL EACH OTHER.
YOU CAN'T JUST SWING IT AROUND WILLY-NILLY, OKAY?
VWOOM
VWOOM
VWOOM
VWOOM

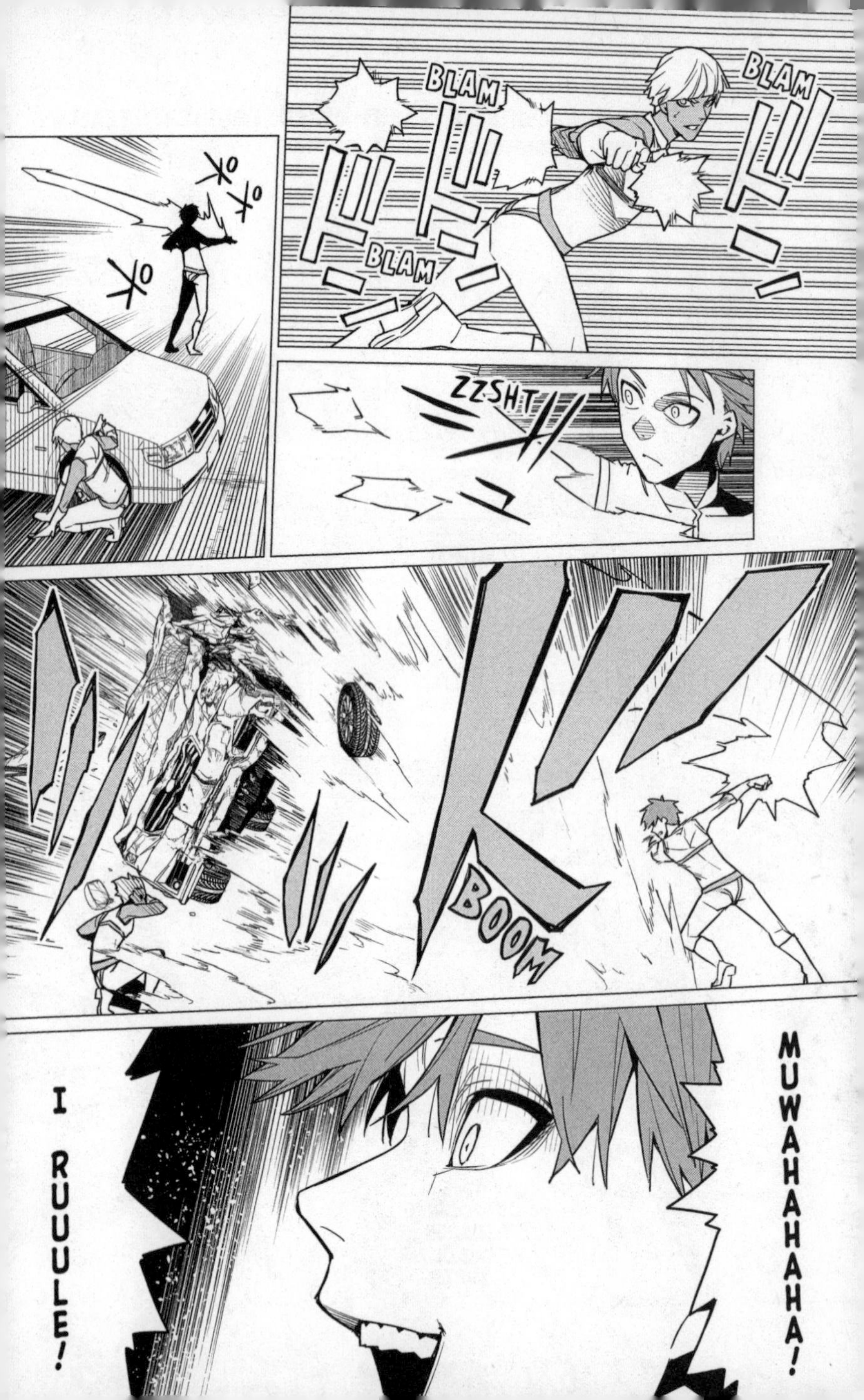
BLAM
BLAM
BLAM
ZZSHT
BOOM
MUWAHAHAHA!
I RUUULE!

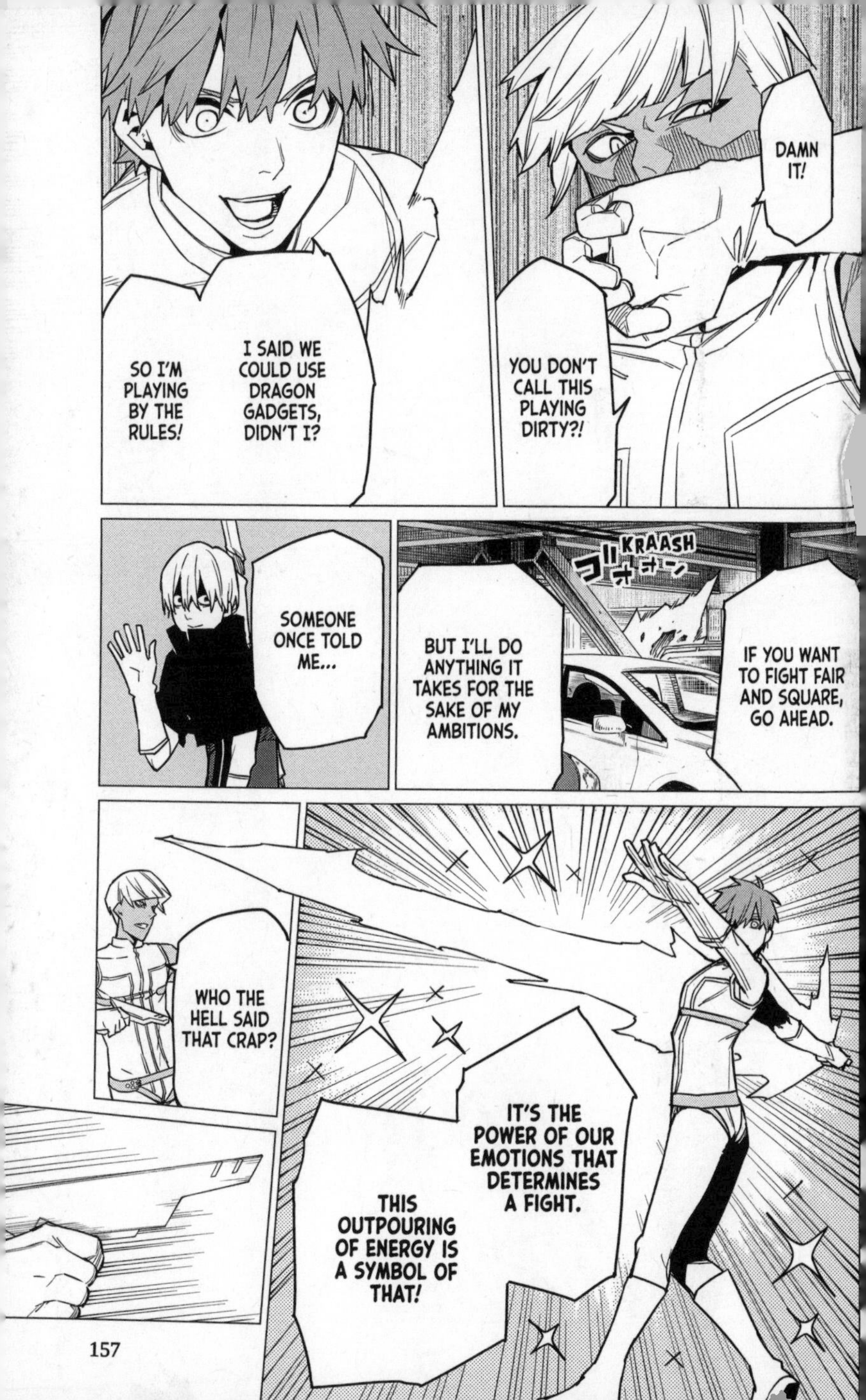
DAMN IT!
YOU DON'T CALL THIS PLAYING DIRTY?!
I SAID WE COULD USE DRAGON GADGETS, DIDN'T I?
SO I'M PLAYING BY THE RULES!
KRAASH
IF YOU WANT TO FIGHT FAIR AND SQUARE, GO AHEAD.
BUT I'LL DO ANYTHING IT TAKES FOR THE SAKE OF MY AMBITIONS.
SOMEONE ONCE TOLD ME...
IT'S THE POWER OF OUR EMOTIONS THAT DETERMINES A FIGHT.
THIS OUTPOURING OF ENERGY IS A SYMBOL OF THAT!
WHO THE HELL SAID THAT CRAP?

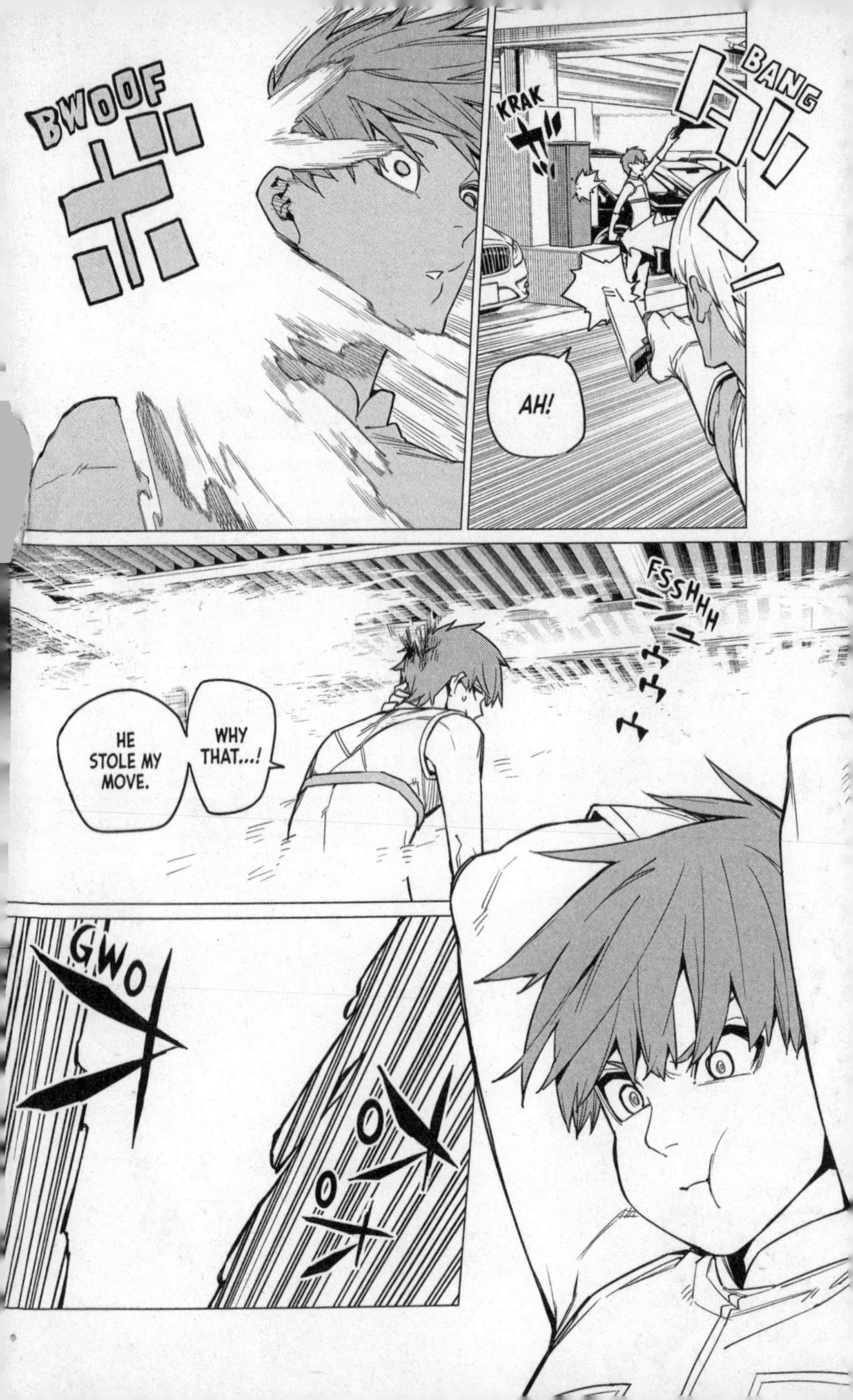
BANG
KRAK
AH!
BWOOF
FSSHHH
WHY THAT...!
HE STOLE MY MOVE.
GWO

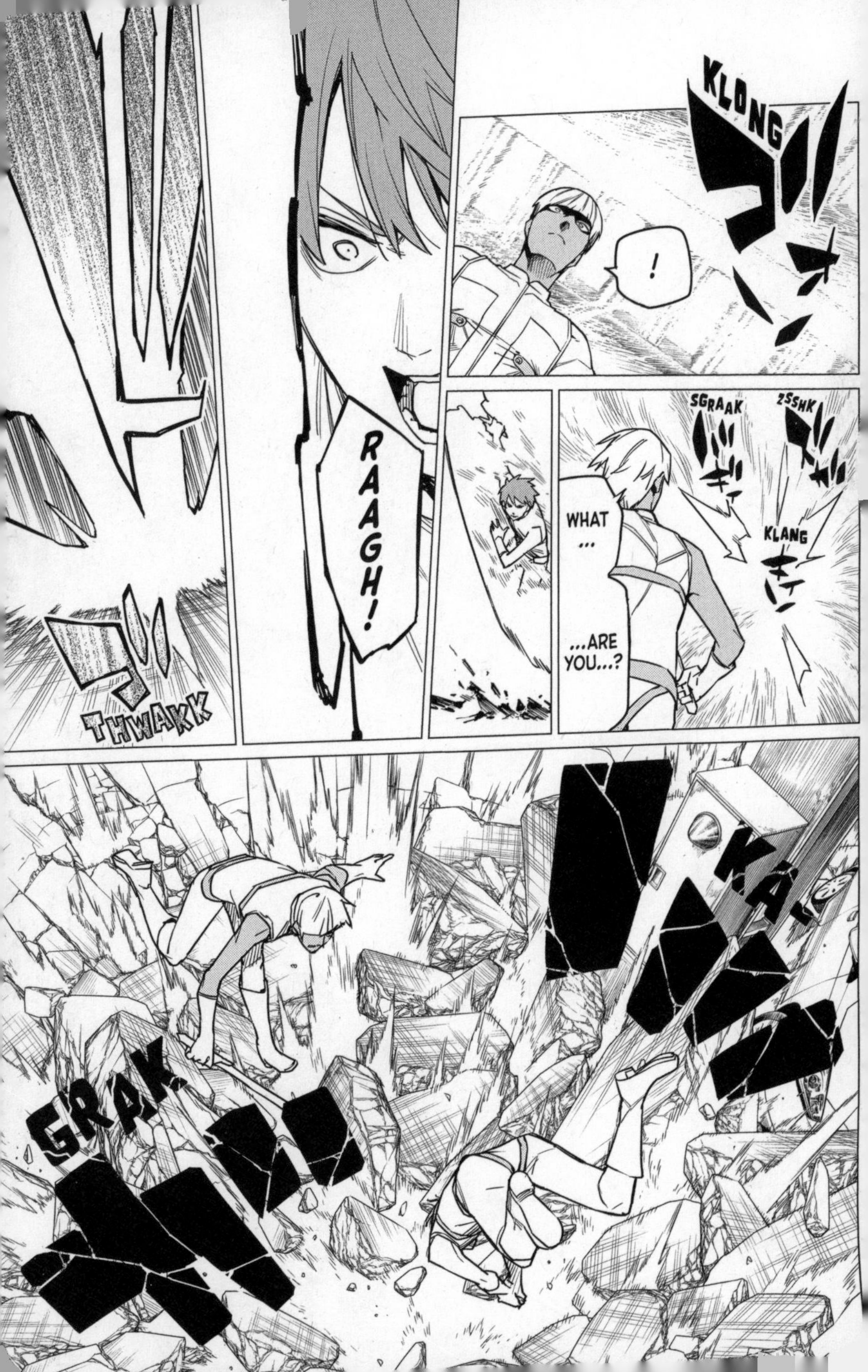
KLONG
!
ZSSHK
SGRAAK
KLANG
WHAT...
...ARE YOU...?
RAAGH!
THWAKK
KA-
GRAK

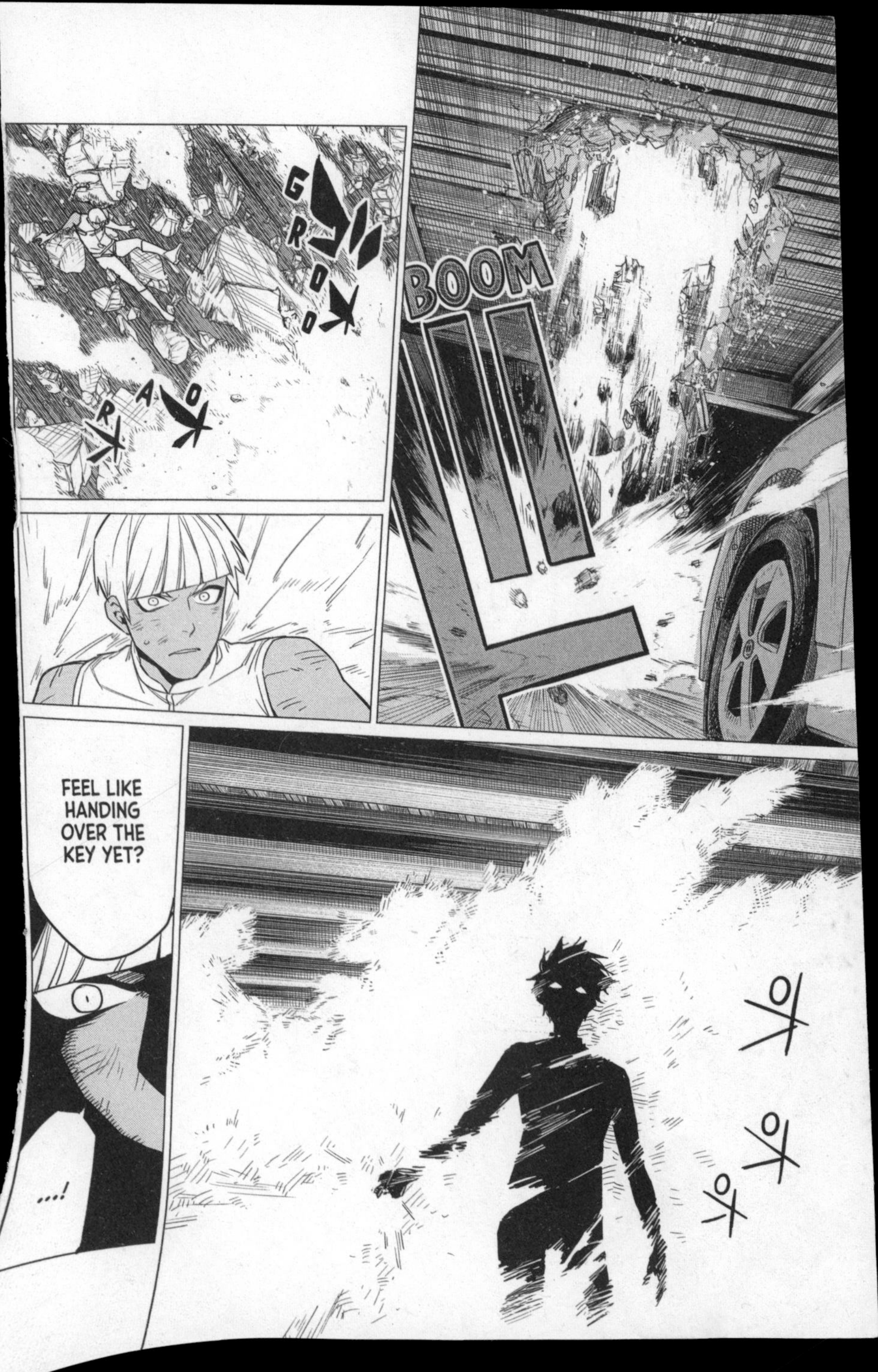
BOOM
GROOOAR
FEEL LIKE HANDING OVER THE KEY YET?
...!

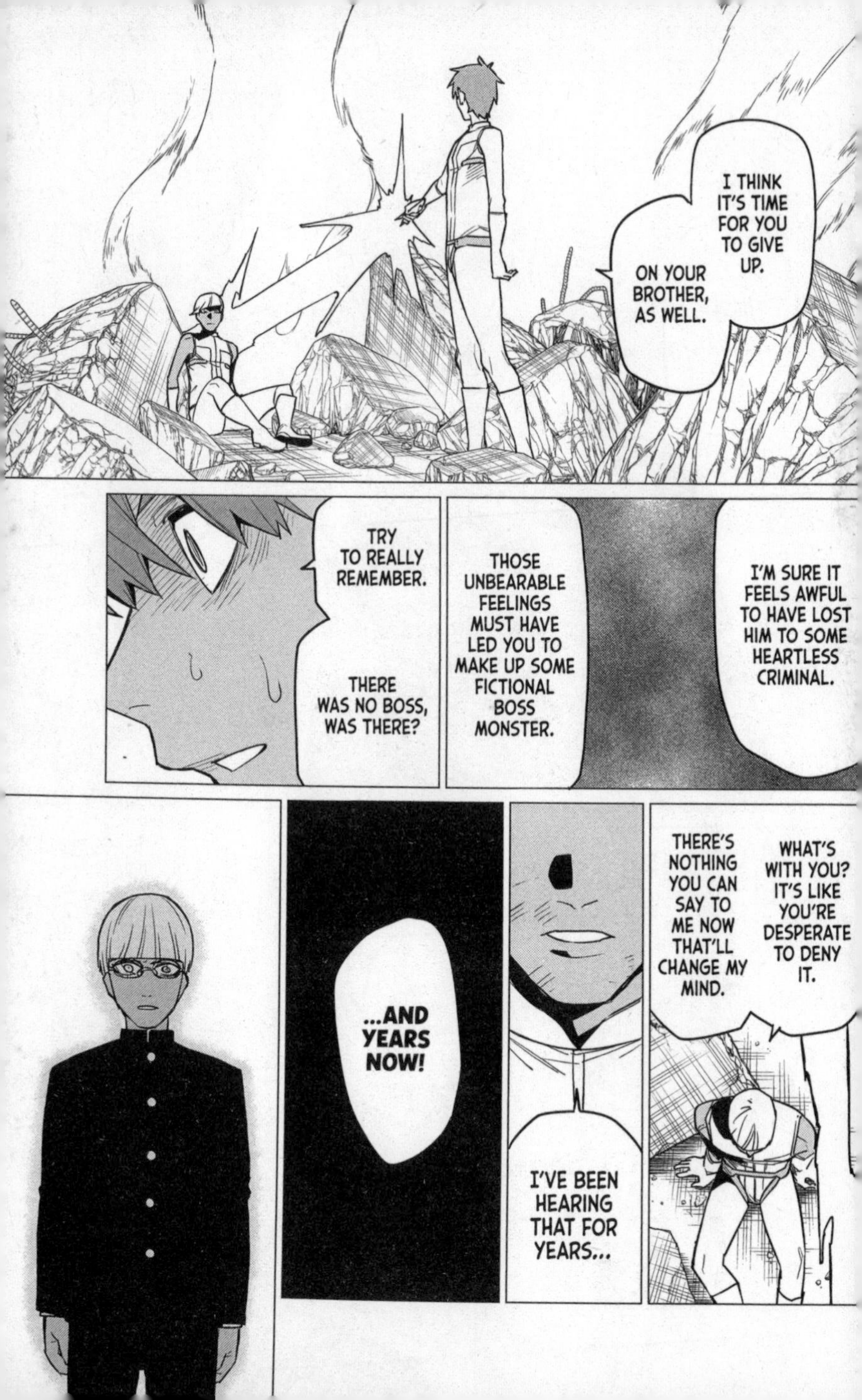
I THINK IT'S TIME FOR YOU TO GIVE UP.
ON YOUR BROTHER, AS WELL.
I'M SURE IT FEELS AWFUL TO HAVE LOST HIM TO SOME HEARTLESS CRIMINAL.
THOSE UNBEARABLE FEELINGS MUST HAVE LED YOU TO MAKE UP SOME FICTIONAL BOSS MONSTER.
TRY TO REALLY REMEMBER.
THERE WAS NO BOSS, WAS THERE?
WHAT'S WITH YOU? IT'S LIKE YOU'RE DESPERATE TO DENY IT.
THERE'S NOTHING YOU CAN SAY TO ME NOW THAT'LL CHANGE MY MIND.
I'VE BEEN HEARING THAT FOR YEARS...
...AND YEARS NOW!

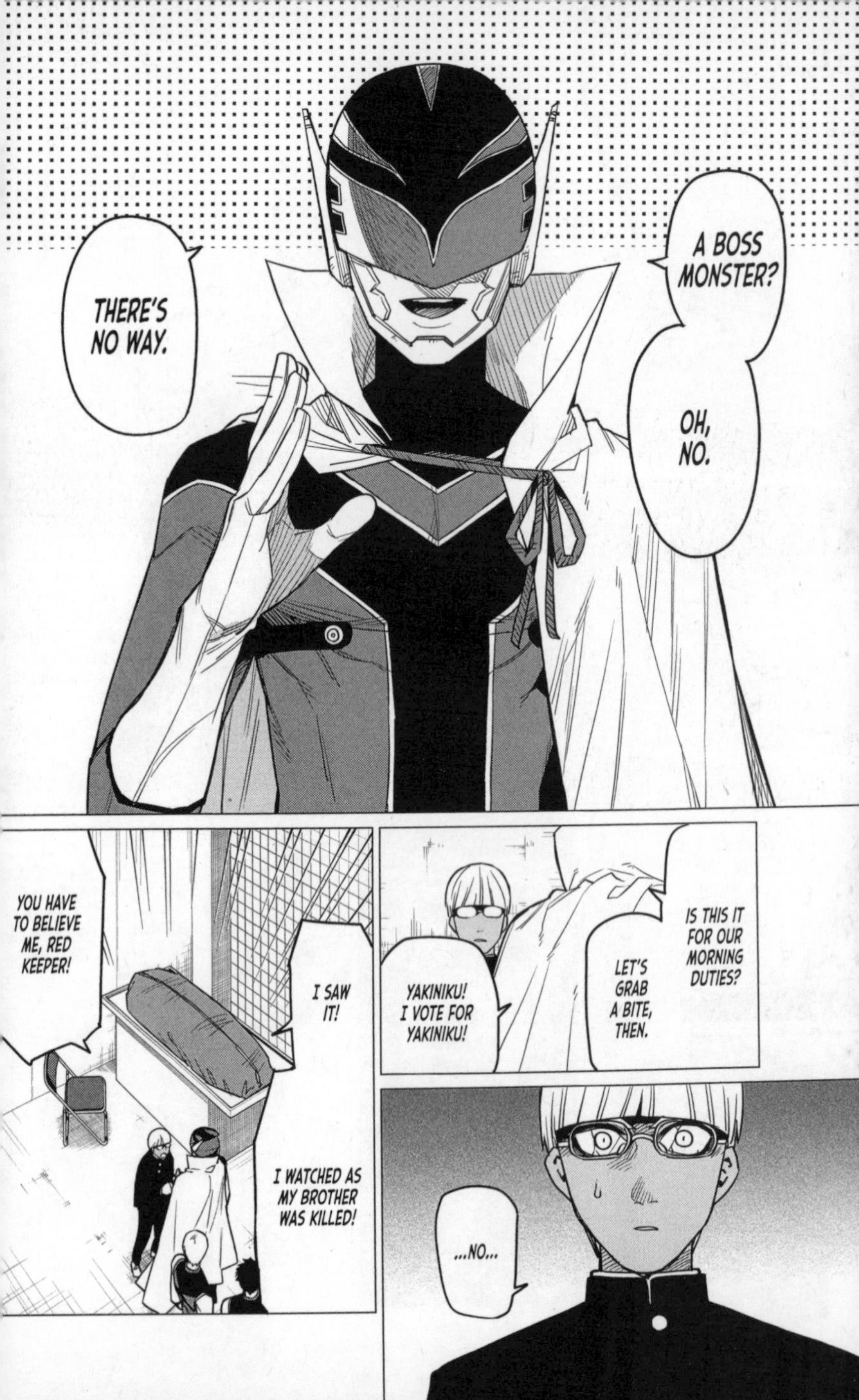
A BOSS MONSTER?
OH, NO.
THERE'S NO WAY.
IS THIS IT FOR OUR MORNING DUTIES?
LET'S GRAB A BITE, THEN.
YAKINIKU! I VOTE FOR YAKINIKU!
...NO...
YOU HAVE TO BELIEVE ME, RED KEEPER!
I SAW IT!
I WATCHED AS MY BROTHER WAS KILLED!

ISN'T IT POSSIBLE THAT YOUR BIG BROTHER GOT KILLED BY AN AVERAGE FIGHTER?

A PLAIN LITTLE FIGHTER, MAYBE.

THERE'S NO RECORD OF A BOSS EVER COMING TO THE SURFACE ASIDE FROM THE SUNDAY SHOWDOWNS.

DIDN'T YOU LEARN THIS IN SCHOOL?

TSK.

GUESS HE CHOSE THE WRONG PATH IN LIFE.

HE WAS NEVER CUT OUT TO BE A RANGER.

I'M NOT JUST AFTER THE BOSS MONSTERS...

HRGH

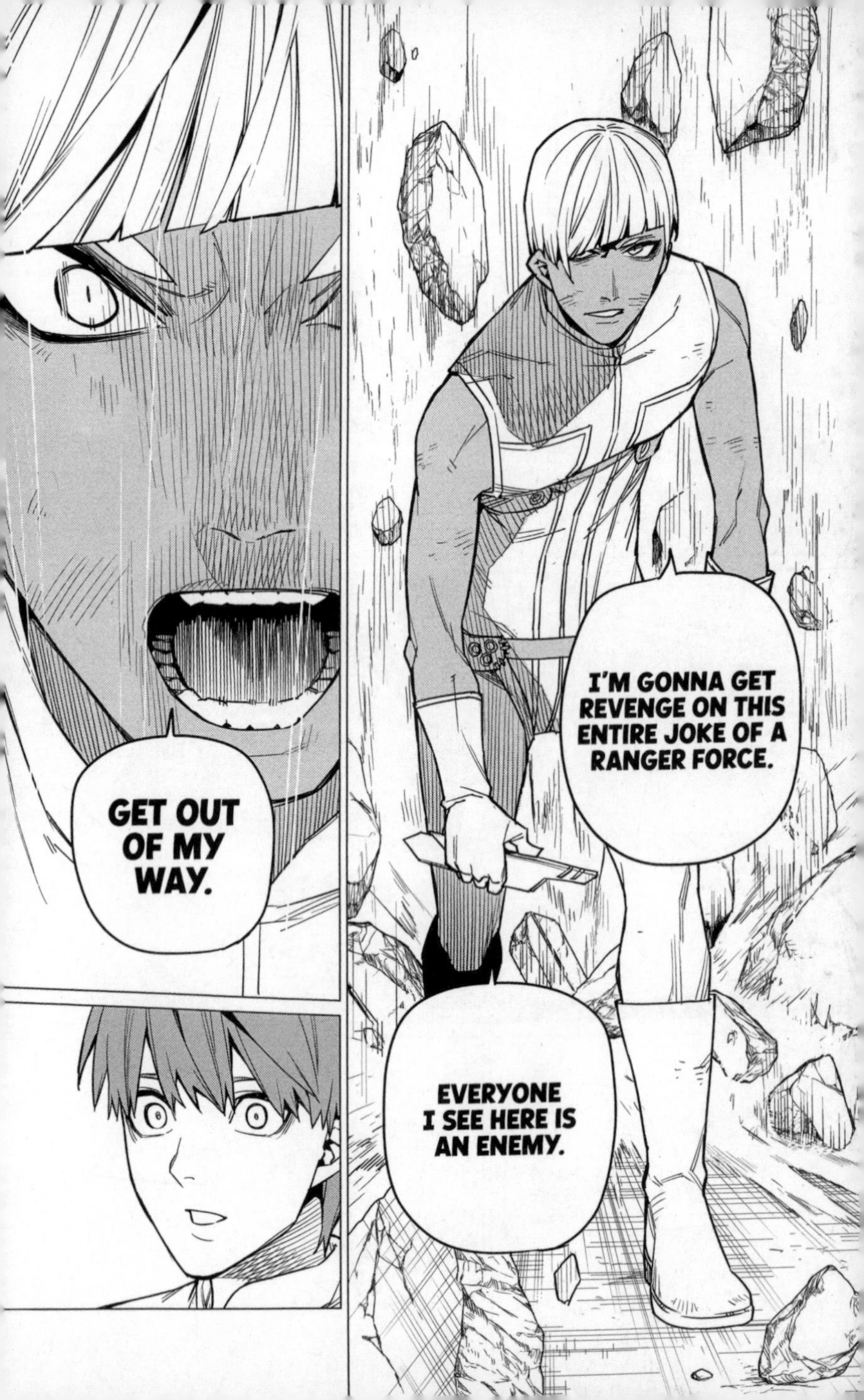
I'M GONNA GET REVENGE ON THIS ENTIRE JOKE OF A RANGER FORCE.
EVERYONE I SEE HERE IS AN ENEMY.
GET OUT OF MY WAY.

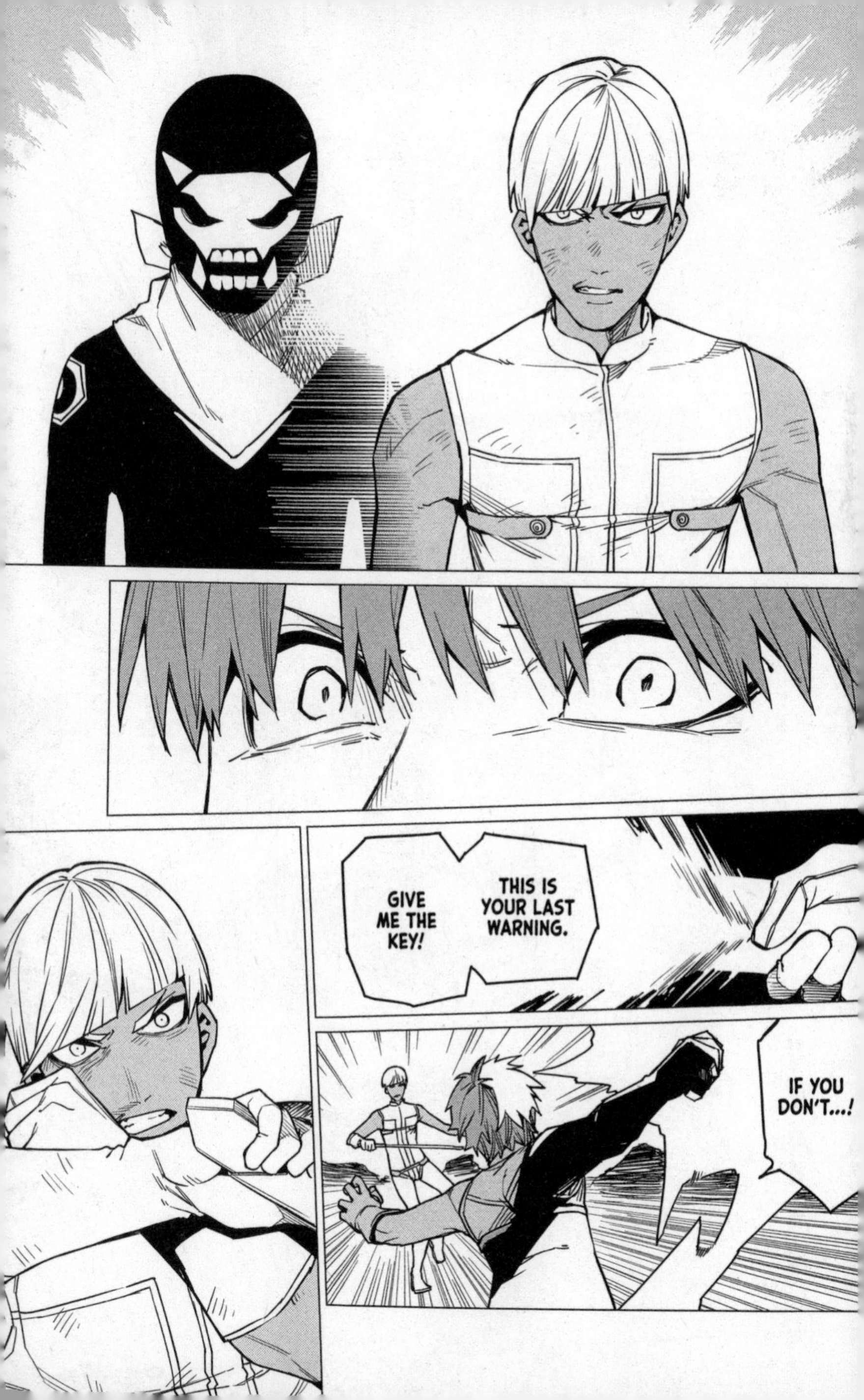
THIS IS YOUR LAST WARNING.
GIVE ME THE KEY!
IF YOU DON'T...!

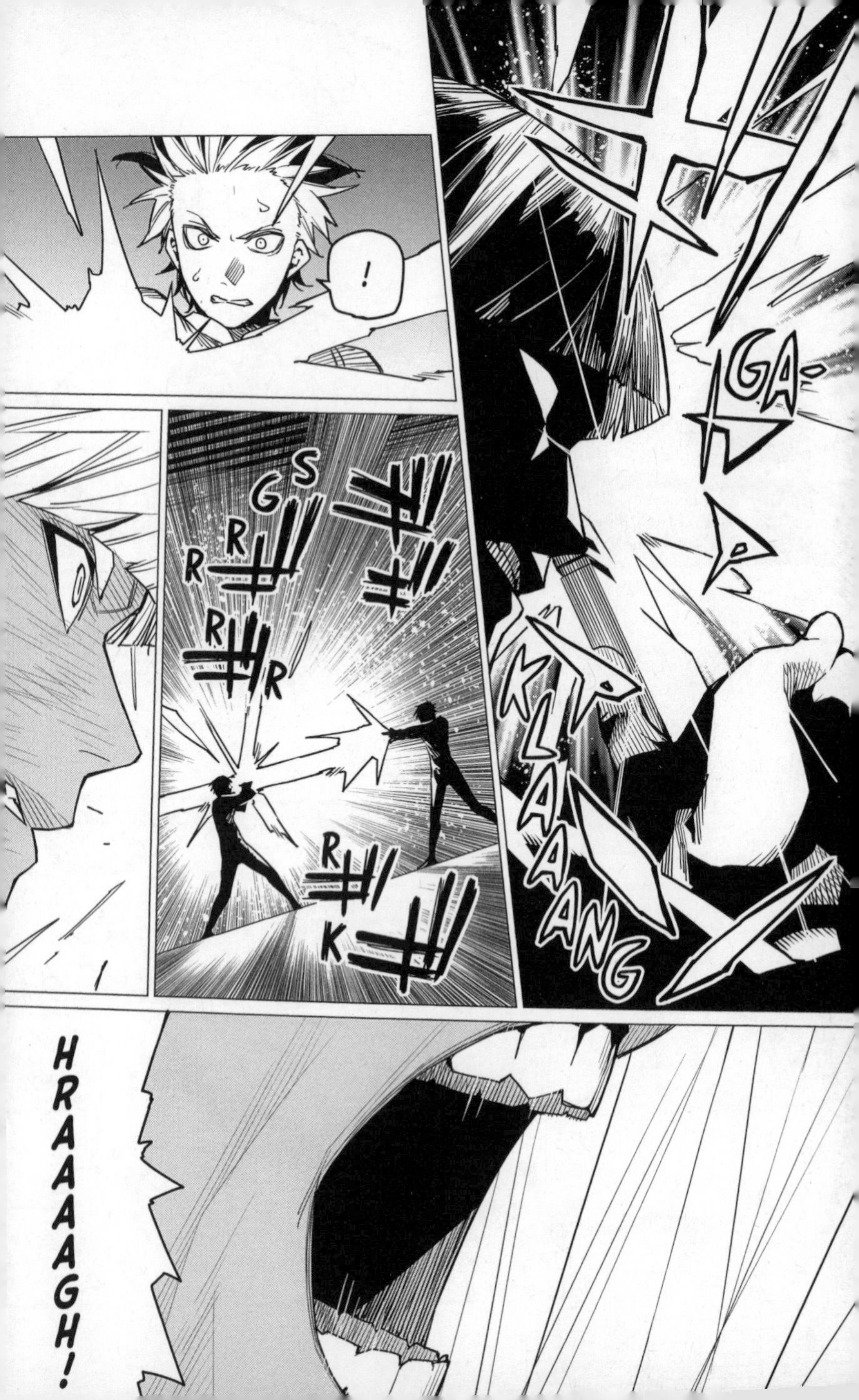
GA-P
KLAAANG
!
SGRRRR
RK
HRAAAAAGH!

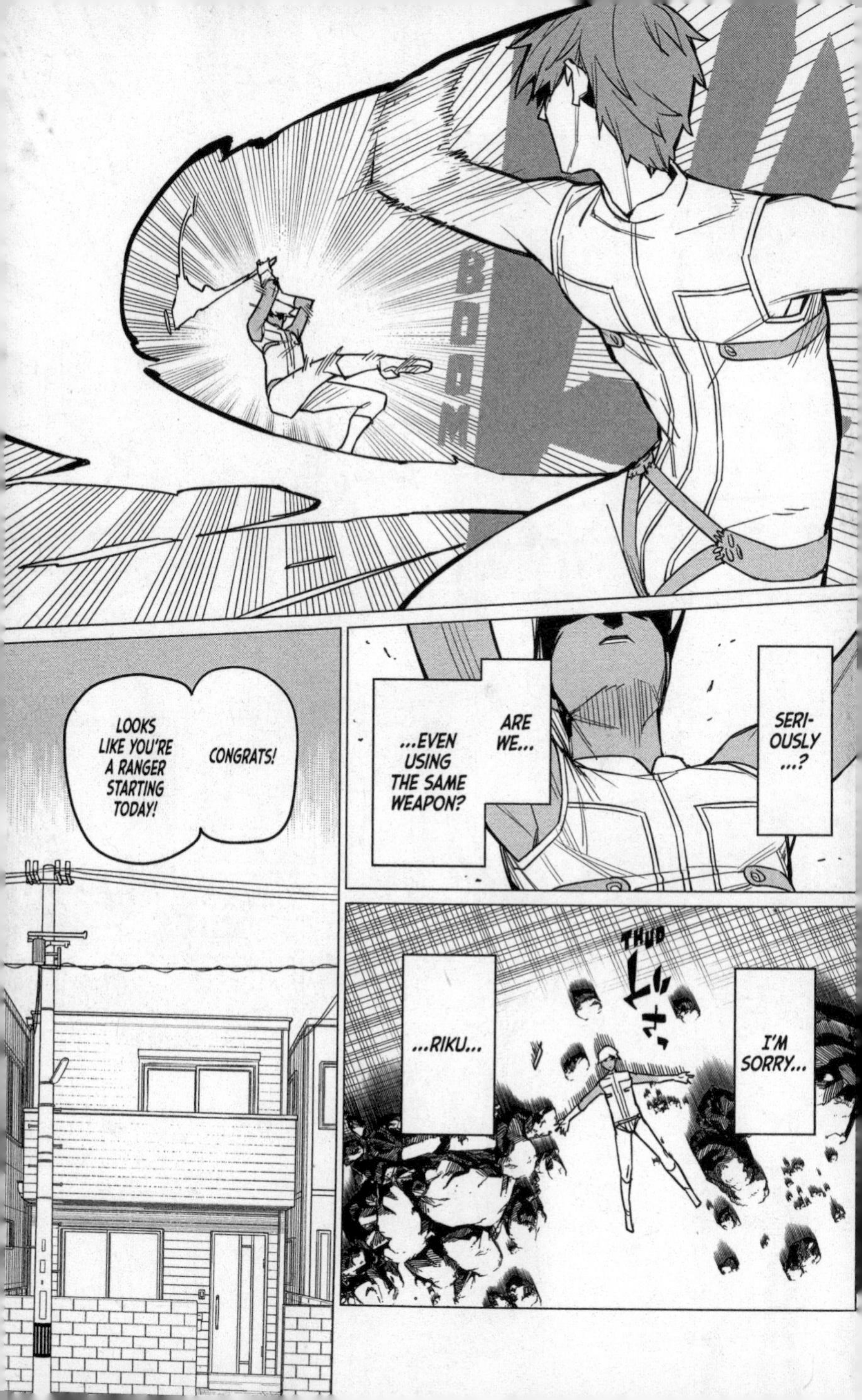
BOOM
SERIOUSLY...?
ARE WE...
...EVEN USING THE SAME WEAPON?
THUD
I'M SORRY...
...RIKU...
CONGRATS!
LOOKS LIKE YOU'RE A RANGER STARTING TODAY!

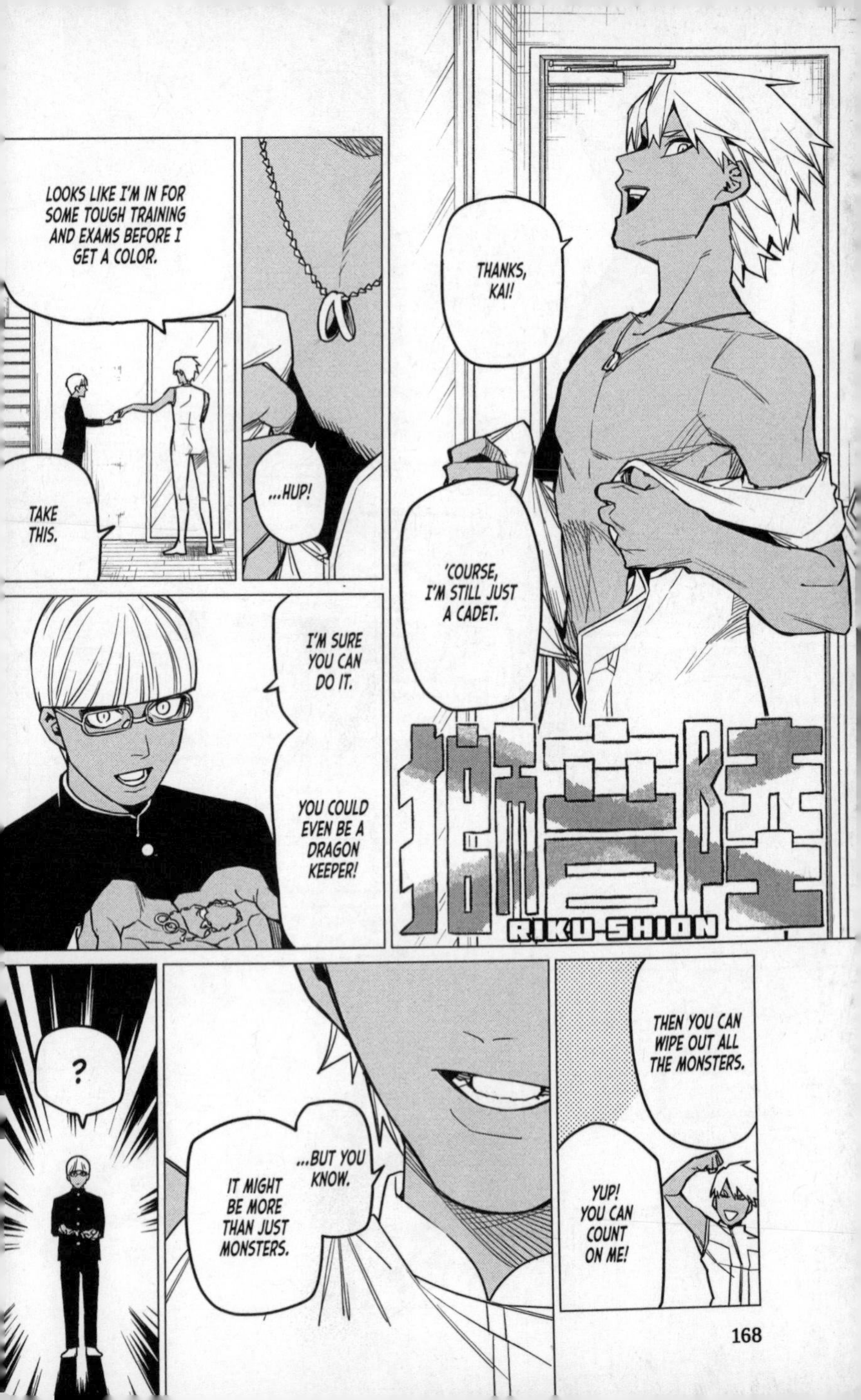
THANKS, KAI!
'COURSE, I'M STILL JUST A CADET.
RIKU-SHION
...HUP!
LOOKS LIKE I'M IN FOR SOME TOUGH TRAINING AND EXAMS BEFORE I GET A COLOR.
TAKE THIS.
I'M SURE YOU CAN DO IT.
YOU COULD EVEN BE A DRAGON KEEPER!
THEN YOU CAN WIPE OUT ALL THE MONSTERS.
YUP! YOU CAN COUNT ON ME!
...BUT YOU KNOW.
IT MIGHT BE MORE THAN JUST MONSTERS.
?

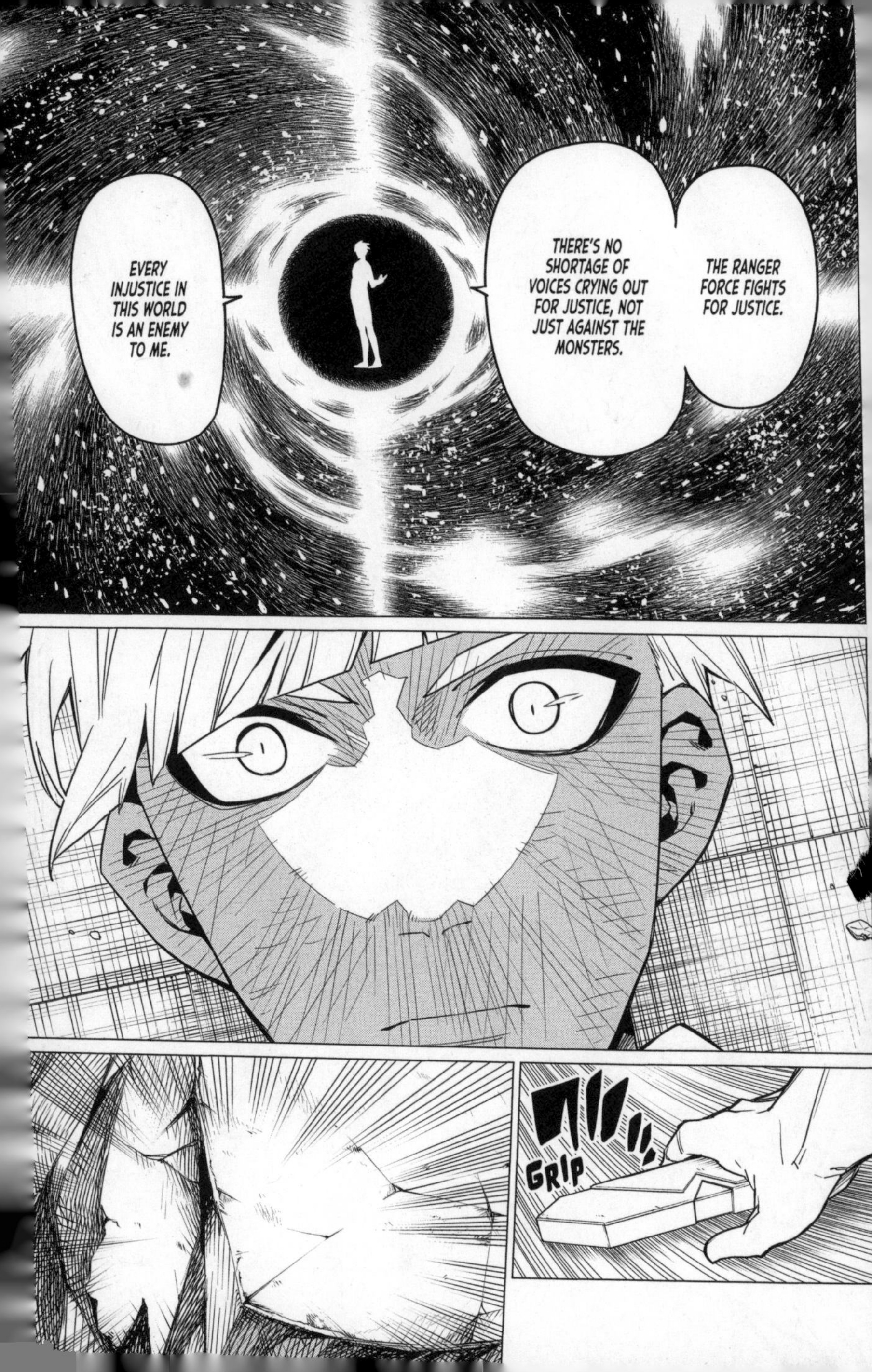
THE RANGER FORCE FIGHTS FOR JUSTICE.
THERE'S NO SHORTAGE OF VOICES CRYING OUT FOR JUSTICE, NOT JUST AGAINST THE MONSTERS.
EVERY INJUSTICE IN THIS WORLD IS AN ENEMY TO ME.
GRIP

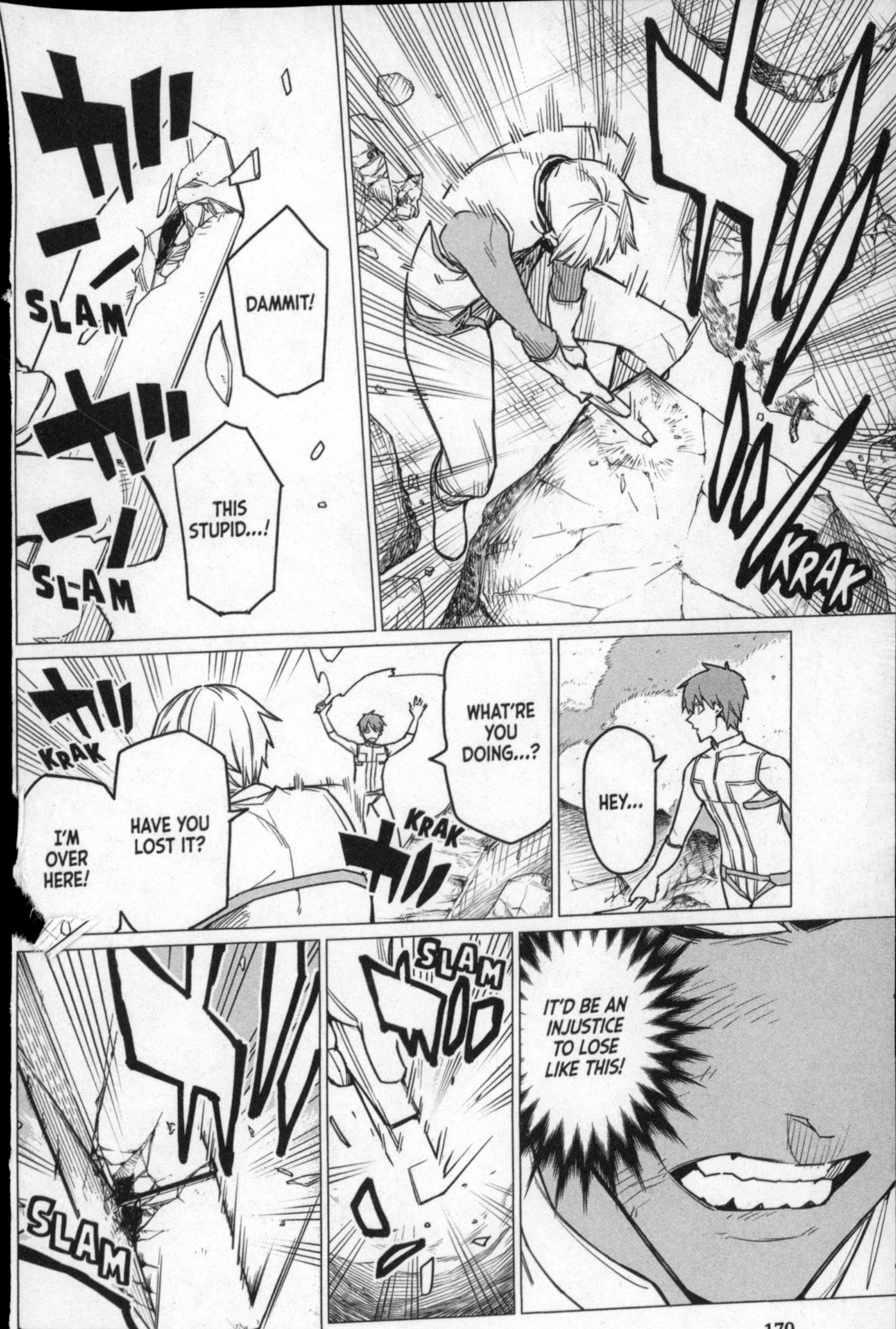
KRAK
DAMMIT!
THIS STUPID...!
SLAM
SLAM
HEY...
WHAT'RE YOU DOING...?
KRAK
HAVE YOU LOST IT?
I'M OVER HERE!
KRAK
IT'D BE AN INJUSTICE TO LOSE LIKE THIS!
SLAM
SLAM